EMPIRE OR INDEPENDENCE

1760-1776

EMPIRE OR INDEPENDENCE

1760-1776

*A British-American Dialogue on
the Coming of the American Revolution*

———◆———

Ian R. Christie

Benjamin W. Labaree

W · W · NORTON & COMPANY · INC · New York

THE TEXT of this book was set in Baskerville on the Variable Input Photosetter. Composition, printing, and binding are by Vail-Ballou Press, Inc.

BOOK DESIGN BY DODI BEARDSHAW ERVIN

Library of Congress Cataloging in Publication Data
Christie, Ian R
    Empire or independence, 1760–1776.
    Bibliography: p.
    Includes index.
      1. United States—History—Revolution, 1775–1783
—Causes. I. Labaree, Benjamin Woods, joint author.
II. Title.
                        6-18-76
E210.C54   973.3'11   75-44341

ISBN 0 393 05556 6

1 2 3 4 5 6 7 8 9 0

CONTENTS

———•—

CONTENTS

ILLUSTRATIONS

———•———

FOREWORD

———•—

WHEN THE PROJECT OF a joint book on the American Revolution by an American and a British scholar was first suggested to us by Mr. John Calmann of Phaidon Press, it appeared to offer certain distinctive attractions. This lay not only in a welcome division of labour in the survey of a vast subject, the secondary literature on which snowballs from year to year. In particular, by allowing the authors to concentrate on their respective national sides of the great controversy that rent asunder the first British Empire, it presented an opportunity for a balanced juxtaposition of analyses of the attitudes of the British governments which made policy on the one hand, and on the other of the attitudes of the colonists who found the activities of these governments unacceptable. In this antiphonal account we hope that we may have succeeded in bringing into sharper relief the conflicting points of view and intractable circumstances which underlay the Anglo-American quarrel leading up to the Declaration of Independence, while at the same time providing an outline of the story which both casts some light on the influence of individuals and gives equal weight to the considerations operating on the minds of men on both sides of the Atlantic. We have been able to present at least some new suggestions regarding the motivation which lay behind policy and action. We are conscious that this interlocking survey of action and reaction leaves the loyalists with only a small role to play in these pages. This in itself reflects the fact that the numerous successive crucial decisions which led to Independence were made not by them but by British ministers on the one hand and American patriots on the other.

The two authors did not meet until after the completion of the text, but we did have the advantage of modern communications. Letters and drafts of chapters crossed the Atlantic and were delivered in less than a week. A single telephone call settled several questions within minutes. And when the text was finished, a brief transoceanic flight enabled one of the authors to join the other for final polishing. During an afternoon stroll through the Hertfordshire countryside we wondered how differently the crisis two hundred years ago might have ended had the British government enjoyed similar advantages of communications. In the eighteenth century it took eight weeks or more for most dispatches to be delivered in America (although one letter reached its destination in four). Colonial governors requesting advice or clarification of instructions rarely received replies in less than four months. Such exchanges sometimes took nearly half a year, by which time fast-moving events in America had often changed the circumstances altogether. How much more responsive to American conditions might Whitehall have been with the instantaneous communications of today? The whole question of colonial representation in Parliament might also have been viewed differently on both sides of the Atlantic under modern conditions of travel and communications. Such musings serve to emphasize the extraordinary handicaps under which the British government laboured in its efforts to administer a farflung empire.

During the correspondence and conversations which attended the composition of this work the two authors came to realize the existence of several interesting contrasts between the staging of our respective parts of the story. At the beginning the British position required a fuller exposition than the American, whereas later on this situation was reversed. Another feature we noted was that on the British side of the story the principal decision-makers were a relatively small number of ministers and officials working against the background of political opinion in the two Houses of Parliament. Among the Americans, on the other hand, major decisions were made at almost every point by large bodies of colonists assembled in local or provincial meetings and responsive to a far broader base of public opinion. We have also noted how little the leaders of each side could understand the thoughts and circumstances across the Atlantic. It has made both of us more appreciative of the opportunities we have had to understand the eighteenth-century experience in each other's country. The extent to which an American and a British historian have been able to produce a composite history of this subject with so little disagreement is a remarkable tribute to the quality of the previous scholarship on the subject to which we owe so much.

ACKNOWLEDGEMENTS

WE ACKNOWLEDGE the gracious permission of Her Majesty Queen Elizabeth II to verify information in the papers of King George III in the Royal Archives edited by Sir John Fortescue. We are also grateful to the following for permission to use manuscript material: The British Library; the Keeper of the Public Records in respect of Crown copyright papers in the Public Record Office; the House of Lords Record Office; the Duke of Grafton and the County Archivist, Suffolk Record Office; the Earl Fitzwilliam and the Trustees of the Wentworth Woodhouse Settled Estates and to the Librarian of the Central Library, Sheffield; the Earl of Dartmouth and the Librarian of the William Salt Library, Stafford; the Curator of Manuscripts at the William L. Clements Library and Dr. John Shy, for making available copies of Viscount Barrington's letters to General Thomas Gage. Mr. E.L.C. Mullins, Secretary of the Editorial Board of the History of Parliament Trust, has kindly given access to transcripts in the Trust's files. We also acknowledge our gratitude for the use of materials in: the Massachusetts Historical Society; the Massachusetts Archives; the Houghton Library of Harvard University; the New England Historic and Genealogical Society; the American Antiquarian Society; the New-York Historical Society; the New York Public Library, the American Philosophical Society; the Historical Society of Pennsylvania; and the Library of Congress.

Finally, we are grateful to Dr. Ivon Asquith and Mrs. Alice Prochaska, who helped to assemble material for this book, and to Mrs. Constance Ellis who typed a part of the manuscript.

IAN R. CHRISTIE
University College, London

BENJAMIN W. LABAREE
Williams College, Williamstown, Massachusetts

April 1975

EMPIRE OR INDEPENDENCE

INDEPENDENCE

1760-1776

I

The Empire at the
Accession of George III

———•◦•———

1. *The British Isles*

AT THE END OF THE Seven Years War, the peace treaty signed at
Paris on 10 February 1763 established British maritime supremacy
and placed Great Britain in the position of the foremost colonial
power in the world. France, the rival of a century, had been overcome decisively, and Spain forced to yield by damaging blows in the
course of a mere few months of hostilities. Reserves of military and
naval power conjured up by the ruthless will of William Pitt had suddenly made plain the formidable resources of which the British people could dispose, within an Empire which appeared firmly based on
both shores of the Atlantic and commanded other important areas
of economic interest, notably in the Indian subcontinent.

In 1763 the heartland of this Empire, the kingdom of Great Britain, had a population of about seven and a half millions. Its centre
of gravity still lay as yet in the south. Below Trent and Mersey the
richest agricultural lands in the island extended from Kent and East
Anglia to Devon and the Welsh border, thick with prosperous villages and towns. Here sprawled the 'great wen' of London, the City
with its adjacent outparishes and villages, where the great waterway
of the Thames estuary formed a gateway to the Continent and to the
shores washed by every ocean of the world, the focal point of a farflung commerce which had fostered the development of an enormous manufacturing and trading community almost unique in its
size and character. The greater London area housed and gave employment to perhaps three-quarters of a million people, a tenth of
the country's population. Of these about 150,000 lived in the
crowded alleys of the City itself, an enormous and fecund concentra-

tion of human energy and expertise, a forcing-house of talent in many arts and crafts, and of mastery of the complex skills of commercial enterprise. None of the few large towns and outports elsewhere in the country could compare with it. Facing the Atlantic, Bristol, the second city in England, had a mere 60,000 inhabitants; Liverpool, growing very rapidly at this time, had about 26,000; Glasgow, the second city of Scotland, built up principally on the Virginia tobacco trade, had about 38,000. Norwich, the major town of East Anglia, with its sea outlet down the Yare, had about 40,000 people, Newcastle on Tyne about 25,000; Edinburgh with Leith on the Firth of Forth, looking out towards the German rivers and the Baltic, over 70,000. Few other towns were anywhere near such size. At the accession of George III Britain was still a pre-industrial country. Half the families in England and more than half in Scotland were primarily engaged in agriculture. The typical community was the village, or the small country town with less than 5,000 inhabitants, and the manufacturing and commercial activities carried on in them were often closely connected with rural life. Exceptional at this time were the great industrial urban parish of Halifax in the West Riding of Yorkshire with its 50,000 inhabitants specializing in the manufacture of woollen cloth, the metalware centre of Birmingham with about 30,000, and Manchester with Salford, the nascent centre of the English cotton manufacture, containing some 20,000 people.

This was a society where the lines of cleavage were vertical rather than horizontal, one based on status and deference and a sense of local community, and not yet split by great divisions of class. No abrupt gap separated rich and poor, rather a steady gradation from the aristocracy and gentry, through numerous levels of the middling sorts of people, to the master craftsmen, journeymen, and casual labourers below. Under George III Robert Mackreth, a coffeehouse waiter, became a wealthy financier and landed proprietor, passing the last twenty-eight years of his life as a member of Parliament, and Lloyd Kenyon, the son of a well-to-do yeoman, rose to be chief justice. While somewhat exceptional these examples reflect the considerable social mobility and opportunity for talent in British society at that time. Another dynamic feature was the growth of population. From about 1740, perhaps owing to a series of good harvests, more children were being born and more of them reached maturity. The average annual rate of natural increase of the population of England and Wales had perhaps been only about one point one per thousand in the half-century up to 1751. It stood at six point eight for the period 1751–81, during which every decade added about half a million people to the population. During those years the population of Scotland increased by well over 50,000 per decade.

To sustain such a growth a progressive agriculture was indispensable. There were no dramatic developments; but the adoption of by now well-tried flexible rotations of crops made possible a steady increase in food production. Cultivation of roots, legumes, and improved grasses provided more fodder, enabled land to carry more stock which enriched the ground with additional manure, in turn raising the yields of both cereal and fodder crops and hence making possible even heavier stocking. The spread of 'alternate husbandry'—the famous Norfolk system—on the light sandy soils of East Anglia and elsewhere, and of 'convertible husbandry', or 'ley farming', on heavier but well-drained lands in Hampshire and other parts of the south, has been described as 'the real breakthrough' in farming technique in this period. Improved stock breeding increased the yield of meat. Moreover, for over thirty years the struggle to survive in an age of plenitude and low grain prices, had forced farmers to raise productivity in relation to cost and weeded out the inefficient. To some extent this had been achieved by such rationalization as the disappearance of some small farms and by enclosure. Enclosure also contributed to food stocks and prosperity by bringing waste lands into cultivation, an increasingly important trend in the 1760s. As the population grew the customary surpluses of wheat for export came to an end, and farmers benefited and were stimulated to expand their undertakings by higher prices for what had now suddenly become a slightly scarce commodity. Conversely, the poor suffered from higher prices of bread. Many of them in the countryside, losing through enclosure the little margin of economic independence they had hitherto enjoyed by virtue of their rights of common, became wholly dependent on wages which lagged behind the price-rise. In consequence, in the 1760s Great Britain was moving into a period of economic tensions and social protest.

Urban markets stimulated agricultural production. To feed London, wheat came by land or water from East Anglia and the nearer counties north of the Thames, cattle and sheep raised in the Midlands were herded southwards to be fattened in the Essex marshes, dairy produce, especially cheese, was brought from the lush grasslands of the south-west and Severn valley. Sheep-farming flourished on the uplands of the Pennines, Lakeland, and the Scottish border, providing not only meat for the townsmen of Yorkshire and Lancashire but wool for the expanding cloth industry of the West Riding, which found an increasing outlet for its wares in the American colonies. Great numbers of sheep and cattle were driven south from Scotland to feed the urban populations of the north and Midlands, and London also. Improvements in turnpike roads during the forty years before 1760, as well as the provision of locks and weirs on rivers, helped to facilitate traffic and so to stimulate it. Ease in the movement of food to towns was an essential precondition of their further expansion.

A growing population and a buoyant agriculture provided the basis for an increasingly diversified national economy, which was also favoured by other circumstances. Since the Union of 1707, Great Britain had been the largest area in Europe free from internal tariff barriers. The country had developed one of the most efficient systems of finance and public credit, of which the twin pillars were the Bank of England and the National Debt, and among the advantages brought by political stability after 1714 had been a degree of security which attracted foreign, especially Dutch, investment. In many areas industry had arisen free from the hampering controls of the old town guilds. The obstructions of state regulation for social purposes had largely lapsed, and the extent to which personal liberty and rights of property had been secured by the political revolution of the seventeenth century had firmly laid the basis of an acquisitive society, and had removed potential brakes on economic development. Free play for individual enterprise, the absence of any sharp class or caste divisions, and the relatively high degree of social mobility, all helped to bring about a fairly wide diffusion of wealth. This in turn facilitated the raising of capital for new ventures, which a small family group, or social, local, or religious circle could often provide. Money spent by the government in the wars in which the country had been involved for most of the previous twenty years assisted economic development, especially in such undertakings as the South Wales mining and metallurgical industries, where the amounts of capital required might have been more difficult to find but for the large profits which passed into the hands of government contractors. In the 1760s a perceptible inflationary effect produced by these wars may also have played a part in the longer-term stimulus of the British economy, though the immediate effect of the return to peace in 1763 was a post-war depression.

By geography Ireland appeared to form part of the metropolitan state. But though in form a separate kingdom under the same sovereign, in some ways it occupied a colonial status, and proximity placed its fortunes all the more closely under British control. Over the centuries the Irish parliament had been deprived of all independent initiative, and legislation, though formally enacted at Dublin, was firmly directed by George III's British ministers. Even if the Lord Lieutenant, their representative, was unable to manage the Irish Lords and Commons, no laws could be passed without the approval of the British Privy Council. The British House of Lords acted as a final court of appeal in Irish cases, and by its own statutory declaration of 1719 the British Parliament claimed full power to legislate for Ireland. In certain ways the Irish economy was subordinated to British vested interests. Irish woollen manufacturers might not be exported either to Britain or the Continent. Irish coarse linens were encouraged by bounties but the finer kinds were penalized by high tariffs on the British market and were altogether excluded from the colonies. Similar checks were placed upon the manufacture of glass. On the other hand Ireland also gained economically from the British connection. There was a growing demand for Irish beef, mutton, butter, and cereals. Except for one or two commodities the Irish could trade freely on the Continent, where they found good markets for foodstuffs, and in these trade relations they gained benefit from British status. Irish butter and other supplies were sold to the West Indies. In peacetime the French navy took much of its provisions from Cork, and though war interrupted this trade, then the increased demands of the British navy largely took its place. Although by and large the living standards of the people of Ireland were below those of Great Britain, the Irish population was growing proportionately even faster than the British. In the twenty years after 1761 it increased by some 750,000, to just over four millions. Dublin, with over 100,000 inhabitants, was the second city in the British Isles. Cork, the metropolis of the provisions trade, rivalled Bristol in population and enterprise. Economically the country was forging ahead rapidly in the mid-eighteenth century.[1] Imports and exports both trebled in the twenty-five years from 1741 to 1766, mainly due to an expansion of trade with Britain. In roughly the same period total rents from land were thought to have doubled. In many ways, directly and indirectly, Ireland supported British power. About an eighth of the revenues received from Irish estates were drawn away by non-resident proprietors to be spent in England. A separate Irish peacetime military establishment provided some 12,000 men at the government's disposal—though a large part of this force was needed to maintain law and order—and in time of war Ireland was recruiting ground for both British and Irish regiments. And not least, Irish migrants swelled the population and resources of the North American colonies.

2. The Overseas Dependencies

By 1763 the tentacles of British power and influence were reaching out in many parts of the globe.

In the East, the British were about to become a territorial power. The East India Company, a great financial and commercial interest, held bases for the purposes of commerce at Bombay, Madras, and Calcutta, and conducted a trade which orthodox mercantilists regarded with some disfavour, for it involved shipments of silver bullion eastwards in return for raw silk and cotton yarn, and luxury goods such as muslims, calicos, and tea. During recent wars against France the Company had found itself obliged to become a military power in order to defend its trade, and to secure the succession or usurpation of friendly Indian princes in the states bordering on its forts. In 1764 the Company's military victory at Buxar put control of much of the Ganges valley in its hands, and in the same year as Grenville's Stamp Act, 1765, by assuming control over the financial administration of Bengal, its servants took the first step towards dominion in India. In London there was much unjustified optimism about the Company in the early 1760s. It was assumed that its growing political power and influence in eastern and southern India assured a rapid increase in the scale of its commercial activities and a corresponding expansion of its profits; whereas its military responsibilities entailed much expense, and illicit private enterprise, even by its own servants, bit into such potential as did exist for commercial expansion.

After the end of the Seven Years War the British held two dependencies in Europe: Gibraltar and Minorca, both chiefly of value as naval bases. Further south, on the West African coast, the French had been required to cede their colony on the Senegal. But the main axis of the British Empire lay across the Atlantic.

In the Western Atlantic and Caribbean the British had long been established in a number of the islands. Jamaica was the principal colony, but in addition sovereignty extended over the Bahamas east of the Florida Strait, the Leeward Islands—Nevis, Antigua, St. Kitts and Montserrat—and the Windward Island of Barbados. The peace of 1763 added Grenada and the Grenadines, and three of the four so-called 'neutral islands' in the Windward group—St. Vincent, Dominique, and Tobago—settled by nationals of both France and Great Britain but hitherto claimed by neither. In the Atlantic wastes to the north the British also held the Bermudas.

Sugar cane was the great staple of the islands. Sugar and molasses were exported in considerable quantities to Great Britain, and also some rum, cotton-wool, cocoa, and dyestuffs, in return for consumer goods and provisions which the West Indians could not provide for themselves. Sugar added to the amenities of life in Britain and formed an important item of re-export trade to parts of the Continent. From North America the planters drew large amounts of foodstuffs and timber. Both strategically and economically the islands were valuable, but also vulnerable. All save Jamaica were small in acreage and population. All lay relatively close to foreign bases and were exposed to French or Spanish attack in time of war. Naval support and garrisons imposed a heavy burden on the metropolitan state, and the high mortality from tropical diseases caused a constant drain in manpower.

On the American mainland the British Empire in 1760 comprised fifteen provinces: Newfoundland, Nova Scotia, Massachusetts (including present-day Maine), New Hampshire, Rhode Island, Connecticut, New York, New Jersey, Pennsylvania, Delaware, Maryland, Virginia, North and South Carolina, and Georgia. Spread along some eighteen hundred miles of the American eastern seaboard, these territories displayed great diversity of climate and resources. Newfoundland was still little more than a base for the fisheries, with no settled government, and only a few thousand settlers clustered round St. Johns and Placentia on the Avalon Peninsula. Nova Scotia was primarily a military outpost and part of the territories which it later included were in course of being wrested from the French. By the peace of 1763 the British added to this American Empire the former French and Spanish territories of Florida and Louisiana east of the lower Mississippi and Iberville rivers, which were erected into the two virtually unpopulated colonies of East and West Florida; the French territory of Quebec, extending along the lower St. Lawrence Valley, with a population of about 80,000; Cape Breton and other islands and territories comprising former French Acadia, lying along the south and west shores of the Gulf of St. Lawrence and north of the Bay of Fundy; and a vast inland area between the Alleghenies, the Mississippi, and the Great Lakes, formerly claimed by the French as parts of Louisiana and Quebec, peopled only by some thousands of Indians and a few hundred French Canadian traders.

At the close of the Seven Years War (known to Americans as the French and Indian War) the thirteen old continental colonies were inhabited by about 1,750,000 persons, of whom around twenty percent were blacks, almost all of them slaves. The population had been doubling every quarter-century for over one hundred years. A further decline in the death rate and continuing immigration from England, continental Europe, and Africa promised a steady increase far into the future. Most of the good tidewater land had long since been taken up, and in some places was already exhausted by intensive cultivation. Consequently, many colonists looked to the interior regions of the continent for their future subsistence, and the coming of peace in 1763 witnessed a renewal of the relentless press of population up river valleys, through mountain passes, onward ever onward into the vast wilderness of the American continent. If one were allowed but a single adjective to describe the Americans at mid-century, 'dynamic' might prove most appropriate. A restless striving, physically, commercially, socially, politically, drove the American on toward the future.

An Englishman surveying his nation's Empire at the close of the Seven Years War would recognize that the thirteen continental American colonies fell into four quite distinct regions. Immediately to the north of newly-acquired Florida was the colony of Georgia, founded in 1732 and inhabited thirty years later by fewer than 20,000 souls. Yet the sea islands offered a promising future, and during the next decade the population would nearly triple. Across the Savannah river lay one of the most prosperous of the colonies, South Carolina, with its lush 'low country' of fertile soil, fulsome rivers, and semi-tropical climate. A population somewhat greater than 150,000 concentrated on the cultivation of two major crops— rice and indigo—and on the extraction of valuable naval stores from the pine barrens of the interior. The port of Charleston served as entrepôt for the region and had long been the centre of the continent's slave trade. In recent years just after the Treaty of Paris, Englishmen could reckon South Carolina as one of the Empire's most salutary colonies. Together with its somewhat less populated neighbour, North Carolina, the two provinces exported during the mid-1760s more than £300,000 worth of commodities to the mother country each year and purchased goods of nearly equal value in return.

The two Chesapeake Bay colonies of Virginia and Maryland rated still higher marks from the mercantilists of London. Over one-third of all Americans, black and white, lived there in the period before the American Revolution, sending immense quantities of tobacco to English houses for re-export throughout Europe. Pig and bar iron and, by the 1760s, considerable quantities of wheat were also exported. At the same time the Chesapeake region proved to be a major market-place for the manufacturers of the mother country. Because its many broad rivers and creeks reached many miles into the interior the Chesapeake planter could load his tobacco and other crops directly on board transatlantic vessels from his own wharf. For this reason no seaport such as Charleston was necessary.

Still further to the north lay the so-called middle colonies, Delaware and Pennsylvania on the Delaware River, New York on the Hudson, and New Jersey, 'a cask tapped at both ends', lying in between. The first two provinces had separate legislatures but the same governor and in many respects the lower counties of Delaware were considered an appendage to their larger neighbour to the north. Pennsylvania ranked fourth in total population behind Virginia, Massachusetts, and Maryland. In what a visitor once described as 'the best poor man's country', the rich lands between the Delaware and the Susquehanna west of Philadelphia, farmers from Germany as well as England raised bountiful crops of wheat, corn, and other produce for markets in other continental colonies and in the West Indies. Philadelphia had already surpassed Boston as the continent's busiest seaport, shipping out the area's agricultural surpluses both as raw materials and as manufactured commodities like breadstuffs, flour, and rum. Very little of Pennsylvania's exports went to the mother country, but the colony's inhabitants proved excellent customers for English wares. New York, despite its advantageous geographical position astride the Hudson and Mohawk valleys, had not yet reached its full potential at the end of the Seven Years War, with a total population that ranked only eighth among the continental provinces. As in the case of the other middle colonies, few of New York's exports went directly to England, for the province produced little of value to the mother country aside from some flax, iron, and furs. But its inhabitants were voracious consumers of English goods. In addition, New York harbour served as an entrepot for a wide area, including the towns of northern New Jersey and many Connecticut communities as well. The city's greatness as a seaport, however, lay far in the future.

New England had long been regarded by the other colonists as almost a single province, although there were recognizable differences between these 'eastern provinces', as they were sometimes called. Except for those towns in Connecticut and Rhode Island which looked down Long Island sound toward New York, most of New England regarded Boston as the centre of its commercial activities. Massachusetts itself numbered well over 200,000 inhabitants at the end of the war, although its population rose only slowly in subsequent years. Its vessels dominated the fishing grounds of the North Atlantic, and its distilleries produced vast quantities of rum, much of which ended up in the fur trade with the Indians or in the African slave trade. But the colony produced few products saleable in the mother country, and therefore its merchants searched elsewhere for the 'returns' with which to purchase the English goods so much in demand. This led to the development of the coastal and West Indies trade. Colonists from New York to Barbados soon became used to the ubiquitous Yankee schooner or sloop shuffling to and fro among the smaller ports of the continent with assorted cargoes. New Hampshire and Maine (the latter a part of Massachusetts) did produce ship timber and masts for the Royal Navy and a miscellany of other lumber products, but they were otherwise insignificant in the economic activity of the Empire. Overall, New England proved fairly good customers for English manufacturers, purchasing annually on the average well over £400,000 worth in the mid-1760s.

An overview of British commerce in the years immediately after the Peace of Paris would therefore show that the continental colonies played an important role in the economic affairs of the Empire. They provided the West Indies with vitally needed fish, provisions, and wood products and served as a major market for much of the islands' molasses. Yankee timber and fish brought Spanish bills and coinage into circulation, as did Pennsylvania wheat shipped to southern Europe. New England rum furnished a necessary commodity in the nefarious slave trade, and its shipyards provided vessels at far less cost than their English counterparts. On the eve of the Revolution, in fact, about one-third of all British merchant vessels were colonial-built. Plantation goods like tobacco, indigo, and rice gave English merchants commodities in considerable demand throughout Europe, and American iron proved an important raw material for the foundries of the mother country. But it was as a market for English goods that the continental colonies proved most valuable. Their inhabitants purchased on the average about £2,000,000 worth of English manufactures and other goods during the mid-1760s, the equivalent of about £1.7s. for every man, woman, and child of the white population. And by the eve of the Revolution the per capita figure climbed to £1.10s. and the total to nearly £3,000,000.

While the great bulk of American commerce functioned within the Empire itself, the colonists took advantage of the various opportunities afforded by the Navigation Acts to trade with the world beyond as well. The foreign West Indies had already become one such region earlier in the eighteenth century, as had Europe south of Cape Finisterre. Americans also traded with the Atlantic wine islands and the coast of Africa. Inevitably some merchants ventured cargoes along routes clearly prohibited by the Acts of Trade. Tobacco and rice were shipped directly to the European Continent, to Dutch and French ports primarily, in exchange for textiles, hardware, gin, brandy, and tea. Other kinds of illicit voyages involved the failure to pay full duties (or any at all) on certain cargoes not in themselves illegal, mostly molasses from the French islands. One wonders, however, whether colonial merchants on the whole violated the customs laws any more frequently than their English cousins. There is little evidence to suggest that American smugglers had any other motive than to maximize profits, and in this respect they were no different from most merchants. In an era when Englishmen smuggled in perhaps as much as seven million lb. of tea (worth at least £700,000) from ports across the Channel each year, the illicit trade of the colonists was not at all unusual.

At mid-century the vast majority of colonists were farmers who owned from fifty to two hundred acres of land, much of it still uncultivated perhaps. It would be only a slight exaggeration to say that as soon as an American farmer had cleared all of the land he owned, he began to consider the possibility of moving on. Of course most of them did not move, but the continuing influx of immigrants and the high birth-rate provided numerous inhabitants who did. Indeed, after a family holding had been divided and subdivided through several generations, there came a time when further division was no longer possible. Then only one son (not necessarily the eldest) could remain on the family farm; the others pushed west, or north, or south toward the unsettled lands beyond. In each generation other young men left the soil altogether and took up a craft or went into business as a storekeeper. And as always the seaports attracted their share of restless young men, bored by the prospect of a lifetime of farming. But when one thinks of American colonists in the 1760s one must think primarily of people living on the land.

Most of the men who worked the soil were subsistence farmers. They produced only incidental surpluses with which to barter for needed supplies. But in each region some of the farmers raised either a staple crop such as rice or tobacco for market in the mother country or a crop like wheat in demand by other colonists. And farmers fortunate enough to be situated within ten or twenty miles of a seaport or large interior settlement could market a variety of surplus foodstuffs directly to the inhabitants and to others who made purchases there. From Pennsylvania north diversification was the pattern; from the Chesapeake south, specialization in a single market crop was more common. But by the middle of the eighteenth century progressive planters like George Washington had begun to experiment with a variety of produce: wheat and other grains, Indian corn, and fruit. But the German farmers of Pennsylvania were about the only practitioners of conservation in the modern sense. They manured their fields, experimented with rotation, and of course let fields lie fallow. For the rest of America's farmers, the Swedish traveller Peter Kalm was astonished at the 'perfect carelessness' with which they treated fields, forests, and livestock. 'Their eyes are fixed upon the present gain,' he concluded, 'and they are blind to the future.' Kalm's judgement of American motives was not altogether accurate, but compared to European farmers the colonists were indeed careless. There was, after all, plenty of land, was there not?

Although agriculture predominated in America, numerous other activities added a dynamic dimension to the colonial economy. Shipbuilding had long since become a complex manufacturing process. It was centred primarily in New England and employed hundreds of artisans skilled in a dozen or more crafts. The large merchant mills around Philadelphia, and later Wilmington and Baltimore, formed the nucleus of yet another manufactury. The millowners purchased wheat outright from the farmers of the area, ground it into flour under water-driven stones, and then packed it into barrels for shipment. These entrepreneurs often operated bakeries as well, preparing bread and biscuits for market. In the Chesapeake region there were large-scale iron manufactures. Alexander Spotswood's works near Fredericksburg, Virginia, utilized 15,000 acres of ore field and two square miles of woodland to feed the furnaces. The Spotswood enterprise turned out twenty tons of iron a week, and in addition to supplying slitting and plating mills in the region it shipped out to England each year pig and bar iron worth £60,000.

In every town and village local craftsmen offered many of the skilled services and finished products needed by their neighbours. In the rural villages craftsmen usually made goods to order only, but in the larger towns they were shopkeepers as well. Some artisans, such as cabinetmakers and silversmiths, served a market far beyond their local communities. Almost all of these activities were subject to various local regulations affecting the quantity, quality, and price of the articles sold. High standards for Philadelphia's flour, Virginia's tobacco, and the rice and indigo shipped from South Carolina, were all rigidly enforced by local authorities. In addition, Parliament had enacted various laws such as the Woollen Act (1699), The Hat Act (1732), and the Iron Act (1750) limiting in various ways economic activities in those fields. Americans evaded these laws with regularity, although they rarely quarrelled with Parliament's right to enact such legislation.

One of America's most serious economic problems came from its chronic shortage of currency. Virtually no coinage was minted in the colonies and their unfavourable balance of trade with the mother country constantly drained off what little Spanish and Portuguese coinage they could accumulate. Commodities like tobacco, rice, and wheat served as 'country pay' in various regions despite wild fluctuations in value. Efforts to set the price of tobacco at 2d. a pound by Virginia in the 1750s met with the royal disallowance, and Parliament nullified the attempt in Massachusetts to establish a 'land bank' in the 1740s as well as to issue a paper currency in the decade following. The lack of currency and of liquid capital remained serious roadblocks to commercial enterprise in the colonies. Despite these and other handicaps, however, the great surge in population stimulated rapid economic development.

As in other parts of the western world the society of colonial

America was comprised of several recognizable ranks or classes of people. Occupation, life style, or in particular, property holdings, marked these distinctions. What a man did and how successfully he did it rather than his family's 'place' determined a white individual's status, however. At the bottom stood the blacks, both slave and free, comprising about twenty percent of the total population as of 1760. Set apart by colour and their condition of servitude, the black peoples performed the most arduous tasks, elevating by their labour all whites to higher rungs on the ladder. Next were the indentured servants, less common now in the mid-eighteenth century. With other landless whites including urban labourers, they accounted for another fifteen percent of the population. The majority of colonists, as we have already noted, were farmers and artisans with holdings large enough to assure their independence. Within such a large category, of course, existed a wide range of conditions, from the bare subsistence farmer of the frontier to the prosperous market farmer, from the village blacksmith or cordwainer to the skillful silversmith or cabinetmaker. At the top stood the wealthy upper class, planters with extensive holdings in land and slaves, merchants with several deepwater vessels and a warehouse full of goods, and the professional men such as lawyers and doctors.

Although a trend toward polarization had begun to appear in some of the seaports by the mid-eighteenth century, most Americans continued to have faith that theirs was a highly mobile society in which a man could rise on his merits. One reason for this social movement was the absence of a titled nobility or landed gentry which handed down estates intact from father to eldest son. On the contrary land was plentiful along the frontiers. At the same time the rapid increase of population provided greater opportunities for all (except as always the blacks). The progression of the economy from a simple subsistence agricultural basis to the more complex mixed economy of the mid-eighteenth century offered still further chance for advancement.

A large number of the immigrants who poured into the American colonies during the eighteenth century came in some degree of bondage. The importation of Africans reached its highest point yet at mid-century, averaging 5,000 a year. Many of the Germans settling in Pennsylvania were redemptioners able to pay a part but not all of their passage money. Scots-Irish came in droves earlier in the century and a few still arrived each year throughout the 1760s and 1770s, joined by Highlanders captured in the various border wars with the English, especially after Culloden in 1746. Quakers also came from England to seek a more peaceful (and prosperous) existence in Pennsylvania. Although several groups, most notably the Germans, have remained distinct for generations, there is much truth in Hector St. Jean de Crèvecoeur's statement that 'here individuals of all nations are melted into a new race of men, whose labours and posterity will one day cause great changes in the world.'[2]

It is difficult to generalize about the quality of life in America at mid-century because of the considerable variations between northern and southern colonies, countryside and urban communities, rich people and poor. But the lives of almost all Americans shared certain common characteristics. For one thing the idea of the extended family persisted throughout the period. Thus many parents and their children shared homes with at least one grandparent, uncle or aunt, at one time or another. Many hands were required to clear the land, cultivate the soil, and make the clothes and other necessaries. Most Americans put a high premium on labour; wages were high; and there was virtually no leisure class. Planters like George Washington usually worked a full day managing every detail of their holdings. Seaport merchants spent little time at the country seats that a few of them were now able to afford. Only the Carolina rice barons retreated during the growing season, as much to escape the heat of the low country as to avoid work.

Urban life presented particularly difficult problems. All but one of the twenty largest towns in the colonies on the eve of the Revolution were seaports. Population estimates vary widely. As of 1760 one historian has ranked Philadelphia first with just under 25,000, New York next with 18,000, and Boston third with 15,631, but only the last is an actual census. The influx of mariners, of farmers coming to market their crops, and of youths seeking excitement merely exacerbated the crowded conditions already plaguing the authorities. As the sources of timber for new construction grew steadily more remote, building costs soared, and as always space was at a premium. The seat of government in most of the colonies was a seaport, and thus was added to commercial congestion the crowd of people attending the governor and council, or sessions of the court and legislature. Seaports also became bases for British military units during the eighteenth century's numerous wars, requiring barracks, fortresses, and other facilities to support both army and navy. Customhouse men and admiralty court justices added to the list of officials, and to the sense of a British 'presence' totally unknown by inhabitants of the rural areas.

Caring for the poor, a group swollen by the large number of widows and orphans of mariners lost at sea, became a major headache for seaport authorities. In Boston, for instance, nearly one out of every three adult women was a widow. Itinerant seamen were also viewed as a potential source of difficulty. Public health problems common to all eighteenth-century cities challenged the ingenuity of civic leaders, but most of the seaports had constructed underground sewers by mid-century and had paved their major streets with stone. Bubonic plague was successfully avoided, but smallpox and yellow fever periodically took heavy tolls. Another urban hazard came from the conflagrations that occasionally swept through the closely packed wooden buildings of eighteenth-century America.

Culturally speaking, Americans of the mid-eighteenth century remained, for the most part, Englishmen after all. Despite the infusion of African, German, French, and Dutch peoples into the colonies the inhabitants still looked primarily to England for their cultural standards. Much of their reading material, their music and art, and even their religious denominations had their origins in the mother country. But at the same time New World conditions altered the shape of English forms, and regional differences were so persistent that one might well question the existence of a single American culture at all on the eve of the Revolution. Throughout the eighteenth century, however, several forces were slowly but steadily eroding the barrier of spatial distance between northern and southern colonies and between tidewater and interior settlements. Better land transportation but particularly the vastly increased coastal trade improved communications throughout the colonies; the constant movement of people themselves created refreshing mixtures of customs. A reliable postal service distributed both personal letters and regional newspapers to distant parts of the continent. By 1763 there were over twenty newspapers published in eleven of the thirteen continental colonies and over the next decade the number would greatly increase. Newspapers and other publications by the colonial printers did much to create a sense of common identity.

The colonies were perhaps most alike in political structure. To begin with all were, of course, *English* colonies, subject to the same rules and regulations of Parliament, the same orders of the Privy Council, and the same royal instructions. Each had a single executive, although some governors were elected (Connecticut and Rhode Island), some were appointed by the proprietors of the colony (Pennsylvania, Delaware, Maryland, and South Carolina till 1763), while the rest were royal governors appointed by the Crown. With only slight variations in composition and duties each colony had a governor's council as well. Most significantly, each of the colonial governments included a lower house of assembly composed of delegates chosen by the various counties, towns, or other local constituencies to represent their interests in the legislative process.

By the middle of the eighteenth century perhaps as many as

three out of four adult white males could vote for representatives. All colonies limited their electorates by applying in one form or another the 'stake in society' theory. In about half of the provinces potential voters had to possess a freehold estate worth forty or fifty pounds, while the other provinces offered as well various alternative means to qualify, including the ownership of a specified amount of personal property or payment of some minimum sum in taxes. Aside from the fact that particular groups were thus disfranchised additional constraints precluded the development of true political democracy in colonial America. Property qualifications for office-holders were higher than for voters. Practical considerations also prevented most artisans and farmers from holding provincial office, for they could not afford to be absent from their work. Besides, many colonists customarily looked to men of wealth and education for leadership in civic affairs. This 'habit of deference' along with the stake in society theory were so deeply ingrained within Americans that both principles survived the Revolutionary era and became integral parts of most state constitutions as they were in the mother country.

In local affairs the small farmers and artisans had a far greater opportunity to wield political power. For one thing those qualified (over ninety percent of the adult white males in many areas and an average of around seventy-five percent overall) could participate directly in town or parish meetings or send delegates to county sessions. Secondly, local office-holding itself was rarely subject to special property qualifications, nor did local officials have to be free to attend distant meetings as did assembly delegates. Such important governmental functions as assessment of property, establishment of budgets and tax rates, administration of welfare, and control of schools were all in the hands of local officials, many of whom were ordinary citizens. In some areas a large landholder or wealthy merchant might hold a disproportionate amount of political power, but in contrast to the provincial level local government was far more broadly based.

The governor enjoyed considerable political influence as direct representative of the Crown and in most colonies actually held more power relative to the legislature than did the King in relation to Parliament. The governor controlled appointment to numerous offices, served as commander-in-chief of his colony's militia, was the head of the Anglican church, and had the right in some colonies to grant land to his supporters. He could veto legislation, dissolve the legislature, and refuse to call it into session. In many of the provinces furthermore, the governor presided over the council, sometimes even when it acted as an upper house, and thus he had an occasional share in the legislative process. With the council the governor exercised considerable power over the judicial establishment of his colony. Plural office-holding was a common occurrence, but rarely did any colonial official approach the record list of offices held by Thomas Hutchinson of Massachusetts, who in 1763 simultaneously served as lieutenant governor, chief justice of the superior court, president of the council (and thus a member of the General Court), and a judge of probate.

Throughout the first half of the eighteenth century the lower houses of assembly steadily expanded their share of political power, usually at the expense of the governor, whom the representatives saw as a threat to their own ambitions. This development resulted not from a preconcerted plan nor from a conscious movement toward the independence actually achieved at a later date. Rather, the legislatures gained strength simply by winning more than their share of single-issue confrontations over a long period. When the governor of Massachusetts, for instance, finally accepted his remuneration as an annual gift rather than holding out for a fixed salary, the legislature had won an important round. Or when Virginia's House of Burgesses insisted on appointing the colony's treasurer (he was in fact the speaker of the house itself for most of the period), the legislature deprived the governor of an important power. In the final analysis it was their ability to initiate legislation that gave the lower houses a distinct advantage. A governor could hinder the process by counter-proposals, veto, or prorogation, but he could not force the assembly to enact his programme. In the first half of the eighteenth century the members of most colonies increasingly modelled their chambers on the House of Commons, demanding all the rights and privileges of that body and claiming that their houses existed by right, not by royal or parliamentary suffrance.

Patterns of political life varied somewhat from colony to colony, but in each certain common characteristics emerged. As we have seen provincial offices remained in the hands of a small élite. Within each colony prolonged struggles for ascendancy between various factions became the normal state of political affairs. The ultimate goal of these power struggles was not to assure the triumph of one ideology over another but rather to attain some self-serving purpose, such as land grants, military contracts, or often simply prestige. In Massachusetts, for instance, Thomas Hutchinson's 'court party' waged political warfare against a 'country party' led after 1757 by James Otis. At stake were such political plums as the house speakership, seats on the governor's council, and places on the judicial bench. The aftermath of the Glorious Revolution of 1689 divided New York into irreconcilable factions—the Morrisites and the De-

Lanceys—who tore at each other's throats for almost a century thereafter. Among the principal weapons was the adaptation by the Morrisites of essays by Trenchard, Gordon, and other opponents of Robert Walpole to assail the DeLancy faction. The printer John Peter Zenger was but one victim of the battle. Like the factional struggle in Massachusetts, New York's political warfare was overtaken by the crisis between England and the colonies in the 1760s and added fuel to that already fiery confrontation. In Pennsylvania the proprietary party so frustrated its opponents in the lower house that the latter sent Franklin to England in an effort to have Pennsylvania taken over as a royal colony. Virginia, politically the most stable of the major colonies at mid-century, was rent by two controversies in the 1750s. The 'pistole fee' protest against the governor and the 'two penny act' struggle with the Privy Council both shook the confidence of younger burgesses in the older leadership and paved the way for such men as Patrick Henry and Richard Henry Lee.

Although the leaders of opposing factions rarely acted in response to a set of ideological principles, by the middle of the eighteenth century the continuing struggle between legislatures and governors did begin to create a body of political ideas that became the foundation for later developments. One principle was that of government by consent of the governed as expressed by their assembled delegates. Secondly, Americans tended to view their constitutions as susceptible to growth and change rather than as fixed documents determined solely by the edicts of kings and parliaments. (This view would change in the 1760s, however.) Colonists shared the fears most eloquently expressed by the English commonwealth man toward political power. They agreed in theory that the best defence against corrupting tyranny was the mixed constitution—the three-legged stool of monarchy, aristocracy, and commons. But in fact the absence of a true aristocracy in America meant that the stool had only two legs, the royal prerogative expressed through the governors and the commons represented by the lower houses of assembly. Thus the all-important balance could not be achieved, and the assemblies therefore saw themselves standing alone as defenders of the people's 'liberty' against the avaricious encroachment of executive 'tyranny'. It is important to realize that many Americans had come to view their political world in this perspective at least a decade before the Grenville administration provided an element of reality to the picture.

In 1760 a visiting Anglican cleric, Andrew Burnaby, predicted that the continental colonies were too disparate ever to become united. The prevalence of slavery in one region, of commercial interests in another, the wide variety of ethnic backgrounds and religious preferences, and the numerous boundary disputes and other frictions between the colonies combined, in Burnaby's view, to preclude a permanent union among them. But as we know Burnaby proved to be a poor prophet. Beyond the fact that the continental colonists shared many experiences together within the Empire they also held a number of values in common. The principle of self-government, and particularly the right of property holders to a voice in their own taxation, had become a tradition by mid-century. So too was the virtual autonomy of local government and the freedom from external control in church affairs. The universal shortage of labour emphasized the value of work, and combined with widespread opportunity, these factors encouraged Americans to be ambitious. 'Getting ahead' became a national obsession long before America became a nation. The colonists shared a common commitment to the future—their own, that of their families, and of their 'country'. People who look forward together are often able to ignore their past differences, at least for a while.

In 1748, at the close of King George's War (as the War of the Austrian Succession was called in America), the wealthy Boston merchant Thomas Hancock wrote to an English correspondent: 'I hope a general peace may be for the good of the nation, tho' I don't think it will prove so to this country.' [3] Hancock was expressing New England's grave disappointment over the return of Louisbourg to the French in 1748 at the treaty of Aix-la-Chapelle. But he also expressed, probably unconsciously, a dilemma that would become increasingly common for all American colonists after mid-century—the distinction between 'nation' and 'country'. For men of the eighteenth century the former term defined one's political allegiance, the latter his geographical home. For most people their country was physically a part of their nation, but for Americans the two were separated by three thousand miles of rolling sea.

At the close of the Seven Years War the continental colonists were proud to claim membership in the world's most powerful Empire. They were proud too of Great Britain's tradition of political liberty and civil rights guaranteed by the constitution, and they accepted with relatively little complaint a subordinate role in the economic system of the Empire because they also shared generously in its profits. Thus the American poet Francis Hopkinson celebrated the British capture of Louisbourg in 1758:

> At length 'tis done! The glorious Conflict's done!
> And *British* valour has the conquest won!
> *Success* our arms, our heroes, *Honor* crowns,
> And Louisbourg an *English* monarch owns. . . .

At the same time that colonists waxed enthusiastically over British victories, however, running through their hearts was a countervailing current—a pride in America itself. In his remarkable essay *Observations Concerning the Increase of Mankind* (1751) Benjamin Franklin predicted that one day 'the greatest number of Englishmen will be on this side the water. What an accession of power to the British empire by sea as well as by land,' he enthused. 'What increase in trade and navigation! What numbers of ships and men!' [4] At the end of the decade Franklin began to see the implications of this prospect somewhat more clearly. 'I have long been of opinion,' he wrote to Lord Kames in 1760, 'that the foundations of the future grandeur and stability of the British empire lie in America, and though, like other foundations, they are low and little seen, they are nevertheless broad and strong enough to support the greatest political structure human wisdom ever yet erected.' [5] In short, America was destined for greatness, said Franklin, and would in time become the seat of empire. In a way that perhaps even he could not quite foresee in 1760, Franklin was right.

3. A Theory of Empire

In the mid-eighteenth century British public men, and especially the younger among them, were seized of a well-established and familiar corpus of received ideas about the nature and the purpose of colonies. These concepts were by no means peculiar only to Great Britain. Western European governments in general believed in the principle of national monopoly in relation to overseas colonies, with all that this implied, and the unanimity of belief and action on this subject had struck that acute observer, Montesquieu, as partaking of the nature of a fundamental law.[6]

Much of the British theory on colonies (as well as the practice) had been elaborated during the later Stuart period, though some strands of thinking reached back even earlier: it is hardly coincidence that Charles Davenant's *Discourses on the Publick Revenues and the Trade of England,* first published in 1698, were reprinted in 1771 in a new edition of his works prepared by Sir Charles Whitworth, the then chairman of the committee of ways and means in the House of Commons. Davenant, Sir Josiah Child, and other late-seventeenth-century authorities on commercial subjects were quoted and followed with respect by many mid-eighteenth-century pamphleteers. And not only were public men conditioned in their thinking by reading these authors and the glosses put upon them by contemporaries, but they could not avoid noting that many of the principles there enunciated were embodied in the law of the land, in the great series of Trade and Navigation Acts of Charles II, and in the consolidating statute of 1696.[7] Discussion was intensified during the 1750s. Many traditional arguments were rehashed and given a keener edge during the decade from about 1752, when the British were faced first with a major war to uphold the interests of the whole Empire against the French in America, and then with the problems of expansion and reorganization created by their overwhelming victory. In particular, the celebrated debate on the respective merits of annexing Canada or Guadeloupe involved discussion of basic principles and drew them to the attention of a wider public.

Renewed publicity was thus given to the general assumption that colonies had no *raison d'être* if they did not contribute to the economic well-being and so to the power of the metropolitan state. A newspaper correspondent gave an illustration of this view in its most brutally forthright form in 1775, when he wrote: 'I have always considered the colonies as the great farms of the public and the colonists as our tenants. . . . It is time to look about us, and keep them to the terms of their leases.'[8] An assumption of this kind placed the colonists in the position of second-class citizens. It was sometimes justified by the further assertion that the colonies were entirely a creation of the British community at home, which had invested capital and labour in developing them, had provided defence against foreign enemies at further considerable expense, and so had a right to expect an economic return.[9] Like many political axioms, this was just sufficient a half-truth to provide a plausible basis for far-reaching conclusions. The assumption bore about as much—or as little—relation to the complex world of reality as the equally unbalanced view declaimed in the House of Commons in 1765 by Isaac Barré and rapidly taken into currency in America, that the colonists owed nothing at all to British support.[10] As a half-truth it was less than fair to the colonists, since it allowed no credit to the human losses and creative activities of several generations of British-American pioneers.

The belief that the colonies should minister to the economic well-being of the metropolitan state involved various other secondary assumptions. It appeared to follow that their economies should be complementary to and not in competition with that of Great Britain. Ideally they should confine themselves to the production of agricultural and extractive commodities, providing their own foodstuffs and otherwise satisfying needs for materials which the British could not supply from home sources. Such materials would be supplied to Great Britain with more certainty, in abundance, and more cheaply, than if reliance had to be placed on foreign suppliers. Moreover, in respect of such commodities Great Britain should become the staple for European trade, drawing the middleman's profits from supplying markets on the Continent. West Indian sugar, spices, cotton-wool, and coffee, and the tobacco, rice, indigo, and pitch produced by the southern mainland colonies fell admirably into this commercial framework. The colonies north of Maryland fitted far less easily into this pattern. Few staples in great demand offered themselves from this region, though potash, pearl ash, and white pine masts from the New England forests might be placed in this category. Their surpluses of agricultural produce and lumber did, indeed, minister directly to the well-being of the West Indies. But in almost all other respects, on the superficial view sometimes taken at the time, they seemed to be economic competitors with the metropolis rather than collaborators—in shipbuilding, in the fisheries, in the carrying trade, in the iron production of the middle colonies. By thinking along these lines most commentators tended to overlook the general contribution the northern colonies made to the prosperity and resources of the Empire as a whole, by the spending power they earned from their extensive trade with the foreign West Indies and the Latin countries of southern Europe, and by the enormous addition they made to the pool of British shipping and seamen. Rare indeed was the writer perceptive enough to point out that the monopoly systems set up by British trade regulation might benefit particular groups of businessmen rather than the nation as a whole.[11] There was even the occasional extremist—not to be taken too seriously—who thought it would be a happy solution if the New England colonies were abandoned and their populations transferred *en bloc* to more southern settlements, or to Ireland, where they would be seen to make a direct economic contribution to the wealth of the Empire.[12]

On another function of overseas colonies eighteenth-century economic writers were almost unanimous, and so were the politicians who took guidance from them. Colonial populations should constitute a captive market for home manufactures, helping thereby to create employment and general prosperity in Great Britain, and they should be actively discouraged from engaging in manufactures themselves.[13] Most parts of the Empire in fact fulfilled this role, making large and steady demands upon home suppliers for manufactured goods of every sort.

All these assumptions entailed a precise and rigid, though not all-embracing, framework of commercial controls, binding the colonies and the metropolitan state into one self-contained economic system, and denying foreign countries any advantages from trade with the colonies. On paper the Navigation Acts and the Acts of Trade formed such a system. Foreign ships were barred from the ports of

British possessions, and British (including colonial) shipping had a statutory monopoly of carrying trade within the Empire. Certain staple commodities could be exported only to other imperial destinations: direct carriage to Europe was forbidden. In this category by 1763 stood rice and sugar (with some exceptions respecting southern Europe), tobacco, cotton wool, indigo, ginger, dye-stuffs, naval stores, molasses, furs, and copper. By the same token the direct importation of most European goods was forbidden. They could be shipped to an American destination only from a British port, ensuring the levying of duties that would raise prices above any similar goods of British manufacture. The Woollen Act and the Hat Act forbade the export of raw wool, woollen yarn, cloth, or beaver hats from any colony, even to another destination within the Empire. Under various Acts white pine trees suitable for masts for the King's ships were not to be cut except under license. Against these restrictions might be set bounties for the encouragement of various extractive industries, notably for indigo, pot and pearl ash, naval stores, and ships' timber. Many colonial products were left uncontrolled. Foodstuffs, horses, fruit, vegetables, pig iron, and many forms of wood products could be sold wherever a market presented itself.

On the whole, up to 1763, this system had worked to the benefit of the colonies. It has been pointed out that 'the Navigation Act of 1660 was the basis for the prosperous shipbuilding industry in America, and that the prohibition of the presence of foreign merchant ships in colonial seaports was largely responsible for the existence in the eighteenth century of a flourishing and extensive American colonial merchant marine.' [14] The general prosperity of the American colonies in the mid-eighteenth century was indisputable. How far this might actually be in despite of the system, because it was often honoured as much in the breach as in the observance, is a question that no contemporary seems to have asked. Evasion of the trade laws occurred and was known, and was generally deplored. Disaster was foreseen if the system was allowed to break down, for it was assumed that then not only would Great Britain lose the advantages to be expected from the colonies, but foreign rivals would gain. This was a lesson drummed home by the most respected seventeenth-century authorities. 'All colonies or plantations', Sir Josiah Child wrote in 1690, 'do endamage their mother kingdoms, whereof the trades of such plantations are not confined by severe laws and good execution of those laws, to the mother kingdom.' [15] A few years later Charles Davenant declared in similar vein: 'Colonies are a strength to their mother-country while they are under good discipline. . . . But otherwise they are worse than members lopped from the body politic.' [16]

Mid-eighteenth-century pamphlets re-echoed such warnings, and to this generally accepted view is attributable in no small degree the heated British reaction to any hint or suspicion that the colonies were thrusting towards independence. Both prosperity and national security were thought to be involved. In the eyes of most people who thought about the matter the colonists were and must remain essentially subordinate. Their interests must always take second place to those of the metropolitan state.[17] Otherwise the unity of the Empire would be dissolved and Britain and the provinces alike would succumb to the dominance of some foreign rival. Such an attitude was wholly incompatible with any concept of an Atlantic empire of equals, such as was soon to cross the minds of Benjamin Franklin and other Americans.[18] Here was a mental barrier not to be overcome until, two generations later, the corroding theories of Adam Smith's *The Wealth of Nations* combined with the dominant economic role of Great Britain as the workshop of the world to undermine the old imperial conceptions. Meanwhile the old orthodoxies held the field. The only change was in the new vigour with which British governments proceeded to apply them in the years after 1763.

II

George Grenville and the Problems of Empire

1. The Issues

WHEN THE GREAT WAR for empire of 1754–63 ended, many men in governing circles in London felt that, next to the peace treaty itself, the most urgent matter awaiting attention was the settlement of America, 'that greatest and most necessary of all schemes'.[1] The war itself had shaped views and sharpened perspectives. For nearly a decade ministers and their officials had grappled with American issues, had struggled to integrate into the general war effort the contributions of the mainland and island dependencies, had tested the sinews and experienced the stresses within the imperial fabric—only to find, when peace was made, new problems piled upon the old. Moreover men in London were more alert, perhaps, than those in Boston, New York, or Philadelphia, to the fact that what had been won had to be held. Four times in seventy years France had proved herself a formidable opponent. Would she not be so again, and all the more inveterate because there was so much she might seek to recover? The war had sharpened concern about the efficient deployment of resources for self-defence at the same time as it intensified the problem of survival in the jungle of international rivalries. Former modes of thought, old habits of *laissez aller,* seemed no longer appropriate. Not only in America but also in Britain the thunder-shock of war triggered an avalanche of change in the attitudes and then in the actions of men.

George Grenville, as the King's chief minister, and as head of the Treasury, bore a primary responsibility for the shaping of policy in the crucial years after the peace. Many of the emergent problems related to his own department, and even those which did not, might have fiscal repercussions. Conceivably Grenville was the wrong man in the wrong place at the wrong time, and a different personality holding the reins might have pursued less abrasive courses of action; yet the logic of the situation drove events strongly forward in the direction they were to follow. Grenville's character displayed both strengths and weaknesses which may have contributed to the growing friction within the Empire. Edmund Burke, knowing and respecting him as a colleague in opposition during the last years of his life, afterwards made an appraisal which seems both shrewd and fair.[2] Grenville suffered from limitations of perspective. With 'a very serious desire to benefit the public' and 'no small study' of detail, said Burke, 'he did not seem to have his view, at least equally, carried to the total circuit of our affairs.' Moving almost straight from a training and early practice in the law to a career of business in government offices, he tended to think 'the substance of business not to be much more important than the forms in which it is conducted'. Without the broad vision that a wider, more varied experience might have given, he lacked the political sensitivity necessary to deal with the imperial conditions of the 1760s:

> Persons who are nurtured in office do admirably well, as long as things go on in their common order; but when the high roads are broken up, and the waters out, when a new and troubled scene is opened, and the file affords no precedent, then it is that a greater knowledge of mankind, and a far more extensive comprehension of things, is requisite than ever office gave, or than office can ever give. Mr. Grenville thought better of the wisdom and power of human legislation than in truth it deserves.

As Burke rightly pointed out, Grenville was to err in good company. Other men also contributed to the shaping of policy. George Montagu Dunk, 2nd Earl of Halifax, Southern Secretary of State with charge of the colonies for most of Grenville's administration, had been an active and ambitious President of the Board of Trade from 1748 to 1761, and the general tenor of his policy had been to extend British supervision over colonial affairs.[3] That stormy petrel of politics, Charles Townshend, had served in junior office since 1749, entering the Board of Trade five years after Grenville had begun his official career at the Admiralty. At an early stage he had formed distinctive views about the restructuring of the Empire, to which he was to adhere with singular consistency.[4] Although a politician of much lighter weight than Grenville or Halifax, his charm and brilliance in the House of Commons made it impossible to ignore him. But it would be an error to identify colonial policy too closely with these men or even a slightly wider circle of personalities. It was Newcastle's Treasury Board which, under the stress of war, had begun

investigations into the shortfall of revenue from colonial trade resulting from neglect in enforcing regulations long on the statute
book. The Secretary of State William Pitt, and the First Lord of the
Admiralty George, Lord Anson, were the men who found the suppression of smuggling in America and the Caribbean to be a step essential to the effective prosecution of the recent war. The Treasury,
the Board of Trade, and the efficient members of the Privy Council
all encountered the problem of colonial currency during the 1750s.
Throughout the latter years of the war imperial reorganization was
being widely discussed at many levels in the government service.[5]

Enforcement of the Laws of Navigation and the Acts of Trade
was a major preoccupation of British ministers as they reflected
upon the post-war settlement of America.[6] This was particularly so
of the new head of the administration. Burke remarked of Grenville
in one of many felicitous passages in his famous speech on American
taxation: [7]

> He conceived, and many conceived along with him, that the flourish-
> ing trade of this country was greatly owing to law and institution, and
> not quite so much to liberty; for but too many are apt to believe regu-
> lation to be commerce and taxes to be revenue. Among regulations,
> that which stood first in reputation was his idol. I mean the Act of
> Navigation. He has often professed it to be so.

By the early 1760s the experience of half a century had shown
that the machinery for enforcing the laws of trade in the colonies
was inadequate, that illegal traffic was considerable, that the law
could be violated almost with impunity, and that if most colonial
trade still flowed in lawful channels, this was due to convenience and
complaisance, not to fear of coercion. Local customs officials were
too few on the ground. Often they received little or no support from
colonial governors. The assemblies deliberately denied them a scale
of fees adequate to encourage zeal in the discharge of their duty.
The sympathies of juries and even of judges made it difficult to
secure convictions in revenue cases. Officers were frequently
harassed with actions for damages and could get little help in resisting violent recovery of sequestered smuggled goods. In particular,
the universal evasion of the duty of 6d. per gallon, laid by the Molasses Act of 1733 on all molasses imported from foreign plantations,
tended to bring the law into contempt. Rows over writs of assistance
and the use of the proceeds of fines to reward informers reduced
the customs service in Massachusetts to a nullity during the first two
years of George III's reign. The multiplicity of authorities in London concerned with the business—the Treasury, the Secretary of
State, the Board of Trade, the Privy Council, the Customs Commissioners—may have contributed to the development of this situation,

but the crucial factor was that before 1760 no one in government had had the will to make the machine work.[8]

From the nature of the case it is exceedingly difficult to arrive at the vaguest estimates of the extent of unlawful trade carried on in North America. Some writers have considered it to be minimal,[9] but there are various contrary indications.

In 1763–4 the Treasury believed annual American imports of foreign molasses to be in the region of 8,000,000 gallons.[10] Unless there was extreme collusion, this figure was confirmed in the evidence at the bar of the House of Commons in 1766. One witness put the annual importation into the New England colonies alone at 4,000,000 gallons. The New York merchant, William Kelly, deposed that, according to replies to enquiries received from merchants at the various ports, the total consumption for North America lay somewhere between seven and nine million gallons, almost all of it French, and scarcely any of it lawfully imported paying duty.[11] The prime cost of French molasses at the port of lading was about 6d. per gallon.[12] Taking the mean of Kelly's figures, and ignoring the small advance in the price for cost of transport from the Caribbean, it appears that the trade in this one commodity alone was worth at least £200,000 on the Atlantic coast, and that in 1763 duty to that same amount was being evaded by violations of the Act of 1733.

Tea appears to have been smuggled into North America on an enormous scale. By one Pennsylvanian estimate in 1757 only sixteen out of 400 chests brought into Philadelphia in the two preceding years had been imported legally. According to one conservative computation, in the years 1760–6 the colonists consumed annually about 1,200,000 lb. of tea: as only 275,000 lb. were imported from England, the balance—more than three-quarters of the total consumption—was smuggled.[13] British officials feared the situation was even worse: among the considerations spurring them to action in 1763 was the belief that only one-tenth of the tea used in America was lawfully imported.[14] The demand for gunpowder in the colonies exceeded British capacity to supply, and large quantities were obtained from Holland or by way of the Dutch West Indies.[15] In March 1764 Grenville declared in the Commons that 'three or four' colonies were conducting a direct trade with France to the amount of £400,000 or £500,000 per annum; and when, at the end of that year, his secretary to the Treasury, Thomas Whately, drew up a justification of the government's measures, he set at £700,000 the estimated annual value of foreign goods smuggled into the colonies—a figure higher than that for the foreign goods imported legally by way of Great Britain.[16]

It was the war which focused official attention upon this situation; but the first clamours for law enforcement arose not in respect of tax-dodging or of illegal traffic with Europe, but over American sales of provisions directly or indirectly to enemy bases in the Caribbean. In some colonies, notably Connecticut, New Jersey, and Rhode Island, customs officials were bribed or pressured into giving false clearances to ships which then made their way to French West Indian ports. Substantial trade went on through the neutral Dutch island of St. Eustatius, and at Monte Christi in Spanish Dominica direct exchanges took place between British and French craft lying alongside each other in the roads. One or two governors connived at the misuse of cartel ships.[17] By 1757 reports on these practices had set on foot a train of investigation which was to lead directly to the Plantation Act of 1764. The Board of Trade made a systematic collation of information received over the previous twenty years, and its members were so alarmed by the result that, a year later after due reflection, they consulted the Commissioners of Customs.[18]

By this time the financial pressures generated by a war in which Pitt was prepared to spend money like water to achieve his aims were already drawing attention to the problems of revenue collection in the colonies. Early in 1758 the Customs Commissioners also received a directive from the Treasury for an enquiry, particularly into the evasion of the Molasses Act: from being a prohibitive regulation this Act had now come to be regarded as a revenue law. Thus by the end of 1759 the Privy Council and all the boards concerned had become seized of the fact that a considerable illegal trade was being carried on by the colonists; that this was depriving the metropolitan country of trade and the government of revenue; and that some of the traffic was directly detrimental to the war effort. Consultations continued during the next two or three years and strong feelings were stirred up in London by further complaints of the failure of customs officials to check trading with the enemy in the Spanish colonies after Spain entered the war in 1762.[19]

Although the peace treaty brought an easing of these problems, a strong impetus had been given to a movement for more effective trade regulation, and the connection of this with revenue was fully grasped. As Grenville was to tell the Commons the following year, the government's 'great object' was 'to reconcile the regulation of commerce with an increase of revenue'.[20] Effective control over colonial trade with foreign countries, especially the ending of illegal direct importation from the mainland of Europe, would add to the revenue collected in Great Britain by way of both customs and excise duties on goods supplied to the colonies. The Customs Commissioners pointed out that a less prohibitive duty on molasses would reduce the incentive to smuggling and open a possibility of obtaining a substantial revenue from this traffic, and the idea of a low tariff on French molasses, giving a preference on the British product, seems to have crystallized by 1763.[21]

Various uses were conceived for such a revenue. A more effective customs service would itself be more costly. One or two politicians, notably Charles Townshend and Lord Halifax, hankered after permanent civil lists for governors and other colonial officials. In general this would help to establish the 'due subordination' of the colonies; in particular it would strengthen local administrative support for the customs officials in their fight against smuggling. But above all, there was a widespread impression by 1763 that the defence of the enlarged Empire was going to cost much more than before, and that some financial contribution towards this charge should be raised in the colonies.[22]

There is much truth in the comment that, 'the decision to keep an army in America was not really *made,* it was simply assumed by the time the preliminaries of a peace settlement had been worked out in 1762.'[23] This is not to say that the decision was unwarranted. The overwhelming British triumph over France and Spain had left a legacy of major military commitments. The most pressing was the permanent control of the gulf and valley of the St. Lawrence—an object dear to the hearts of informed New Englanders.[24] Almost as urgent was the need to take physical possession of other vast territories ceded by the Bourbon powers, which must not be left open by default for these states later to resume occupation.

Relations with the Indians entailed policing operations, for which the army was indispensable. In earlier days the imperial government had hardly had a native policy. Frontier relations had been left to the provinces, with the result that almost all the tribes were hostile in 1754. The French success in winning Indian alliances forced London to evolve a policy and to enter into commitments. By 1760 frontier diplomacy had done much to detach the Indians from the French, but at the cost of promises to protect them both from unscrupulous traders and from squatters and landspeculators who coveted their hunting grounds. Military officers operating in the interior sent repeated recommendations that the army should be employed for this purpose; otherwise peace would not be kept on the frontier. If the British government did not directly foresee the great Indian rising of 1763–4, which ravaged the border settlements round the headwaters of the Ohio, nevertheless it and its agents were alive to the dangers and tried to evolve schemes to counter them. In 1760 it intervened to restrain Lieutenant Governor Fauquier of Virginia from making land grants in the upper Ohio valley. A year later it condemned local encouragement of white settlement in the Mohawk valley. It vetoed General Amherst's plans for a settlement to support the garrison at Niagara. At the end of 1761 it sent out a general instruction to all governors not to grant lands or encourage settlement in areas where Indian interests were involved and to refer all applications to Whitehall. In this context the army began to be seen as having a policing role, protecting Red Men against Whites: it was not cast for the role of a defence force against the Indians.[25]

Various other considerations contributed to the decision to maintain an American military establishment. There is evidence that men in governing circles contemplated the possible use of the army to control the mainland colonies, but no indication how far this idea had entered into ministerial decisions: the troop dispositions of the early 1760s had no relevance for any such intention. In the autumn of 1763 support of customs officials was explicitly added to the duties of the military, but troops were not deployed to fulfil this role. It has been suggested that internal political pressures made army reductions difficult for George III and his ministers, and that therefore no less than fifteen regiments were pushed away into North America, where they would be less likely to rouse the traditional hostility in Britain against a standing army.

More clearly, part of the political price of parliamentary approval for an increased army establishment was the promise given in 1763, that although the first year's expenditure in America must be found by the British taxpayer, for the future the burden would be placed on the shoulders of the colonists.[26] The case for this was understandable. During the past nine years Great Britain had expended over £82,000,000 on the war. Between 1756 and 1762 the annual national expenditure had almost doubled. The national debt had also more than doubled, and the annual interest charge had increased by well over £2,000,000. Taxation in Britain would inevitably remain higher than before the war, and this was only palatable if it were understood that some part of the future burdens would be shared by the colonists, who had hitherto made no direct contribution to the upkeep of peacetime regular army establishments.

Colonial paper money raised issues which had attracted the attention of the imperial government for some years before the accession of George III and which became pressing soon after Grenville's appointment to the Treasury. Years earlier the growing concern of Boston businessmen over unrestrained issues of paper legal tender in Rhode Island had eventually led to the New England Currency Act of 1751. This statute restricted issues in the four northern colonies to such amounts as were necessary to meet either war expenditure or the current service of government, and specified that such paper should be legal tender for public obligations only and not for private transactions.[27] A precedent for imperial intervention had thus been established when the currency problems of Virginia began to cause friction in the 1750s.

At that time the economy of the Virginia plantations rested partly on advances of credit from London business houses which have been estimated at over two million pounds. British merchants naturally expected to be repaid in sterling, and they felt cause for alarm when a Virginian Insolvent Debtors Act of 1749, empowering debts to be discharged in local currency at an advance of twenty-five percent, slipped through the vetting procedures of the Privy Council. A Virginian amending Act of 1755 giving courts the right to fix the rate of exchange in cases of debt failed to get royal confirmation owing to legal technicalities and neglect in Whitehall, and therefore, though normally implemented by the provincial courts, was challengeable and not felt to be an adequate safeguard. As Virginian bills of credit declined in value, by 1758 British creditors felt themselves liable to lose £20 on every £100 of debt discharged under Virginia law. After a long series of complaints, at the beginning of 1764 the Board of Trade undertook a general investigation of paper money in all colonies not controlled by the Act of 1751.[28]

2. The Measures of 1763–1764

A complex array of American problems thus faced the administration during 1763. Two steps were taken before Lord Bute resigned the Treasury. The new army establishment received parliamentary approval; and Grenville, during his last month as First Lord of the Admiralty, conducted through the Commons a Bill to tighten procedures against smuggling and to extend to American waters the provisions of the British Hovering Acts.[29] Soon after Grenville took over the Treasury in mid-April, his Board and the Customs Commissioners began discussions about improving the American revenues. In mid-July the commissioners returned a report showing that the receipts from colonial duties collected under the Plantation Act of 1673 and the Molasses Act of 1733 averaged a mere £1,800 a year, less than a quarter of the cost of the service, which they put at £7,600 for 1763. Immediate administrative action followed. Absent officials were ordered back to their posts, strict instructions issued about the punctilious discharge of all their duties, additional appointments were authorized, and a substantial naval force of over forty vessels was detailed to assist in the suppression of smuggling. In mid-September a further report from the Customs Commissioners provided a comprehensive basis for Treasury drafts of what was to become the Plantation (or Sugar) Act of 1764.[30] About the same time, calculating that other sources of revenue in America would have to be tapped, the Treasury Board instructed the stamp commissioners to prepare a scheme for a colonial stamp tax.[31] Until early in the following year the question seems still to have remained open whether some of the funds so raised might be used for colonial civil lists.[32]

Meanwhile, during the summer of 1763 the Southern Secretary and the Board of Trade were busy settling government and land tenure in the American and Caribbean territories ceded to Great Britain by the peace of Paris. Grenville's brother-in-law, Lord Egremont, having succeeded Pitt as Secretary of State in October 1761, was by now familiar with American problems, especially those of the frontier, and although the Board of Trade was duly consulted, its members added little to the main outlines of policy drawn up by Egremont and his staff. On Egremont's death in August 1763 Halifax took control of the southern department. He made no change of substance in these plans, which were finally approved by the Privy Council and promulgated by proclamation on 7 October.[33]

Parts of the conquered territories on the mainland were apportioned between four provinces. The remainder of former French Acadia, with Prince Edward and Cape Breton Islands, was annexed to Nova Scotia. Three new governments were proclaimed for East and West Florida and for Quebec. In all these areas governors were empowered to make land grants on terms expected to facilitate the rapid peopling of their provinces. But in some respects the most significant provisions in the proclamation were those establishing an Indian reservation in the vast area of the Great Lakes and the Ohio basin. The western boundary of Quebec was confined to the headwaters of the Ottawa river. South of the St. Lawrence, while not abrogating the claims of various colonies under old charters, the government forbade settlement for the present west of the Alleghany watershed. In the area beyond, the operations of British traders were to be strictly controlled. Lawful entry required a licence, trade was to be conducted only at designated points where British army detachments would exercise police functions, and bond for good behaviour was to be given. Military officials and the staff of the British Indian Agency were authorized to return criminals and fugitives to the seaboard for trial.[34]

The proclamation gave formal sanction to an *ad hoc* policy for the interior which had been emerging for several years at the hands of local military commanders and of the Indian superintendents, Sir William Johnson and John Stuart, who had held these posts since the mid-1750s. It implemented a principle to which the Board of

Trade, then headed by Halifax, had committed itself at least six years before—that 'the only effectual method of conducting Indian affairs . . . [would be] to establish one general system under the sole direction of the crown and its officers.'[35] It reflected a determination to conciliate the Indians, 'by every act of strict justice and by affording them protection . . . for their hunting grounds.'[36]

Common humanity played its part in this policy. Viewing the matter with more detachment than the frontiersmen, who tended to regard the Indians as savages to be cleared off the rich lands they believed were the white man's goodly heritage, British officials considered that the natives equally deserved justice and protection and held property rights in their lands which should be acknowledged. But other material considerations also shaped their policy on settlement. Ministers wished the tide of migration to flow not west but north and south. They were alert to the political and economic advantages of the rapid peopling of Nova Scotia and the three new colonies. A thickly-populated province could more easily defend itself. An inflow of English-speaking settlers in the north would help to hold in check the French Canadians, whose loyalty must remain doubtful, at least for a time. Wheatlands in Quebec, coal mines in Cape Breton, the fisheries of the gulf of St. Lawrence were all assets awaiting development; the last of these would add to the reserves of seamen on which that vital factor of British ascendancy, sea power, was based. Planners looked to the Floridas for rich yields of sub-tropical and Mediterranean-type produce, and larger populations in all these areas would create new markets for British goods.[37] By contrast, no advantage—indeed disadvantage—was anticipated from westward migration. John Pownall of the Board of Trade, reflecting on American affairs in the summer of 1763, noted that the establishment of inland colonies might 'induce a necessity for such remote settlements (out of the reach of navigation) to ingage in the production and manufacture of those articles of necessary consumption which they ought, upon every principle of true policy, to take from the mother country, and would also give rise to a separation of interests and connections, in other points, not consistent with that policy.'[38]

Grenville's plans for regulation and revenue came before the Commons in a series of financial resolutions in March 1764 and passed into law a few weeks later as the Plantation Act, 4 George III, c.15. The description 'Revenue Act' sometimes applied to this measure tends to obscure its essential nature. The main content of its forty-seven clauses clearly placed it in the sequence of the great Acts of Trade and Navigation of the previous century; few of them were concerned with taxation and those which were also involved trade regulation.[39] While in part the new regulations served particular vested interests, it would be a mistake to overlook the concern with general imperial objectives which animated Grenville and his colleagues. Their essential task as they saw it was to foster the economic resources of the Empire and to deny other powers any advantages from it. Whately wrote afterwards in defence of the Act: [40]

> To encourage the consumption of our own produce and our own manufactures, in preference to those of other countries, has been at all times an undisputed maxim of policy; and for this purpose, high duties and even prohibitions have been laid upon foreign commodities, while bounties have been granted on our own. The general tendency of the Act . . . is to extend the same principle to the *American*, as is followed in respect to our home trade and consumption.

In oblique reference to the known or suspected violations of the Trade Acts which the Plantation Act was partly intended to curb, he stated the contemporary assumption: 'If [colonies] were allowed to transfer the benefits of their commerce to any other country than that from which they came, they would destroy the very purposes of their establishment.' [41] In effect, the inhabitants of the colonies should still contribute to the general welfare of the whole as if they continued to live within one single geo-political unit: [42]

> They, the subjects still of the same country, should continue to act as they must have acted, had they continued its inhabitants, and that their produce and their consumption should be for the benefit of that country, in preference to any other.

On this understanding of the matter Britons in Boston were entitled to similar but no more favourable trade contacts with foreign peoples than Britons in London or Edinburgh—a principle difficult to maintain against either the facts of geography or the enjoyment of particular commercial advantages by those Britons who remained in Great Britain.

Many provisions of the Plantation Act and of a group of other statutes associated with it were intended to foster American enterprises which would add to the resources and prosperity of the Empire, both as a trading nation and as a Great Power. In the days of sail, hemp and flax were 'strategic materials': bounties were intended to promote expansion of production, but also to act as a disincentive to the development of a native American linen industry. A British import duty of 7*d.* on beaver skins was reduced to 1*d.* as an encouragement to both fur traders and British makers of hats. Rice culture in South Carolina and Georgia was fostered by the leave granted to export rice direct to any foreign-controlled part of the New World south of Georgia. The benefit of this concession was ex-

pected to be all the greater, since inferior and spoilt grains unacceptable in European markets might now be disposed of more readily as
food for slaves. The abolition of a British import duty of 3*d.* per lb.
on whale fins would give the New England whalers operating in the
gulf of St. Lawrence so great an advantage that the British whaling
industry based at Poole would have to be discontinued. Nevertheless
the government defended the decision on grounds of national interest, 'when the inhabitants of *America* and of *Europe* [were] look'd
upon as one people.' The North American rum manufacture was
given protection in the domestic market by an absolute prohibition
on the importation of foreign rum. Foreign sugar entering British
colonies was subjected to a stiff protective duty. This last measure
was partly intended to help the British West India planters, but it
also had a more purely regulatory function. Treasury officials could
think of no better way of combatting the abuse practised by unscrupulous merchants, whereby foreign sugar reached the British Isles
from America under colour of being British-grown and then attracted a drawback on re-export—to the detriment of the revenue
and of everyone involved in the legitimate trade from the planter to
the British exporter.[43]

Clauses in the Plantation Act relating to textiles reflected the government's intention to apply the principle of preference for native
over foreign manufactures. European and East Indian fabrics re-
exported from Great Britain to the colonies became dearer, both by
the abolition of British drawback on export and by the imposition of
an American import duty. In a number of instances the tax-burden
in America still remained lower than that falling on purchasers in
Britain; and if the colonists had to pay more for French lawns and
cambrics, at least they could lawfully buy them, which their fellow-
subjects in Britain could not do.[44]

Much of the Act was aimed directly at the suppression of illegal
commerce carried on by the mainland colonies with Europe and the
foreign West Indies. Such trade was under ban for several reasons.
It interfered with the British monopoly of colonial markets for manufactured goods, with the first call on various colonial staples which
contemporary theory assigned to the metropolitan state, and with
Britain's function as the centre for the export trade in these commodities. The list of these products, which already included tobacco,
sugar, indigo, and other items, was greatly extended in 1764: coffee,
pimento, cocoa, whale fins, raw silk, hides and skins, pot and pearl
ash, iron, and timber were added to the schedule of 'enumerated'
goods which could lawfully be shipped only to Great Britain or another British colony. Illegal trade also meant revenue lost to the
Treasury. Finally statesmen feared the deplorable consequence that

other countries, especially the dangerous rival, France, might draw the benefits from the colonies which should add to the sinews of British strength. In so far as this happened, the American provinces were, in ministerial eyes, 'no longer *British* colonies, but colonies of the country they trade to.' [45]

It was in order to deal with these problems that the Act of 1764 laid down a much more full and rigid code of procedures, with elaborate documentation of cargoes and confirmation of bonds, in the hope that officials might then be able to check smuggling and the passing of foreign goods as British. The Act reaffirmed that all laden ships arriving in the colonies from Europe should have taken aboard the whole of their cargo at a British port; the only goods excepted were wines from the Atlantic islands, salt for the fisheries, which might be loaded anywhere, and horses, provisions, and linens shipped in Ireland. Elaborate systems of bonds and certificates were prescribed to ensure that enumerated goods leaving American ports were not discharged at prohibited destinations. Customs administration in the colonies was tightened. New penalties were laid down for defaulting officials. A substantial degree of protection from harassing actions for damages was extended to those who performed their duty. Local contrivances to prevent the prosecution of smugglers in vice-admiralty courts were overriden by a clause giving customs officers the option to choose such a court, where there was no jury likely to be biased in favour of the defendant. In an unrealistic effort to strengthen this jurisdiction the government set up a superior vice-admiralty court at Halifax. The statute confirmed the application of the Hovering Acts to American waters and clarified the law regarding apportionment of the proceeds of seizures, a matter which had been under challenge in the colonial courts.[46]

Lastly, as the preamble showed, the Plantation Act was a revenue measure, which modified and extended the system of American port duties. The export duty of 7*d*. per cwt. on colonial rice extended to shipments now authorized to foreign territories in the New World; this trade was therefore expected to add to the revenue.[47] Legislation on wines was intended to end a situation in which the colonists obtained most of their wine from the Atlantic islands free of impost and were discouraged by high duties from shipping European wines by way of Great Britain. The latter were now made cheaper by tax concessions amounting to over £7. 10*s*. per ton; most of the remaining levy of £4 would be charged on export from Britain, but an import duty of 10*s*. per ton was to be collected in America in order to provide a cross-check in the custom-house accounts. Wines from the Atlantic islands were henceforth to be charged £7 per ton on entry into the colonies. Treasury officials calculated that the island vintners, for long enjoying a virtual monopoly, had heavily overcharged their American customers and would be forced to reduce prices by the competition of European vintages. They believed, too, that most of the tax on island wines would thus fall in fact on the producers, not the colonial consumers, and that in the end Americans would get their wine supplies more cheaply than before.[48]

Similar assumptions underpinned the change made by the Act in the import duty on foreign molasses entering the colonies. In 1764 ministers accepted the view that the duty of 6d. enacted as a prohibition in 1733, but never enforced, was impracticable as a revenue measure. North Americans felt any duty would be a burden on the trade. West Indians wanted a high duty, principally in hopes of embarrassing their rivals, the French sugar planters. Agreeing that the molasses trade was an important North American interest, the Treasury in effect turned down the West Indian plea, and pitched on a 3d. duty as the level of tax likely to bring in the highest yield. In theory British molasses thus received a preference in the North American market, but in fact most of this molasses was distilled by the British planters, and the North Americans were almost wholly dependent on supplies from the French islands. Treasury officials assumed that the 3d. rate would be only slightly higher than the cost of smuggling under the conditions of law enforcement they hoped to achieve, and that therefore the illegal trade would wither. They produced convincing arguments to demolish colonial allegations that the rum trade and all the attendant activities in New England and New York would be ruined by the duty; and, in particular, they calculated that the main burden of the tax would fall not on the colonial consumers, but on the foreign producers, who would either have to sell their molasses more cheaply or else pay more for the essential provisions they took in exchange.[49]

A resolution approving colonial stamp duties in principle was accepted by the Commons on 9 March 1764. There was no direct opposition, though the American merchant, John Huske, pleaded for preliminary consultation with the colonists, a step the Treasury had in mind for its own purposes.[50] Grenville's staff still lacked the information on which to base a Bill and only gathered it during the latter part of the year. While this was Grenville's main reason for postponing action till 1765, it is possible that he hoped to obtain some sort of general consent from the colonial legislatures and thus establish a precedent for consultations. It has been suggested that, playing for time, Grenville deliberately misled the colonial agents and their principals, by holding out a possibility that the colonies might themselves raise the money and thereby avoid a parliamentary tax. This seems most doubtful. One agent, Jasper Mauduit (Massachusetts), reporting at second hand, used ambiguous language which could be so construed. Another, Edward Montague (Virginia), reported clearly in this sense.[51] However, the majority of the agents seem not to have done so.[52] Moreover, the suggestion is inherently unlikely. It does not square with Grenville's sense of the dignity of his office or of Parliament. The proposition would have been clean contrary to his firm convictions about the way the constitution worked; for he believed that no authority except Parliament could constitutionally grant money to the Crown, and the idea that the Crown might keep up forces with money not controlled by Parliament was anathema to him.[53] The account of the debate on 9 March by Nathaniel Ryder contains no mention of such a suggestion: he reported merely Grenville's statement that 'he would likewise wish to follow to a certain degree the inclination of the people in North America, if they will agree to the end.' [54] Two months later, after meetings with Grenville, Charles Garth, agent for South Carolina, appeared to understand clearly that the issue before the assemblies was 'whether, or how far, to approve or disapprove'; and his report of Grenville's belief that the only way to deal with the matter was by parliamentary enactment is devoid of any ambiguity.[55]

Before the end of the session pressures from the Board of Trade and from interested groups culminated in the passage of one further important measure, a colonial Currency Act. This legislation was prompted above all by the question of Virginia debts. Three conflicting interests were involved. The planters who dominated the Virginia House of Burgesses defended local paper legal tender mainly as their safeguard against supposedly avaricious merchant creditors. The Glasgow tobacco traders favoured a local paper currency because their investments were tied up in local book credit, but wanted a carefully controlled emission on the assumption that this would prevent oscillations in the rate of exchange. London merchants demanded a situation in which their debts could be collected in money of sterling value and would not be adversely affected by exchange fluctuations. Members of the Board of Trade sympathized with this last view and were led by a simple quantity theory of money to regard all paper emissions as unsound and undesirable.[56] Almost everyone involved was misled into believing that there was a direct correlation between issues of paper currency and its fall in value. Hardly anyone else came as close to the mark as Lieutenant Governor Fauquier did when he claimed that the root of the trouble in Virginia was overspending on imports.[57] As a consequence of this the balance of payments had tilted heavily against Virginia, and a shortage of sterling bills of exchange and specie sent the exchange rate soaring. The general economic crisis of the early 1760s added to the difficulty, for anxious merchants in Britain, themselves dunned by their creditors, sought urgently to call in loans extended to their colonial customers in more prosperous years. Influential members of the Board of Trade had no grasp of these complexities, failing to note that legal tender paper formed only part of the circulating medium in the colonies, that issues in the middle colonies had not produced disorder in the exchange rates, and that the critical factors were improvident spending by one or two provinces and the unpleasant results of a consequent tangle of debt in a period of recession. Since the study of currency problems was still rudimentary, perhaps they can hardly be blamed. But the result was unfortunate. When North America merchants led by Anthony Bacon demanded immedate legislation to protect their debts, members of the Board threw their weight into the scales in favour of a restrictive Bill. The resulting Act prohibited further issues of legal tender paper money in all the colonies south of New England, and so created the situation that a desirable medium of exchange would gradually disappear as the current issues successively fell due for redemption.

3. The Reaction in America

In Boston, Massachusetts, on a late February day in 1761 James Otis, Jr., confronted Jeremiah Gridley, an old friend who represented the government before the Superior Court, Chief Justice Thomas Hutchinson presiding. At issue were the writs of assistance which permitted customs officials to break into buildings where they suspected smuggled goods to be concealed. 'Otis was a flame of fire,' reported John Adams. 'Then and there was the first scene of the first act of opposition to the arbitrary claims of Great Britain. Then and there the child Independence was born.' [58] Adams recalled the scene more than fifty years after the event. His estimate of Otis might well be doubted, and yet this statement reveals his profound and lasting opinion that the claims of Great Britain were indeed arbitrary. Still more significant was his conviction that American independence had resulted from opposition to those claims, not from a willful or capricious urge on the part of the colonists to set out for themselves. In the end it was not what Great Britain intended by its policies that mattered, but what intentions the Americans suspected. Tyranny like beauty might be said to lie in the eye of the beholder. By 1774 thousands upon thousands of American colonists became convinced that Great Britain's goal was to enslave them. 'This radical change in the principles, opinions, sentiments, and affections of the people,' Adams recalled, 'was the real American Revolution.' [59]

It was not the substance of the question heard before Judge Hutchinson that had impressed John Adams so much that day, for colonial courts had been authorized to grant such general search warrants since 1696. Nor could Adams have been pleased by the outcome, because Otis eventually lost the case. Rather, it was Otis's argument that Adams admired. Gridley pointed out for the government that such writs had been authorized by Parliament as far back as the reign of Charles II. In rebuttal Otis seized the opportunity to note that Gridley's vaunted precedent came 'in the zenith of arbitrary power' under the Stuarts. It mattered not to Otis that Parliament had authorized the writs; they violated the constitutional principle that a man's home was his castle, safe from unreasonable search. Both the writs themselves and the Navigation Acts they enforced were illegal, Otis concluded, for 'an act against the constitution is void.' [60] Inhabitants of Massachusetts Bay had occasionally challenged the authority of Parliament in the seventeenth century. One such contention had contributed to the loss of its original charter in 1684. But similar confrontations had been avoided in the eighteenth century. In his vehement objection to a specific exercise of British authority in America, therefore, Otis had made a break with the immediate past. The significance of his action would become patently clear within three years.

In the 1770s, as the crisis with Great Britain was tearing the Empire apart, many colonists looked back with nostalgia to the days before 1763. That year became a symbolic watershed separating an earlier era of happy contentment from the almost unrelieved argument and confrontation that ensued thereafter. Within a twelvemonth new statutes and orders would make major changes in the relationship between the American colonies and the mother country. The decision to garrison ten thousand British troops in America during peacetime was a disturbing departure from previous custom. The Proclamation of 1763 abruptly halted migration west of the Appalachians and even uprooted settlers already there. The Sugar Act (as the Plantation Act has been called in America) in 1764 not only tightened day-to-day enforcement of the Navigation Acts but altered judicial procedures as well. Additionally, the law broadened imperial control over the whole range of colonial commerce, expanded the list of enumerated articles exportable within the Empire only, and levied duties on the importation of sugar and other plantation articles with the explicit intention of raising a revenue. At the same time Parliament had extended currency restrictions even more stringent than those imposed in New England to the other continental colonies, putting an end to their emission of paper money.

The assemblies of several colonies had learned of Grenville's plans only through their agents in London and not until the autumn and winter of 1763-4. Within a year eight assemblies adopted resolutions protesting the new measures, particularly the Sugar Act, for it had the greatest immediate effect upon their welfare. None of the remonstrances reached Parliament in time to alter the ministry's programme, however, nor had Grenville shown any genuine interest in opinion from America on the subject, for that matter.[61]

Rhode Island's assembly drew up its response in January 1764. The tiny seagirt colony took a commercial stance by pointing out that its inhabitants purchased each year English goods to the value of £120,000. To earn funds for these imports Rhode Island had only its commerce with the West Indies, from which it annually imported some 14,000 hogsheads of molasses. Some was traded to other colonies in exchange for British goods, but most was distilled into rum and sold throughout New England or exported to the African coast. In Africa rum had undercut French brandy as a desideratum in the slave trade, and had generated an annual profit of £40,000 which was remitted to England. Most of this molasses, the Rhode Islanders conceded, came from the French West Indies, because the British West Indies could neither absorb all of the surplus produce of the northern colonies nor supply them with enough molasses to maintain their distilleries and commerce. In short, the ministry's determination to collect a 3d. per gallon duty on molasses would disrupt Rhode Island's means of purchasing British goods, throw its distillery workers and shipwrights out of work, and destroy the effectiveness of its merchant marine as a nursery of seamen.[62]

Once the text of the new law reached America, the tenor of protest against it changed. So too was the direction of those protests altered. Rhode Island had sent its remonstrance through Governor Stephen Hopkins (its actual author) to the Board of Trade. In October 1764 New York drew up a lengthy petition to the House of Commons. (Years later the Earl of Dartmouth would chastise the colonists for taking their protests to the streets instead of humbly petitioning Parliament for redress of grievances.) New York carried the argument onto new ground. 'An exemption from the burden of ungranted, involuntary taxes must be the grand principle of every free state,' the New Yorkers wrote. 'Without such a right vested in themselves, exclusive of all others, there can be no liberty, no happiness, no security; it is inseparable from the very idea of property,' they concluded, 'for who can call that his own which may be taken away at the pleasure of another?'[63]

New York's assembly recognized Parliament's authority to regulate the commerce of the Empire and even to enhance the interest of the mother country at the expense of the wealth of the colonies. The assembly staunchly denied that its protest arose from any desire for independence. 'Of so extravagant a disregard to our own interests we cannot be guilty. From what other quarter can we hope for protection?' The colonists cited their unstinting support of the mother country in time of war at the cost of both blood and treasure, and they noted that in compensating the colony for some of its losses Parliament had recognized how great a sacrifice New York had made. The petitioners pointedly asked why funds for support of the army in America were not being sought by Crown requisition. 'Should a more incorrigible spirit be imputed to us than to the Parliament of Ireland,' without a trial requisition? [64]

The petitioners then turned to commercial arguments. Much of their objection to the Sugar Act followed lines traced in the Rhode Island remonstrance, but then New York broadened the argument by objecting to the prohibition against the American lumber trade to Ireland. Such a ban would adversely effect the linen trade. But the colonists also protested against the principle adopted in enforcing the acts of trade. 'When we consider the wisdom of our ancestors in contriving trials by juries,' they noted, 'we cannot stifle our regret that the laws of trade in general change the current of justice from the common law and subject controversies of the utmost importance to the decisions of the vice-admiralty courts.' [65] The New York petition also criticized the Currency Act. Ever since the reign of William III the province had issued paper currency as an emergency wartime measure. Without it the colonists could not have cooperated in the conquest of Canada, 'that grand stroke which secured to Great Britain the immense dominion of the continent of North America.' Furthermore, the petitioners reminded Parliament, New York had granted Sir Jeffrey Amherst a loan of £150,000 to enable the British commander to carry on the campaign of 1759.[66]

The colony of Virginia, late in the year 1764, also sought redress not only from the House of Commons but from the King and the House of Lords as well. The petitioners sought from each body a recognition of their right to make their own laws governing internal matters and taxation. They based their claim on their British heritage and what they considered a fundamental principle of the British constitution, 'that the people are not subject to any taxes but such as are laid on them by their own consent, or by those who are legally appointed to represent them.' [67] Since the colonists could not by the nature of things be represented in Parliament, that body could have no right of taxation in America. Furthermore, Virginians had taxed themselves since the beginning of the colonies, the petitioners asserted, and they had responded whenever the Crown had by requisition sought their financial aid in time of war. Like Rhode Island and

New York, Virginia argued against the Sugar Act and Currency Act on grounds of expediency as well, but the major thrust of its case rested, as did New York's, on principle.[68]

Perhaps no one of the new British measures would have stirred up such widespread protest in the colonies. But taken together and during a period of sharp post-war depression, the package caused real hardship not fully understood by British officials, who were either unaware or uncaring of the circumstances of American trade. The scarcity of northern produce marketable in Great Britain sent merchants searching for 'returns' in other parts of the Atlantic world as a means of paying for needed British manufactures. Every new restriction, such as that on lumber, or wine, or molasses, ultimately impaired the colonists' ability to purchase British goods. Overzealous naval and customs officers applied the letter of the new law to coastal vessels bringing small cargoes from one colony to another, an action that sometimes doubled the time and costs of these short passages. Private merchants added their protest in letters to English correspondents. 'I need not say much of future dealings,' wrote the Philadelphian Samuel Rhodes in June 1764, 'for I fear that all our trade with you must come to an end . . . , if your legislature will carry into execution those resolves.' [69]

In the summer of 1764 James Otis, Jr., gave the American case its fullest and most learned statement in a pamphlet entitled *The Rights of the British Colonies Asserted and Proved*. His reasoning was sometimes hard to follow, his arguments seemingly contradictory in places, but the document moved inexorably to a single conclusion— 'the imposition of taxes . . . in the colonies [by Parliament] is absolutely irreconcilable with the rights of the colonists as British subjects and as men.' Furthermore, Otis recognized no distinction between an external tax on trade alone and an internal tax. Neither was valid. Yet Otis admitted with a candour that confused some of his supporters that 'the power of Parliament is uncontrollable but by themselves, and we must obey. They only can repeal their own acts.' For subjects or subordinate provinces to refuse obedience to such acts on the basis of their own judgement was treason. But 'to say the Parliament is absolute and arbitrary is a contradiction,' Otis continued. 'The Parliament cannot make 2 and 2, 5: omnipotency cannot do it.' As soon as the members of Parliament realized that they had acted in violation of God's natural laws they would repeal the offending law. Such had been the case in the past. 'See here the grandeur of the British constitution! See here the wisdom of our ancestors!' said Otis. The Massachusetts lawyer suspected that Parliament had been misled by various British governmental officials posted in America, and he made several specific references to the former Governor

Thomas Pownall, whose pamphlet *The Administration of the Colonies* had enjoyed considerable popularity in London as an authentic view of British America.[70]

In one form or another almost all the basic elements of the protest mounted by colonists in the decade to come could be found in Otis's pamphlet: the claim of constitutional exemption from parliamentary taxation; the warnings that new regulations would disrupt colonial trade; the appeal for redress by petition; the suspicion that Parliament had been misled. Only one element was missing in 1764—violence. Execution of the Stamp Act the following year would precipitate that ultimate form of protest in the streets of Boston, New York, and other colonial towns.

III

The First Crisis over Taxation

———•——

1. Grenville Completes His Programme

BY THE TIME Parliament reassembled in January 1765 Grenville's preparations for the colonial Stamp Bill were well advanced. Whately had gathered information from colonial agents and American friends. Lord Halifax had secured returns from governors listing 'all instruments made use of in public transactions, law proceedings, grants, conveyances, securities of land or money.' Evidence was also noted that the colonists disputed the proposal on constitutional even more than on economic grounds: the Lieutenant Governor of Massachusetts himself sent over elaborate arguments against it.[1] Consequently, from the start ministers and officials were drawn to defend the measure not merely as an equitable levy upon the colonists, but as an assertion of authority to which they believed Parliament had an indisputable claim.[2] Grenville discussed both aspects at length when introducing the Bill in committee of ways and means on 6 February. He pointed out that if Parliament could not tax, then neither could it legislate in other ways. He held forth on the 'virtual' nature of representation in Parliament, and denied that colonial charters could convey any exemption from parliamentary authority. He gave a list of precedents from 1673 onwards. After a detailed consideration of colonial debts and taxation he dismissed the colonists' claims to be unable to bear the burden. He argued that neither the colonies themselves nor the home government could fairly apportion shares of taxation to be raised in different provinces, and that a system of stamp taxes would fall fairly upon different communities in accordance with the respective wealth of each. Furthermore the tax was cheap to collect and did not require a large force of officials to enforce.[3]

In a full House the parliamentary opposition did not as a body challenge the measure.[4] Criticism came mainly from individuals with colonial connections or commercial constituents, and 'a few of the heads of the minority who [were] sure to thwart and oppose the minister in every measure.'[5] William Beckford, wealthy London merchant and West India planter, took the lead, and was possibly the sole speaker to hint that the colonists had an exemption by constitutional right from taxation by Parliament.[6] Other members opposed the Bill on grounds of expediency. 'We are working in the dark,' argued Isaac Barré, one of the few M.P.s with a firsthand knowledge of North America, 'and the less we do the better. Power and Right: caution to be exercised lest the power be abused, the right subverted, and 2 millions of unrepresented people mistreated and in their own opinions slaves.'[7] Richard Jackson, agent for Connecticut, conceded the right of taxation, but argued from precedent that such a power should only be used with discretion, if they were to preserve among the people of the colonies, 'a continued confidence in the legislature that is essential to the well-being of government.'[8] Sir William Meredith, M.P. for Liverpool, pointed out the irresponsibility of the mode of taxation proposed, which might be considered its most objectionable feature:[9]

> The safety of this country consists in this with respect that we cannot lay a tax upon others without taxing ourselves. This is not the case in America. We shall tax them in order to ease ourselves. We ought therefore to be extremely delicate in imposing a burden upon others which we not only do not share ourselves but which is to take it far from us.

But the advocates of caution could not prevail, and a motion to cut short the proposal was lost by 245 votes to 49. Irritation at colonial questioning of parliamentary authority undoubtedly contributed to this result: three days later Whately referred to the Bill as 'the great measure of the sessions . . . on account of the important point it establishes, the right of Parliament to lay an internal tax upon the colonies.'[10] For the same reason the Commons refused to receive colonial petitions against the Bill.[11] By mid-March it had reached the statute book.

The Stamp Act laid duties on various documents used in court proceedings and for appointments to public offices, on mortgages and other business documents, certificates of clearance for ships, liquor licences, playing cards, dice, pamphlets and newspapers. Charges on entry to the legal profession were set higher than in Great Britain. On the other hand, in response to colonial representations, Treasury officials proposed charges on land transfers, small bonds, probate, wine and spirit licences, and on appointments to

various offices below the British rates, and exempted military and
naval appointments, appointments as justice of the peace, and licences and certificates of marriage.[12] Duties were to be paid in
money of sterling value, not in local currency. To facilitate legal proceedings against defaulters, the precedent in the Plantation Act was
followed, and officials were empowered to take cases to vice-
admiralty courts. This provision was justified on the ground that in
Britain also, there was 'no safety in trusting the breach of revenue
laws to a jury of the country' where the offence was committed, and
cases were commonly brought to London for trial.[13] Treasury officials estimated that in a full year this measure would add more
than another £100,000 of revenue to the £60,000 expected from
duties under the Act of 1764.[14] They took pains to refute colonial
contentions that the taxes would draw sterling money out of
America, pointing out that by statute the funds collected were to be
spent there on defence. Moreover Great Britain was still bound to
remit large sums *to* America for this purpose; the net effect of the
taxes was simply to reduce the amount remitted.[15] The Act was
scheduled to come into operation on 1 November 1765.

The Grenville ministry's second Plantation Act, enacted in May,
corrected shortcomings in the Act of 1764 and developed further
some of the principles of policy expressed in it.[16] The statute prescribed a long, detailed list of bounties on various sorts of timber
reaching Britain from the colonies. The right to export rice to
American territories south of Georgia was extended to North Carolina, and the sale to northern Europe through Great Britain was facilitated by the introduction of a bonded warehouse system. An
error in the 1764 Act was acknowledged by the re-authorization of a
direct trade in timber from the colonies to southern Europe and
Ireland. The government refused a similar concession on colonial
iron, apart from permitting direct dispatch to Ireland; but it tried to
open the market by repealing a clause in the Iron Act of 1750 for-
bidding reshipment of this iron either in the British coastal trade or
for re-sale abroad. Tariffs on coffee and sugar were readjusted,
principally to assist the West India interest, and with the same object
another clause required ships leaving American ports in ballast to
give bond against any illegal trafficking in molasses or sugar which
might be taken on board later in the voyage. In an attempt to meet
colonial complaints about interference with local traffic under the
Act of 1764, the statute exempted from obligation to obtain clearance certificates and cockets small undecked vessels of up to twenty
tons, plying between different parts of the same colony, provided
these carried only produce not liable to duty and sailed not more
than a league from shore. The government also attempted in this

Act to clarify and authorize the scales of fees to which customs officers in America were entitled.[17] Accepting criticisms about the remoteness of the superior vice-admiralty court at Halifax, ministers prepared plans, left unimplemented until two years later, for a system of district courts at Boston, Philadelphia, and New York or Charleston, which would be within relatively easy reach of any point along the American coast.[18]

During the spring of 1765, at the request of the commander-in-chief, General Gage, the ministry also secured the passage of an American Mutiny and Quartering Act.[19] It has been forcibly argued that such a measure was both inexpedient and unnecessary; that, generalizing from one or two untypical circumstances, Gage and his staff anticipated increasing difficulties over desertions, troop movements and billeting, and were afraid to rely for the future on the *ad hoc* working arrangements which had operated in the past.[20] However, they presented a pressing case for legislation, and the government rather naturally responded to the opinions of its experts. Unfortunately the response was confused. While the resulting Act was unexceptionable in its treatment of desertion and the requisition of transport, on quartering it fairly deserved the description of 'abortion'.[21] Because of his concern for troops on the move through sparsely populated areas where there was little accommodation of any kind, Gage had wanted sanction for billeting in private houses. This was illegal under a statute of 1679: George III immediately saw political danger in the proposal.[22] It was vehemently opposed by the colonial agents, and an abandonment of this old principle was unacceptable to the Commons. All Gage obtained was power to requisition vacant houses and outbuildings to be fitted up as temporary barracks in case of need. At the same time the Act placed firmly upon the colonists the burden of fitting and provisioning with various necessaries barracks, whether temporary or permanent, to make them 'as much like public houses as possible'.[23] When troops were so quartered, local magistrates were to provide firewood, bedding, candles, salt, vinegar, cooking utensils, and a ration of beer, cider or rum; and the provincial authorities were to reimburse them for the expenses so incurred.[24]

With the close of the 1765 session the outlines of the new colonial policy were clear. It had grown naturally out of the preoccupations of the men in charge of government in London, and from the circumstances with which they found themselves faced. Foremost loomed the problem of meeting the greatly increased defence costs of a vastly extended Empire. A letter from the Connecticut agent, Jared Ingersoll, summarizing the substance of various discussions he and other agents had had with Grenville, fairly reflects ministerial attitudes at the time the Stamp Bill was going through its legislative stages: [25]

And now Sir in order to give you . . . an idea of the conferences, s[en]timents and reasonings upon these subjects, on this side the water, you will be pleased to imagine to yourself a few Americans with the Minister . . . and after much time spent in enquiry, various observations and remarks, he saying to them as follows, You will be pleased, laying aside all consideration of past services on your part or on ours, they have both been very great, to consider what is the present state of things; there is an immense national debt, not less than one hundred and forty millions lying heavy on this nation, for which an annual interest is paid; by the best informations we can get the whole of the public debt now in arrear of all the colonies together is about eight hundred thousand pounds. The civil establishment here for the support of government is eight hundred thousand pounds a year—that of all the colonies together we find to be about forty thousand pounds per annum only. You say you are comparatively poor to what we are; 'tis difficult measuring this point, but however opulent some in these kingdoms are 'tis well known the many can but just live. The military and naval establishment here is immense, but without considering that, the amount of the expence of the army now placed in America and which is thought quite necessary, as well on account of the trouble with the Indians as for general defence against other nations and the like in so extensive a country, is upwards of three hundred thousand pounds a year. We shall be glad to find that the Stamp Duty now laying on America shall amount to forty or fifty thousand pounds and that all the duties together, the post office and those laid upon Molasses and other ways shall amount to one hundred thousand pounds a year, so that there will not only not be any money brought away from America by means of these duties, but there will be a ballance of more than two hundred thousand pounds sent over every year from England to be spent in America. You say the colonies think they can, and that they are willing to do something in the common cause;—is this too much? We think it is not, but if on trial we find it is, we will certainly lessen it. As to our authority to lay these duties or taxes—to us 'tis so clear a point that to be sure we dont care to have a question made of it. And dont you yourselves even want to have us exercise this authority in your turn? Dont some of you complain, and perhaps very justly, that in the late war, while some of you did much, others did but little or perhaps nothing at all—and would not that be the case again was you left to defend yourselves? No doubt it would, unless you were erected into one power by a union of the whole, but that is a measure we dont think you yourselves, was you in our steads would think adviseable; and there are many reasons why you should wish not to have the country defended by your own children. A soldier's life is not only a life of danger, but in a proper sense is a base life, whereas you have all a chance in that opening country to raise your families to be considerable in time by a diligent attention to your natural and proper business.

To all this the Americans answer, truly Sir we must own there is a weight in your arguments and a force in your reasonings—but after all we must say we are rather silenced than convinced. We feel in our bosoms that it will be for ever inconvenient, 'twill for ever be dangerous to America that they should be taxed by the authority of a British Parliament by reason of our great distance from you; that general want of mutual knowledge and acquaintance with each other,—that want of connexion and personal friendship, and we without any persons of our own appointing, who will have any thing to fear or hope from us, to speak for us in the great council of the nation—we fear a foundation will be laid for mutual jealousy and ill will, and that your resentments being kindled you will be apt to lay upon us more and more, even to a degree that will be truly grievous and that if that should be the case that twill be hard under all the circumstances, very hard to convince you that you wrong us, and that unknown and very unhappy consequences will ensue.

To this the Minister replies:–

Come, suppose your observations are entirely just, and indeed we must own there are inconveniences attending this matter; what then is to be done? Perhaps you will say let the colonies send members to Parliament; as to that in the first place the colonies have not told us that they desire such a thing, and 'tis easy to see there are many reasons why they should not desire it. The expense would probably be very great to 'em; they could not expect to be allowed to have a majority of members in the House, and the very inconveniencies which you urge with regard to the people in America would in many respects and to a degree take place with regard to their members. What then? Shall no steps be taken and must we and America be two distinct kingdoms and that now immediately, or must America be defended entirely by us, and be themselves quite excused or be left to do just what they shall please to do? Some perhaps will do something and others nothing. Perhaps from the nature of our situations it will happen and must be expected that one day we shall be two distinct kingdoms, but we trust even you wont say you think yourselves ripe for that event as yet. You are continually increasing in numbers and in strength; we are perhaps come, at least, to our full growth. Let us then leave these possible events to the disposal of providence. We own on our part we dont choose to predict, nor yet to hasten the time of this supposed period, and think it would be to our mutual disadvantage for us to attempt a separation.

Let us, then, instead of predicting the worst, hope that mutual interest as well as duty will keep us on both sides within the bounds of justice. We trust we shall never intentionally burden you unreasonably; if at any time we shall happen to do it by mistake, let us know it and I trust it will be remedied.

British ministers felt they had reason on their side. They were anxious to strike an equitable balance in the sharing of the Empire's financial burdens. Perhaps they were unduly sensitive to the likelihood of trouble at Westminster if they did not do so. Perhaps they were too confident that the body exercising power would always be guided by sweet reasonableness. But if there are various grounds on which their policy can be criticized, one at least can be dismissed. It was not nurtured by any sinister Tory authoritarian plot such as haunted the fevered imaginations of some politicians both in Britain and in America during the years that followed. British policy did, however, raise the spectre of authority; for imperial reorganization on the scale which, from the viewpoint of London, seemed necessary for continued survival after 1763, inevitably involved the use of power in ways which had not hitherto been customary; and the basis of that power therefore became a focus of controversy.

It would be incorrect to see in the developments described above an inevitable progress towards the revolutionary crisis: an element of free will exists in most human situations. However, it might be said, that in making their decisions, the British politicians did not perceive the full range of choice before them. The grounds for action seemed compelling, and the action followed. The grounds for inaction at first hardly obtruded upon their notice at all, and when they did their urgency was far from being clearly apparent. Very few members of Parliament realized that government action in these years raised problems of a political—as distinct from a legal—character, regarding consent and consensus among British Americans. Not even Americans in London like Benjamin Franklin or Ingersoll, who became involved in the making of appointments or who accepted appointments in the new colonial stamp administration, had fully grasped this fact. Those few men who did, such as Isaac Barré, Richard Jackson, or Sir William Meredith, carried no weight in the nation's councils.[26] Had William Pitt stood forth at this time and deployed their arguments with the full weight of his great prestige and personal authority, perhaps the history of the next few years might have been different. But Pitt, like Achilles, sulked in his tent. No more apparently than any other leading politician did he sense the emergence of an issue of crucial importance for the future of the Empire he had done so much to consolidate.

2. *America Resists*

The Americans had of course known for some time of Grenville's plan to introduce a bill establishing stamp duties in the colonies (see pp. 41–2 above). Contemporary observers and subsequent historians

have disagreed over Grenville's motives in postponing the new legislation for a year. But at least some of the assemblies considered the
delay an opportunity to express their views on the matter and to
propose alternative means of raising a revenue. Seven colonies sent
special instructions to their agents in London, and despite the failure
of earlier efforts, several assemblies also petitioned the King and/or
Parliament in opposition to the proposed Stamp Act. Rhode Island
now advanced its argument from the grounds of expediency used
against the Sugar Act to the claim of constitutional rights. Other colonies raised the question of requisitions as an alternative to the
stamp duties, and in February 1765, four colonial agents including
Jared Ingersoll and Benjamin Franklin made such a proposal directly to Grenville. But all to no avail.[27]

In mid-April 1765 colonists received the text of the Stamp Act
indicating that the new taxation would become effective on 1 November. They also learned that Parliament had refused to consider
American petitions. Many must have shared the indignation of
New York's conservative jurist William Smith, who would later become a loyalist. In late May he wrote to General Robert Monckton
that 'when the Americans reflect upon the Parliament's refusal to
hear their representations. . . , and find themselves tantalized and
condemned, advantages taken of their silence heretofore, and remonstrances forbidden in time to come . . . , what can be expected
but discontent for a while and in the end open opposition. . . . This
single stroke,' Smith concluded, 'has lost Great Britain the affection
of all her colonies.' [28]

In Virginia Patrick Henry arrived from his Piedmont county to
take a seat in the House of Burgesses. The session was nearly over;
only thirty-nine of 116 members remained. Just what Henry said to
the House has long since become obscured by historical legend. According to an impartial witness, the young firebrand declaimed that
'in former times Tarquin and Julius had their Brutus, Charles had
his Cromwell and [I do] not doubt some American would stand up
in favor of his country.' The implication that George III was a tyrant
and would meet a violent end similar to other tyrants apparently
worried no one present save the speaker, who rose to call Henry to
order and label his allegations treason. The young delegate immediately apologized and swore his eternal loyalty to the King.[29]

What Patrick Henry did achieve at Williamsburg was to propose
several resolutions, the exact number and text uncertain, which the
House proceeded to adopt. The first two statements merely established the historical basis for Virginia's claim, already made in its
petitions of 1764, and now repeated, that 'the taxation of the people
by themselves, or by people chosen by themselves to represent them

. . . is the only security against a burthensome taxation, and the distinguishing characteristic of British freedom. . . .' A fifth resolution, adopted by a one-vote majority after furious debate but rescinded the next day, apparently went much further than any previous statement made in the colonies. Here the historical record again is obscured by legend. The impartial observer of the previous day's proceedings described the fifth resolution as declaring that anyone supporting Parliament's claim to tax the colonies 'should be looked upon as a traitor and deemed an enemy to his country.' Henry's own account of his fifth proposal reveals a far less extreme version, a mere assertion that Virginia had 'the only and sole exclusive right and power' to lay taxes there, hardly new ground in 1765 nor worth the trouble of rescinding. The item expunged was apparently one of two additional resolutions which the House had hotly debated on the previous day. Ironically, both the *Newport Mercury* and the *Maryland Gazette* (the first newspapers to report Virginia's proceedings) included a version of the controversial last resolution as though it had been permanently adopted.[30]

One cannot be sure what effect if any the publication of Virginia's real and alleged resolutions may have had in other colonies, but in September Rhode Island adopted a set modelled closely on those of the southern colony. The Rhode Islanders went further, however, by declaring that they were not bound to obey a law 'designed to impose any internal taxation whatsoever upon them', except those enacted by their own general assembly. And in a final resolve the assembly called upon all officers of the colony to proceed with their business 'in the same manner as usual, [i.e., without conforming to requirements of the impending Stamp Act] and that this Assembly will indemnify and save harmless all the said officers, on account of their conduct, agreeable to this resolution.'[31] Now at last rhetoric gave way to resistance. During the autumn of 1765 eight other colonies also considered the implications of the Stamp Act, but only New Jersey's assembly joined Rhode Island in offering support to officers pursuing their duties 'in the usual manner'. The remaining colonies merely stated constitutional objections without calling for overt disobedience, but in so doing most were moving considerably beyond their previous arguments based on expediency.[32]

And now the colonies were ready to act together. When Massachusetts suggested in early June that they all send delegates to a congress in New York the following October, New Hampshire alone declined, although governors prevented three others from electing delegates. Among the twenty-seven men from nine continental colonies were James Otis, Robert R. Livingston, John Dickinson, Caesar Rodney, and Christopher Gadsden, all of whom would play prominent roles in the decade to follow. Dickinson apparently submitted several drafts of a statement to initiate discussion. The delegates debated whether to include a specific acknowledgement of Parliament's authority over the colonies, such as its right to regulate commerce, for instance. The more conservative members lost the argument, and the document stated only that the colonies owed 'all due subordination' to Parliament, a safe enough generalization. What the congress meant, made clear in a memorandum left by one of the delegates, was that Parliament had only the right to exercise a 'general superintending power' over the colonies, which included the regulation of trade but excluded 'levying external and internal duties and taxes' or any other legislation that violated the colonists' constitutional rights.[33]

The foundation of the American constitutional argument rested firmly on the belief, shared by almost all Americans, that only the colonists' representatives could exercise the power of taxation, since the revenue thus raised was considered a free gift to the Crown from the people. English writers countered these claims in several pamphlets which enjoyed wide circulation in the colonies and which prompted an immediate response. This exchange of views, the so-called 'great debate' on British colonial policy, involved some of the most experienced and articulate advocates on both sides of the Atlantic. Thomas Pownall, former governor of Massachusett, was swept into the debate by his proposed revision of imperial affairs published as *Administration of the Colonies* in 1764. In the superstate he proposed Parliament became the well-spring of all political power, 'the true and perfect representative' of Great Britain and the colonies both. Pownall asserted, if he did not precisely prove, that Parliament had the right to tax the colonies.[34] The best written pamphlet of the great debate was probably *The Objections to the Taxation of our American Colonies . . . Briefly Consider'd,* by Soame Jenyns, M.P. for Dunwich and a member of the Board of Trade when he wrote his work. Jenyns brushed aside the American arguments for their 'insolence' as much as for their 'absurdity', and he cited the examples of numerous English towns and categories of individuals to prove that taxation did not require consent.[35]

The question of representation however, remained central not only for Americans but for the British ministry as well. Thomas Whately, secretary to the Treasury and the man who drafted the Stamp Act, raised this issue for the Grenville administration in his pamphlet *The Regulations Lately Made. . . ,* published in 1765. He fully agreed that the principle 'is common to all *British* subjects, of being taxed only with their own consent, given by their representatives.' Whately in fact went further than any of the American assemblies in declaring that 'no new law whatever can bind us that is made without the concurrence of our representatives. The Acts of Trade and Navigation, and all other acts that relate either to ourselves or to the colonies are founded upon no other authority. They are not obligatory,' he concluded, 'if a Stamp Act is not.' [36] Whately of course insisted that the colonists were in fact represented in Parliament. 'All British subjects are really in the same [situation]; none are actually, all are virtually represented in Parliament; for every member of Parliament sits in the House, not as representative of his own constituents, but as one of that august assembly by which all the Commons of Great Britain are represented.' [37]

However persuasive such a definition of 'representation' might have been to readers in England, where by Whately's own assertion nine-tenths of the people were not electors, the idea of 'virtual representation' was meaningless to Americans. Indeed, one of the fascinating aspects of the American Revolutionary era is to note how basic concepts such as political representation had come to acquire different meanings on opposite sides of the Atlantic. In each continental colony representatives from distinct geographical entities—towns, counties, or parishes—comprised the legislature. They were often called 'delegates', a term which emphasized their special responsibility to those who elected them. Residency requirements, annual elections, and occasional instructions prevented representatives from forgetting the source of their political powers.

The American position found its most articulate spokesman in Daniel Dulany, a nativeborn Marylander considered by many the most brilliant lawyer in America. Through years at Eton, Clare College, Cambridge, and the Middle Temple Dulany had become familiar with the English point of view. In less than a decade he would in fact become (or remain?) a loyalist. But now in the summer of 1765 he set about to challenge the defence of Grenville's policy in a pamphlet of his own, entitled *Considerations on the Propriety of Imposing Taxes in the British Colonies.* . . . Whately had cited, in *The Regulations Lately Made,* the case of numerous lessees, copyholders, and inhabitants of cities like Leeds and Birmingham, as examples of non-electors in England who were virtually represented in Parliament and therefore subject to its taxation. Dulany took aim on Whately's argument that by analogy American non-electors were similarly represented and thus equally liable. 'The notion of a virtual representation of the colonies . . . is a mere cobweb, spread to catch the unwary and entangle the weak.' [38] The Englishmen cited by Whately as non-electors in one capacity could and often did qualify as electors in some other capacity. 'The interests therefore of the non-electors, the electors, and the representatives, are individually the same.'

Parliament could not oppress non-electors without oppressing electors and its own members as well. Furthermore, if English non-electors were not taxed by Parliament they would not be taxed at all.[39]

By contrast colonial non-electors had no other means of qualifying; theirs was a total incapacity. In addition, the electors of Great Britain and the inhabitants of the colonies had no intimate relationship or mutuality of interests such as bound together electors and non-electors in the mother country. 'On the contrary, not a single actual elector in England might be immediately affected by a taxation in America.' In fact, Dulany suggested, acts that oppressed the colonies might even become popular in England 'from the promise or expectation that the very measures which depressed the colonies would give ease to the inhabitants of Great Britain.' [40] Furthermore, the concept of 'virtual representation' ran counter to the basic American practice that legislators were agents of their particular constituents, not representatives of the nation as a whole.

Dulany then moved on to probe new ground in the relationship between England and her American colonies. He agreed that the colonies were dependent and that Parliament had the authority to hold them in subordination.[41] From this premise he concluded that Great Britain had the right to regulate colonial commerce by duties on imports and exports if Parliament so wished, even if a revenue were incidentally produced.[42] But the authority to maintain the inferiority of the colonies did not give Parliament licence to seize the property of Americans, as a tax for revenue would do, or to command them in everything else. 'There may very well exist a dependence and inferiority without absolute vassalage and slavery.' Parliament's power was in fact limited, in Dulany's view, 'by the powers vested in the inferior . . .', specifically the power to impose internal taxes conferred upon the colonies by their charters.[43] Although Dulany did not pursue the matter further, he in fact stood on the very brink of formulating a new federal principle by his suggestion of a nation superintended by an authority whose powers were limited by equally valid powers of inferior member states. 'I acknowledge dependence on Great Britain,' Dulany concluded, 'but I can perceive a degree of it without slavery, and I disown all other.' [44]

Like all such exchanges the 'great debate' raised more questions than it answered, providing grounds for the publication of further pamphlets on both sides of the Atlantic. Had not Dulany suggested that the Americans would accept external but not internal taxation? (No, he had not, if one notes his definition of taxation as a measure *designed* to raise a revenue rather than one that produced an incidental revenue in pursuit of another end.) By their denial of 'virtual representation' were the Americans not seeking the privilege of sending actual representatives to Parliament? (No, as numerous writers suggested, actual representation could not, because of the distance, fulfill the American expectation that representatives maintain close and continuous touch with their constituents.) If, as Dulany conceded, Parliament could *legislate* for the colonies, could it not legislate taxes? (No, Dulany insisted, legislation and taxation were two separate functions of Parliament, only the latter requiring the consent of the people affected.) Was not the colonists' suggestion that restrictions on their commerce also harmed the British a tacit admission that the American and the British interests did indeed coincide? (Yes, and so did colonial boycotts of British manufactures as a means of putting pressure on Parliament seem to imply a kind of 'virtual representation'. But the inconsistency was too vague to be exploited.)

While the orators talked, and the pamphleteers wrote, other Americans turned to more direct means of expressing their opposition to Grenville's Stamp Act. Violence was nothing new in colonial America, particularly in Boston and other seaports, where Pope's Day and other celebrations often generated a little turmoil in the streets. But with the exception of the Revolution of 1689 popular uprisings in America were rarely directed toward political ends. Yet Americans were fully aware of the writings of Robert Molesworth, Benjamin Hoadley, John Trenchard, and Thomas Gordon, among others, who built upon the seventeenth-century work of John Locke and Algernon Sidney a convincing rationale for the use of force as a last resort in defence of liberty. Whig ideology had emphasized the need for prompt action at the first indication of abuse of power. The corruption of public officials, maintenance of large standing armies, or the levying of taxes without consent were some of the common signs of potential tyranny. By the 1760s, however, most Britishers had enough confidence in their Parliament to agree with William Blackstone's argument that the people's right to remove the legislature existed in theory only and was no longer of practical value. But Americans who were separated by 3,000 miles from England could not so easily share this confidence in Parliament. Upon reading Blackstone's judgement, the young Massachusetts lawyer Josiah Quincy, Jr., asked himself 'whether a conclusion can be just in theory, that will not bear adoption in practice.' [45]

In Boston as in other seaports the problem was how to prevent the Stamp Act from taking effect as scheduled. Repeal seemed unlikely, and would in any case not come before November. Meanwhile letters from England reported that various officials had been appointed stamp distributors and would soon receive stamped papers upon which numerous legal documents were thereafter to be printed. Surely the first signs of tyranny seemed at hand. When a small group of Boston shopkeepers and artisans met together as 'the Loyal Nine' that summer, the *Boston Gazette* and other newspapers had been carrying protests against Grenville's new policies for over a year. The Nine had no intention of overthrowing the government or of separating Massachusetts from the Empire; they merely hoped that by forcing Andrew Oliver, the apparent distributor for Boston, to resign his office the law might be rendered a dead letter.[46]

Oliver was the Secretary of the colony, a member of the Governor's Council, and a man of considerable property in his own right. To persuade him to resign, the Loyal Nine arranged with Ebenezer Mackintosh, leader of Boston's South-End mob, to put on a convincing demonstration. On the morning of 14 August Bostonians awoke to discover Mr. Oliver hanging in effigy. A crowd gathered, then marched to the waterfront where Oliver had recently constructed a commercial building. This they demolished in the belief that the Secretary intended to house his stamp-office there. The next stop was his fine mansion, where the mob hoped to receive Oliver's terrified resignation. But by the time the people arrived, the Secretary had understandably departed for safer grounds. In its anger and frustration the crowd wrecked what they could of the mansion, ripping out interior woodwork, smashing all the windows, and destroying much of the furniture. When Lieutenant Governor Thomas Hutchinson made an effort to calm the crowd, he and the sheriff were driven away in a hail of stones. The next day Oliver resigned the commission that he had not yet received, and the crisis appeared resolved to the satisfaction of the Loyal Nine and their supporters.

But instead of satisfying the crowd Oliver's resignation seemed only to whet its appetite for larger game: Thomas Hutchinson. The Lieutenant Governor had long been an unpopular figure. Born to a wealthy old-line New England family, Thomas had all the right credentials for political leadership in Massachusetts. But one difficulty stemmed from the fact that he held several offices simultaneously. And his hard-money policies had alienated influential leaders of the province's country party. Hutchinson himself, as spokesman of the so-called court party was used to the rough-and-tumble of factional politics and to the opposition of James Otis's followers. He was also a rather pompous, sometimes arrogant, fellow, not accustomed to compromise. Hutchinson had more recently angered the 'popular' leaders in 1764 by intervening to water down the General Court's protest against Grenville's taxation programme. Although in fact he was opposed to Parliament raising a revenue in America on grounds of expediency, Hutchinson became a prime suspect on Otis's list of Americans who had misled the ministry into adopting its new policy. In those August days of public anxiety Hutchinson altogether made a plausible target of public resentment.

On the night of 26 August the mob turned vicious. First it attacked the homes of the deputy registrar of the Admiralty Court, William Story, and of Benjamin Hallowell, the comptroller of the customs office. Private papers, books, and fine furnishings were all destroyed, and much of the decorative woodwork torn off the walls. Hutchinson's mansion was next on the list. The Lieutenant Governor described his loss a few days later:

> Not contented with tearing off all the wainscot and hangings and splitting the doors to pieces they beat down the partition walls . . . , cut down the cupola . . . , and began to take the slate and boards from the roof. . . . The garden fence was laid flat and all my trees &c. broke down to the ground. . . . Besides my plate and family pictures, household furniture of every kind, my own my children and servants apparel, they carried off about £900 sterling in money and emptied the house of everything whatsoever . . . , not leaving a single book or paper in it and have scattered or destroyed all the manuscripts and other papers I had been collecting for 30 years together besides a great number of public papers in my custody. . . .[47]

Enemies as well as friends of Hutchinson shared his horrified reaction; yet they all seemed powerless. Gradually, however, a semblance of order returned to Boston as the more moderate citizens condemned the proceedings and took steps to prevent such extreme outbursts in future.

Opposition to the Stamp Act turned to violence or the threat of it in other communities as well. At Newport, Rhode Island, the inhabitants ransacked the homes of Augustus Johnston, incoming stamp distributor, and two other citizens well known as advocates of submission to Parliament. New York's distributor promptly resigned before sharing a fate similar to Oliver's, but Maryland's stampman was more stubborn, and lost his house for his pains. By 1 November not an official could be found who was willing to distribute stamped paper in any of the continental colonies except Georgia, where the Governor achieved a partial compliance for a brief period.

Meanwhile, the merchants of several ports had advanced their own particular means of opposition: the boycott. Begun more as economy measures than as political protests, local agreements to cut back on the purchase of luxuries led more or less directly into a series of more broadly-based agreements against the importation of British manufactured articles until repeal of the unwanted acts. By September 1765 a number of individual merchants had already cancelled their orders for spring goods from London, and many others soon followed. At the end of October two hundred New York merchants took the first coordinated step by agreeing among themselves to make all their English orders contingent upon repeal. Soon the merchants of Philadelphia, Boston, Salem, and several lesser ports fell into line. Perhaps the American community of merchants could exert sufficient economic pressure upon the mother country to bring about their desired political end. The fact that trade conditions called for retrenchment made the sacrifice more apparent than real.[48]

Successful in the negative sense of preventing the use of stamps, the colonial leaders next faced the problem of maintaining 'business as usual,' for technically not a vessel could be cleared, not a court order issued, nor a newspaper printed without the use of stamped paper. Within two months most of the ports were operating in open defiance of the law. Closed courts, however, benefited the debtors of colonial America, and it is not surprising that there was little popular interest in keeping them open. Only in Rhode Island did the courts continue without interruption, although they reopened in several other colonies before repeal of the Stamp Act was announced. But the courts did little business during that long winter of uncertainty, for lawyers were reluctant to bring cases to trial under such irregular circumstances.

Resistance to the Stamp Act had sprung up simultaneously in numerous localities throughout the colonies during the summer and fall of 1765. Not until the year was nearly out did these various groups succeed in exchanging views and coordinating their opposition, for the colonies had no tradition of cooperation, no machinery nor institutions through which to work. Only the newspapers (none of which ceased publication because of the Stamp Act) and postal service linked the colonies together. The Stamp Act congress was in itself an extraordinary act of unity. But gradually through the autumn and winter local groups calling themselves the 'Sons of Liberty', apparently from a complimentary phrase by Colonel Isaac Barré, began to associate with like groups elsewhere. The name itself recalled the concern for liberty that dominated the writings of Trenchard, Gordon, and Hoadly. The rise of the Sons of Liberty tended to regularize colonial opposition and to limit its goal to repeal of the Stamp Act. Its members repeatedly pledged their loyalty to King George and showed little malice toward Parliament as a whole. It was Grenville's ministry, misled perhaps by erroneous informants, which was the villain of the piece. The Stamp Act agitation was, in the opinion of one recent historian, 'a classic instance of limited forceful resistance. The fundamental authority of the state, as embodied in the monarch, was not contested; and the distinction between this authority and that of individual malefactors was consciously drawn.'[49] Resistance, no matter how violent in some instances, had not yet become revolution.

IV

The Rockingham Ministry
and the Colonies, 1765-1766

---

1. The Evolution of Policy

DURING THE SPRING OF 1765, for reasons unconnected with America, George III's relations with the leaders of the Grenville ministry reached breaking point. In July, with the help of his uncle the Duke of Cumberland, he succeeded in forming a new administration.[1] The Marquis of Rockingham accepted the Treasury, but real leadership rested—for so long as he lived—with Cumberland, whose prestige and experience far exceeded that of most of the ministers. The royal duke was regularly present at cabinet meetings, set the tone of approach to various questions, and may without serious exaggeration be regarded up till his death on 31 October as the head of the ministry he had created.[2]

No one at first realized the nature of the approaching storm. When, at the end of August, the cabinet considered Lieutenant Governor Fauquier's report on the Virginia Resolutions, they dismissed them as the effervescent gesture of a small, youthful minority in one colonial legislature, which would be repudiated when the sober majority of the House of Burgesses reconvened.[3] Routine instructions to governors about the administration of the stamp taxes were sent out on 14 September, in ignorance of the upsurge of colonial opinion and action which were to make the whole scheme impracticable.[4]

This is not to say, however, that the ministers had no thought for the colonies. Perhaps inevitably in hindsight, the story of this government has been dominated by the Stamp Crisis leading up to repeal; but independent of that, the ministers had an American policy—one which was under tentative consideration almost from the moment they took office and which was brought to fruition

weeks after the Stamp Act had been repealed. From the start they
were preoccupied with an economic situation steadily deteriorating
both in Britain and in America. Businessmen individually and in
groups lobbied the Board of Trade and the Treasury, and their representations fell into place alongside the flood of complaints from
the colonies against British commercial legislation and taxation. The
statesman who legislates for trade and finance in a period of economic recession is doomed to condemnation whatever he does; and
in the situation that developed in the summer of 1765, it is not
surprising that the ministry rapidly formed an impression on the
basis of the information thrust upon it that Grenville's measures
were to blame. Within a few weeks the cabinet was contemplating
drastic amendments.[5] At that stage the Stamp Act was merely one of
a number of colonial economic questions which ministers were considering in a more general context. But for the dramatic events at
Boston and elsewhere it seems likely that their thoughts would have
turned to a policy of modification with the object of lightening the
fiscal burden on the colonies; and in the event, this wider perspective they were already beginning to form helped to shape their response to the colonial demand for repeal.

Two circumstances in particular reflected the ministers' response
during the summer and early autumn of 1765. Rockingham busied
himself with measures to restore the traffic in Spanish bullion in the
West Indies. In October the London merchant John Huske, a native
of New Hampshire and M.P. for Maldon, probably after unofficial
discussions with members of the administration, put forward a comprehensive scheme for reinvigorating imperial trade, including the
establishment of free ports both in the West Indies and on the North
American mainland, and a reduction of the molasses duty to 1*d.* per
gallon.[6]

The British economic situation was as much in their minds as the
American. Rockingham, as a leading Yorkshire magnate, was deeply
concerned about the prosperity of the West Riding woollen industry.
The Staffordshire connection of the President of the Board of
Trade, the Earl of Dartmouth, made him alert to the problems facing the manufacturers of iron and other metalwares in the West
Midlands. Newcastle had long-standing political links with various
London merchants, some of whom were engaged in the North
American trade. The West India interest was a powerful lobby with
which all politicians had to reckon. Sensitive to the narrowness of
their political base, the leading ministers were anxious to cultivate
support outside Parliament. But not the least of the motives at work
was the political mileage to be gained from a successful reversal of
the previous administration's policies. To save the country from eco-

nomic ills and at the same time to rub the face of one's opponent in the mud is a prospect apt to attract most politicians.[7]

As the American crisis developed, it was perhaps important that Rockingham, Conway, and Grafton were all conciliatory men by temperament. Conway and Grafton were admirers of Pitt and probably aware that he disapproved of the Stamp Act. The ripe political experience of the Duke of Newcastle, the Lord Privy Seal, inclined him strongly to avoid any confrontation over constitutional rights.[8]

Nevertheless, when first news of the Boston riots reached London early in October, with clear indications that the colonial complaint stood on constitutional rather than economic grounds,[9] the cabinet's response, very different in tone from the well-meaning consideration it had begun to give to commercial grievances, was to order the use of force to restore obedience to the law. But for gubernatorial weakness and the dispersal of British troops far from the centres of disturbance, these orders might have precipitated a military conflict within a few weeks.[10] While Cumberland was probably responsible for this firm line, he did not stand alone, for the Lord Chancellor condemned the riots as rebellion and came to cabinet on 31 October prepared to demand military enforcement of the Stamp Act, 'in support of the sovereignty of the British P[arliamen]t over the colonies'.[11] Cumberland's death caused a postponement of this meeting and perhaps alone prevented the cabinet from committing itself a second time, and irrevocably, to an immediate armed conflict in North America.

With Rockingham's emergence as effective head of the administration, a more moderate tone began to prevail, and various indications combined to convince him and some of his colleagues that the malaise arose principally out of the economic situation. In this the strong representations of British merchants played a major part.[12] At the same time Benjamin Franklin, moving into the position of leading spokesman for America in London, exerted pressure of another kind. On 10 November he dined with Rockingham and doubtless reiterated the argument he had already impressed on Dartmouth, 'that the general execution of the Stamp Act would be impracticable without occasioning more mischief than it was worth, by totally alienating the affections of the Americans from this country, and thereby lessening its commerce.'[13] In early November it was still understood in London that the government would stand by the Stamp Act;[14] but by the end of the month Rockingham was converted to the merchants' point of view and could be fairly sure of carrying more than half the cabinet with him. Difficulties still lay ahead. Dissidents both of cabinet rank and below it in the administration had to be overcome, and beyond loomed the problem of win-

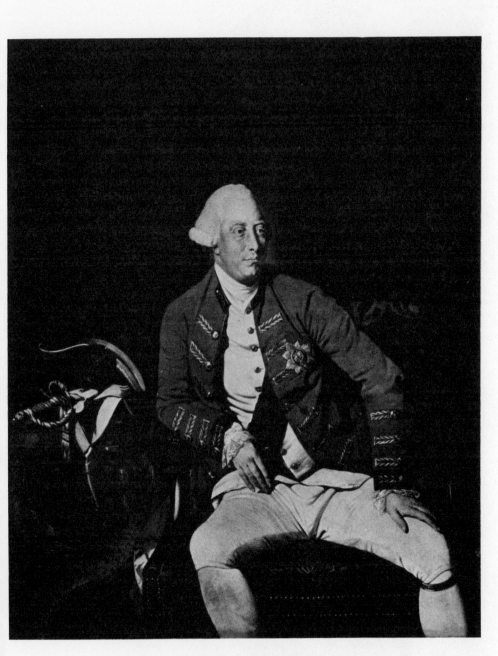

King George III (1738–1820) at the age of thirty-three. *After Zoffany. Oil,*
c. 1771. By permission of the Marquess of Zetland.

George Montagu Dunk,
second Earl of Halifax (1716–1771);
detail with, at left, an under-secretary.
*Attributed to H. D. Hamilton. Oil.
National Portrait Gallery, London.*

George Grenville (1712–
1770) in his robes as Chancellor of the
Exchequer. *By William Hoare. Oil.
Christ Church, Oxford.*

The Marquis of Rockingham (1730–1782). *By the studio of Reynolds. Oil.*
National Portrait Gallery, London.

The Old Custom House, London, centre of the economic life of the Empire. By
Maurer Engraving 1714. Reproduced in Old and New London by G. W. Thornbury.

Canada, and the limits of West Florida. *By Daniel Paterson, assistant quarter-master general. Manuscript map, 1766. The British Library, London.*

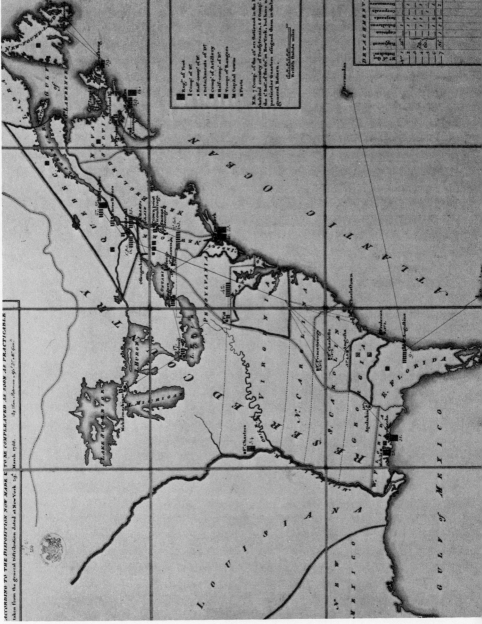

THE GREAT FINANCIER, OR BRITISH ECONOMY FOR THE YEARS 1763, 1764, 1765. Grenville, first Lord of the Treasury, holds the balance, which one of his subordinates is loading with candle ends and other rubbish. Pitt, supported by a crutch, upbraids him for sacrificing conquests abandoned at the Peace of 1763, and behind him unrepresented America groans under the burden of Grenville's taxes. *Engraving. Department of Prints and Drawings, British Museum, London.*

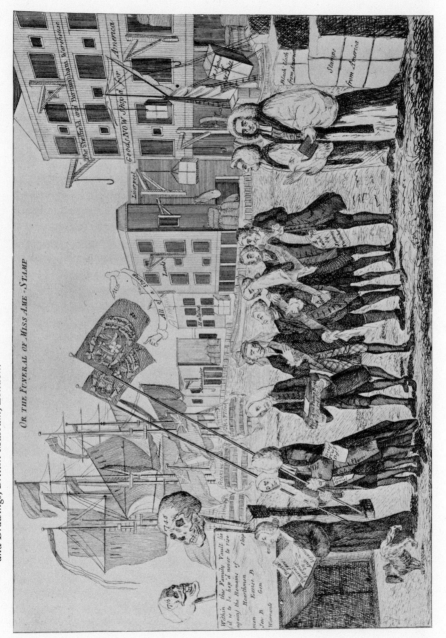

THE REPEAL, OR THE FUNERAL OF MISS AME-STAMP. Members and supporters of the former Grenville administration attend the interment of the Stamp Act. Grenville carries the coffin. In the background ships named after the Marquis of Rockingham and his colleagues prepare to resume the trade with the colonies. *By B. Wilson. Engraving, 1766. Department of Prints and Drawings, British Museum, London.*

William Pitt, first Earl of Chatham (1708–1778), in his peer's robes. *After R. Brompton. Oil. National Portrait Gallery, London.*

ning the approval of Parliament. As Franklin shrewdly observed, the ministers were 'truely perplex'd how to act . . . as, if they relax, their predecessors will reproach them with giving up the honour, dignity and power of this nation.' [15]

Popular pressure out of doors was a potential lever against these obstacles, and Rockingham's desire for public support, combined with a sense of identity of views, seems to have been the basis for the close cooperation which developed between him and the leaders of the commercial interest during December 1765. Together with Barlow Trecothick, chairman of the body of London merchants trading to America, Rockingham shaped the circular in which an appeal was made for a nationwide campaign of petitions to Parliament. This document made it clear that there would be no discussion of constitutional issues. The Stamp Act, for reasons regarding which no analysis was offered, was taken to be an obstruction to American commerce, and its repeal was sought as a means to a purely commercial end. Parliament was to be left in no doubt that this action was demanded by public opinion, and that the prosperity—perhaps the internal security—of the country depended upon it.[16] Only by such tactics could Rockingham hope to overcome the resistance of his dissidents, the strong defence of their policies which the ex-ministers would undoubtedly present in Parliament, and the much more general reluctance which could be expected in both Houses to approve any step appearing to diminish the authority of Parliament over the colonies.

The first step was to neutralise the opposition within the ministry. Certain key men in both Houses were strongly averse to any hint of a surrender on the constitutional point. In particular, disaster threatened from the hostility to concession of the two leading lawyers, Lord Chancellor Northington in the Lords, and the attorney general, Charles Yorke, in the Commons. Both men had to be persuaded that a declaration of Parliament's legislative rights and strong verbal condemnation of colonial excesses would be a sufficient vindication of British authority over the colonies, and that this authority would not then be jeopardized by repeal. Charles Townshend, the Paymaster General, was another formidable debater with a concern for the due subordination of the colonies, whose goodwill had to be gained. This situation explains the extraordinary procedure adopted by Rockingham during December and January. American affairs were withheld from the cabinet, and the tough debate over policy took place in a series of *ad hoc* meetings, usually held at the Marquis's house. Alderman Sir William Baker and Barlow Trecothick sometimes attended as spokesmen for the commercial interest. Neither Newcastle nor Northington were summoned to these meetings.

Both men would have played havoc with Rockingham's delicate task of edging his colleagues into some form of consensus, Newcastle by his fussily obstinate objection to declarations of constitutional right and Northington by his opposition to repeal; and Northington might also, by reports to the King, have brought further embarrassing pressure from that quarter. At the same time this unofficial committee, through the inclusion of back bench and even non-parliamentary representatives of commerce, provided a means by which influential opinion could be brought to bear against the resistance of Townshend and Yorke.[17]

During these discussions Rockingham faced demands which could have gravely exacerbated the crisis—demands for a Declaratory Bill framed in far stronger terms than those ultimately adopted, and for an amending Bill which would leave some parts of the Stamp Act in operation. Until a late stage Yorke desired a specific declaration of the power of taxation, and there was also pressure for the inclusion of penalties of high treason for any future impeachment of Parliament's authority.[18] By 2 January the idea of a Declaratory Bill, along the lines of the Declaratory Act (Ireland) of 1719, was generally agreed, as was 'the intention of giving the colonies every possible relief in trade and commerce . . . hand in hand with declarations of authority or censures of the riots and tumults.' But the ministers were deadlocked on the Stamp Act. '*All*,' Rockingham wrote to Newcastle, 'would agree to various amendments and curtailings of the Act. *Some as yet* not very many to a suspension and *very few* to a repeal.'[19] On 11 January, only three days before Parliament reassembled, reliable reports forecast that some token stamp duties would be retained.[20]

During a brief parliamentary sitting before Christmas the ministers had been able to stall; but on 14 January they were still in disarray.[21] The firm tone of the King's speech reflected their agreement on strong affirmations of parliamentary authority but gave no hint (none was possible) of their intentions regarding the Stamp Act.[22] Opposition leaders believed that proposals to repeal it had been laid aside.[23] They were wrong. But it seems probable that, up to 14 January, Rockingham, determined as he personally was to push for repeal, could not see his way clear in face of the dissent of some of his junior colleagues and the known opposition of the Lord Chancellor. Time was running short, for in a few days the ministry was bound to declare itself or else collapse in confusion. In the event Rockingham was relieved of his worst immediate difficulties by the intervention of William Pitt.

Pitt turned the Commons debate of 14 January on the address into a nine-day wonder. But there is no doubt that his irruption upon the scene was the beginning of a calculated campaign for return to office. While dissociating himself in the most forthright terms from Grenville's policies, Pitt threw out lures to the Scottish M.P.s who had formed the core of Bute's party and who constituted part of the squadron described as the 'King's Friends'. At the same time he manœuvred in such a way as to promote the disintegration of Rockingham's ministry, several leading members of which would have preferred to have him at their head, and he avoided identifying himself too closely with Rockingham's policies. How far this last consideration determined his line of argument can only be surmised; but by not merely denouncing the Stamp Act, together with the rest of Grenville's works, as ill-advised and inexpedient, but in addition declaring it to be unconstitutional, or even illegal, he created a confusion which temporarily aided at the same time as it embarrassed Rockingham. Pitt's attempt to distinguish direct or internal taxation from port duties and other legislation outraged the lawyers (and indeed delivered him into their hands), and his championing of American resistance evoked a more widespread anger and indignation among members of the House.[24]

Several results of moment for America arose from this affair. Henceforth, if only by comparison, the ministry's policy appeared less yielding, and some of the reaction which it might otherwise have evoked seems to have been expended against Pitt himself. It seems possible, as has been suggested, that 'Pitt's speech gave Rockingham the moral courage openly to avow the policy already formulated in the recess. Perhaps also it cooled his more stubborn supporters.'[25] One immediate sequel into which Rockingham was stampeded by his Pittite secretaries of state, an overture to Pitt believed essential in the light of the first dazzling appraisal of his performance, had, as Pitt doubtless hoped, a weakening effect upon the administration.[26] This may have sobered both Townshend and Yorke. Townshend may not have worried much about his future prospects, but Yorke certainly did and knew that he could hope for little from the Grenvillites or Pitt if the Rockingham ministry were to collapse. At any rate, whatever their reasons, both men soon abandoned their obstructive tactics. Townshend, who had been strongly for the Stamp Act before the Christmas recess, came into the plan of repeal on 19 January.[27] Yorke, upon whose support Rockingham perhaps rightly professed to believe 'the whole depends', gave his agreement at a political dinner at Rockingham's on the 20th. However, he exacted his price— one more or less already agreed by the inner policy-making group— the adoption of a series of firmly-worded resolutions asserting British supremacy and condemning colonial excesses, which struck dismay into Newcastle's wing of the ministerial coalition.[28] On the 24th

Yorke called on Newcastle to explain his position; 'very warm', the Duke wrote, 'and said, my notions about the American affairs, were *insanity;* I think, he talked more like a madman than I did.' [29]

Dependent as Rockingham was on his leading legal officer in the Commons, the most he could do was press Yorke into various verbal concessions. One of these was important, for it involved the exclusion of any specific mention of taxing powers in the proposed Declaratory Bill. Any such wording would alienate Pitt and so put the government's plan in jeopardy when it reached the Commons. Yorke was made to understand that Rockingham too had reached his sticking point. He was not prepared to face the dire consequences at home of failure to repeal. Despite a threatened secession of many members of the court party, he believed the Commons would agree to repeal by a great majority. If it did the ministry would be proved to be firmly in the saddle. If it did not, 'I wish no man so great a curse, as to desire him to be the person to take administration and be obliged to enforce the Act.' In oblique but emphatic terms Rockingham warned Yorke that his failure to cooperate would make him responsible for economic collapse and social catastrophe in Great Britain, as well as for the end of the ministry and perhaps also of his ambitions to be Lord Chancellor.[30]

According to Franklin the Marquis may have gained some leverage from yet another argument—that after the repeal of the Stamp Act an alternative revenue might be obtained by the establishment of an American loan office to manage an American paper currency to take the place of the provincial issues which the Currency Act of 1764 had been intended to restrain. Franklin and Thomas Pownall jointly submitted a plan to Rockingham and had an interview with him about it early in December.[31] A year before Franklin had sought to head Grenville off stamp taxes with this proposal, but to no avail; now he expounded it to more receptive ears. His friend John Huske later brought in a Bill, apparently with the tacit support of the ministers, but in face of opposition it was postponed till the next session.[32] Although there seems to be no other evidence, Franklin's statement that Rockingham used the scheme to catch at support appears not improbable.

Be that as it may, after tense arguments, barely forty-eight hours before the day fixed for detailed consideration of American business in the Commons—aided perhaps by the near approach of this deadline—the Marquis, displaying a firmness with which he is rarely credited, had imposed on the cabinet and underministers a compromise policy which many of them, even he himself, disliked in part, but which all but one, at least grudgingly, would support in Parliament. The Stamp Act should be repealed. This would satisfy the colonists' demand for action. At the same time the principle of Parliament's legislative supremacy would be upheld in word if not in deed. It followed that the case for repeal must be presented to Parliament on purely economic grounds. Of the cabinet ministers only Northington still remained obdurately set against repeal, and the difficulty this might cause in the House of Lords would have to be overcome as best it might.

2. *The Parliamentary Campaign*

On 17 January the House of Commons had received over twenty petitions from London and other commercial centres. On the 27th it shelved consideration of the petition from the Stamp Act congress, in order to avoid discussion of the fundamental constitutional challenges which that document posed, which would have irreparably damaged the government's chances of implementing its policies.[33] On the 28th it proceeded to the examination of papers and witnesses. First, for three days, members read and heard evidence about colonial disorders.[34] This was business which the more liberal-minded ministers could not avoid if they were to keep the support of their more authoritarian colleagues. Nevertheless it involved a threat to their programme, for the information presented to the House tended to confirm the allegations of Grenville and his friends about the rebellious state of America and the signs there of a conscious move towards independence. This impression inevitably built up prejudice against the concession of repeal at which the government aimed. The risks became evident on 3 February, when the ministers moved the first of their resolutions, to the effect that Parliament 'had, hath, and of right ought to have full power and authority to make laws and statutes of sufficient force and validity to bind the people of America, subjects of Great Britain, in all cases whatsoever.' Isaac Barré, seconded by Pitt, moved to delete the last four words, on the ground that they implied Parliament's right to tax, which both denied. The whole situation, the motion, and the amendment were considered at length with the utmost seriousness. 'A fuller House I don't recollect to have seen', Charles Garth, M.P. and colonial agent, wrote to his American correspondents, 'and it is to the honour of Parliament, I must add, that I believe there never was a debate so temperate, serious, solemn, and parliamentary, without the least appearance of party faction (disunited and divided as we are), intermingling in the arguments upon the question on one side or the other.' Faced with a subject of transcendant national importance, the House of Commons displayed an appropriate sense of occasion, and the debate continued until nearly four in the morning.

The members' conviction of their full power and authority was such
that scarcely ten voices were heard for the amendment when the
question was put, and Barré saw it was useless to press for a division.[35] In the Lords the Declaratory Resolution was carried by 125 to
5. Lord Chief Justice Camden's elaborations of Pitt's constitutional
arguments were torn to shreds by two far more eminent lawyers,
Northington and Mansfield, and only four young peers, Shelburne,
Poulet, Torrington, and Cornwallis, had the temerity to vote with
him.[36] On this question the opposition had no quarrel with the ministers.

Pittite tactics may indeed have spared the ministry one embarrassment. The opposition might well have moved to add to the Declaratory Resolution a specific reference to taxation of the kind
which Rockingham had already insisted on deleting. However, the
discussions on the motions by Barré in the Commons and Camden
in the Lords tended to pre-empt the issue, fixing in everybody's
minds the assumption that the words 'in all cases whatsoever' included the taxing power.[37]

From this point onwards the threat to the government's policy
began to show itself. Affirmations of authority could as readily lead
away from repeal as towards it. Of this the ex-ministers were well
aware. If they could now turn the sense of the two Houses away
from the direction in which the government sought to impel it, they
might achieve a number of aims: the vindication of their own legislative achievements, now about to come under attack; the destruction
of the ministry, since few of its members would remain under the
constraint of resolutions which would force upon them an immediate direct conflict with the colonies; thereby, perhaps, their own
reinstatement in office, in the absence of any alternative group of
men to whom the King could turn; and finally the preservation, as
they saw it, of the imperial structure—for in their view a Declaratory
Act would be a meaningless pretence if the substance of Parliament's
authority were conceded by repeal of the Stamp Act. The last of
these considerations was naturally the one they presented as their
public motive for action; how the others may have ranked in their
minds can only be guessed.

The ministers themselves were sufficiently aware of the danger
and had taken at least some of the steps open to them to avert it.
From mid-January, if not earlier, George III's personal influence
with his court servants was already being employed on behalf of the
government.[38] At Rockingham's request the King also tried unsuccessfully to overcome the opposition to repeal of Northington.[39]
What caused the Marquis greatest concern was the sudden
emergence of Bute in direct opposition to the policy of repeal and

the threatened secession of many of his friends and other members
of the court group in both Houses. Some of these men may have
been trying to bid up their price with the ministry, but many were
genuinely convinced that the policy of repeal was a recipe for disaster. Bute believed the alternative to enforcement was, 'to sit tamely
by and see our country, this great empire crumble into pieces.' [40]
The King's promptings failed to override the conscience and conviction of numbers of his servants—probably even the sanction of dismissal which he was afterwards blamed for not using would not have
done so—and with large-scale defections the ministry's position became precarious in both Houses, but especially in the Lords. Grenville and his friends felt correspondingly encouraged and in early
February they set out to demolish the ministry and its American policy.

The ministers introduced the rest of their assertive resolutions in
the Lords on 4 February and in the Commons on the following day.
The Lords' proceedings began quietly with acceptance of a resolution, that dangerous tumults and insurrections had occurred in
America in defiance of the government and legislative authority of
Great Britain. The ministers next defeated an opposition amendment to their second resolution, which would have declared that the
resolves of colonial assemblies had 'caused' (instead of 'greatly encouraged') these disorders. The third resolution of which they had
given notice was then withdrawn—this would have led up to an
address to the King for instructions to governors to punish rioters
and maintain the authority of Crown and Parliament; clearly it
would have stood in the way of conciliation.[41] Their fourth resolution, that colonial governors should recommend to their assemblies
compensation for those whose property had been destroyed in the
riots, provoked an ominous situation: Grenville's and Bute's friends
combined to carry by 63 votes to 60 an amendment substituting the
word 'require' for 'recommend'. To outsiders it seemed significant
that the Lord Chancellor, Lord Chief Justice Mansfield, and even
the King's brother, the Duke of York, deserted the ministers on this
question.[42]

In the Commons on 5 February the ministers fought off an opposition amendment to their first resolution introducing a specific
reference to the Stamp Act, carried the second without challenge,
and obtained leave (as in the Lords the day before) to withdraw the
third. On the fourth they ran into trouble and suffered the indignity
of losing control of their programme. Their proposal that governors
be instructed to recommend compensation was attacked from both
sides, the Grenvillites seeking to insert the word 'require', Pitt and
the Master of the Rolls both denouncing it as inexpedient, without

precedent, and constitutionally dangerous. In the end the ministers accepted in place of their own a neutrally worded resolution offered by Grenville, that a 'full and ample' compensation ought to be made. Grenville, having thus captured the initiative, then carried two further resolutions—one pledging support to those who had attempted to uphold parliamentary authority in America, the other providing for indemnity for those who by reason of the Stamp riots had been obliged to break the law and transact business without stamped paper. This last resolution carried a sting, for although Grenville agreed to withdraw a form of words clearly making the indemnity conditional on payment of the duties outstanding, the substitute phrase 'under certain [proper] restrictions', moved by one of his henchmen, implied that this condition would be required.[43]

On 6 February the opposition triumphed again in the Lords. Lord Weymouth, a member of the Bedford-Grenville connection, introduced a resolution of support for American officeholders, similar to that carried by Grenville in the Commons, and the ministers were defeated by 59 votes to 55 in resisting an amendment further strengthening its terms by introducing a specific reference to the Stamp Act. On this occasion Bute electrified the audience in the galleries as well as the House, when he declared that British authority in America must be upheld by more than mere resolutions, and that if the ministers acted on other principles 'even the wishes of a king whom he loved and adored, should not sway or determine him to act contrary to the duty he owed as a free member of Parliament.'[44]

Taken together with a narrow government victory on a Scottish election petition in the Commons on 31 January, these events signalled a concerted defection of many members of the Bute party, suggesting that the government had lost control of Parliament and was on its way out. Grenville was encouraged to make a decisive attack, and Rockingham was spurred to desperate remedies. When the Commons resumed business in committee on 7 February Grenville moved for an address to the King expressing indignation at the events in America and pledging support for the enforcement of all 'the laws of this kingdom'. As ministers saw, such a resolution would be a direction to enforce the Stamp Act. Pitt, supporting them, drew a lurid picture of bloodshed in the colonies resulting from peremptory orders the ministry would have to send, perhaps only a week before Parliament resolved to repeal the Act.[45] The opposition were confident of success. The disaster into which they now plunged was thus all the more unexpected. It was due perhaps, more than anything else, to Rockingham's use of the last available political engine, Crown influence. After an audience that day the Marquis spread the word that the King had authorized him to declare his support for repeal. At least one observer believed that this report had brought an accession of strength to the ministry; [46] and it is otherwise puzzling to understand how opposition groups which had counted their numbers at over 200 [47] should have been able in the event to bring only 134 to the division, while the government rallied the remarkable total of 274 votes.

Thereupon arose an incident which was afterwards taken to have sinister political overtones but which, in the light of all the facts, appears to have sprung from nothing worse than an unintentional indiscretion on the part of George III. Personally the King preferred modification to repeal of the Stamp Act. However, he was prepared to back the ministers on repeal as against enforcement, and at a time when he was under severe political stress, he appears to have failed to grasp that 'modification' would imply enforcement and was not therefore a distinct possible course of action. His anxiety not to be misrepresented led him to reveal his preference for modification and to allow one of his courtiers to spread this news with the added gloss, which it seems likely he had not authorized, that he was 'not for the repeal'. Rockingham required an immediate retraction, without which his position would have become untenable. In the end the effect of the episode seems to have been 'to neutralize the king's opinion as a factor in the decision of Parliament', and on the whole the ministers gained from it.[48]

Having thus cleared the air, on 11 February the ministers opened the proceedings in the Commons which were to prepare the ground for repeal.[49] During much of the next week the House sat till nearly eleven each night, and the efforts of a stream of well-prompted witnesses, 'all primed', wrote one of Grenville's supporters, 'to say everything against the Stamp Act and neither to answer nor to know anything on the other side',[50] were devoted to exposing the disastrous consequences likely to ensue in both America and Great Britain if the Stamp Act were not repealed. A number of points were repeatedly hammered home: the decline of trade; the inability of the colonists to pay huge outstanding debts; the danger of large-scale unemployment and social disruption in Great Britain. Great play was made of fears of calamitous long-term consequences if the colonists turned to manufacturing for themselves goods they could no longer afford to import from Great Britain, and their capacity to do this was systematically exaggerated. Threats of social disorder may have been all the more real to the country gentlemen in Parliament, especially those from the west country, owing to their knowledge of widespread discontent and threatened disturbances over high grain prices.[51] How far they were impressed by the spectre of colonial military potential in the event of a conflict is more dif-

ficult to guess. There is no doubt, however, that one or two ministe-
rialists thought this an important card to play,[52] and the brief notes
by the opposition M.P., R.A. Neville, of Conway's summing up of
the evidence begin: '5000 all the forces in America. The Americans
150,000.'[53] Even an intervening debate on the army estimates was
used to cast further discredit on Grenville's begetting of the Stamp
Act.[54] On 21 February the ministers marshalled the evidence and
after a strenuous debate, lasting till two in the morning, carried their
resolution for repeal by a great majority.[55]

In retrospect Parliament's decision appears commendable. The
alternative was an immediate civil war, for which the government
was entirely unprepared. Yet considerations of statesmanship played
little part with the backbenchers, and it is hard to deny that they
were led in blinkers by the nose. The case on which the government
sought consent for its policy was illusory. The Stamp Act—even the
whole of Grenville's legislation—was not really the cause of all the
economic ills which it was claimed repeal would remedy. Great Britain, America, and Europe also, were all affected by a general post-
war depression in the early 1760s. In some instances the colonists'
difficulties were due to a long-term situation as debtor communities
in their relations with Britain, but to a great extent they arose from a
spending spree during the last years of the war, which had left them
with a heavily adverse balance of payments—the same phenomenon
had also helped to depress the Caribbean trade with the Spanish
main. The emphasis placed by the government and the commercial
witnesses upon Britain's dependence on trade with America was deliberately exaggerated: although this commerce was important, exports to America in 1764 amounted to only about one-eighth of British exports as a whole. The irrelevance of Grenville's colonial
taxation to the flow of trade is also apparent in other ways: the
decline had begun at least twelve months before the Stamp Act and
the colonial boycott which it triggered came into operation, and contrary to forecasts that repeal would immediately double the annual
rate of exports to the colonies, the figures dropped still further during 1766.[56] The charge that Grenville and his Treasury officials were
so ignorant of their business that their taxing measures wrecked
trade simply does not hold water.[57]

Much of the fury of Grenville and his colleagues sprang from
their feeling that the ministers were successfully burying the real
issues from sight and unjustifiably blackening their reputations in
the process. In their view the economic arguments for repeal were
rubbish. In the final analysis their contentions come down to the
argument that, if six million subjects in Britain had to pay
£3,000,000 a year for the upkeep of the armed forces (quite apart

from another £2,000,000 annual interest on that part of the national debt incurred in winning a war which brought great benefit to the colonists), then one and a half million subjects in America could well afford to pay slightly over £150,000 yearly in support of the military and naval establishments, a figure in any case cancelled out by the amounts the government paid in subsidies to encourage various colonial undertakings.[58] But few would believe the Grenvillites. The opposing theory of the crisis was so deeply rooted, that Grenville failed utterly to find effective witnesses to testify on his side of the question in the House of Commons.[59]

The Grenvillites also believed that abandonment of the Stamp Act in the context of recent events—that is, as a surrender to coercion imposed on imperial officials which was associated with formal colonial denials of Parliament's constitutional power to impose taxation—would mean the virtual destruction of Parliament's authority, however much this might be proclaimed in a Declaratory Act.[60] Because of this, regardless of the financial nonsense of the proposal, Grenville and his friends pressed for modification rather than repeal, even if all that was left was a peppercorn of duties on dice and playing cards which would cost much more to collect than they would yield.[61]

The seven resolutions passed in committee were reported to the House on 24 February. The Declaratory Bill and Repeal Bill founded on the first and last resolutions were introduced on the 26th and swiftly passed through their legislative stages. Grenville's party kept up until the end a campaign of criticism and obstruction, but in divisions on report and on the second reading of Repeal, the ministry maintained its majority of more than a hundred.[62] Before the Bills went to the Upper House on 5 March, Rockingham again pressed George III to exert his influence among his court servants,[63] and the King may have persuaded the Lord Chancellor to abandon his opposition. In the Lords the ministers were able to muster a safe though not overlarge majority. The crucial fact in their favour was that the repeal was a finance Bill, an attempt by the Lords to amend it would flout long-standing constitutional precedent, and their rejection of it would provoke a dispute of a fundamental nature concerning the superior powers of the Commons in financial legislation.[64] Northington came down firmly against any such confrontation, and his action may have been decisive in securing repeal.[65] Both Bills received the royal assent on 18 March.

Meanwhile neither the ministers nor the merchants had lost sight of the problems of commercial regulation which had first come under discussion the previous summer. The Committee of the Whole House on colonial affairs was kept in being after 21 February, to hear further evidence preparatory to 'a compleat revision of all the commercial laws', and the North American and West Indian lobbies, which did not see eye to eye, were encouraged by the government to compose their differences.[66] British merchants sought to encourage trade between Jamaica and Spanish America, in order to vend British, European, and Asiatic luxury goods in return for bullion, dyestuffs, and other raw materials. The North Americans wanted a lowering of the molasses duty to increase the profits of importation and facilitate sale of their timber and provisions. Both groups sought free ports in the West Indies as an aid to opening the Spanish American trade. The West Indians had reservations about a low molasses duty, though they eventually gave way on this point, and were worried in case free ports opened up a destructive foreign competition with their main cash crops, especially sugar.[67] The ministers for their part, anxious to encourage the British export trade to North America, regarded the tax burdens imposed by Grenville in the Plantation Act of 1764 and other measures as a contributory cause of economic stagnation, which must be removed for fear the colonists should be forced into developing their own manufactures.[68] They overcame West Indian obstruction by concessions, which included the lifting of restrictions on the rum trade and on imports of cotton, a reduction of duties on British-grown sugars entering North America, and the safeguard that any sugars imported into Great Britain via Dominica or the mainland colonies should be burdened with the discriminatory duties on foreign sugar.[69]

On 27 March the House of Commons in committee heard evidence on the American trade, particularly in support of a lowering of the duty on molasses to 1d. per gallon. On 12 April this proposal, and also a plan for the warehousing of foreign sugars, coffee, cotton, and other commodities in transit in America, seems to have been agreed 'with no difficulty' at a meeting of M.P.s at the house of the Chancellor of the Exchequer. However, ministers ran into trouble with a scheme originating with John Huske for direct importation into the colonies of wines, fruits, and olive oil from southern Europe and the Atlantic islands, paying modest duties at American ports. This idea, like the suggestion for free ports, ran counter to the principles of the Navigation Acts—'oversetting every American idea that ever was established', the attorney general's brother wrote some weeks later—and it had to be dropped.[70]

Apart from this all the government's proposals were approved by resolution by 8 May.[71] Two Bills based on these resolutions, one for establishing free ports, the other for altering various American customs duties, went through their stages during the next three weeks in a thinly-attended House, the first completing its readings on the

28th, the second on the 30th.[72] During the discussions on the Plantation Duties Bill, Charles Garth, agent for South Carolina, moved unsuccessfully to insert a clause permitting owners of small decked vessels engaged solely in coastal traffic to post bonds for twelve-month periods, in order to escape the onerous obligation under the Act of 1764 of giving bond on each lading.[73] Both Acts passed swiftly through the Lords and received the royal assent on 6 June.

The Plantation Duties Act of 1766 repealed or modified various duties enacted in 1764.[74] In particular it introduced a flat-rate import duty of 1d. per gallon on all molasses entering a British colony whether from a British or a foreign plantation, and it replaced American import duties on East Indian and French textiles with British duties levied before export. In order to encourage re-export trade through North American ports, imports of sugar, coffee, and indigo from any source and of pimento from British colonies were to pay duty only if sold for local consumption, but might enter free if warehoused and re-exported under bond within twelve months. Consignments of these goods entering Great Britain could similarly be warehoused for re-export and would then attract only minimal duties. In order to stop North American merchants from passing off foreign as British sugar on the British domestic market, all sugar reaching Britain from North America was to be taxed as foreign, unless re-exported. Finally, in an attempt to impose more effective checks on illicit trade between the American colonies and Europe, the Act required shippers to give bond not to discharge even cargoes of non-enumerated goods laden in America or the West Indies at any port in mainland Europe north of Cape Finisterre and the Spanish Biscay coast. By the inadvertent ill-drafting of this clause the ministers rendered technically illegal much important direct trade between North America and Ireland in corn, flax seed, barrel staves, and other articles, that had come into being under the terms of previous statutes.[75] Little was left of the revenue legislation of the last two years, and Grenville and his colleagues lamented that their whole plan of getting money from the colonists had been torn in shreds.[76] On another point also their wishes were brushed aside. The ministry rounded off its settlement of the American crisis by enacting a blanket indemnity for all who had failed to carry out the provisions of the Stamp Act before its repeal.[77] They accepted amendments from the colonial agents in Parliament eliminating the provisions about conditions to which the opposition had tried to pledge the Commons four months before.[78]

If the Rockingham ministry had made a great concession for peace within the Empire by the repeal of the Stamp Act, and if its Declaratory Act was widely regarded as a mere verbal claim to a

power which would not again be exercised,[79] nevertheless it yielded
less in principle than leading American spokesmen desired. Ministers seem to have taken at their face value Franklin's assurances that
the colonists did not object to indirect taxation (perhaps because this
could not be clearly separated from trade regulation).[80] The substi-
tution of the 1d. duty on molasses replaced a quasi-regulatory measure, giving a preference to the British product, with one purely intended to produce revenue, which proved indeed to be extremely
effective. After 1766 the colonists still had to pay a whole range of
duties laid by Parliament on goods they imported for their own consumption. The Plantation Act of 1764 laid a charge on wines from
Britain of ten shillings a ton, and on those from the Atlantic islands
of £7 a ton; foreign refined sugar paid 27 shillings per cwt. and
unrefined five shillings, indigo sixpence a pound, and coffee almost
£3 per cwt. British-grown coffee was charged seven shillings per cwt.
under the Act of 1766 and pimento a halfpenny a pound.[81] The revenue from these sources was to average about £30,000 a year during
the decade before the American War of Independence.[82] It is by no
means clear that the ministers had finally abandoned John Huske's
schemes for revenue-producing importations of wines, fruits, and
olive oil from Europe,[83] and they also appear to have still had in
mind the further possibility of raising a revenue from the administration of an American loan office.[84]

At the end of a crowded parliamentary session the government
left in abeyance consideration of a curtailment of the jurisdiction of
admiralty courts in the colonies and of naval officers' powers to press
sailors in American ports.[85] While these salves to colonial opinion
were not forthcoming, by a routine renewal of Grenville's Mutiny
and Quartering Act the ministers prepared the ground for a new
conflict in America. In another instance also they showed a lack of
sensitivity to colonial feeling: by an Act which received the royal assent on 14 May they extended to Scotland the provisions of an earlier statute authorizing the transportation of felons to North
America.[86] Some problems they ignored altogether. Friends and opponents alike chided them for failing to seek relief for British finances in other ways when the American taxes were abandoned.
Lord Hardwicke thought the ministers ought to resort to the old
method of requisitions and consider Grenville's suggestion that
bounties be reduced, and Thomas Whately afterwards publicly demanded to know why they had not made requisitions.[87] The government seems to have given no thought to policy for the American wilderness or to means of reducing military expenditure in America,
though it welcomed incidental economies achieved by Gage in the

course of concentrating some of his troops nearer to trouble spots on the seaboard.[88]

The ministerial reshuffle in July 1766 which brought William Pitt, as Earl of Chatham, to the head of affairs, cut short the new experiment in colonial administration. The Rockingham ministry was not given time to test the efficacy of its policies. There may be some doubt whether its principles of action, so far as they appeared by the early summer of 1766, formed a really effective basis for lasting harmony within the Empire. However, perhaps if these ministers of conciliatory temperament had remained in office, they would have been less likely to provoke abrasive situations than proved to be the case with their successors.

3. The Legacy of Colonial Discontent

News of the Stamp Act repeal was met throughout the American colonies with genuine relief and joy. Celebrations organized by the Sons of Liberty broke out up and down the coast and in the larger towns of the interior. In most cases renewed expressions of loyalty to the King shared the spotlight with a sense of triumph. Several colonial assemblies took pains to send resolutions to both George III and Parliament in thanks for the relief. Perhaps for the first time since 1763 Americans recognized that they had friends as well as opponents in the mother country. Isaac Barré, already a hero for his stand against passage of the Stamp Act, was joined by William Pitt and the Marquis of Rockingham as the champions of repeal. In future years the colonists would overestimate the strength and misinterpret the motives of these and other friends, but for the moment they rejoiced that they did not stand alone. Unquestionably they regarded repeal as a vindication of their position, even as an acknowledgement of its essential rightness. Many of the Sons of Liberty groups disbanded, their members looking forward to the peace and prosperity that must surely ensue.

Despite the optimism in both England and America a number of basic issues continued to separate the colonies from the mother country. The Declaratory Act, for one thing, took a position that no Son of Liberty and few other Americans would accept had they fully comprehended its meaning. Most colonists seemed to share the confidence James Otis showed at Boston when he asserted to the town meeting that the act had nothing to do with taxation. This view gained further support from the fact that many colonial agents down-played the significance of the new law in their letters to America. And those colonists familiar with reports of Pitt's speech of

14 January were surely encouraged by the distinction he was supposed to have made between legislation and taxation. Yet a few colonists remained sceptical. John Adams wondered 'whether they will lay a tax in consequence of that resolution.' [89] The Providence Sons of Liberty cautioned their counterparts in New York that no thanks were owed to English merchants for repeal of the Stamp Act, because they had acted only 'from principles of convenience to themselves, at the same time holding fast the deleterious doctrine of a certain supremacy of the British people over the Americans. . . .'[90] Virginia's George Mason was equally annoyed by what he considered a condescending tone in letters from English merchants who cautioned Americans against further disruptions.[91]

The Stamp Act crisis had not modified the view many Americans held concerning the relationship between the colonies and their mother country. Indeed, some writers had advanced still further into new ideological ground. In a pamphlet entitled *An Enquiry into the Rights of the British Colonies* (1766), Richard Bland of Virginia took up Daniel Dulany's suggestion that sovereignty within the Empire did not rest solely within Parliament but was divided. Bland had sat in Virginia's House of Burgesses since 1742, played a major role in the 'pistole fee' controversy of the 1750s, and had written several pamphlets and other political tracts on various matters. He was also an expert on the early history of Virginia. From his review of seventeenth-century settlement Bland considered that in coming to America the first colonists were merely exercising their natural right to quit one country in favor of another. In so doing, Bland asserted, 'they recover their natural freedom and independence: the jurisdiction and sovereignty of the state they have quitted, ceases, and if they unite, and by common consent take possession of a new country, and form themselves into a political society,' he concluded, 'they become a sovereign state, independent of the state from which they separated.' [92]

The Virginian noted, however, that these settlements had not been established *in vacuo* but rather in accordance with the terms of charters or compacts made with the sovereign and binding on both parties. It was evident to Bland that the first colony, his own Virginia,

> had a regular government before the first act of navigation and were respected as a distinct state, independent, as to their *internal* government, of the original kingdom, but united with her, as to their *external* polity, in the closest and most intimate LEAGUE AND AMITY, under the same allegiance. . . .[93]

It is not that Bland spoke for a significant number of Americans in the spring of 1766; he probably did not. They would have agreed with him, however, that as colonists they had certain rights, and when Bland concluded, as he did, that 'rights imply equality', he pointed the way toward the idea of a federal empire that other Americans would accept in the ensuing decade. And as the ideological position of the colonists gradually changed along lines first traced by Dulany, Bland, and a few others, the gulf separating them from Blackstone's concept of an omnipotent Parliament yawned ever wider.[94]

Another unresolved matter concerned the Quartering Act. Stationing regular troops in America during peace-time had touched upon a sensitive spot to begin with. While no organized protest erupted, colonists remained uneasy. Five colonies, including New York, Massachusetts, and South Carolina, managed to evade the requirements of the Quartering Act in one way or another. In New York a number of British troops maintained strategic outposts along the frontier as well as occupying barracks in the city. There too was located General Gage's headquarters. When by the end of its session in December 1765 the New York assembly had refused to comply with the Quartering Act, both Gage and Governor Sir Henry Moore anticipated serious trouble.[95]

In May 1766, after proroguing the body until repeal of the Stamp Act, Gage and Moore renewed their requests for bedding, utensils, and other supplies called for under the Quartering Act. In June the assembly finally agreed to furnish all of the essential items save for the rations of spirits. But in so doing the legislators made clear that they were responding to a request by the Crown and not to Parliament's Quartering Act. The distinction of course was of great significance to them. 'You will be pleased to observe that my message is treated merely as a requisition made here,' Governor Moore reported, 'and that they have carefully avoided the least mention of the act on which it is founded, and it is my opinion that every act of Parliament, when not backed by a sufficient power to enforce it, will meet with the same fate here. . . .'[96]

Gage seemed satisfied with this partial compliance, and Moore himself was prepared to let the matter drop, but not so the new Secretary of State for the southern department, Lord Shelburne. In immediate response to Governor Moore's report Shelburne wrote back in early August that 'as it is the indispensable duty of his subjects in America to obey the acts of the Legislature of Great Britain, the king both expects and requires a due and cheerful obedience to the same. . . .'[97] But when the governor presented Shelburne's letter to the assembly in the autumn, they steadfastly refused to take further action in compliance with the Quartering Act. Moore reported the news to Shelburne in mid-December. Had he dissolved the House and called for new elections, he wrote, 'the same members would have been returned again, [and] a flame would have lighted up throughout the Country.' [98]

In the wake of the Stamp Act both British and American nerves had become so sensitive to the constitutional relationship between them that almost any issue appeared to threaten the position of one side or the other, and sometimes both. A few examples will illustrate the point. We remember that Parliament had in its repeal of the Stamp Act also declared that sufferers in the various riots be compensated for their losses. Colonial governors were instructed to recommend such action to their respective assemblies, but none of the legislatures complied with much enthusiasm. New York granted relief to the British commander of Fort George while rejecting a request one-ninth as large from Lieutenant Governor Cadwallader Colden. New Hampshire and Rhode Island refused to comply, and Massachusetts managed to add insult to injury in its proceedings. Throughout the first session of 1766 the General Court stalled along, squabbling the while with Governor Francis Bernard, who had characteristically employed a stick instead of a carrot in bringing up the matter of payments. When the General Court finally acted late in the year, it indeed voted funds to compensate Thomas Hutchinson, Andrew Oliver, and others. But the act also proclaimed a complete pardon for all persons indicted or convicted for participation in the disturbances.[99] The governor realized that to veto the measure would deprive Hutchinson and the others of their funds, and so he reluctantly approved it.

Another source of friction that lingered on in the wake of Stamp Act repeal stemmed from the Currency Act of 1764. The law had required the several colonies south of New England to retire their outstanding paper money on schedule, and it prohibited future emissions of currency for legal tender. Compared with the Stamp Act the measure met with little organized opposition at first, although as we have noted, New York complained of the legislation in its petition against the Sugar Act. Pennsylvania instructed its agent to work for repeal, and complaints were sounded in South Carolina, Virginia, Maryland, and New Jersey as well. The law had no effect on New England, since paper currency in those colonies had already been restricted in 1751. Even before repeal of the Stamp Act several of the middle colonies turned their attention to the Currency Act. In January 1766 the assembly of Pennsylvania complained to the House of Commons that the process of retiring currency on schedule had already caused a serious shortage. Furthermore, as its neighbours Maryland and New York complied with the law, shortages there further strained Pennsylvania money. Late in 1766 Maryland enacted a scheme to put into circulation about £40,000 in interest-bearing bills. Because they did not have to be accepted as legal tender, these bills met the requirements of the Currency Act.[100]

New York, however, had incurred a far larger debt during the French War than had Maryland and could not solve its currency crisis so easily. Faced with the requirement of retiring over £300,000 in paper by the end of 1768, the colonial assembly anticipated a critical shortage of currency. Governor Moore sought permission from the Board of Trade to approve an emission of £260,000 as an exception to the Currency Act. The Board granted Moore's request as an emergency measure, but it required the assembly to include a clause suspending implementation until Crown officials could determine Parliament's view of the whole matter. The assembly objected strenuously to the suspending clause, however, as an unwarranted interference in its legislative rights. In November 1766 the New Yorkers countered with a proposal to issue half the original amount of currency without providing a suspension clause. Governor Moore demurred, and there the matter rested.[101] Like numerous other public questions in the months after the Stamp Act repeal the subject of paper currency was soon swept up into the more general power struggle between English and American political forces.

To make matters worse a group of New York merchants chose the late autumn of 1766 to circulate a petition complaining against the Sugar Act and the recent revision of it enacted that spring. Apparently the work of one William Kelly, a merchant who claimed connections with Charles Townshend, the petition gained nearly 250 signatures when endorsed by Henry Cruger, an influential member of the council. The petitioners made so bold as to suggest that they be allowed a 'free and unrestrained exportation of all the lumber and produce they raise and can spare, and an ample importation of sugar, rum, and molasses, to supply the various branches of the trade. . . .' With greater frankness than circumspection the petitioners went on to criticize the mother country's commercial policy toward the colonies in almost every particular, warning that the recent acts would ruin colonial trade and prove 'highly pernicious' to Great Britain itself.[102]

The New Yorkers then wrote to their counterparts in Boston seeking support for their position. A group of Bostonians who had formed themselves into a society to advance the interests of trade were quick to respond with a petition of its own. The New Englanders emphasized the effect of various regulations on the fisheries, while endorsing the New Yorkers' protest as well. The Bostonians forwarded their grievances directly to their colonial agent Dennys DeBerdt; the New Yorkers had handed theirs to Governor Murray to be forwarded to the Board of Trade.[103] One could hardly expect such gratuitous criticism of the Empire's very foundations to receive a cordial reception in Whitehall, especially coming as it did on the heels of what the ministry considered a reasonable reform of previous regulations.

Yet another festering sore and a serious one at that involved the enforcement of the acts of trade in the various ports of America. Smuggling, it should be remembered, had been a practised art of long standing throughout the Atlantic mercantile world. High duties and many restrictions encouraged a lively illegal commerce into England from nearby French and Low Country ports. English smugglers played for keeps, and running battles with revenue cutters were not an infrequent occurrence. Similar conditions of commerce in America—a myriad of regulations, high duties, and the opportunity offered by numerous coves and creeks—produced a similar response. American merchants smuggled goods for the same reason as their English cousins did, to maximize profits, not to protest authority. Yet like almost every other point of friction between the mother country and her continental colonies, the enforcement of the Navigation Acts was soon viewed in ideological terms on both sides of the Atlantic. Indeed, passage of the Sugar Act of 1764, although primarily an economic measure, seems to have been inspired partly from British indignation over American smuggling. And discussion in the mother country of subsequent measures of enforcement pointed to trade violations by Americans as evidence of disloyalty toward the mother country. Americans might have wondered whether English smugglers were seen in similar terms.

The colonists met the new enforcement provisions of the Sugar Act with the same spirit of opposition that earlier laws had generated. Naval officers patrolling the coast under the act could command little popular support in the pursuit of their new duties. On one occasion the fort at Newport, Rhode Island, fired on the naval schooner St. John as its captain was trying to seize a suspected smuggler. In New York the commanding officer of the sloop-of-war Hawke was jailed on grounds of an improper seizure. The Royal Navy had long been unpopular in America for its habit of impressing colonial seamen without clear legal authority to do so. A statute of 1708, 6 Anne ch. 37, prohibiting the practice was apparently still on the books. But British men-of-war stationed in American waters constantly lost crew members to better-paying billets on board colonial merchantmen, where treatment was also somewhat less harsh. Some evidence suggests that colonial shipowners deliberately enticed sailors off British warships in order to weaken the navy's enforcement of the acts of trade. Attempts at impressment both angered and frightened the

sailors and other inhabitants of seaports from Falmouth to Charleston, and such activities seriously disrupted local commerce. The arrival of the frigate *Maidstone* at Newport in June 1765 scattered local
vessels like chickens running before a fox. When the search officers
picked up a few unfortunate sailors from a vessel entering the harbour, the populace was so furious it seized the warship's boat and
burned it on the town common. One would hardly expect from
naval officers like these the well-tempered spirit of enforcement
needed to create respect for the customs laws. The *Annual Register*
wondered how colonial trade could survive at all under the zealous
policing by 'these new-fangled custom-house officers'.[104]

Mobs continued to assault the regular customs officers and to
'liberate' impounded vessels and goods whenever possible. When
Rhode Island's customs collector, John Robinson, made a seizure
within Massachusetts waters in April 1765, he not only found himself in jail but he became as well a pawn in the long-standing power
struggle between Governor Francis Bernard of Massachusetts and
John Temple, the surveyor-general of customs. A more general animosity pitted royal naval officers against the established customs service in an unseemly rivalry for the spoils of condemnation proceedings. In addition to lowering the impost on foreign molasses to a
collectable level, the Sugar Act also levied a new duty on madeira
wines. New Englanders had developed a considerable taste for madeira, which they purchased with cargoes of fish and pipe staves;
now they deeply resented this blatant favouritism accorded the London wine merchants. After 1764, in short, customs officers not only
had to crack down on the smuggling of molasses, a hard enough assignment, but were also required to collect a new and unpopular
duty on wine. The service as it was then constituted simply could not
handle these additional demands.[105]

One attempt to help the service, in addition to bringing in the
navy, was the establishment of a new vice-admiralty court at Halifax.
Customs officers could bring cases there to avoid the judicial favouritism toward local merchants that occasionally marred proceedings in the vice-admiralty courts long established in the major seaports of the continent. The new law also shifted the burden of proof
to the accused merchant, and if the judge found probable cause for
the seizure, even without sufficient evidence for a conviction, the defendant was charged with court costs. The statute also gave additional protection to the King's officers against suits for false arrest.
Along with these changes in procedure, which also applied at the established courts, the tribunal at Halifax introduced another innovation. Justices of the continental vice-admiralty courts had almost in-
variably been native-born Americans, who lived among their

countrymen and were accustomed (perhaps too much so) to their ways. The new presiding officer, however, was to be Dr. William Spry, an Englishman who had never before been in America. The opening of his court at the end of September 1764 boded ill for the merchants of the continental colonies.[106]

Americans had accepted the jurisdiction of the colonial vice-admiralty courts since their establishment in 1696 with only a minimum amount of grumbling, partly because colonial courts boldly usurped or undermined admiralty jurisdiction whenever possible. As long as the acts of trade were clearly regulatory in nature, the courts enforcing them were at least tolerated. But the Sugar Act of 1764 purported to collect a revenue, and along with their general objections to the law itself, Americans brought their ideological guns to bear on the courts that were to enforce the new act. In England violations of the acts of trade were tried before a jury. Now that revenue rather than regulation became the issue, this procedural inequality generated additional protest among Americans. In his instructions to the representatives of Braintree, written in October 1765, John Adams concluded that 'the most grievous innovation of all, is the alarming extension of the power of courts of admiralty . . . where one judge presides alone!' The new provision, Adams wrote, was 'directly repugnant to the Great Charter itself'.[107]

As in so many of the issues raised by Grenville's new policies, the Americans came to view the confrontation in ideological terms. Not even repeal of the Stamp Act itself could create sufficient good-will to convince skeptical colonists that they too should make a contribution toward more cordial relations. As the year 1766 came to a close numerous points of friction continued to mar the relationship between the mother country and her sensitive continental colonies.

V

Charles Townshend and
the Colonies

———•◦•———

1. Townshend Forces the Pace

THE LEGACY OF colonial affairs which Chatham's administration in-
herited from Rockingham in July 1766 was by no means so simple as
Edmund Burke was afterwards inclined to describe it, or as some
historians until fairly recently assumed it to be.[1] Resentment in political circles at the colonists' refusal to shoulder part of the burden of
American defence was a potential embarrassment whenever Parliament should reassemble. Ministers felt under pressure to find funds
of some kind in America. As early as September the new Treasury
Board under the lead of the Duke of Grafton and his Chancellor of
the Exchequer, Charles Townshend, called for a report on colonial
quitrents and for comprehensive returns of colonial income and expenditure.[2] Among its papers were drafts of schemes for further ex-
tensions of port duties shelved by the Rockingham ministry.[3] During
the autumn the unexpected extent of American expenditure
aroused alarm in the administration.[4] Burke gained an impression
that even Chatham would 'return to the principles of the Stamp Act',
and in October Grenville's confidant, Whately, notified him that the
ministry was planning án American revenue from quitrents to meet
military expenses.[5] These statements form a useful illustration of
prevailing impressions, though neither was correct in detail. There is
no evidence that Chatham's ministry contemplated American internal taxes. Shelburne, the southern secretary with charge of colonial
affairs, linked the scheme of a revenue from quitrents with the
funding of provincial civil lists from which leading colonial officials
could be paid.[6] If the ever-swelling cost of the army in the colonies
was to be partly met by America, it would not be from quitrents:

port duties and a tighter enforcement of customs seemed the obvious methods. Rockingham had continued port duties. Franklin had suggested they were acceptable. A debate on the army estimates on 26 January made the matter urgent. Grenville exploded in defence of his Stamp Act, denounced the repeal, and moved that the colonies should pay the costs of their own defence. Feeling the sense of the House, Townshend gave his pledge that an American revenue would be found, and indicated that he meant to work 'by degrees' and with 'great delicacy' towards the point where it would meet the whole expense.[7]

Right on cue, it seemed, the petition from the New York merchants included a suggestion that foreign rum should be admitted into the colonies at a moderate tariff which would produce a revenue. But the petition made such extensive criticism of trade laws only recently confirmed, with modifications intended to meet colonial complaints, that Shelburne foresaw Grenville would seize upon it as yet another sign of rebellion.[8] Combined with further reports of the province's refusal to comply with the Mutiny Act it created the worst impression: Chatham feared that 'the torrent of indignation in Parliament' would become 'irresistible'. The arrival a day or two later of the news that the Massachusetts assembly had usurped the royal prerogative of pardon by its grant of indemnity for rioters in its Act providing compensation for sufferers from the Stamp Riots added further to the ministers' difficulties. Grenville, anxious to rake up every possible issue against them, pounced on it as a matter requiring urgent parliamentary consideration.[9]

On 14 February ministers discussed New York's defiance of the Quartering Act. Shelburne, the responsible departmental minister, felt out of his depth and anxious about the dangers of provoking a civil war within the Empire; at the same time he sensed the difficulties of inaction, for the opposition would certainly exploit any sign of ministerial weakness. His colleagues felt the same. Everyone, he reported, was 'strongly for enforcing' but nobody would 'suggest the mode', and the King himself had no proposal to offer.[10] Privately (perhaps adopting a suggestion from the Secretary-at-War) Shelburne favoured the dispatch of a military officer as governor of the province, with authority to billet troops in private houses if the assembly refused to retract.[11]

The petition from the New York merchants was read in the Commons on 16 February. Opposition spokesmen clamoured that it confirmed their worst fears of the previous session: nothing would satisfy the colonists but 'an absolute repeal of all regulations and restrictions and in the end independence upon Great Britain'.[12] Two days later army expenditure was again debated, and Barrington, the

Secretary-at-War, explained that a large part of the extraordinaries for the previous year arose out of the difficulty of maintaining posts in the American wilderness. Grenville called for economies, and once more Townshend hinted at port duties.[13] The coincidental impact of these various issues was, to say the least of it, unfortunate.

On 17 February Chatham from his sickbed at Marlborough, eighty miles from London, advised his colleagues that the disobedience of New York in respect of the Mutiny Act was too important to be dealt with administratively but must be referred to Parliament.[14] In point of political tactics this was certainly wise, for it reduced the chances of the government's leaving itself open to subsequent censure, over a question about which, as soon appeared, there was widespread concern. On the 25th Grenville's ally in opposition, the Duke of Bedford, moved in the Lords for papers on America, and the debate, which ranged widely over all the current problems, appeared to disclose considerable unanimity. Whately reported that, 'the re-establishment of the civil authority which has of late been much weakened in the colonies is now the prevailing object amongst men of all denominations.' Even Lord Chancellor Camden declared that after the passage of the Declaratory Act the government was bound to uphold the taxing power.[15]

On 2 March Chatham returned to London, and then collapsed. Lacking his guidance, on 6 March the cabinet had a wrangling, inconclusive discussion about the contumacy of New York.[16] The ministers' sense of urgency was possibly sharpened by knowledge of a private letter in which Gage had written to Barrington: 'I think I may tell your Lordship . . . with great truth, that the colonists are taking large strides towards independency, and that it concerns Great Britain by a speedy and spirited conduct to shew them that these provinces are British colonies dependent on her, and that they are not independent states.'[17]

At this meeting Shelburne's own proposal for giving the governor of New York authority to billet in private houses was turned down unanimously, 'as being a free quarter in point of principle and as [at] once highly exceptionable both here and there'. Conway pressed for a local port duty to meet the quartering expenses, but everyone else agreed this involved too many inconveniences. Townshend favoured an address to the Crown requesting that royal assent should be withheld from all Bills passed in the province until the legislature complied fully with the Mutiny Act. His colleagues shrank from such an interdiction unless it were sanctioned by Act of Parliament. Little support was shown for a fourth proposal, for an Act directing moneys to be paid to the order of the governor out of the first sums raised for the service of the province. Shelburne also submitted to the sick Premier's judgement his own draconic solution, not yet aired in the cabinet: a statute reciting the Declaratory Act, stigmatizing the action of New York as in disregard of it, granting a general pardon for past offences, and providing that from three months after the arrival of the Act, failure to obey a parliamentary statute should be an offence of high treason and any questioning of Parliament's authority a misprision of treason. Shelburne pointed out that the deadline for discussion was the following Thursday, evidently hoping either that Chatham would be sufficiently recovered by then to attend the cabinet meeting, or that he would vouchsafe him guidance. Of these five proposals neither the first nor the fourth were so severe as the third, which was ultimately implemented. Shelburne's own final suggestion indicates that he himself was by no means a voice for moderation in this business.

At the next meeting on 12 March, with Chatham still absent, the ministers adopted the modified form of Townshend's proposal for dealing with New York.[18] At the same time they found themselves facing an ultimatum. Anxious to checkmate Grenville's attacks, which might otherwise derive great support from the known desire of the House of Commons to obtain 'a revenue of some sort from the colonies',[19] the Chancellor of the Exchequer insisted upon an early agreement to three propositions: the withdrawal of troops from the interior and the return to the provinces of responsibility for control of Indian affairs, both of which steps might reduce expenditure; and the imposition of some American port duties. Townshend's knowledge that his only possible supplanter, Lord North, had declined his office, emboldened him to back his demands by threats of resignation.[20] Doubtless he was well aware that the Secretary-at-War had been planning troop withdrawals in consultation with Gage for many months and had been constantly urging them on the Secretary of State since the end of the previous summer.[21] Townshend's stand placed him in collision with Shelburne's pet schemes for revenue from quitrents, to be partly gained from the settlement of inland colonies. 'It appears to me', Shelburne wrote to Chatham the following day, 'quite impossible that Mr. Townshend can mean to go on in the king's service.'[22]

Letters from New Jersey posed a fresh problem at the next cabinet meeting on Wednesday, 18 March (from which Townshend absented himself, perhaps in order to reinforce his ultimatum). Was notice to be taken of defiance of the Mutiny Act elsewhere? The governor's report accompanying the province's Barracks Bill set the conduct of the assembly in an invidious light. Shelburne's impulse was to suppress as much of the comment as possible and even limit disclosure to Parliament to the Bill itself. A number of his colleagues agreed with him on the ground that, 'as everything relative to New York is laid before the House in the fullest manner, it would be more prudent to confine what is done to that province only.'[23]

Here American matters stuck for a time, and the reasons can only be conjectured. The cabinet was preoccupied with the affairs of the East India Company. It was split by disagreements, Conway disliking the sanctions proposed against New York and Shelburne the American economies demanded by Townshend, while Grafton, according to later evidence of his attitude, may have been reluctant to agree to American port duties. Probably the ministers hoped that Chatham would recover and settle these disputes; but delays involved embarrassments. At the end of March they only averted a 'strong resolution and address' in the House of Lords by assurances that legislation to enforce colonial obedience to Acts of Parliament was in preparation: fortunately for them Rockingham and his friends refused to support attacks by the Bedford-Grenville alliance.[24] On 10 April, helped once more by the abstention of the Rockinghams, the ministers defeated by 63 votes to 36 a critical motion by Bedford calling for the immediate reference to the Privy Council of the Massachusetts Indemnity Act.[25] Only a quick recommendation by the law officers, directed against the Act, prevented Grenville from springing a similar awkward motion in the Commons three days later.[26]

However, even those ministers who were most reluctant to provoke the colonists felt that they could not ignore the strong feelings against America in Parliament.[27] Townshend continued his pressure on his colleagues by threats of resignation: his financial anxieties were doubtless increased by the collapse early in April of the attempt to secure an early planned withdrawal of troops from the wilderness.[28] Meanwhile he continued to work on his financial schemes and seems to have wrung a reluctant consent from his cabinet colleagues; opening his budget on 15 April he talked yet again of American taxes.[29] On 13 April the New York Barracks Act was disallowed, and ten days later Shelburne referred to the law officers various queries concerning Townshend's plan for disciplining the provincial legislature.[30] The driving force of Townshend's personality thrust his colleagues into the decisions he wanted, and any hesitation they may have felt was tempered by the knowledge that failure to assert parliamentary authority might place their political position in jeopardy. Indeed, on 6 May, they were hard pressed and obtained a majority of only nine in the Lords (excluding proxies) when the combined opposition suddenly attacked in both Houses their handling of the Massachusetts Indemnity Act.[31]

During the spring Shelburne successfully resisted pressure for immediate military withdrawals; but by the beginning of May, Townshend, having got his way over port duties and over the treatment of New York, secured the Treasury Board's approval for another of his schemes, the establishment of an American Board of Customs to impose efficiency on the service in the colonies and support it in the face of its many local difficulties. Now he made a further demand. By this time it was clear that Shelburne's plan for a revenue from quitrents to support the executive officers in the colonies was impracticable.[32] Shelburne's failure was Townshend's opportunity. He now required cabinet support for a colonial civil list, to be funded from parliamentary taxation. Without this he declined to lead on the government's business in the House of Commons. During the next few days he again threatened resignation; and on 8 May, in the midst of a debate on East India business, he delivered his famous 'champagne speech', a premeditated move clearly aimed to support his pretensions to the premiership, tilting as much against his colleagues as the opposition.[33] Meanwhile, to colonial agents and their friends, he justified his schemes for port duties, declaring an American army 'and consequently an American revenue' to be 'essentially necessary' for defence against foreign enemies. He brushed aside pleas that no force was necessary there, 'declaring peremptorily that the moment a resolution should be taken to withdraw the army . . . he would resign.'[34] Chatham in full health might have curbed him. No one else could do so. But if he resigned and went into opposition, who was to carry the government's business through the Commons against the combination of himself, Grenville, and Dowdeswell? It was no time for the administration to jettison its leading orator. By 13 May opposition in the cabinet to Townshend's civil list plan had cracked sufficiently for him to feel confident that he could force it through by presenting his more reluctant colleagues with a *fait accompli* in the form of a pledge given to the Commons.

On that day Townshend opened a debate on the American papers with a comprehensive survey of colonial issues, touching upon the Massachusetts Indemnity Act (about to be disallowed), the colonial reactions to the Mutiny Act, and various public proceedings in America 'inconsistent with a proper respect to and dependence upon Great Britain'. This speech, 'masterly', 'so consonant to the character of a man of business, and so unlike the wanton sallies of the man of parts and pleasure', seems to have been clearly intended to stake his claim to the leading position in government.[35] Of the three outstanding issues, the first was in the hands of the Privy Council and he recommended leaving alone both that subject and any public disputation over authority. New York, he declared, appeared to be the province most disobedient in respect of the Mutiny Act, and he considered an act of power necessary to strike awe into those there who opposed parliamentary authority. There was he believed a conspiracy: 'There are in several of the assemblies a set of factious men closely cemented together upon a fixed plan from motives of self-interest to establish their popularity in their own country upon the ruin of the dependency of the colonies upon Great Britain.' At the close he moved three resolutions concerning quartering, the last being a motion for a Bill restraining the New York legislature until it complied with the Mutiny Act. During the course of the debate he discussed at some length his intention of establishing a colonial civil list in order to strengthen the operation of the executive and judicial branches of government, of financing this by various American port duties, estimated to yield between £30,000 and £40,000 a year, and of setting up his proposed American Customs Commission, to give effective supervision to the service in the colonies. He suggested that some of the duties would be charged on wines, fruits, and olive oil from Spain and Portugal, direct importation being authorized by a modification of the Navigation Acts. Others would be imposed on china, glass, paper, and red and white lead, supplied to the colonies from Great Britain.[36] These tax proposals corresponded closely with plans which the New Englander, John Huske, had passed to Rockingham early in the spring of 1766 and which he had resubmitted to Townshend on 9 April.[37] In reply to criticisms from Grenville, Townshend explained that a suggested tax on tea could not be discussed until East India Company affairs were settled (though he outlined his plan for it), and that fishery interests made a proposed tax on salt impracticable.

Taxation was not the immediate business before the Commons, and although Grenville took occasion to criticize these proposals, the main weight of his attack was pressed on other grounds. He thought an order by Act of Parliament to the treasurer of New York province a better method of dealing with the quartering issue. He demanded parliamentary compensation for loyal colonists who had been denied relief in their colonies after suffering losses during the Stamp riots, and in particular he urged a test for aspirants to office in America, requiring them to acknowledge the subordination of the colonies to Great Britain. Though friends of Rockingham disliked Townshend's proposals on quartering, they were equally hot against the Americans. Dowdeswell 'spoke against the whole as insufficient', suggesting an Act to authorize billeting in private houses, and Sir George Savile and Lord John Cavendish called for strong measures rather than 'acts of Parliament against acts of assembly . . . making paper war'.[38] It has been noted that, 'the sole recorded comment on

Townshend's proposed duties in the only known debate on his American taxation measures was the complaint by George Grenville that they were inadequate. no criticism of taxes either in principle or in detail was voiced by any follower of Chatham or Rockingham.' [39] So little did Rockingham feel Townshend's policies incompatible with those of his own party, that in July, when he briefly hoped to form a new administration, one of his closest colleagues suggested offering Townshend office with the leadership in the Commons.[40]

The New York resolutions were reported on 15 May. Once more Townshend achieved a great personal success in debate, and an attempt to recommit them was defeated without a division. The Bill founded upon the resolutions passed smoothly through all its stages, but by the time the Act was ready for transmission to New York the assembly appeared to have complied sufficiently with the Mutiny Act.[41]

In mid-May the drama of party conflict on American issues shifted briefly to the House of Lords. The government was hard pressed. On the 13th the Massachusetts Indemnity Bill had been disallowed. However, a strong body of legal opinion held that it should have been declared void *ab initio*. Ministers deplored the reopening of this question, for the course now advocated would bring in question the legality of any recompense already paid under its provisions to victims of the Stamp riots in Boston, would revive the issue of *parliamentary* compensation, and would in general exacerbate relations with the Bay Colony. Nevertheless, calculating that the government might be defeated in the Lords and shaken into a state of collapse, on 22 May the Rockinghams joined the other opposition groups led by Grenville and Bedford in pushing this embarrassing proposal. The ministry just managed to scrape home by a majority of six votes, including those of the King's two younger brothers. Upon a renewal of the attack in somewhat different terms on 26 May, in preparation for which Newcastle strenuously whipped up possible support, this margin was cut to three. A few days later the ministers did better, beating off a motion by the combined opposition for the establishment of representative government in Quebec by 73 votes to 61. The ministry had survived; but the opposition had made its point. Grafton, as *de facto* head of the administration in Chatham's absence, was shaken into thoughts of resignation. This episode heralded the beginnings of his efforts to recruit new strength which, six months later, brought in the heads of the Bedford party, and increased the number of men in the key places in administration who were hard-liners on American questions.[42]

Colonial taxation did not come before Parliament until June. This was partly due to the government's continued preoccupation

with the affairs of the East India Company and the need to settle
these before an American tea duty could be planned. But the main
reason appears to have been Grafton's continued reluctance to sanction American taxation, more especially when linked with Townshend's explosive scheme for a colonial civil list.[43] On 23 May, ten
days after Townshend had publicly pledged himself in the House of
Commons, Grafton merely conceded that the plan for a civil list
might be applied in New York. On the morning of the 25th he was
still reluctant to request the King's formal approval for the wider
plan applying to all the colonies.[44] But he was in an impossible position, for Townshend held the fate of the ministry in the hollow of
his hand—his resignation would have been fatal to its existence.
Perhaps Grafton hoped that even at this stage Chatham might still
step in and scotch a proposal he felt so pregnant with undesirable
consequences. If so, his conviction, after seeing Chatham on 31 May,
that Chatham would not make an early recovery from his strange
mental malady caused him to abandon his opposition to a measure
which he may have feared might infuriate the titular head of the
ministry.[45] One concession only he had managed to wring from his
headstrong subordinate some time during the course of the discussions: in the hope that cheaper tea would make the measure acceptable to the Americans, full customs drawback was to be granted on
all the tea sent to the colonies.[46]

On 1 June Townshend at last brought forward his colonial taxes
in committee of ways and means. In deference to Grenville's objections, the proposals about wine, fruit, and oil were now dropped as
incompatible with the Navigation Acts. Tea was to bear an import
duty of 3*d.* per lb., giving an anticipated annual revenue of £20,000.
Townshend expected another £17,000 a year from duties on paper,
glass, red and white lead, and painters' colours. These duties were to
be applied in the first place to making 'a more certain and adequate
provision for the charge of the administration of justice and the support of civil government', where the ministry might think this necessary. The second charge on them was to be colonial defence. At the
same time, however, Townshend abandoned £60,000 of revenue
collectable in London on tea exported to America. Part of his deal
with the East India Company involved reductions of duties on tea to
both internal and colonial consumers. By Grafton's insistence on a
full drawback on tea sent to America the Treasury lost revenue from
duties amounting to about 9*d.* per pound.[47]

All the evidence—or rather lack of evidence—points to the subsequent passage of Townsend's Revenue Bill without challenge in
the House of Commons. So late in the session attendance was very
thin, but various leaders of the Rockingham group were still active

in the House. The glass duty was marked down for criticism, but this was probably in support of some vested interest. In the Lords Grafton ostentatiously marked his disapproval of the Bill by refusing to speak in support of it.[48] On 29 June both it and the companion measure authorizing the establishment of the American Board of Customs received the royal assent.[49]

For what had Townshend schemed in the months before his unexpected death on 4 September, and for what was the Empire to be thrown into fresh confusion? On his own estimate the net sacrifice of revenue under these arrangements was about £23,000. Falling in with the sentiments of a great part of the House of Commons, he had avoided any check to his own popularity, and he had achieved three aims.

British tea had been made cheaper on the colonial market—it was hoped that it might now compete successfully with Dutch supplies smuggled in from Amsterdam or St. Eustatius. The prosperity of the East India Company, which supplied the tea, was a primary object of the government, which expected to levy some £400,000 a year from the Company under the bargain with it which Townshend had been principally responsible for making.

Cabinet and Parliament had accepted the new principle of a colonial civil list and had put this measure into operation. The need for it appeared to have been demonstrated by the powerlessness of the colonial executives during the Stamp riots. The common approval of it in governing circles is reflected in the optimistic comment by the retired Under Secretary of State, Edward Sedgwick, a former subordinate of Lord Halifax: 'Without it, it was absurd ever to think of preventing smuggling or collecting any revenue whether old or new. But now we may hope to see the laws observed and many evils corrected which have hitherto been incorrigible.' [50] It would be an error to assume that this plan simply arose as a result of Townshend's peculiar psychological stresses. The object, though not the means, had been studied since the end of the previous summer, Shelburne had cooperated in investigating it, and in February wrote about it to Chatham in terms which implied that Chatham had long since given it his blessing.[51] Townshend's late contribution to the plan—one which disquieted Grafton and possibly also Shelburne and Conway— was to give it a radical twist by finding the money for it from port duties when the proposal to supply funds from quitrents proved abortive. If the yield from port duties proved sufficient, then some revenue would also be available to serve his own original purpose of finding more money in America for defence, and this was written into the preamble of the Revenue Act.

Finally, Townshend had edged forward a modest step towards

the ultimate goal he had mentioned in Parliament on 26 January only in respect of defence: the establishment of an American revenue adequate to cover all expenditure.[52] Anyone might have guessed as much at the time; and to the colonists the implications of executives completely relieved from financial dependence upon their assemblies appeared formidable. No wonder the Act created consternation in America!

2. *The Townshend Crisis in America*

The year 1767 brought a series of blows to those Englishmen and Americans who genuinely longed for a permanent settlement of the disputes between the mother country and her continental colonies. In one sense the Americans brought some of their new difficulties upon themselves. New York's foot-dragging in complying with the Quartering Act, the usurpation by Massachusetts of the Crown's pardoning power, and the continuing opposition in both these colonies to the Sugar Act of 1764 and its later amendments—all were viewed in England as examples of colonial ingratitude. As numerous Americans saw it, however, they had little reason to be grateful, for they had at last recognized that repeal of the Stamp Act had come as a response to English needs rather than as an act of justice to the Americans. By the end of 1767 the colonists would have still less cause for gratitude.

Ironically, one of the most disturbing new measures, the New York Suspending Act, became a dead letter before reaching America. During the months after New York's assembly granted limited assistance to Gage's troops in July 1766, its members became increasingly apprehensive about the possible consequences of their obstinacy. When Governor Moore renewed his request for funds to support the troops in early June 1767, the assembly responded almost immediately. The legislators voted the sum of £3000 for the governor to spend as he wished without restriction but also without acknowledging the Quartering Act or enumerating the supplies to be purchased. With greater discretion than accuracy, Moore reported to Shelburne that 'his Majesty's troops in this city will have the provision made for them which is prescribed by the Act of Parliament. . . .'[53] Shelburne in turn chose to regard the action of New York as a mark of 'subordination and constitutional obedience' to Parliament and dropped further consideration of the matter.[54]

In suspending the assembly of New York until it complied with the Quartering Act, Parliament wielded that supremacy over colonial legislatures which it had long claimed and had most recently reaffirmed in the Declaratory Act. New York made a good target, not only because of its blatant disregard of a parliamentary act but also because the colony had no charter on which to claim a right to legislative freedom. Furthermore, it was an established principle in existing colonial charters that provincial laws must conform to those of the mother country in every particular. Whether Shelburne was wise in pursuing the principle of parliamentary supremacy in the case of New York is another matter, however. Although New Yorkers seemed willing to leave well enough alone, at least for a while, colonists elsewhere picked up the implications of the Suspending Act. The issue took its place in the firmament of American opposition thereafter.

Meanwhile, South Carolina and Pennsylvania had joined New York in calling for repeal of the Currency Act. The movement had support from the London merchants trading with North America, and in January 1767 a group of them sat down with several colonial agents to plan their strategy. But news of New York's continuing obstinacy in the Quartering Act affair and the petition of its merchants against trade regulations soured the merchants as well as the ministry against the possibility of reform. Despite a strong rationale for a colonial currency drawn up by Benjamin Franklin, the whole question was pushed aside in favor of a colonial revenue. In the remaining months of that year and into 1768 one colony after another sought permission to issue a paper currency, but each request was summarily rejected by the ministry. Most of the colonies then turned to alternative means of providing a larger circulating medium. Some adopted variations of Maryland's scheme to emit bills not of legal tender. Others established land banks to issue currency based on mortgages. Although none of these issues provided money that was acceptable in payment of British debts, they nevertheless increased the amount of currency circulating in the colonies and to that extent eased the problem aggravated by the ministry's firmness. Ironically, the British position itself eased considerably in the early 1770s, but by that time other problems had reached the explosive point. The removal of the colonists' grievance concerning paper currency mattered little in the grand scale.[55]

The year 1767 brought a deepening crisis in the struggle to enforce the acts of trade all along the Atlantic seaboard. Hardened to the obstinacy of New Englanders, British authorities now found that merchants everywhere gave vent to their anger at enforcement procedures. At Charleston, South Carolina, an ugly episode broke out in May 1767 when Captain James Hawker of the sloop-of-war *Sardoine* attempted to board a coastal schooner. The schooner's crew forced the first boarding party overboard to the cheers of the crowd, but then Hawker himself took over. '[I] went into the bow of the foremost [boat] myself, with the British flag in my hand,' he later explained, 'but sorry I am to say it, that instead of having that respect paid which was due it . . . , it received the highest insults.' Although Hawker too was greeted with 'cutlasses, axes, stones, clubs, etc.' he managed to inspect the papers of the suspicious schooner and found them satisfactory. The naval officer had asserted his right to board any vessel in the harbour, but at a considerable risk to his personal dignity and that of the authority he represented.[56]

Meanwhile, the Grafton ministry searched about for ways to strengthen enforcement of the customs service in North America. In June, 1767, Parliament authorized the establishment of an American Board of Customs Commissioners. As implemented under suggestions from the Treasury during the summer the new legislation provided for a board of five salaried commissioners, supported by clerks, a legal officer, and other assistants to supervise the entire customs service throughout the continental colonies. After considerable discussion, Boston was selected as the Board's home in preference to New York or Philadelphia. Although no reason for the choice was given, Boston was notorious for its disregard of the Navigation Acts, and the ministry probably wished to make an example of the town. Two other proposals for improving the administration of the colonies did not take effect till the following year: the creation of a separate office of Secretary of State for the Colonies and the establishment of three additional vice-admiralty courts modelled on the Halifax court of 1764. The Grafton ministry hoped that together these measures would improve administrative procedures and restore a healthy respect for British law in the colonial ports.[57]

Through no fault of their own the customs commissioners arrived at Boston on a somewhat inauspicious day—the fifth of November, on which gangs from the North End and South End traditionally did battle. Perhaps the rain dampened their spirits, or possibly a truce had been arranged; in any event there was no riot in Boston that Pope's Day. But of course the townspeople could not allow the arrival of the commissioners to go unobserved altogether. A crowd carrying the traditional figures of the Pope, the Pretender, and the Devil greeted the officials at the wharf and led them through the streets, the escorts bearing signs across their chests proclaiming 'Liberty, Property, and no Commissioners'. The effigy of the devil apparently bore a strong resemblance to Charles Paxton, a particularly disliked official and was burnt after the march had ended. Nevertheless, James Otis went before the town meeting to call for law and order. 'Humble and dutiful petitions and remonstrances,' he proclaimed, would 'sooner or later be heard and meet with success, if supported by justice and reason.'[58]

At least four of the five commissioners had had some experience in the customs service (Little is known of one member, William Burch.) Charles Paxton, John Robinson, and John Temple had all served in America. Temple in fact was the son-in-law of a prominent Boston merchant, James Bowdoin, and as surveyor-general he had shown an understanding that at times bordered on neglect of duty in enforcing the acts of trade. The senior member of the group, Henry Hulton, had been plantation clerk with the commissioners in London, and seemed eager to establish friendly relations with the Bostonians. At the same time, however, the commissioners knew that their problems would not be easily solved. Noting that there was not a single British soldier nor man-of-war within the province of Massachusetts Bay, they wrote to Commodore Samuel Hood at Halifax for assistance. They also asked Governor Bernard to seek troops from General Thomas Gage. Thus even before any major disturbances broke out, the customs commissioners sought what one of them described in a private letter as a strengthening of the hands of government.[59]

Bernard knew better than to ask for troops without approval of the Council, and the councillors in turn would as surely refuse consent. The commissioners therefore turned once more to Hood, who obliged by dispatching his own flagship, the fifty-gun *Romney*, to Boston harbour along with a smaller warship. Hood instructed Captain Corner to take extraordinary precautions against the desertion of his crew and to avoid a confrontation with the populace. The Commodore should have warned Corner against impressing any Bostonians, but perhaps he thought the captain had enough sense not to create such provocation. The first sign of trouble ahead came on the second anniversary of the Stamp Act repeal. For several evenings crowds had roamed the streets menacing the homes of the commissioners. Then on the morning of 18 March effigies of Paxton and John Williams, the inspector-general, were hanged on Liberty Tree. That night a mob once more surged through the streets, threatening the governor's official residence and ending up at Williams' house in the North End. There they dispersed without committing any damage, but the message was unmistakable: the Bostonians were ready for a repetition of the Stamp Act riots if such action became necessary.[60]

A number of other incidents added to the mounting tension during the spring. Daniel Malcom, 'a little trader' in the estimate of Governor Bernard, had long been a thorn in the side of the customs officers at Boston. Expecting a cargo of madeira in March, Malcom tried to make an 'arrangement' with the officers concerning the duties, but his overture was brushed aside. In due course the vessel ar-

rived, paused overnight in the harbour, and came up to the wharf
the next day in ballast! Although certain that at least sixty pipes of
wine had been unloaded the previous night, the customs officials
could find no witnesses to testify. The month following, John Hancock's vessel *Lydia* arrived, and the customs collector assigned two
tidewaiters to see that no goods were unloaded until official entry
had been made. When one of the officers became curious about the
schooner's cargo, he exceeded his instructions by snooping around
below decks. There he was caught by the schooner's crew; Hancock
was summoned; and the hapless officer was hustled out of the hold.
Again the customs officials had been bested in irritating fashion by
Bostonians, and naturally they looked for an opportunity to even the
score.[61]

Meanwhile, British authorities contributed a little irritation on
their own. Shortly after the *Lydia* incident the ship-of-war *Romney* arrived at Boston. Incredibly, Captain Corner almost at once began
impressing sailors from incoming vessels. The General Court immediately complained to Governor Bernard, who managed to effect a
modification of Corner's activities but not a cessation. On 10 June an
angry crowd, apparently armed with stones, forced a press gang to
surrender its latest victim. Thomas Hutchinson, rarely a spokesman
for the claims of colonists against Great Britain, was willing at least
to vent his indignation in a letter to Richard Jackson in London:

> It is unfortunate that in the midst of these diff[iculties] the *Romney*
> has been pressing Seamen out of all inward bound vessels and altho
> he does not take men belonging to the Prov. who have families yet
> the fear of it prevents coasters as well as other vessels coming in
> freely and it adds more fewel to the great stock among us before. It is
> pity that in peaceable times any pressing should be allowed in the col-
> onies.[62]

The stage was set for a showdown between the customs officials and
the townspeople of Boston, and it was not long in coming.

Hancock's sloop *Liberty* had arrived from Madeira with a cargo of
wine. On 10 May the captain made entry at the customs house for
twenty-five pipes of wine, far below the vessel's capacity. Inasmuch
as Hancock had recently boasted that he would defy the customs officials, they naturally suspected he had had his men smuggle a part
of the cargo ashore. But the customs officials could find no evidence
of wrong-doing, and the tidesmen placed on board had denied observing any irregularities in their sworn reports. There the matter
rested, as Hancock ordered the *Liberty* to be loaded with a valuable
cargo of whale oil and tar for the London market. Technically, shipowners were required to take out a permit before loading, although
the customs officers had never enforced the rule because it served

no necessary function in the pursuit of their work. But having been outwitted by Hancock before, the customs officers now took advantage of this chance to even the score and perhaps make a profit by sharing in the condemnation of the valuable cargo and vessel.[63]

On 10 June, the customs collector Joseph Harrison boarded the sloop to affix the mark of the broad arrow as symbol of its seizure. But because a crowd had gathered to protest the proceedings the comptroller Benjamin Hallowell feared for the vessel's safety and requested assistance from Captain Corner. At last the crowd had an opportunity to vent its rage against the dreaded *Romney*. As a boat-crew from the warship struggled to free the *Liberty* from its mooring and tow it to safety, the mob showered stones down upon the exposed sailors. After considerable difficulty, however, they succeeded in hauling their prize out into the harbour behind the *Romney*. Frustrated in its effort to protect Hancock's vessel from what they considered an unwarranted seizure, the crowd then turned on the nearest available targets, Harrison and Hallowell themselves. The hapless officials were pursued through the streets of town, their houses stoned, and a fine pleasure boat belonging to Harrison burned on the common. The next day these and other customs officials sought asylum on board the *Romney* for their families and themselves. Shortly after, they were transferred to Castle William, in the harbour, from whence they attempted to conduct their business thereafter.[64]

The *Liberty* affair would have been significant enough had it ended there, but it did not. On the very day that the *Liberty* was seized, one of the tidesmen who had been stationed on board when the vessel arrived in May, apparently informed the collector that he wished to change his report about what had happened that first night. Now he was prepared to testify that while below decks he had heard the sounds of cargo being unloaded. The customs officials must have welcomed this new development. Their case against Hancock for loading without a permit, while legally sound, was not a serious charge. But the smuggling of wine which officials estimated was worth £3,000 made Hancock and five alleged accomplices each liable for triple damages. Now the case was worth over £50,000, which the governor, the Crown, and the informants might share if the case were successfully prosecuted.[65]

Unfortunately for the customs officers the one voice the tidesman recognized belonged to a man who had since died, and the other tidesman had apparently been home drunk that night. Nevertheless, the customs commissioners were determined to prosecute an additional case against Hancock as a wine smuggler. Once a wealthy but virtually unknown figure outside of his own colony, John Hancock now became a familiar name throughout America as his Boston friends circulated regular reports about the case during the lengthy trial. John Adams made much of the fact that Hancock risked losing his property 'without due process of law,' inasmuch as the case was being prosecuted in the vice-admiralty court without benefit of a jury. Having made little progress by the spring of 1769, however, the attorney general decided to drop the case. In exchange for his newly-gained continental reputation, John Hancock had lost one sloop (its cargo had been returned to him). News of the *Liberty* riot provoked the ministry into sending troops to Boston, greatly increasing tensions there.[66]

The merchants and other inhabitants of American seaports had more on their minds during the winter and spring of 1767–8 than customs commissioners, admiralty courts, and impressments. Passage of the Townshend Act establishing duties on a number of imported articles had come at a time when trade was languishing. At first little direct notice was taken of the legislation *per se*. In late October the Boston town meeting voted to circulate an agreement pledging its signers to favouring American goods over more expensive importations from England. But dutied articles were not singled out as special targets, although some items like tea were proscribed as luxuries. Nor did Boston immediately adopt a non-importation agreement. James Otis asserted, according to Governor Bernard, that opposition to the new duties would be 'imprudent at that time,' 'when every other town . . . in America seemed to acquiesce in them.' Otis was apparently right; while a number of other New England towns adopted Boston's non-consumption idea, the Townshend Act itself was ignored.[67]

Then during the winter months there appeared in the leading colonial newspapers a series of 'Letters from a Farmer in Pennsylvania', twelve articles in all. The author was in fact John Dickinson of Pennsylvania, the lawyer who had drafted the resolves adopted by the Stamp Act congress two years before. Dickinson's articles met with such acclaim that they were soon published as a pamphlet, first at Philadelphia, then at Boston, New York, and Williamsburg, in seven different editions. By 1769 Dickinson's work was printed in London, Dublin, and Amsterdam as well. *Letters from a Farmer* took a place along side Dulany's *Considerations* as one of the most influential publications of its time.[68]

In his first letter Dickinson attacked the parliamentary act suspending the New York assembly for its failure to comply with the Quartering Act. Dickinson considered New York's original behavior as imprudent, but at the same time he saw the Quartering Act for what it was, taxation by order of Parliament. The Crown might have considered the affair an act of disobedience to the Crown alone and by its prerogative restrained the royal governor from calling the assembly together until satisfaction was assured. But for Parliament to assert its supreme authority in a matter of taxation was to Dickinson 'as much a violation of the liberty of the people of that province, and consequently of all these colonies', as if Parliament had sent an army to compel compliance. The author closed with a call for statements from other colonial assemblies protesting the suspending act.[69]

In his next letter Dickinson turned to the subject of the Townshend duties. He immediately put to rest any doubt about the nature of these levies. 'That we may legally be bound to pay any *general* duties on these commodities relative to the regulation of trade, is granted,' he wrote, but because Americans were prohibited from purchasing paper, glass, tea and the other items elsewhere than from Great Britain, 'any *special* duties imposed on their exportation *to us only, with intention to raise a revenue from us only,* are as much *taxes,* upon us, as those imposed by the *Stamp-Act.*' Those who argued that Americans could make sufficient quantities of their own paper and glass simply did not realize how few paper mills and glass-houses there were. Besides, accepting the duties on these commodities would then encourage Great Britain to tax those articles, such as iron and steel, which the colonists were prohibited from manufacturing. Having accepted the duties on principle, the Americans would then have no grounds for protest. Dickinson closed with a reminder of the central issue—'whether the Parliament can legally take money out of our pockets, without our consent.' [70]

In subsequent letters, Dickinson developed these themes further, countering the effort made by critics in newspaper letters to distinguish the Townshend duties as 'external' and therefore more acceptable. 'The Farmer' hastened to point out that the new measure drew money from the Americans without their consent. 'What *tax* can be more *internal* than this?' he asked. He answered those who thought the Townshend Act of no consequence because the duties were so small. 'If they have the right to levy a tax of *one penny* upon us, they have the right to levy a *million* upon us.' Dickinson attacked the bill's stated goal of 'making a more certain and adequate provision for defraying the charge of the administration of justice and the support of civil government . . .', that is, the maintenance of a civil list independent of colonial legislatures. A free people must keep the purse strings in their own hands, he warned; 'where this is the case, *they* have a *constitutional check* upon the administration, which may thereby be brought into order *without violence.*' The implication was clear enough. He also deplored the fact that while English judges held their commissions during good behavior, their American counterparts served only at the King's pleasure and were thus dependent upon the executive power. And for the first time a writer of continental stature attacked the whole programme of maintaining British troops in America at the colonists' expense but without their consent.[71]

Perhaps the most significant aspect of John Dickinson's *Letters from a Farmer in Pennsylvania* was the increasingly strident tone of his language. The relatively moderate phrasing of his early letters gradually changed as he warmed to his task. By Letter VI (published in early January 1768) he was cautioning his readers to be watchful lest they be enslaved by 'artful rulers', just as the Caesars had destroyed Roman liberty under the guise of old and venerable titles. Just three weeks later in Letter IX Dickinson's plot theory took a more specific turn. Having noted that in England the major threat to liberty had come from 'arbitrary designs of the crown', in America 'the time may come when we may have to contend with the *designs of the crown and of a mighty kingdom.*' Then we will discover that our judges are 'totally dependent on *that crown* and *that kingdom*—sent over perhaps *from thence*—filled with *British prejudices*—and backed by a STANDING *army*—supported out of OUR OWN pockets to "assert and maintain" OUR OWN "dependence and obedience".' And in his final letter Dickinson warned his readers against 'bad men' in America, who 'serve as decoys for drawing the innocent and unaware into snares.' [72]

Dickinson was at first somewhat vague in his recommendations for remedy. Petitioning the Crown and Parliament, to be sure, and if those efforts failed, he suggested in Letter III, 'let us then take *another step* by withholding from Great Britain all the advantages she had been used to receive from us.' In his last letter the Pennsylvania Farmer exhorted his readers to reaffirm the unanimity they had established during the crisis of two years before. Dickinson shared the common American belief that the threat of non-importation had helped to bring about repeal of the Stamp Act, and now he seemed to suggest a similar threat might bring similar results.[73]

As the last of the Farmer's Letters were appearing in the Boston newspapers during February 1768, the General Court of Massachusetts addressed petitions to George III and the ministry seeking repeal of the Townshend duties. At the same time it sent to its sister assemblies a 'circular letter', informing them of its petitions and the reasons therefor. Compared to Dickinson's letters, the Massachusetts letter, although written by Samuel Adams, was phrased in moderate tones and broke no new ideological ground. But by officially calling upon the other legislatures to adopt similar measures, the New Englanders incurred the displeasure of the new Secretary for the Colonies, the Earl of Hillsborough. What concerned him most was that 'an unwarrantable combination' of the colonies would endorse the Massachusetts denial of unrestricted Parliamentary authority. He promptly dispatched a circular letter of his own, ordering each colonial governor to prevent his assembly from supporting Massachusetts, even by dissolving the body if necessary. At the same time he sent Governor Bernard instructions to require the General Court to repeal its letter of February, on pain of dissolution.[74]

As so frequently happened during the growing crisis between Great Britain and her colonies, action taken by the ministry produced precisely the result it sought most fervently to avoid. Most of the assemblies were in adjournment when Massachusetts dispatched its letter, but as they convened for spring sessions, one by one they considered the New Englanders' message. Virginia's House of Burgesses returned an encouraging reply and then drew up its own still firmer letter to the various colonies. New Jersey and Connecticut had time to approve the Massachusetts resolution and Pennsylvania to table it before Hillsborough's order reached the colonies. When told by Governor Bernard to rescind its circular letter, the Massachusetts house refused by a vote of 92 to 17.[75]

Toasts to the 'Glorious Ninety-two' rang through the colonies to join 'Number Forty-five' in honor of John Wilkes. Paul Revere's famous liberty bowl, inscribed to the '92,' weighed forty-five ounces and held forty-five gills. Enthusiasts not up to handling ninety-two toasts could settle for forty-five without compromising their patriotism. Almost every successful political movement has had its own bit of mystique—special toasts, songs, poetry, and of course heroes. It was during the summer of 1768 that the American protest against Parliamentary power first acquired these trappings on a semi-permanent basis. When the mechanics of South Carolina drank to the hope 'May the ensuing members of Assembly be unanimous, and never rescind from the resolutions of the MASSACHUSETTS NINETY-TWO,' they were not only speaking to their own legislature but in a sense replying to the New Englanders. Philadelphia's patriotic poet 'Rusticus' invoked 'Columbus' himself to advise the inhabitants of the land he discovered:

> With Resolution still your Plan pursue,
> Support the glorious Number Ninety-Two;
> On that the Basis of your Bliss depends,
> On that the safety of your Lives and Friends;
> Fresh Schemes are laying to disturb your Peace
> Your Rights to wound, and Injuries encrease;
> . . . .
> Yet thus in brief—Be resolute and true
> And safely trust to Number Ninety-Two.

By the end of the summer of 1768 the inhabitants of Massachusetts might well have thanked the Earl of Hillsborough for his contribution to colonial unity.[76]

Toasts and songs and poetry would not bring about repeal of the Townshend duties, but perhaps economic protest would. In early March 1768 a group of about one hundred Boston merchants gathered at the British Coffee House to consider the 'present embarrassments' of trade. The non-consumption movement had considerably reduced their sales of English goods. As much for this reason as to protest the Townshend duties themselves the group adopted an agreement not to order any European goods (except for salt, hooks, and other items necessary in the fisheries) for twelve months or until the duties were repealed. The resolution was then circulated among the other merchants in Boston and neighbouring towns. The idea gained support in Salem, Marblehead, and Newburyport, but Portsmouth, New Hampshire, turned it down and a number of prominent Bostonians refused to sign. Meanwhile, merchants at New York agreed to accept no British goods sent after 1 October 1768, contingent upon a similar agreement by the merchants of Boston and Philadelphia. The New Englanders agreed, but the Pennsylvanians suspected that the more wealthy New York merchants would take advantage of the period before the deadline to stock up on English goods. John Dickinson delivered a plea for unity to the group, but the Philadelphia merchants rejected the plan. With that decision any chance for a boycott to take effect in 1768 was lost.[77]

In the summer, however, Boston merchants began to lay plans for the coming year. In early August a committee drew up yet another non-importation agreement not only in protest to parliamentary taxation but as a retrenchment in the face of a scarcity of money, poor fishing, and heavy taxes. The resolution established a one-year boycott of English goods (fisheries materials excepted) beginning on 1 January 1769. In addition, the signatories agreed not to import any goods subject to the Townshend Act until those duties were repealed. New Yorkers went still further at the end of August by agreeing not to import any goods shipped from England after 1 November until repeal of the Townshend Act. Furthermore, they made plans to store all cargoes sent in violation of the boycott and to label as 'enemies to this country' all subscribers who failed to observe the agreement.[78]

The New York group sent its resolutions on to Philadelphia, where a furious battle had raged in the newspapers ever since the merchants' refusal to join the earlier boycott. Joseph Galloway, the conservative speaker of the assembly, defended the decision in anonymous newspaper contributions while John Dickinson continued his attack. In September the merchants decided to petition the King and the two Houses of Parliament for redress but to go no further. In November some of them signed a petition asking the merchants of London to intercede with Parliament on behalf of the colonists. When the time arrived in the spring of 1769 to order goods for fall delivery, the Philadelphians had still not received a favourable response from any of their petitions. Brushing aside their earlier caution, they agreed on 10 March not to accept any goods sent from England after 1 April (with a few exemptions) until repeal of the duties. At a later session they decided to return all cargoes shipped after the deadline and to publish the names of any violator as 'an enemy of the liberties of America'. Now at last the three major ports of the colonies were united in their commitment to apply economic pressures on the mother country, and during the spring of 1769 merchants in most of the other ports along the Atlantic entered into similar agreements.[79]

While the merchants struggled to achieve some sort of non-importation agreement among themselves, the ordinary inhabitants of the colonies refused to stand idly by awaiting a decision. The non-consumption movement, begun in 1767 in the face of hard times, now became a protest against the Townshend Act. Townspeople throughout the colonies drew up their own agreements not to consume various imported articles, but soon the movement focused on tea. Not only was the duty of 3d. per pound likely to raise a large revenue, but tea was widely regarded as a luxury and in some sense a symbol of old-world decadence. Legally the colonists could import tea only from England, but because of its relatively high cost in London, merchants had smuggled it from Holland and France in vast quantities (just as the English did themselves). The illicit trade was centered at New York and Philadelphia, and so inhabitants there could ban 'dutied tea' at little sacrifice. New Englanders were not so fortunate, because it was more difficult for them to obtain the Dutch variety. Instead, they were exhorted by newspaper patriots to try 'labradore', 'evergreen', or other varieties derived from native American plants. The ineffectiveness of voluntary abstinence is suggested by the frequency with which communities had to reaffirm earlier prohibitions.[80]

Meanwhile the merchants had an equally difficult task in enforcing their own agreements. For one thing, a number of prominent importers refused to sign up: at Boston the sons of Lieutenant Governor Thomas Hutchinson and their friends the Clarkes were among the most obstinate. Another was John Mein, who was also printer of the conservative Boston Chronicle. When proscribed as an enemy to his country in August 1769, Mein took revenge by publishing from custom-house records a list of cargoes and owners in violation of the agreement at Boston. The fact that most of the offenders were, like Mein himself, ideologically opposed to non-importation did not make the record look any better to unknowing inhabitants of interior towns or other seaports. Criticism against Boston mounted steadily. 'I will not sacrifice my interest to serve the publick any longer,' stormed one shopkeeper in Worcester. Particularly embarrassing was the continuing importation of tea into Boston, over half of it by the Hutchinsons. Even though they were finally forced to cease in early 1770 they proved that New Englanders would buy dutied tea if nothing else were available. This lesson would be remembered by Sam Adams and his supporters in the fall of 1773.[81]

Notwithstanding their difficulty in enforcing a one-year ban on the importation of English goods, the more enthusiastic Boston merchants decided in the autumn of 1769 to extend their boycott until Parliament agreed to repeal *all* its revenue acts, including the duties on molasses and wines. Logically, the Bostonians had a good case, for the 1*d.* per gallon duty imposed on the importation of both English and foreign molasses in 1766 was clearly a revenue measure. But it had met with little specific opposition, perhaps because it was viewed by many as an acceptable modification of the 3*d.* per gallon duty levied by the Sugar Act of 1764. Also, the colonists had been used to paying, or evading, a duty on foreign molasses since 1733. Why merchants acquiesced in the wine duty is also hard to explain, except that protest against all parts of the Sugar Act had been made more difficult by repeal of the Stamp Act. Indeed, collections under the Sugar Act rose from about £26,700 in 1766 to nearly £40,000 in 1769, almost half of which derived from molasses and another £6,500 from wines. Sugar itself accounted for nearly £13,000 in duties for 1769.[82]

Both necessity and habit worked against Boston's proposal to extend colonial protest. It was hard enough to give up dutied tea. But sugar was fast becoming a staple, and molasses, as the basis for rum, was essential for both the domestic market and for trade with the Indians and Africa. Besides, as the Philadelphians pointed out, the duties on wine and molasses '[have] unfortunately been so long neglected', that the merchants were loath to make their repeal an object of non-importation. New Yorkers also refused to go along, and the Boston suggestion died, but at least the merchants there had extended their boycott from its original deadline of 1 January until repeal of the Townshend act.[83]

Effectiveness of the non-importation agreements is difficult to assess because of the normal fluctuations of commerce over any short span of years. Total imports from England had averaged about £2,000,000 in the years 1767–8, before the boycott, but in 1769 they dropped to £1,360,000. New York achieved the most effective boycott, goods arriving there dropping in value from £483,000 to £73,500. Both Philadelphia and Boston cut imports by a little more than half, but in all the southern colonies imports for 1769 were in fact higher than ever. A different way of looking at the matter, however, shows that collections under the Townshend Act fell from £13,302 in 1768, its first full year, to £2,727 in 1770. Almost three-quarters of these moneys were paid at Boston, New York, and Philadelphia, southern and other ports accounting for the rest. In short, the northern ports were reasonably successful in cutting down purchase of English goods overall, while the southern ports more effectively boycotted dutied articles. Given the fact that the non-importation movement depended entirely upon the pressure of public opinion to enforce compliance without the support of even quasi-governmental bodies, the results were reasonably significant in terms of American unity. Whether they made an important impact in England, however, is another matter.[84]

VI

The Grafton Ministry
Marks Time

— · —

1. Hillsborough's Heavy Hand

FROM JULY 1767 TO JANUARY 1768 Grafton's major preoccupation was the strengthening of what had now become in effect his administration. The intricate political manoeuvres which followed concern this study only insofar as they revealed that no party felt able to leave the impression that it might be lax towards America. Demands made by Grenville provoked Rockingham into a passionate repudiation of any insinuation that he would give up 'the superiority of this country over its colonies.' [1] Grafton's overtures ended in the recruitment of members of the Bedford party, whose influence in the administration tended towards a harder line on colonial questions.

In this reshuffle, at the insistence of Grafton, responsibility for colonial affairs was separated from the work of the southern secretary and placed in the hands of Lord Hillsborough. An experienced politician and—perhaps significantly—a friend of Halifax, Hillsborough had already proved himself an active and diligent administrator as President of the Board of Trade, first during the Grenville ministry and then for the first six months of Chatham's premiership. There seemed no doubt that he would effectively discharge duties which Grafton felt to be too great for Shelburne's office. At the same time, as a friend of Lord North, the Chancellor of the Exchequer, and as a man who regarded himself as unattached to any of the political factions, Hillsborough provided a balance against the Bedford group. Personally Hillsborough was a cheerful, likeable man, full of bonhomie and good feeling, who had managed to make and sustain lifelong friendships with such diverse men in very different parts of the political spectrum as George Bubb Dodington, George Grenville, and Henry Fox. However, as Franklin's descriptions show, his character was coloured by a certain Celtic emotional vehemence, and he tended to overreact when under pressure.

When Parliament re-assembled on 24 November 1767, Grafton and his colleagues avoided any mention of America in the King's speech and address. This was an extreme provocation to Grenville, who harangued about the need to enforce British supremacy. On the 27th he again launched into a tirade about events reported in the *Boston Gazette*, describing them as 'treasonable, rebellious, etc.', but the ministers turned aside his motion for an enquiry without a division.[2] However, in mid-December Grenville's stock rose and the ministers were correspondingly embarrassed when news arrived of the Boston resolutions in favour of a commercial boycott. After Christmas a more anti-American spirit affected the tone of both administrative and parliamentary business.[3] The colonial office had reports about illicit trade on its files, notably one from Gage, and the paucity of colonial contributions to imperial defence was highlighted by the debate on the army extraordinaries on 22 February.[4] It could have been clear to the Treasury that, owing to smuggling, the molasses duty was bringing in less than half the estimated yield.[5] The concurrence of these circumstances may have led the ministers to hustle through before the dissolution of Parliament the Bill prepared by Townshend authorizing the establishment of four district vice-admiralty courts as an additional means of combatting smuggling. The Bill received the royal assent on 8 March.[6]

By early spring Hillsborough had familiarized himself with the American business, and firm decisions on policy were beginning to emerge. Almost immediately he repudiated schemes for interior colonies which Shelburne had taken up the previous autumn.[7] Probably as a result of his association with Halifax five years earlier, he was wholly committed to the policies embodied in the Proclamation of 1763. He expressed his concern for the protection of the Indians from abuse and violence with passionate decision, demanding retribution upon the savage brutality of those who murdered them. He pushed through the transfer of responsibility for Indian trade relations to the provinces in the belief that fear of the consequences of their own neglect would spur them to action, and he confirmed that no settlements should be allowed west of the modified boundary line then being negotiated with the Indians. Linked with these measures was a reduction of the military posts in the interior, which would bring some financial saving.[8] Questions left unsettled by Shelburne for eighteen months were thus cleared out of the way in fewer weeks.

Other initiatives were less successful. Hillsborough was eager—

perhaps too eager—to press ahead with the establishment of representative government in Quebec and resented the discouragement he met in the cabinet.[9] On economic grounds he would have liked to see the repeal of Townshend's Revenue Act and pressed this policy on North within a few weeks of taking office; [10] but almost immediately such a concession became politically impossible in view of colonial denunciations of parliamentary supremacy.

From the early spring of 1768 this defiance increasingly worried Hillsborough, particularly with respect to Massachusetts. He regarded the province's circular letter against the Revenue Act as 'seditious', and it is possible that his sharp reaction, already described above,[11] owed a good deal to alarmist letters from both Bernard and Gage. In a dispatch of 18 February addressed to Shelburne, which reached Whitehall on 15 April, Bernard pointed out how the Bostonians had shifted their ground in such a way as to reject parliamentary authority which they had accepted two years before. On top of this Gage's private letter to Barrington in the same mail, which was passed to Hillsborough next day, foretold a move towards independence: [12]

> From the denying the right of internal taxation, they next deny the right of duties on imports, and thus they mean to go on step by step, till they throw off all subjection to your laws. They will acknowledge the King of Great Britain to be their King, but soon deny the prerogatives of the Crown, and acknowledge their King no longer than it shall be convenient for them to do so.

Henceforward, from summer 1768 to the spring of 1770, British ministerial attitudes towards the colonies oscillated through a period of growing tension followed by relaxation. In .particular, Hillsborough began to edge towards a course of action intended to assert British authority which would probably have produced civil war in either 1769 or 1770 but for the restraining influence of the King and of his cabinet colleagues and the unfavourable turn of international affairs.

On 8 June, in the light of reports of disturbances received up to that date, Hillsborough ordered Gage to send one regiment, or such force as he considered necessary, to Boston to give support to the civil power and the customs officials. To the same end, in the following month he ordered the naval rendezvous on the North Atlantic station to be moved from Halifax to Boston. For some reason his dispatch to Gage did not arrive until September, by which time it had been overtaken by events.[13]

Bernard's reports of the *Liberty* riots reached Hillsborough on 16 and 19 July. They threw him into near panic, made worse three days later, when he received the uncompromising Virginia protests against the Townshend Acts.[14] The cabinet discussed the situation on 27 and 28 July,[15] and on the 30th, having secured the assent of all the ministers except Shelburne, Hillsborough ordered the immediate dispatch of two regiments from Ireland. In a private letter by a later packet, Barrington urged Gage to concentrate a force capable of commanding the situation decisively, or none at all.[16] The American secretary thus committed the government to a course of action which neither Conway nor Shelburne would have dared to contemplate: for the first time a substantial military force was deployed in order to enforce the law laid down by Parliament. At the same time the cabinet decided to end an arrangement whereby Amherst held the governorship of Virginia as a sinecure, and on his sinecure declining to go there in person, appointed in his place an energetic administrator in the person of Lord Botetourt.[17]

As the summer wore on Gage bombarded Hillsborough and Barrington with pleas for decisive action against rebellion, and with analyses of the weaknesses of executive government in Boston which the governor's letters also clearly revealed.[18] 'Warm and spirited resolves with speedy execution in consequence thereof, will be the only effectual means to put a stop to the seditious spirit and daring threats of rebellion so prevalent in this country', Gage wrote to Barrington on 28 June.[19] There followed a series of monitory pronouncements: 'I know of nothing that can so effectually quell the spirit of sedition . . . as speedy, vigorous and unanimous measures taken in England to suppress it'; [20] 'You have tried forbearance, moderate and conciliating measures, to little purpose, they have encreased the storm instead of laying it. . . . I am only to hope that the measures taken at home . . . may be vigorous, speedy, and above all unanimous; for the Americans rely much on finding firm and powerfull friends amongst you: and will by no means believe, that the Acts which have been passed concerning them, or the orders that have been lately transmitted, have been the sense of the nation'; [21] 'The constitution of this province [of Massachusetts] leans so much to the side of democracy, that the governor has not power alone to remedy the disorders which happens in it.' [22] Early next year, when the battle for strong measures was already lost in London, he again advised Barrington: 'The cause of Britain should be supported with spirit and vigour. If that is not now done, your Lordship will soon find, that America will rise in her claims.' [23]

Hillsborough greatly respected Gage's opinion, and as Barrington showed Gage's private letters to him both to George III and to Hillsborough, this constant pressure could not but have an effect.[24] During the autumn Hillsborough became increasingly inclined to

some decisive stroke of policy, and Bernard's letters helped to reinforce the impression that he was dealing with a dangerous but nu-
merically insignificant 'faction' at Boston.[25] It seems evident that the
Bedfordites in the cabinet were of similar mind. On the other hand
the Chathamites could foresee only disaster from forcing a crisis.
Camden wrote to Grafton from Bath on 4 October: [26]

> The issue is now joined upon the right, which in my apprehension, is
> the most untoward ground of dispute that could have been started:
> fatal to Great Britain, if she miscarries: unprofitable if she succeeds.
> For it is (as I believe your Grace thinks with me, it is) inexpedient to
> tax the colonies, as we maintained, when the Stamp Act was repealed.
> After both sides are half ruined in the contest, we shall at last es-
> tablish a right, which ought never to be exerted. . . . As a member of
> the legislature, I cannot bring myself to advise violent measures to
> support a plan so inexpedient and so impolitic. . . . There is nothing
> I dread so much as a war with America.

By this time the leaders of the wing of parliamentary opposition
headed by Rockingham held very similar views. Dowdeswell, in a full
and fair analysis, predicted a collision and in effect counselled surrender in the last resort: 'A contest with the colonies, supported as
they will be by the enemies of this country, must be destructive to us
in the first place.' If necessary the port duties should be abandoned:
'If we come off at last with a loss those must answer for it who have
wantonly and unnecessarily revived the question, and I believe now
profess that these duties were laid merely as a test to the Americans.' [27] Newcastle's last political testament to the young men he had
joined at the end of his career was to eschew 'the measure of con-
quering the colonies', as one 'that must totally destroy all connection
with [them].' [28] And at the end of October 1768 Rockingham himself
avowed his belief in the need for conciliation: [29]

> I own I feel just as angry at the dangerous madness of some in
> America, as at the passion and obstinacy of some at home, and my
> only reliance is, that there are still at home those who will adhere to
> their avowed maxims of justness and mildness towards the colonies—
> and that in the colonies there are still as many, who will cooperate
> with them by checking a conduct in the colonies which has every now
> and then broke out in the most dangerous and offensive manner.

But not all the party were so moderate. The attitude of Rockingham's Yorkshire ally, Sir George Savile, was equivocal, and Newcastle, perhaps with Charles Yorke particularly in mind, had fears
that 'the ministerial measure of forcing the colonies, may be a little
adopted by some of our best friends.' [30] When Parliament met,
Americans in London noted that the Rockinghams refused to take a

lead in pressing for the repeal of the Revenue Act.[31] On the other wing of opposition Grenville stood equally firmly, but in the context of his own past policies, for the maintenance of Parliament's full legislative sovereignty. Yet at the same time he stated his desire to avoid extreme measures, and blamed 'those in England who have weakly or wickedly misled the subjects in America, and not . . . the colonies themselves, who have done no more than any other people would have done, to whom an immunity from taxes had been holden forth, and who had been encouraged as they have been.' This was a slap at Chatham; and yet, in his acknowledgement of the limits of coercion, he echoed Chatham's spirit: 'The respect and affection of its subjects is the basis on which every wise government must be founded.' [32] Nevertheless, the dynamic of events in America wholly escaped him. Like Dowdeswell [33] he regarded Chatham as the source of all dissension.

During September and October men in government circles knew not what to expect. Boston appeared to them on the point of open rebellion, and ministers expected resistance there to the troops sent from Halifax and Ireland. George III commented on first news about the Massachusetts convention: 'I see [that] the tendency of the town of Boston to cast off that constitutional dependency on the mother country (which must be supported) is now openly avowed.' But he vetoed Hillsborough's panic suggestion that still more troops should be sent, on the two grounds that Gage did not appear to think this necessary, and that forces sufficient to curb civil disturbances must be kept in the British Isles.[34] 'War is apprehended from every quarter', William Knox wrote to Grenville on 27 September.[35] 'They saw the event with horror,' the special agent for Connecticut wrote afterwards, 'yet seemed to think it absolutely necessary to meet the danger and hazard everything rather than recede in the least degree from the plan they had adopted.' [36] The relief when news arrived that the troops had landed at Boston without incident was correspondingly great.[37]

Meanwhile the ministry itself was in confusion. The general dislike of Shelburne among his colleagues and Shelburne's deliberate stand against their views on America led to pressure for his dismissal. Thereupon Chatham emerged briefly from his seclusion to resign, and Shelburne hastily followed suit, to be replaced by the politically unaligned professional diplomat, the Earl of Rochford. For a moment it seemed as if Granby and therefore Camden would go too, in which case Grafton would not have stayed and some substantially different administration would have had to be formed. George III, still wary of Grenville, managed to avert this collapse. Minimal changes followed. Bristol, a follower of Chatham, took the Privy

Seal, but without a seat in the cabinet, where the Chathamite contingent thus fell in number from five to four.[38]

Parliament met on 8 November 1768. The King's speech declared Boston to be apparently 'in a state of disobedience to all law and government', involved in measures 'subversive of the constitution, and attended with circumstances that might manifest a disposition to throw off their dependence on Great Britain.' [39] In the debate on the address Grenville once more defended his Stamp Act and called for measures to uphold British authority. He denounced Camden and Chatham for misleading the colonists with false constitutional doctrine. At the same time, he showed himself ready to play party politics, by an attack on Hillsborough's April circular, which he denounced as unconstitutional. North was clearly in tune with the feeling in the Commons when he declared, in words which burned themselves into the minds of American patriots, that he hoped the House would never think of repealing the Revenue Act, *'till we saw America prostrate at our feet.'* [40]

During the next few weeks ministers laid American papers before both Houses, but were careful to confine them to the affairs of Massachusetts. There in Hillsborough's view a faction required frightening, if not coercing; the indirect evidence seems clear that he wished to pursue charges of treason against the men who had called together the Massachusetts provincial convention.[41] On 15 December he moved in the Lords a series of resolutions condemning votes and proceedings of the provincial assembly and the Boston town meeting as illegal, unconstitutional, and subversive, and recording that the council and magistrates of the colony had failed in their duty to suppress disturbances. No significant dissent was voiced during the debate. On behalf of the ministers the Duke of Bedford then proposed and carried an address to the King, requesting that all steps should be taken to secure information about acts of treason or misprision of treason in Massachusetts, with a view to trials taking place before a special commission in Great Britain. George III congratulated Grafton on a result which he thought would impress the colonists with the Peers' unanimous determination to maintain British authority while showing 'a desire with temper to let them return to their reason, not with violence to drive them.' The Commons deferred their concurrence till after the Christmas recess. Most of the ministers seem to have regarded this move as no more than a gesture, for later, during the debates in the Commons, one spokesman declared it was merely to show 'what government could do if pushed to it.' [42]

Meanwhile Hillsborough also tried cajolery. In late November he called together the colonial agents, to inform them that 'if they would waive the point of right, and petition for a repeal of the [Townshend] duties as *burdensome and grievous,* Administration were disposed to come into it.' As the agents felt they could not abandon their instructions about the issue of right and must refer back to their constituents, this attempt to open the way to an immediate face-saving solution failed of its purpose. In other conversations Hillsborough reiterated his view, that the government was by no means irrevocably committed to Revenue Acts, especially Townshend's, but that the colonial insistence on rights made repeal impossible for the time being.[43]

Further papers about the disturbances at Boston were laid before the Commons on 20 January. These were debated during the following week, the government carrying by 213 votes to 80 a motion to agree with the Lords' resolutions and securing concurrence in the Lords' address by 155 to 89 in a thin House at the end of a long and exhausting sitting. An attempt by Rose Fuller and Thomas Pownall to recommit was beaten off on 8 February by 169 to 65, and the address was presented to the King on the 13th.[44]

Hillsborough, dissatisfied with his colleagues' decision to treat the address as a mere gesture, and disappointed in his approach to the colonial agents, felt obliged to elaborate more far-reaching measures for dealing with colonial unrest. On 13 February 1769 he submitted them to the cabinet. He proposed that the appointment of the Massachusetts council be vested in the Crown, and that any future denial by the assembly of the Declaratory Act should be of itself an avoidance and forfeiture of the charter. Bernard was to be given discretion to call the next general court outside Boston, at Salem or Cambridge, his services were to be recognized with a baronetcy, and he was to be recalled on leave for consultations. Troops might be withdrawn from Boston if Gage saw fit. In addition, four New York councillors should be removed, and resolutions passed by the New York assembly were to be erased or a *praemunire* be enacted against those principally involved in them. Since provision for the civil establishment already existed in Virginia and in the West Indies, Townshend's Revenue Act should be repealed in respect of them, and the other provinces informed that it would cease to apply to them when they had made suitable permanent provision themselves. At the prompting of Barrington, and in the light of Gage's reports about Boston, Hillsborough suggested a tightening up of the colonial Mutiny and Quartering Act, with penalties for magistrates who failed to act, and full powers to use private houses for billeting where necessary if colonial authorities did not provide more eligible accommodation.[45]

On the 15th Hillsborough submitted these proposals to George

III. The King himself considered them excessive. He thought that royal appointment of the Massachusetts council might in the end, perhaps, become necessary, 'but till then ought to be avoided as the altering charters is at all times an odious measure.' The threat to the colony's charter contained in the second proposal he condemned as 'of so strong a nature that it rather seems calculated to increase the unhappy feuds that subsist than to assuage them.' He made no comment about the Quartering Act. To most of the other suggestions he gave agreement; but he considered the conduct of Virginia too offensive to merit relief from the Townshend Act immediately, remarking that, 'any hint that could be given that those colonies which submit to that law and make proper establishments for the governors and other services expressed in the . . . Act, may another year be exempted from every article of it except the tea duty.' He added that there seemed ground for a dissolution of the commission of the peace in Massachusetts, as the only way to remove magistrates who had failed to uphold the civil power.[46]

Predictably Camden, Conway, and Grafton were critical,[47] and it is possible that the King's comments partly reflected their views. At any rate no more was heard of the first two contentious suggestions, or indeed of others. Only the proposals concerning Bernard seem to have been approved. The cabinet spurned the idea of an extended Quartering Act, and directed Barrington to pilot through the Commons a simple re-enactment of the existing provisions. In committee of the House on 15 March, Barrington took it upon himself to offer a modified form of the idea he had suggested to Hillsborough, only to be slammed from both sides of the House: 'Court and opposition, who have never agreed—in anything else—joined in rejecting my proposal', he wrote to Gage a few days later. The Act in its final form included two new clauses moved by Thomas Pownall, intended to conciliate colonial opinion. One stated that it should not operate in any province which had itself enacted acceptable arrangements which had been approved in the Privy Council. The other empowered local commanders of troops and magistrates to reach mutual agreement on issues not settled by the Act.[48]

The cabinet was split over the question what to do about the Townshend Act. Franklin reported in January: [49]

> The majority really wish the Duty Acts had never been made; they say they are evidently inconsistent with all sound commercial and political principles, equally prejudicial to this country as to America; but they think the national honour concern'd in supporting them, considering the manner in which the execution of them has been oppos'd. They cannot bear the denial of the right of Parliament to make them, tho' they acknowledge they ought not to have been made.

For the most part, this disagreement was kept out of public view. Through much of February, March, and April, the Commons was otherwise occupied, with debates concerning Wilkes and the Middlesex elections. The colonial agents, inhibited by their instructions to insist on colonial rights, which they felt would be futile, refrained from any petition for the repeal of the Act: [50] on 14 March they saw the Commons reject a representation from the New York assembly without a division.[51]

On 19 April Thomas Pownall moved for a committee to consider the Act, using arguments apparently tailored to attract support from the Rockinghams. He took the principle of parliamentary supremacy as laid down in 1766 to be axiomatic and pleaded that the colonies merely wished to hold 'under this supremacy' those rights which they had hitherto enjoyed. He condemned the colonial civil list provisions of 1767 as 'a revocation of the rights and privileges of the legislatures of those colonies, as they [had] been permitted hitherto to enjoy them.' Traditionally from the beginning they had exercised 'the same check and controul upon the servants of the public', through the power of the purse, as Parliament had done. It was unjust to impose in Virginia and the West Indies a levy for purposes for which a provision already existed. In any case the yield in revenue was negligible; the practical effect was merely to destroy trade and the cordial relations between Great Britain and the colonies.[52]

Against this motion North and Dyson argued, in substance:

> That they were equally concerned for the unhappy breach between the two countries and wished as much as anybody . . . [for] a reconciliation . . . they thought it absolutely necessary to assert and maintain their superiority over them; that that supremacy was denied, and their authority disputed, and while this was the case, it was not, in their opinion, a time to make concessions.

They foretold that a course of surrender would lead to demands for the repeal of the Act of Navigation, 'the basis of the wealth and power of Great Britain'.[53] In Burke's rejoinder one colonial agent detected a lurking ambiguity, suggesting that the Rockinghams preferred to exploit the issue for party ends. '[They] do not', he wrote, 'seem through the sessions really to have wished the repeal of the Act, but rather that it should remain to embarrass the present ministers, and as a means to their destruction, to whom they hope to succeed.' In that event, he thought, they would themselves take credit for its repeal.[54]

An alternative proposal by Barré, for a resolution that it would be proper next session to make a revision of laws respecting the colonies passed since 1761, found little support when opposed on similar grounds. At that point Conway, still a cabinet minister, broke front bench solidarity. He knew that by this time the cabinet had in mind the repeal of at least some of the Townshend duties, he was anxious to hold out a prospect of conciliation to the colonists, and he proposed that the House should pledge itself for next session to reconsider the Townshend Act alone. He received support from his nephew, also a placeholder, and from Sir George Savile, Beckford, Jackson, Gray, and other independents, while George Grenville opposed in a factious speech demanding that the ministers make a clear statement of policy. North closed the debate by carrying the question for the order of the day without a division.[55]

At that stage the question whether all the duties laid in 1767 should be repealed still remained unresolved in the cabinet, though about half its members so desired. But on 1 May Grafton, though Premier and head of the Treasury, allowed his own proposal to abolish all the duties to be set aside (by five voices to four at a meeting at which one of the colleagues he might have counted on for support was absent) in favour of a decision to retain the tea duty.[56] The discussion revealed a straight cleavage between the Chathamite section of the cabinet and the rest. Tension between the two sides was heightened when Hillsborough wrote into the minute and his subsequent dispatch assertions of authority and condemnations of colonial faction, with gritty references to men 'with factious and seditious views . . . enemies to the peace and prosperity of Great Britain and her colonies', which his more pacific colleagues had not intended should be associated with the cabinet's proposal.[57] Mutual confidence was destroyed, and eight or so months later Camden, Grafton, and Granby broke with the ministry, while Conway gave up his seat in the cabinet. It was thus left to North to carry the repeal of all Townshend's duties except that on tea in the early part of 1770.

How far the ministers' decisions were affected by their embarrassments over Wilkes and the Middlesex election dispute remains an open question. American agents thought these domestic tensions predisposed them to concession. In the summer of 1769 Johnson of Connecticut reported unofficial probings about colonial demands which suggested 'an intention to get out of the controversy as easily as they could.'[58] But he noted on the other side of the coin that this time by contrast with 1766 the ministry was not embarrassed by commercial pressures. A vast Russian demand for goods stimulated by the Russo-Turkish war, new openings for exports to France, the canal boom in Britain, and various evasions of the colonial non-importation agreements, all combined to reduce the effect of those agreements on British commerce.[59] Meanwhile, ministers, though resenting the boycott, were growing increasingly confident that colonial opposition would fizzle out, and that a partial repeal of the Townshend Act was therefore admissible.[60]

2. *The Boston Massacre*

As a result of the *Liberty* riot the customs officials had fled Boston and taken refuge on board the *Romney* and thence in Castle William. News of these developments strengthened support in England for Hillsborough's military solution to the crisis and prompted the ministry to send out two regiments from Ireland. Meanwhile, Gage himself had responded to the plight of the customs commissioners by giving Governor Bernard in effect a blank check with which to authorize two regiments of troops stationed at Halifax to come to his assistance. As a result of these decisions, therefore, the major parts of four regiments of British regulars converged on Boston during September 1768.[61]

When Bernard had dissolved the House of Representatives in June for its failure to rescind the circular letter, he stretched the truth by saying that he could not reconvene it without specific permission from England. The Boston leaders took him at his word and called a town meeting in mid-September to discuss what they considered an impending crisis facing the colony. James Otis, it is said, urged the gathering to take up arms, and in fact the town's arsenal of 400 muskets was brought out of storage. But his suggestion that they be distributed was roundly defeated. (Jimmy was a little 'tetched', it was recognized.) The meeting did issue a call for a 'convention of towns' to meet in place of the fall legislative session, which Bernard had cancelled. Over 100 towns responded by sending delegates, comparable to the degree of participation at a regular meeting of the General Court. Although this virtual usurpation of the executive's prerogative to convene the assembly seemed to Bernard an ominous portent, the convention made no real effort to conduct itself like a legislature. By sending delegates at all, however, the towns of Massachusetts demonstrated their belief in a right to regular 'legislative' sessions.[62]

The authorities seemed surprised that the troops who landed at Long Wharf on the first day of October were met with no opposition, and yet one wonders what they expected from ordinary, unarmed citizens in the face of massed and fully equipped regulars. Up King Street the soldiers marched to the beating of drums and whistling of fifes. Tall grenadiers, with bearskin caps, the officers with gold and silver trim on theirs; men of the battalion with three-cornered hats in black, their officers with crimson sashes over their shoulders; sergeants with long battleaxes; drummers; flag-bearers;

rank upon rank they came past the customhouse, down Queen Street, and finally onto the Commons. A large crowd had turned out to watch. There would be time enough later for the inhabitants to show their resentment. For the first time a British army took up its post in America not to help defend the colonists against the common French and Indian opponents but to maintain the authority of the mother country within a fractious colony. And out in the harbour his Majesty's warships rode with springs to their cables so that their broadsides could command the town that lay before them.[63]

Bostonians had their first chance for opposition when Lieutenant Colonel William Dalrymple began looking for places to quarter his troops. Bernard had hoped to use the so-called Manufactory House, but the tenants refused to vacate. When asked about alternative possibilities, the selectmen told the colonel that it was not their problem. One regiment camped out on Boston Common; the other occupied Faneuil Hall and the Town House. The British had to tread carefully, for any officer using force or compulsion in violation of the Quartering Act could be cashiered out of the army if convicted before two justices of the peace. Gage did not have much confidence in Massachusetts justices. Bostonians remained adamant; friction began to develop between citizen and soldier; and desertion mounted. In mid-October Gage came from New York to handle the problem of quarters personally and incidentally sat for his portrait by John Singleton Copley. The Council finally agreed to let the troops have the Manufactory House, but the tenants still refused to leave. An angry crowd gathered to prevent their forcible eviction. By renting warehouses and other buildings (some indeed from anti-British merchants) and using Castle William for one of the regiments that arrived from Ireland in mid-November, Gage finally succeeded in getting all of his troops under some sort of cover before the cold New England winter set in.[64]

Aside from a few minor incidents the season passed rather quietly, for Boston. Yet the soldiers found garrison duty among inhabitants who obviously resented their presence a highly distasteful assignment. And for their part Bostonians considered the constant parading to fife and drum an irritating disturbance and the occasional challenge from sentries an intolerable insult. Nor was the populace easy at having to witness on their Common the administration of military justice—firing squads for deserters, up to 1,000 lashes for lesser offenders. Sam Adams began collecting reports of incidents between soldiers and civilians for publication in New York and elsewhere under the title 'Journal of the Times'. In early June 1769 Gage received authorization from Hillsborough to remove any or all of the troops from Boston 'if you shall judge it expedient'. The general was prepared to order out two regiments, but as he explained to the colonial secretary, it would take time to arrange other places for the remaining regiments and to find the necessary transports. 'I hear of no riots or commotions in any of the colonies, or that any are likely to happen,' Gage concluded, 'and I know of no reasons at present that should induce me to detain the two [remaining regiments] any longer in this country.' But Governor Bernard was about to be relieved of his duties and wished to avoid responsibility for approving complete withdrawal. Nor was his successor Lieutenant Governor Hutchinson prepared to assume that responsibility either. Two regiments therefore remained at Boston, not so much as the result of a decision as for the lack of one. This lapse would in time lead to a major disaster.[65]

Through the summer of 1769 petty clashes between the troops and inhabitants increased. Bostonians enticed soldiers to desert, and the strict counter-measures pursued by the officers created more friction. In the exchange of abuse between the two sides, the inhabitants had every advantage. The justices favoured the Bostonians, especially Richard Dana, before whom many of the disputes were heard; the soldiers were vastly outnumbered; they were exposed in the line of duty to a never-ending stream of insults from passersby; and not frequently they were assaulted by stones, snowballs, and 'dirt'. Most difficult of all, perhaps, was the fact that soldiers on duty had virtually no weapons for self-defence except those that, like bayonets, swords, or muskets, might legally be classified as 'deadly'. And the law constrained them from using such lethal force against unarmed inhabitants unless ordered to do so by civil, not military, authorities, or as a last resort to save their own lives.[66]

Not all of the trouble in Boston resulted from clashes between soldiers and civilians during 1769. James Otis and the customs commissioner John Robinson were involved in a coffee-house brawl in September that left the outspoken lawyer badly bloodied. John Mein, the loyalist printer who had exposed the violators of non-importation, barely escaped a mobbing in late October. Later that same day the crowd rounded up a sailor suspected of having informed on his sloop, gave him a coat of tar and feathers, and forced him to confess to his 'wrong-doings'. As for Mein, he took refuge first with the garrison and then on board the warship *Hope*, eventually sailing for England. Throughout the early months of winter violence increased against merchants who refused to observe the boycott of British goods. One such episode in late February 1770 degenerated into an assault against the house of a citizen who fired his musket into the crowd, killing a young boy. The youngster's funeral, like that conducted by the Wilkesites for William Allen after

Interior view of the House of Commons. *By Cole. Engraving. Reproduced
in* Eighteenth-Century London Life, *by Rosamond Bayne-Powell.*

John Dickinson (1732–1808). *By Charles Willson Peale. Oil. Historical Society of Pennsylvania, Philadelphia.*

Augustus Henry, third
Duke of Grafton (1735–1811). *By
Pompeo Girolamo Battoni. Oil.
National Portrait Gallery, Lon-
don.*

Charles Townshend
(1725–1767). *Attributed to I. Gos-
set. Wax. National Portrait Gallery, London.*

The BLOODY MASSACRE perpetrated in King-Street BOSTON on March 5th 1770 by a party of the 29th Regt.

Engrav'd Printed & Sold by Paul Revere Boston.

Unhappy Boston! see thy Sons deplore,
Thy hallow'd Walks besmear'd with guiltless Gore:
While faithless P——n and his savage Bands,
With murdrous Rancour stretch their bloody Hands;
Like fierce Barbarians grinning o'er their Prey,
Approve the Carnage and enjoy the Day.

If scalding drops from Rage from Anguish Wrung
If speechless Sorrows lab'ring for a Tongue,
Or if a weeping World can ought appease
The plaintive Ghosts of Victims such as these;
The Patriot's copious Tears for each are shed,
A glorious Tribute which embalms the Dead.

But know, Fate summons to that awful Goal.
Where JUSTICE strips the Murd'rer of his Soul:
Should venal C——ts the scandal of the Land,
Snatch the relentless Villain from her Hand,
Keen Execrations on this Plate inscrib'd,
Shall reach a JUDGE who never can be brib'd.

The unhappy Sufferers were Mess.rs Sam.l Gray, Sam.l Maverick, Jam.s Caldwell, Crispus Attucks & Pat.k Carr
Killed. Six wounded; two of them (Christ.r Monk & John Clark) Mortally

---

Broadside of 12 March 1770 describing the Bloody Massacre perpetrated
a week earlier in King Street, Boston. *Published by the Boston Gazette, with engraving by Paul Revere, 1770. Courtesy of the New-York Historical Society, New York.*

Thomas Hutchinson (1711–1780). *By Edward Truman. Oil. Massachu-setts Historical Society, Boston.*

General Thomas Gage (1721–1787). *By David Martin. Oil. Lord Gage, Firle Park, Lewes, Sussex.*

Wills Hill, first Earl of Hillsborough (1718–1793), in later life. *By John Downman. Oil. By permission of Lord Salisbury.*

Lord North (1732–1792) in his robes as Chancellor of the Exchequer. *By Nathaniel Dance. Oil. National Portrait Gallery, London.*

BRITANNIA IN DISTRESS. On the right of the picture leaders of the opposition commiserate with poor Britannia, while on the left members of the government offer their remedies. *Engraving, 1770. The British Library, London.*

the St. George's Field affair, quickly turned into a popular rally. It could only be a matter of time before these tensions would explode in a clash between civilian and soldier.[67]

A brawl between ropemakers and soldiers in early March foretold trouble, as each side prepared for the showdown to come. On Monday, 5 March it happened. A late winter chill settled with the disappearing sun upon the town. A thin moon cast its pale light over the hard packed snow. Soldiers of the 29th Regiment, bayonets fixed on their long 'Brown Bess' muskets, stood guard at their posts. A tense expectancy filled the air. By mid-evening small bands of townsmen armed with clubs began roaming the streets. Off-duty soldiers were out too. Down King Street at one corner of the Custom House Private Hugh White stood sentry, a gang of young apprentices taunting him. Finally he fetched one of the youths a terrific clout with his musket. The boys yelled still more loudly. 'Damned rascally scoundrel lobster son of a bitch.' As the yelling crowd hurled chunks of ice along with their epithets at the sentry, shouting 'kill him, kill him', and daring him to fire his musket, White edged back toward the Custom House door and bellowed for help.[68]

A few blocks away another throng, mostly armed with clubs, gathered in Dock Square, summoned by the cry of 'Fire! Fire!', the eerie whistling of the mob, and the clanging of churchbells all over town. Word spread fast that soldiers and citizens were fighting in King Street, and the crowd surged toward the Custom House. Meanwhile, Thomas Preston, captain of the day, wondered from headquarters across the way what he could do for Private White, now cut off by the mob. Fearing for the sentry's life, Preston ordered a corporal and six grenadiers to the rescue, and he himself set off in their wake. The group reached White safely, but then the crowd closed in, sealing off the line of retreat. The soldiers loaded their muskets, formed a line, and tried to stand their ground against the mounting pressure of the crowd, now an estimated 300 or 400 people. More snowballs. More whistles and shrieks. More taunts from out of the darkness—'Damn you, you sons of bitches. Fire!' Preston assured those nearest him that his troops would not shoot, and in fact he placed himself in their line of fire. Then a club came hurling through the air and knocked one of the guards flat. He struggled to his feet and fired his musket, apparently into the air. The crowd reeled back, but after a pause came more shots. And men began to fall, mortally wounded, onto the icy street before the Custom House. Four died that night and a fifth man several days later.

Lieutenant Governor Hutchinson courageously stepped forward to calm the crowd and urge that the troops withdraw first. He as-

sured the populace that 'the law shall have its course', and a warrant
was issued for the arrest of Captain Preston. To the astonishment of
many, he and his men received a fair trial (too fair said those who
suspected the jury was packed with loyalists) and were all acquitted
save two, who were allowed to plead benefit of clergy to charges of
manslaughter. Under great pressure of public opinion Colonel
Dalrymple had withdrawn his troops to Castle William in Boston
harbour several days after the 'massacre'. Hutchinson was furious
but made no serious effort to intervene in the evacuation. By the
time Gage learned of the move it was too late to reverse the decision.
Bostonians had achieved their objective of removing the troops, but
at what cost? [69]

The leaders of Boston also used the episode as proof to other
colonists that their earlier reports of oppression from the troops
were not exaggerated. The *Boston Gazette*'s account of the 'massacre',
complete with black border and featuring four coffins, circulated
through the colonies and was widely copied. The radical printers
Edes and Gill also published an official report drawn up by the
merchant James Bowdoin and a special committee of the town, and
several other accounts appeared as well. Paul Revere engraved and
printed without permission a sketch of the scene by Peter Pelham,
inaccurate in many details but dramatic in its overall effect. The
facts of the shooting itself were startling enough not to require such
embellishment but were highly susceptible to both natural and deliberate distortion. Within weeks the entire continent knew that 'the
streets of Boston have already been bathed with the BLOOD of innocent Americans! Shed by the execrable Hands of the diabolical
Tools of Tyrants!' The Boston Massacre took its place in the legend
of American history, to be commemorated each year as a patriotic
day until the Fourth of July supplanted it after 1776. [70]

In one of those odd coincidences of history the day of the Boston
Massacre was also the day that Parliament rescinded all of the Townshend duties save that on tea. News of the decision reached the colonies in mid-April 1770, although in fact Americans had been expecting such action ever since Hillsborough's circular letter of the
previous May. Partial repeal put the American merchants in a difficult position. Purists insisted that as long as Parliament continued
to levy taxes on the colonists the ideological victory had not yet been
won, but realists contended, perhaps with one eye on their dwin-
dling stockpiles of English goods, that four-fifths of a loaf was better
than none. Besides, perhaps Parliament would rescind the remaining duty if the colonists ended their boycott. [71]

The merchants at New York were the first to weaken. Popular
pressure urged a continuation of the boycott, but by mid-June im-

porters favouring a reopening of trade gained control of the merchants' committee. Within weeks they agreed to the importation of all goods save tea. Philadelphians were indignant at this weakening of 'that union of the colonies on which their safety depends . . . We think you have in the day of trial deserted the cause of liberty and your country,' they concluded. Having unburdened themselves of those sentiments, however, the Philadelphians soon rescinded their own boycott, just in time to get orders off for spring goods. Boston held out against the New York defection, but the addition of Philadelphia was too much to withstand. By mid-October the merchants there also capitulated; except for a continuing boycott against tea, the great non-importation movement of 1768–70 had come to an end.

Whatever the actual effect of non-importation on the decision-making process in Great Britain (and it does not seem to have been very great) the movement ratified the earlier faith Americans had placed in economic boycott at the time of the Stamp Act crisis. The colonists would reaffirm their confidence in this approach four years later in the wake of the Coercive Acts. Secondly, despite petty jealousies and an inglorious demise in the face of partial repeal, the non-importation movement nevertheless represented a degree of sustained cooperation between the merchants of the several commercial colonies. Every bit of experience with such endeavours contributed to the breakdown of isolation that had separated the American provinces throughout the first century and a half of settlement.

VII

Aftermath of the Boston Massacre

1. Whitehall: Period of Frustration

EARLY IN 1770 after the resignation of Grafton and his friends, the reorganized administration, now headed by Lord North, took up the project of conciliation agreed by the cabinet the previous May. At this stage ministers still believed that colonial affairs were settling into equilibrium. On 5 March—the same day that King Street, Boston, ran with blood—after a suitable petition from London merchants trading with America had been arranged, North brought forward in the Commons the government's proposal for the repeal of all the Townshend duties except that on tea. None troubled themselves to defend Townshend's memory when North censured his Act for taxing British manufactures, declaring 'it must astonish any reasonable man to think how so preposterous a law could originally obtain existence from a British legislature.' North observed that the government might have proposed repeal of the tea duty also, but for the steady opposition to British authority in the colonies: lenity merely encouraged them 'to aim at independent government.' On good evidence he suggested that the non-importation agreements would soon break down.

Both friends and opponents of American claims attacked the measure. Thomas Pownall pointed out that the reference to civil lists in the preamble of the Townshend Act was so alarming to the colonists, that the whole Act should be got rid of, and therefore moved for repeal of the tea duty also. Grenville declared there had been no rational system behind government policy since 1766. He opposed any concession but withdrew from the Chamber with his followers rather than jeopardize relations with his new allies in opposition, the

Rockinghams, by voting against partial repeal. Barré pleaded in support of total repeal the interest of the East India Company, for the prosperity of which a free traffic in tea to the colonies was essential. On the other hand Barrington and Welbore Ellis, representing conservative opinion in the House, declared that no part of the Act should be repealed in view of 'the ill-conduct of the colonies'. Barrington lamented after the debate: 'This country has I fear lost all sort of authority over America.' [1] Rockinghamites, Chathamites and independent critics of the government managed to muster the respectable total of 142 votes, but North carried the day with a majority of 62.[2] The partial repeal passed rapidly through its legislative stages and became law the following month.[3]

This Act fixed the line of publicly declared policy towards the colonies for the following three and a half years. Ministers assumed that the non-importation agreements would collapse without their making surrenders of legislative powers which they felt to be inadmissible. They were anxious not to trouble the House of Commons with further debates on America which might cause colonial issues to be taken up for the purpose of party warfare and so accentuate the conflict with the colonies, and were not deflected from this plan by news of the 'massacre'.[4] The remaining discussions of American questions during this parliamentary session were provoked by the opposition.

On 26 April, in the wake of news of the 'massacre', Trecothick moved for papers on disputes between the military and the people of Boston, preliminary to a general assault on the government's policy. On 8 May Pownall attacked the powers Gage exercised as commander-in-chief of ordering troops into any area irrespective of the wishes of the provincial governor, but withdrew his motion after a government undertaking to have the matter referred to legal opinion.[5] The next day Edmund Burke led the opposition's main attack on the government's colonial policy. As one American agent reported: 'For three hours he very ably discussed all the conduct of administration relative to the colonies for three years past, which he insisted had been futile, inconstant, contradictory, absurd, and pernicious . . . but pointing out no plan for the future.' As a contribution to solving the imperial problem this was a worthless exercise, and such a piece of petty point-scoring reaped its just reward in an opposition defeat by 199 to 79. A parallel move in the Upper House on 18 May produced a 'cold, feeble, and unanimated' debate, with neither side apparently 'much in earnest': ministers warded off a motion of censure by 60 votes to 26. So far as appears from the record, the most sensible and balanced contribution was made by Rockingham. Eschewing party polemics, he went to the heart of the matter: 'I candidly confess . . . that government has a very delicate part to act . . . to maintain the due authority of the mother country, and yet satisfy the demands of the Americans is no easy circumstance.' But he had no better suggestion to offer than that the ministers should avoid standing on punctilios, 'nor set an inconsiderable tax by any means in competition with the trade and the affection of America.'[6] Apparently it did not occur to him that the revenue duties of 1766 were just as objectionable on principle to the colonists as those of 1767.

Before the end of the session North's government undertook one further piece of legislation for America, which displayed its willingness to respond to colonial pressures so long as these did not involve challenges to Parliament's legislative supremacy. Recently two New York currency Bills had been disallowed as *ultra vires,* in terms of the Currency Act of 1764. But the ministers were persuaded that New York had a case. In May they pushed through Parliament an Act empowering the New York assembly to issue bills of credit redeemable for public debts at the colony's Loan Office and Treasury, though not to be full legal tender in private transactions.[7] This modification of the Act of 1764 marked the Board of Trade's first retreat away from its rigid hard-money policy of the 1760s, and presaged the growth of a greater sensitivity in future years to the currency needs of the American colonies.

With the ending of the parliamentary session of 1770, American issues virtually disappeared from the agenda of Parliament for the next three years. Not until 1774, in the aftermath of the Boston Tea Party, were they again the subject of major debate. A prolonged lull appeared to have intervened in the Anglo-American crisis. It seemed on the surface almost as if ministers felt that if they studiously ignored the imperial problem it would disappear.

Behind the scenes this was far from being the case. The ministers had made their partial concession during the spring for tactical reasons, but the June dispatches seemed to indicate that the object, the disintegration of the colonial boycott, had not been achieved. This added fuel to the provocation of the Boston Massacre, and the cabinet began once more to consider more decisive action against the patriots of Massachusetts, whom they regarded as the instigators of all trouble in America.

There is little doubt that Hillsborough was again the moving spirit. Foiled in 1769 by the influence of Grafton and his friends in the cabinet, it seems most probable that, under what the American Secretary regarded as new provocation justifying his earlier advice, he should attempt to renew his policies after the political reshuffle of the past winter had removed his critics from office. Halifax, at this time holding the Privy Seal in the last year of his life, may well have encouraged him. Through Barrington he knew that Gage regarded the inaction of 1769 as disastrous.[8] And so, on 12 June 1770, acknowledging Gage's reports about the Boston Massacre, Hillsborough ordered him to set Castle William in a state of defence and gave indirect hints of steps intended to strengthen the executive government in Massachusetts. The same day he wrote in similar cryptic style to the lieutenant governor.[9]

Ten days later, on 22 June, the Privy Council referred to its plantation committee papers and a report on disorders in Massachusetts extending over the past three years.[10] On the 26th and 27th the leading members of the government serving on the committee went through the papers and took verbal evidence from Francis Bernard, Benjamin Hallowell, late customs comptroller at Boston, John Robinson, one of the American commissioners of customs, Joseph Harrison, collector at Boston, and other people recently returned from Massachusetts. On 4 July the committee adopted a report animadverting upon the 'seditious and libellous' publications uttered in the province, the violence used against customs officers, the 'illegal' proceedings of the town meeting and the provincial convention in 1768, the non-importation agreement, the declarations and doctrines inculcated by the assembly, and the conduct of the council. It formed a comprehensive indictment. Anticipating that the assembly's answer to Lieutenant Governor Hutchinson's message of 7 April 1770 might encourage the people of the province to further violence, and noting that instructions issued on 15 May by the Boston town meeting to their representatives showed 'an evident disposition to support by force the unconstitutional doctrines, which have been inculcated', the committee made three formal recommendations. In endorsement of Hillsborough's action it approved the placing of Castle William in a state of defence as a place of refuge for royal officials. It proposed that Boston be again made the rendezvous for the naval forces stationed in North American waters, instead of Halifax. Furthermore it added: [11]

> that the weakness of magistracy and the inefficacy of the law may be most effectually redressed by the interposition of the wisdom and authority of the legislature; wherefore the committee humbly submit to your majesty, that it may be adviseable . . . to recommend the consideration of the state of the province of Massachusetts Bay to Parliament.

On 6 July the Council issued formal orders to the Admiralty, the Ordnance, and the Secretary-at-War, implementing the first two of these recommendations.[12] The same day Hillsborough sent a copy of the Order in Council to Hutchinson, making no comment about future action, but instructing him not to make the text public in any way.[13] On the 7th he ordered the Admiralty to change the naval rendezvous immediately for the purpose of supporting civil order and checking illicit trade.[14]

There seems good reason to believe that, at this stage, Hillsborough had gained control of policy and that the cabinet as a whole contemplated resort to some of the tougher measures which had been shelved in 1769. In that year the government had attempted a bluff. Bluff would not do again, and the reticence maintained in July 1770 suggested that the ministers were anxious to avoid such imputations. Nevertheless, however 'close in all their proceedings' they managed to be, secrecy was not a virtue of eighteenth-century governments. Merely by cross-examining some of the witnesses about the questions put to them, the agent for Connecticut formed a shrewd suspicion that alterations to the constitution of Massachusetts were contemplated.[15] Thomas Pownall passed on the same intelligence to an American correspondent on 14 July, and as his brother was one of Hillsborough's under-secretaries, this information perhaps deserves the more credence. He gave circumstantial detail about discussions of proposals for a separation of the conciliar functions between two bodies, an executive council to be appointed at pleasure and a legislative council whose members should have tenure during good behaviour. An independent salary for the governor was 'certainly intended', and he feared a formal limitation of the governor's control over the military.[16] On the other hand William Bollan, agent for the Massachusetts council, had gathered by 9 July 'that some severe measures proposed by Lord H. had been rejected by the far greater part of the council', and on the 13th the secretary to the plantation office told him there was no intention of proceeding against the charter.[17] The first point seems possible—the second much less likely, not only in the light of Pownall's detailed comments, but also of evidence in the second Lord Hardwicke's papers that, as foreshadowed in Hillsborough's letter to Gage of 12 June, questions had been referred to the lawyers for consideration.[18] Furthermore, unless the plantation secretary had rightly preserved the secrecy which ought to have been expected of him, it is difficult to understand the firm tone of Hillsborough's letter of 31 July to Hutchinson or the exultant tenor of his dispatch to Gage of 4 August: [19]

> I think I can now confidently assure you that right principles and purposes with regard to America are adopted by all the king's confidential servants; and I make no doubt that the measures which will be pursued at the opening of the next session of parliament will warrant me in this information.

There can be no doubt as to what both he and Gage regarded as 'right principles and purposes'. That same day he instructed Hutchinson to abide by his instructions to hold the Massachusetts General Court at Cambridge instead of Boston, observing that the doctrines current in the assembly tended to destroy the power of the Crown and must not be suffered to have effect.[20]

Hillsborough appears to have been on holiday in Ireland through most of September,[21] but the intention to bring Massachusetts under closer royal control was not forgotten. On 3 October he wrote to Hutchinson: 'I am persuaded that all those who wish well to the community and who do not mean to concur in the dangerous designs of a few desperate men will see the necessity of such a further explanation and reform of the constitution of the Massachusetts Bay as shall have the effect to restore the dignity of the King's government and the authority of the supreme legislature.'[22] On 15 November the Connecticut agent wrote that he thought a Bill modifying the Massachusetts charter was in preparation.[23] On 2 January 1771 he explicitly confirmed this news and at the same time explained the delay in bringing it forward:[24]

> The Bill . . . has been settled and approved by many principal officers of state; yet so strong have been the applications against it, and such the representations of the injustice and the ill-consequences which would attend it, such is the situation of things, and let me add, to do justice, such is the moderation of *some* of his Majesty's ministers, that I believe that it will go no further at present.

Two circumstances in particular may have determined the outcome. One was Boston's peaceful acquiescence in the discharge of Captain Preston.[25] The other was indeed the 'situation of things'. In the summer of 1770, on orders from Madrid, the Spanish authorities at Buenos Aires forcibly removed a small token British garrison from Port Egmont in the Falkland Islands.[26] Hillsborough's first task on returning to his desk at the end of September was to warn Gage and all governors of the possibility of a war with Spain.[27] This was no time for a trial of strength with Massachusetts, nor had the ministers, engrossed in diplomatic issues which split the cabinet, leisure and energy to take up the subject. About the end of November Barrington received yet one more plea from Gage for vigorous action: 'I think it must be plain to every man, that no peace will ever be established in that province, till the king nominates his council and appoints the magistrates, and that all town meetings are absolutely abolished.'[28] On 3 December he replied: 'I cannot tell you whether anything has yet been determined in our cabinet concerning America. Everybody's attention is fixed on our negotiation with Spain; nobody here can tell how it will end.'[29]

In late January the Spanish government gave up the contest and disavowed the action of the viceroy at Buenos Aires. Most of the legislative session still lay ahead. But the ministry brought in no Bill to regulate the affairs of Massachusetts. Direct evidence as to why they let the matter drop has not been found, but it seems probable that the sudden flare-up of an international incident in which war was only narrowly averted, weakened their confidence and made them pause over the possible consequences of confronting Massachusetts, and perhaps America, until the final reverberations of their quarrel with Madrid had died away.[30] Possibly also relaxation of tensions with the colonies contributed to the decision. By the beginning of 1771 the non-importation agreements appeared to be on the verge of final collapse. The peaceful outcome of the Preston trial was reassuring, and Hutchinson's letter of 5 December reporting on this, received in London on the 30th, also recorded his view that the state of affairs in his province was more favourable than for eighteen months past.[31] Also, as a result of the diplomatic crisis, the momentum built up by Hillsborough had been lost. For the time being only one element was salvaged from his policies for strengthening royal administration in Massachusetts. Hutchinson, now governor, was allotted a salary of £1,500, and Andrew Oliver, the new lieutenant governor, one of £300, to be paid out of the proceeds of the American tea duty.[32]

2. America: The Growth of Suspicion

Historians of the American Revolution have often referred to the three-and-one-half year span between the Boston Massacre and the tea crisis as a period of calm. Yet like most historical generalizations the term is valid only in a relative sense. Although no major crises erupted, beneath the surface a number of issues old and new continued to disturb relations between Great Britain and her continental colonies. Perhaps the period is most significant for its missed opportunities, for the failure of leaders on both sides of the Atlantic to reassess imperial functions and take steps to eliminate points of friction wherever possible. They would never have so good a chance again. 'There seems now to be a pause in politics,' Boston's Samuel Cooper wrote to Benjamin Franklin in January 1771. 'Should [the British] government be so temperate and just as to place us on the old ground on which we stood before the Stamp Act, there is no danger of our rising in our demands.' Cooper could not speak for all Americans of course, but as a member of Boston's radical élite he knew that were England to make further concessions a renewal of American agitation would gain little popular support.[33]

On the bright side of the picture was the restoration of trade between England and America on a greater scale than ever. In the three-year period 1771–3 the colonies altogether purchased over £9 million worth of British goods, up from £5.4 million during the previous three-year period and almost double the annual average for the entire decade of the 1760s. In the first year after the end of non-importation New England merchants alone imported over £1.5 million, most of which poured into the formerly ill-behaved port of Boston. Whatever their politics the Yankees of Massachusetts still favoured the manufactures of the mother country, and the merchants of the region were first and foremost still businessmen interested in a profit. Despite the continuing Townshend duty on tea that commodity comprised an important part of the cargoes bound for Boston, over 500,000 lb. in the years 1771–3 not including the special shipment by the East India Company at the end of the period. 'The article of tea is so generally and openly sold in this town,' one patriotic Bostonian wrote, 'that was it in my way as it is in some other people, I would sell it myself.' Future loyalists and patriots alike shared in the profits; even John Hancock's ships freighted cargoes of the once-banned commodity for various local shopkeepers. The knowledge that Bostonians would buy dutied tea if available was not lost on radical patriots like Sam Adams. Well might he have concluded as early as 1771 that the only way to prevent the consumption of du2tied commodities was to block them at the waterfront.[34]

In contrast New York and Philadelphia imported almost no tea from England after the end of non-importation. Yet the commodity was abundantly available in both towns, freely advertised with prices listed in the weekly newspapers. As Thomas Hutchinson explained to Hillsborough in mid-1770 the New Yorkers 'have no occasion for [tea] from England, their Dutch trade being under no restraint.' And from Philadelphia, collector John Swift reported that 'smuggling was never carried to such a height as it has been lately,' a statement suggesting that other commodities besides tea were being run illegally into the Delaware. Indeed, while imports of English goods at Philadelphia increased a little in the years after non-importation, the advance was not so great as in New England. And at New York, the figures hardly grew at all. But the southern colonies remained good customers of the mother country as well as providing the major share of exports from the continent to England in the form of tobacco, rice, and indigo. In the first three years of the 1770s British re-exports of southern tobacco jumped by fifty percent over the previous decade's annual average.[35]

A quick survey of the three southern-most colonies during the period 1770–3 suggests that the 'pause in politics' which Samuel

Cooper observed in Massachusetts was more apparent than real in many provinces. One does not have to scratch the surface very deeply to find political disputes. In Georgia, for instance, Governor James Wright provoked a minor crisis when he dissolved the Commons House in early 1771 and vetoed the next session's choice of speaker, both actions within his rights as governor but rarely exercised before in the province. The following year the Reverend John J. Zubly, already a veteran political commentator from his Savannah pulpit, criticized Wright's behavior in his pamphlet *Calm and Respectful Thoughts on the Negative of the Crown . . . ,* one of the first publications directly to challenge the extent of royal authority in the colonies.[36]

In South Carolina a somewhat different dispute broke out between the governor and the house of assembly. In December 1769 that body had appropriated a sum equivalent to £1,500 to be remitted to Great Britain 'for the support of the just and constitutional rights and liberties of the people of Great Britain and America'. This unusual appropriation was in fact a gift to the Wilkesite Society of the Supporters of the Bill of Rights, an act of generosity that no northern colony had taken. The resolution provoked a furious dispute between the royal governor and conservative council on the one hand and the impetuous house of assembly on the other that continued intermittently throughout the so-called period of calm. At issue, among other matters, was whether the house had the right to appropriate money for whatever purpose it thought valid for the public good beyond as well as within the boundaries of the province. Despite additional instructions issued by the Privy Council to prevent such irregularities the assembly of South Carolina persisted in its defiance until it had worn down one colonial governor, Lord Charles Greville Montagu, and forced Lieutenant Governor William Bull to take a more conciliatory stance. Unresolved until overtaken by the events of 1774, the dispute in South Carolina, like that in Georgia, became in the apt phrase of one historian 'a bridge to revolution'.[37]

In North Carolina still another issue split the colonial government into two camps. A law of 1768 had empowered the courts to attach all property owned by non-residents of North Carolina against the debts they owed any inhabitant of the colony. British merchants who had invested heavily in Carolina lands brought about a royal instruction requiring the governor to reject any law which contained this so-called 'foreign attachments' clause. Throughout the first years of the 1770s the assembly persisted in defying the governor by including the disputed clause in every relevant statute, and it rebuffed his efforts at compromise. Like other quarrels of the

period, the 'foreign attachments' clause was rendered a dead issue in
1774 by other more momentous events. But each of these disputes
indicated how sensitive members of colonial legislatures had become
in defence of procedures they considered to be theirs by right.[38]

Direct political or military confrontation between the continental
colonies and the mother country was avoided for two years after the
Boston Massacre. The number of political pamphlets published on
subjects directly pertaining to the imperial dispute declined from
twenty-four in 1769–70 to only five during 1771–2. But persistent
colonists found other ways to express their continuing concern. Certainly the great interest in the Wilkes affair reflected an apprehen-
sion for something more than the political fate of one individual.
Americans concluded that if English petitions on behalf of Wilkes
should fail, their worst suspicions of executive tyranny would be sub-
stantiated. George III's contempt for the petitions of the City of
London and of Westminster in 1770 therefore did not go unnoticed
in America. 'Is this the virtuous, the religious k[ing] who was to
bring back the Golden Age and to banish vice and impiety from the
realm [?]' asked the *Boston Gazette*. No one could accuse the printers
Edes and Gill of letting up during the period of calm! [39]

Still another issue, one which began long before the political controversy between England and her colonies, erupted in Virginia during the 1770s. This was the question of whether the Church of England would appoint a bishop to preside in America. Rumours to
that effect had excited opposition among the various dissenting sects
in the colonies intermittently throughout the eighteenth century.
Most recently, such a possibility seemed imminent during the Stamp
Act crisis. Concern was greatest in New England, where Congrega-
tionalists, Baptists, and Quakers vastly outnumbered the Anglicans.
At stake was not only a continuation of the dissenters' domination of
society but also, they were convinced, their religious liberty itself. In
New York, where the Anglicans were far stronger, the movement
had strong support from the Reverend Samuel Johnson, one-time
President of King's College, New York, Sir William Johnson (no
relation), wealthy land-holder and superintendent of Indian affairs,
and numerous other influential men of the colony. In England the
Archbishop of Canterbury, Thomas Secker, gave the plan his fullest
backing. At his death in 1768 he left £1,000 to further the project.[40]

Key to the plan's success, however, lay in the hands of the Anglican clergy of the southern colonies, among whom interest in an episcopate had never been very strong. In 1770 the Church of England
clergy in Maryland petitioned the King and archbishops to settle a
bishop in their colony, and in the same year the proposal gained the
support of James Horrocks, the influential President of William and

Mary College in Virginia. But at a convention the following year only a handful of the colony's Anglican clergymen endorsed the idea. Richard Bland, himself an Episcopalian as well as a staunch defender of American 'liberties', ridiculed the proceedings in a letter to an English friend. In his conclusion he probably spoke for many of his fellow Anglicans in America: 'I profess myself a sincere son of the established church, but I can embrace her doctrines without approving of her hierarchy, which I know to be a relick of the Papal Incroachments [sic] upon the Common Law. . . .' But the harder the northerners argued for the plan through pamphlets, letters, and personal appeals, the more suspicious both clerics and laity in the southern colonies became. Like other issues of the period the attempt to establish an American episcopate had no clear resolution; it simply became absorbed into the larger political dispute, contributing one more element to the gradual estrangement between mother country and her continental colonies.[41]

Another irritant that continued through the early years of the 1770s was the customs establishment. Although partial repeal of the Townshend Act reduced the number of articles liable to a duty, collections during the four-year period 1770–4 produced a revenue that averaged slightly over £40,000, considerably higher than that of the previous six years, and not an inconsiderable sum when profits from seizures, fees, and various other charges were thrown in. Out of this revenue came the governors' salaries for Massachusetts and New York, stipends for assorted lieutenant governors, attorneys general, and chief justices, as well as the salaries of all the admiralty judges. Although the total fell far short of Grenville's original goal of £200,000 for support of the army, the North ministry saw in it, not without reason, the promise of a considerable potential revenue in future, enough perhaps to achieve a truly independent civil establishment in all of the colonies.[42]

Despite the lessening of tensions that accompanied partial repeal, collecting these sums and carrying out the other tasks associated with enforcement of the Navigation Acts remained as difficult an assignment as before. Collector John Hatton at the New Jersey district of Salem and Cohensy could testify to that. Hatton had been known as an easy mark among the smugglers of the Delaware River region, and it therefore must have come as a surprise when in the fall of 1770 he decided to investigate a vessel reportedly unloading its cargo into small pilot boats off the entrance to the bay. He and his son overtook one of the boats and boarded it, but when the wind died, they were in turn overwhelmed by bargeloads of irate sailors who gave them a severe beating. Hatton himself was then jailed on a charge of wounding one of his assailants, but he sent his son to warn the Philadelphia collector to watch for the recaptured boat. There the young man was attacked by another band of sailors, his bandages ripped off, and his previous wounds given a thorough coat of tar and feathers. For more than an hour young Hatton was beaten, pilloried, and dragged through the streets by a rope around his neck. He was then left for dead on the New Jersey side of the river, but in time miraculously recovered. That no customs officials were actually killed during these years was more the result of British resilience than of American restraint.[43]

The following autumn smugglers on the Delaware attacked the custom-house schooner itself. A mob of more than thirty men, armed with clubs and cutlasses, climbed aboard the vessel, which was anchored with its prize for the night. They gave captain and crew a severe beating and threw them into the hold, after which they cut away the rigging and sails and made their escape in the prize. 'We have too much reason to believe that they were some of the principle [*sic*] merchants in this City in disguise,' concluded the collector of Philadelphia. He considered it strange that, despite a bright moonlight during the attack, none of the customs officers could identify the assailants.[44]

One of the most significant episodes of the period was the attack on the schooner *Gaspée* in Narragansett Bay in June 1772, for it revealed how bitter attitudes had remained toward enforcement of the Navigation Acts even during these years of relative calm. Rhode Islanders had never accepted outside authority with much grace. It will be remembered that in 1764 Newporters had opened fire on the customs schooner *St. John* from their harbour battery. Then, five years later, the sloop *Liberty,* the same vessel that had been seized from John Hancock the previous summer, was patrolling Rhode Island waters under the command of William Reid, viewed by one American as 'an infamous detested tool, pimp, and informer. . . .' Reid so enraged the Newporters that a group cut his vessel from its moorings, stripped it of rigging and armament, and scuttled it in the harbour. These were serious offences, but the vessels and men involved were in the customs service, where such risks were a part of the routine.[45]

In the spring of 1772, however, a far more ominous confrontation, one between Rhode Islanders and the Royal Navy, was in the making. Lieutenant William Dudingston, R.N., apparently under orders from Admiral John Montagu of the Atlantic Station, patrolled southern New England waters in the naval schooner *Gaspée.* Like many another naval officer, Dudingston showed little consideration for his victims as he carried out his instructions with literal exactitude and he added minor irritating practices of his own, such as sending his prizes all the way to Boston for trial. In an exchange of vitriolic correspondence Governor Joseph Wanton challenged Dudingston's authorization to cruise within Rhode Island's waters, but the lieutenant refused to present his papers. Dudingston forwarded Wanton's complaints to Admiral Montagu, who thereupon lectured Wanton as to what was expected of provincial governors. 'As to your attempt to point out what was my duty as Governor,' Wanton cooly responded, 'please to be informed that I do not receive instructions for the administration of my government, from the King's admiral stationed in America.' [46]

In June the war of words turned to violence. On the afternoon of the 9th Dudingston set off in pursuit of a vessel heading for Providence, but he had the misfortune to run aground as the tide ebbed. His quarry reported the situation to John Brown, a prominent merchant of Providence, who promptly readied eight longboats for a night attack on the helpless schooner. Lieutenant Dudingston was painfully shot by the party boarding the *Gaspée*. Its crew members were bound up and rowed ashore in their boats, along with the wounded captain. The Rhode Islanders then put the hated *Gaspée* to the torch and burned it to the waterline. The governor offered a reward for information leading to the conviction of the miscreants, without result. [47]

The special investigatory commission appointed by George III got off to a bad start when the battery at Newport refused to salute the arrival of Admiral Montagu aboard his flagship. Governor Wanton explained with a straight face that budgetary considerations limited salutes to certain holidays! Whereupon the admiral withdrew in a huff. Nothing came of the investigation except that Dudingston was chastised for his intemperate zeal in enforcing the acts of trade and his imprudence in refusing to show the governor his original orders. But the appointment of this commission did have another, wholly unintended result. The *Gaspée* commission was authorized to send all persons it might accuse in the affair to England for trial. The Virginia House of Burgesses, though distant from the scene and little involved itself in such incidents, nevertheless took exception to 'the principles and authority' of the commission. In March 1773 that House appointed a committee of correspondence to keep itself informed of all acts and other decisions of Parliament or the ministry affecting the colonies and 'to keep up and maintain a correspondence and communication with our sister colonies respecting these important considerations.' The House of Burgesses promptly invited all of the other colonies in North America to establish similar committees. [48]

Despite the absence of confrontations such as had marked the

Stamp Act crisis and the non-importation protests, relations between England and America remained tense throughout the first years of the 1770s. Competing resistance groups in New York took advantage of the lull to settle their differences and to close ranks. The new leader was Alexander McDougall, a shipmaster turned merchant who gained fame (or notoriety) as the author of a stinging attack on the General Assembly in December 1769 for having complied with the Quartering Act. His broadside was declared libellous, and like the hero John Wilkes, McDougall was himself briefly jailed. When forty-five virgins serenaded the incarcerated patriot with forty-five songs, one cynic suggested that they were all forty-five years old. Isaac Sears and John Lamb, formerly at the head of the opposing faction, joined in support of McDougall after this episode.[49]

In Philadelphia, disillusionment with the merchants' cautious behavior during the Townshend crisis led to a major shift in political alignments. The White Oaks ship-carpenters abandoned their support of Joseph Galloway and his Quaker party to join the Presbyterian camp of Charles Thomson, but they were unable at first to establish an effective political organization. However, anti-British leaders like John Dickinson and Thomson had at least succeeded in undercutting Galloway's support among the electorate. One sign of Dickinson's strength was adoption by the Pennsylvania assembly in March 1771 of a petition he drafted to the King requesting repeal of the remaining Townshend duty on tea. Although it came to no avail, the effort at least expressed a continuing opposition to the principle of taxation without representation.[50]

The most dramatic political development during the period took place at Boston. Orations marking the anniversary of the Boston Massacre each year were supplemented by other towns with their own annual lectures. But these efforts at maintaining public concern had no coordination. Consciously or not, Samuel Adams borrowed an idea of religious dissenters in England when he suggested in September 1771 that correspondence societies be established in the several colonies. Adams' original goal was to maintain contact with groups in England who opposed alleged tyranny in the mother country, but through the next several months he and his associate Dr. Thomas Young saw the plan as an excellent means of uniting the various towns of Massachusetts. 'We are brewing something here which will make some people's heads reel at a very moderate age,' wrote Young in late August 1772. When word came in September 1772 that henceforward the justices of the Superior Court in Massachusetts would be paid by the Crown from American customs revenue, it reawakened dormant anxieties about a civil list of corrupt officials independent of control by the people. At the last of a series of town meetings called in November to inquire into the matter of the judges' salaries, Adams moved the appointment of a 'Committee of Correspondence . . . to state the rights of the colonists and of this province in particular . . . , to communicate and publish the same to the several towns in this province and to the world as the sense of this town. . . .' The resolution closed with a request that each town communicate its sentiments on the occasion. The Boston town meeting adopted the proposal without dissent.[51]

After three weeks of work in sub-groups the Committee of Correspondence presented to the town meeting on 20 November a document drafted largely by Adams entitled 'The State of the Rights of the Colonists', as well as 'The Enumeration of the Violations of our Rights'. These documents were unanimously adopted and sent to all of the other towns in the province inviting their comment. Under three major headings the committee spelled out the rights of the colonists as men, as Christians, and as subjects. Although no new theoretical arguments were advanced, the document closed on an ominous note: 'The colonists have been branded with the odious names of traitors and rebels, only for complaining of their grievances. How long such treatment will, or ought to be born[e], is submitted.'[52]

The list of infringements opened with a repetition of the argument against the Declaratory Act and parliamentary taxation. It then quickly moved on to a topic that particularly concerned Massachusetts—the appointment of numerous new officials to collect that revenue, positions not provided for in the colony's charter. These officers have been 'invested with powers altogether unconstitutional', the document stated, and then it catalogued a long series of abuses allegedly committed by the customs establishment. Worse still, 'fleets and armies have been introduced to support these unconstitutional Officers in collecting and managing this unconstitutional revenue. . . . Introducing and quartering standing armies in a free country in times of peace without the consent of the people' had always been regarded as a violation of the rights of freemen. And to complete the offense, the moneys collected had been used for 'the most destructive purposes', to render the governor, the judges, and the King's attorney totally independent of the legislature, thus destroying that equilibrium 'without which we cannot continue a free state'. The list of infringements also denounced the suspension of New York's assembly, the extension of admiralty court jurisdiction, efforts to establish an American episcopate, and a number of lesser threats real or imagined.[53]

The 'Boston pamphlet', as the published form of these various reports was called, went to the selectmen of the province's 260 towns and districts, where it received an unexpectedly enthusiastic reception. For the first time in the movement to resist British policies, people on the grass-roots level in the smaller communities were being asked to take a stand. By the summer of 1773 over half of the colony's towns and districts had responded in some positive fashion to the Boston pamphlet. While many of these communities had previously expressed interest in imperial affairs, some became involved in the question for the first time. Few towns went so far as the town of Pownallborough in Maine, which declared that 'our Forefathers soon as they landed here considered themselves as beyond the jurisdiction of the Supream Authority of the relm of England'. Most responding communities agreed with Marlborough, that they were 'engaged in one Common Cause, viz. that of Asserting and Maintaining our Rights.' Before the end of 1773 over fifty communities had established their own committees of correspondence, while many more maintained contact with the Boston committee through other channels. The foundation for unified opposition was already established in Massachusetts before the tea crisis.[54]

An equally significant though less intentional consequence of Boston's initiative in November 1772 was the provocation of the governor. Alarmed by the spreading popularity of the Boston pamphlet, Hutchinson convened the General Court in early January 1773 and used the occasion of its opening session to deliver a rebuttal to the Boston documents. Before the governor broke off the battle of words in March, he and the assembly had fought it out through three months of charges and counter-charges. Hutchinson reportedly 'reduced himself to a most ridiculous state of distress,' seeking the assistance of various conservative and moderate leaders of Boston. For their part leaders of the Massachusetts assembly attempted to enlist the help of both Daniel Dulany and John Dickinson, to no avail. Hutchinson's debate with the assembly of his colony marked the first effort by an American to formulate a comprehensive defence of Parliament's claim to supremacy over the colonies.[55]

Hutchinson attempted to demonstrate to the assembly that 'from the nature of government, there must be one supreme authority over the whole,' and that in the British Empire that supreme authority rested with Parliament. He could find no support for the claim that the Massachusetts charter granted the colonial legislature sole power to make laws. By their voluntary removal to America, Hutchinson averred, the colonists had relinquished their English right to elect the men who legislated for them in Parliament. The governor then threw down a challenge to the assembly. 'I know of no line that can be drawn between the supreme authority of Parliament and the total independence of the colonies, as it is impossible there should be two independent legislatures in one and the same

state.' He could not bring himself to believe that independence was
what the leaders of Massachusetts had in mind. 'If you can conceive
of any other constitutional dependence than what I have mentioned;
if you are of opinion that upon any other principles our connexion
with [Great Britain] can be continued, communicate your sentiments
to me. . . .' [56]

The assembly did not need an invitation to take up the gauntlet.
Samuel Adams, John Hancock, and the radical lawyer Joseph Hawley drafted the response. It was indeed difficult, they agreed, to
draw a line between a universal authority for Parliament or none at
all. If such a line could be drawn the Massachusetts assembly would
nevertheless hesitate to do so without the consent of the other colonies 'in Congress'. But if no such line existed, the authors concluded,
then the colonies were either 'the vassals' of Parliament or they were
totally independent. Surely it could not be supposed that the
founders of Massachusetts intended that their descendants be reduced to a state of vassalage. Rather, it was their belief that 'the colonies were by their charters made distinct states from the mother
country' under the same King. Independence from Parliament was
certainly a less dreadful prospect than submission to an 'absolute,
uncontrolled power'. The assembly closed with a reassertion of its
allegiance to the King, 'our rightful Sovereign', and the promise that
as long as 'the people of this province be left to the free and full exercise of all the liberties and immunities granted them by charter,
there would be no danger of an independence on the Crown.' [57]

Here at last was new ground indeed. Ignoring (or rejecting?) the
line first traced by Daniel Dulany and Richard Bland toward the
concept of a dual sovereignty within the Empire, the Massachusetts
leaders took up Hutchinson's challenge and carried it to what for
them was its logical conclusion—an assertion that Parliament had not
even a general superintending power over the colonies which in turn
were bound to Great Britain only by their allegiance to the King. In
subsequent exchanges Hutchinson could never quite undo the damage caused by his insistence on an 'either-or' construction of the
problem. Not only had he deprived himself of a middle ground, but
all of the other moderate Americans who sought a place to stand between absolute independence from Parliament on the one hand and
unlimited submission on the other were similarly deprived. In the
all-important struggle for men's minds that played such a decisive
part in the coming of the American Revolution, Governor Thomas
Hutchinson had lost a strategic round for his side. Perhaps most
seriously Hutchinson was criticised by both friends and foes as the
one responsible for having reopened the quarrel. The charge is un-
fair, perhaps, for the governor was actually responding to the Bos-

ton pamphlet, but he chose to use the House of Representatives as his forum, thereby assuring maximum publicity for a debate which he ultimately lost in the eyes of most observers. 'Whether the governor will be thanked by [the British] administration for his speech . . . you can best tell,' wrote Boston's Samuel Cooper to the former Governor Thomas Pownall in London. 'It is certain he has gained nothing by it here.' [58]

Hutchinson's troubles with the assembly were in fact just beginning. For years he had feared that some of his letters to English officials might fall into hostile hands and be used against him. After the publication of several letters from his predecessor Francis Bernard to Lord Barrington in 1769, Hutchinson's anxiety deepened. In the spring of 1773 there came into the hands of Benjamin Franklin, then serving in London as colonial agent for Massachusetts, a group of letters written by Hutchinson and his brother-in-law Andrew Oliver to the subminister Thomas Whately. Franklin had come to believe that certain royal officials in America were more responsible for the imperial crisis than was the British ministry, and Hutchinson was one of his prime suspects. He therefore forwarded the letters to the leaders of Massachusetts apparently to bolster his claim, but with the understanding that they would be shown only among a small group and not be published. That was easier said than done. Within a few weeks in June rumours about the content of the letters began to fly, inaccurate versions appeared, and finally, in response to public demand, so they said, the patriots published the letters in the newspapers and in pamphlet form.[59]

The people of Massachusetts already viewed their governor as a dangerous threat, but the letters seemed to confirm their suspicions. In one Hutchinson asserted that 'government had been too long in the hands of the people' in Massachusetts. In others he urged Parliament to punish those who opposed English policies. In the most damaging letter he stated that 'there must be an abridgment of what are called English liberties' in the colonies for their own good. Although the letters disclosed little that Hutchinson had not already said publicly, the fact that an American-born governor should share such views with English government officials through private letters (complete with warnings to keep their contents secret) heightened the aura of intrigue. A series of resolutions adopted by the house led to a petition that the King remove both Hutchinson and Oliver from office for conduct obnoxious to the people.[60] The bill of particulars ran as follows:

> There has long been a combination of evil men in this province, who have contemplated Measures and formed plans to raise their own fortunes and advance themselves to posts of power, honor, and profit

to the destruction of the character of the province, at the expense of the quiet of the nation, and to the annihilating of the rights and liberties of the American colonies. . . . The said Thomas Hutchinson and Andrew Oliver have been some of the chief instruments in the introduction of a fleet and army into this province to establish and perpetuate their plans; whereby they have not only been greatly instrumental in disturbing the peace and harmony of the government and causing unnatural and hateful discords and animosities between the several parts of his Majesty's Dominions, but are justly chargeable with all that corruption of morals in this province, and all that confusion, misery, and bloodshed which have been the natural effect of the posting of troops in a populous town. . . .

'The people are highly incensed against the two impeached gentlemen,' reported Samuel Adams a few days later. 'Even some of their few friends are ashamed to countenance them.' [61]

In New York, Philadelphia, and Boston patriot forces closed ranks during the period of calm. At Newport, Rhode Island, blood had been spilled; in Virginia the House of Burgesses called for unified action in opposition to British policies; and in the back-country of Massachusetts the ordinary people of the province expressed their support of Boston. Before the year 1773 was out these signs of unity would face a stern testing.

VIII

Crisis over Tea

———•◦•———

1. Whitehall Hears the Low Rumble of Distant Thunder

DURING THE EARLY PART OF 1771 Hutchinson's reports about the state of his province were reasonably reassuring, and in the wake of the crisis over the Falkland Islands, the British cabinet seems to have drifted into a decision, perhaps never clearly formulated, to wait and see if the unrest in Massachusetts would die down of its own accord.[1] This inaction could be, and was, misunderstood. In early February Franklin gathered the impression that 'the doctrine of the right of Parliament to lay taxes on America is now almost generally given up here, and one seldom meets in conversation with any, who continue to assert it', but feelings about the dignity of Parliament would prevent any formal renunciation.[2] 'With regard to America', W. S. Johnson reported on 15 March, 'it is the general opinion that nothing should be done at present. It is enough that they know that goods are going out there, this spring, to the amount of more than a million sterling.'[3]

Despite occasional minor signs of friction the calendar of the Secretary of State's correspondence during 1771 gives an overall impression of routine uninterrupted by any serious tension between Great Britain and the colonies.[4] In the summer ministers even contemplated the possibility of reducing the American military establishment from fifteen to ten battalions, in the hopes of limiting colonial military expenditure and at the same time providing a larger force in the British Isles.[5] This idea was hurriedly quashed by the commander-in-chief. Gage pointed out that, although perhaps garrisons at St. Augustine and Halifax might be safely halved, withdrawal of five regiments would leave him with no force to be assembled to meet any emergency. The only large concentration of troops left would be the four regiments in Canada, and these were

hardly sufficient to hold the province. Little would be saved finan-
cially. The cost of provisions would have to be met wherever the five
regiments were stationed, and their removal from America would
make little difference to the ordinary, very large contingencies in his
command, which arose from 'the support of the distant posts, repairs of storehouses, magazines, barracks and works in all the garrisons', which were numerous, their provisioning, and the expenses of
Indian diplomacy.[6] It is possible that this information weakened the
stand Hillsborough was making throughout this year against the
projects of landspeculators for the establishment of an inland colony
in the Ohio basin. He consistently objected to these schemes on the
grounds which had been adduced as justifications for the Proclamation Line of 1763; [7] but his position was being steadily undermined
by the argument that an inland colony would reduce the costs of occupation of the interior, and still more by the success of the projec-
tors in buying the goodwill of various ministers and officials by substantial shares in the enterprise.[8]

Illicit trade remained a recurrent problem. During the autumn
of 1771, for instance, Hillsborough received information from Hutchinson, that an estimated five-sixths of the tea consumed in North
America was being imported illegally, much of it from Dutch
sources. Hutchinson estimated the total consumption in America at
about six and a half million pounds. Such figures, if anywhere near
correct, indicated an annual loss to the revenue of over £60,000.[9]
Even if they were grossly exaggerated, which seems likely, there is
little doubt that less than half the tea entering America was paying
the duty. It seems probable that a renewed emphasis on the inter-
ception of 'free trade' at sea led to the series of incidents around
Rhode Island, which provoked some of its inhabitants to the destruction of H. M. S. *Gaspée* in June 1772.[10] It was to strengthen colonial
administration against this, as well as other forms of insubordination, that Hillsborough during the last weeks of his tenure at the
colonial office arranged for salaries out of the proceeds of the tea
duty to be paid to legal officers and judges of the superior court in
Massachusetts and to chief justices in other royal colonies: he thus
bequeathed another festering legacy to his successor when he left office in the summer of 1772.[11]

Reports of the attack on the *Gaspée* reached London on 16 July.[12]
On 10 August the attorney and solicitor general reported that a
charge of high treason would lie and might be tried either in England or in Rhode Island.[13] At this point Hillsborough resigned, defeated in his stand against the Ohio colony and the victim of in-
trigues for political leverage within the cabinet.[14] His successor, Lord
Dartmouth, the step-brother of Lord North, was thought likely to be

less 'firm' in dealing with colonial insubordination.[15] In fact he was no more prepared than Hillsborough to tolerate lawlessness, especially in a business which the attorney general considered of 'five times the magnitude of the Stamp Act'.[16] Further steps were taken at two cabinet meetings on the 20th. Hillsborough's dispatches were cancelled, and the ministers approved the proposal for the special commission of enquiry, of which mention has already been made.[17]

Nearly a year was to elapse before it finally became clear to the new American secretary and his colleagues that this operation was abortive, and the commission was powerless to uncover responsibility for the destruction of a King's ship.[18] Long before then other issues had become uppermost in the minds of the ministers.

Dartmouth held entirely orthodox views about the constitutional problems of the Empire, and he soon became increasingly concerned about the course of events in Massachusetts. Commenting on 2 September on the complaints raised in the assembly against the Crown salary paid to Hutchinson, he remarked: 'I must confess that I have always been taught to believe that the providing for the support of the American governors and other officers of the crown in the colonies independent of the people was a measure equally for the honour and dignity of the crown and for the welfare of those colonies.'[19] On 9 December, having heard of the exception also taken to the grants of salaries to the judges, he commiserated at length with Hutchinson about the 'unhappy mistake' concerning the supremacy of Parliament which had 'for some time past possessed the minds of so many of the people under your government.' He hoped that before long reason and good sense would prevail and the 'veil of error' be lifted.[20] This optimism did not survive the news of the Boston declarations of rights and infringements, and the first reports of supporting town resolutions from other parts of the province.[21] Presumably with the King's approval Dartmouth brought them forward for the attention of the cabinet on 1 February; but his minute laconically noted that 'consideration of the Massachusetts papers was deferred', and there is no trace of further action.[22] On 3 February he still hoped that 'truth and conviction [would] prevail over prejudice and error'; but that hope died with the arrival on 29 March and 7 April of news of the outcome of Hutchinson's constitutional debate with the General Court.[23] Persuasion, Dartmouth realized, would achieve nothing. The addresses of the assembly and council were 'replete with doctrines of the most dangerous nature'. Some action would have to be taken.[24] Others agreed. North a year later, defending the Massachusetts Charter Act in conversation with Hutchinson, declared that 'it ought to have been done the last session, upon the declaration of independence, both by the council and the house', and he explained that delay had been due to 'the state of affairs here in England'. In April 1773 North was in no frame of mind to make concessions to the colonies about the tea duty or anything else; and he claimed afterwards that although there had been opposition to specific measures proposed by the ministers, all parties agreed in the need for a change, 'in order to prevent the colony from entirely throwing off their dependence.[25] This mood of grim concern was doubtless intensified by a string of alarmist letters from a place-seeking informant at Boston, Joseph Ward, who painted a dramatic picture of a conspiracy aimed at rendering America entirely independent of Great Britain,[26] and by a further complaint by Hutchinson in a private letter of 19 April to John Pownall, which may have reached London about the end of May.[27] On 2 June Dartmouth wrote to Hutchinson, that the King concurred with the unanimous opinion of his ministers, that the authority of Parliament must be supported and that the declarations of the council and assembly in their dispute with Hutchinson would have to be laid before it— which could not then be done until the following session.[28] Shortly afterwards, ignoring protocol, the colonial secretary sent a direct personal reply to a private letter in which Speaker Thomas Cushing of the Massachusetts assembly had given a detailed exposition of the province's grievances. Stressing that he wrote merely in his private capacity, he described the assembly's constitutional claims as 'wild and extravagant doctrines . . . which appear to me so utterly inconsistent with any pretensions to a share in the privileges and advantages of British subjects that I could never subscribe to them.' They were nothing less than a declaration of independence, and he could see no possibility of British concessions on taxation until they were rescinded. He reaffirmed his belief in the principle of parliamentary supremacy, but in a tacit plea for compromise, he drew a distinction between the theoretical possession of this power and its exercise: 'If my wishes and sentiments could have any weight with a British Parliament, the exercise of that right . . . should be suspended and lie dormant till some occasion should arise . . . in which the expediency and necessity of such exercise should be obvious.'[29] News of the publication at Boston of Thomas Whately's correspondence with provincial officials, on which the Massachusetts assembly founded its demands for removal of both the governor and his deputy, simply added one more black mark in Dartmouth's book against the province.[30]

However, other urgent matters pressed upon the attention of the ministers. It is not unlikely that, during the autumn and winter of 1772-3, once again the international situation prevented the cabinet from bringing forward measures to deal with the situation in Mas-

sachusetts. A *coup d'état* in Sweden by the Crown with the support of
the pro-French faction known as the Hats threatened such an extension of French influence, that in October the southern secretary,
Lord Rochford, gave his colleagues reason to expect that a serious
diplomatic crisis was imminent.[31] Russia was believed about to con-
clude a peace ending the war with Turkey in which she had been involved since 1768, and in that event was expected to intervene in
Sweden. Her action would appear certain to bring in France. In that
case Great Britain could hardly stand aside and see her last possible
allies in Europe fall under French dominance. On 7 October the
cabinet agreed to Rochford's proposal, that in the event of the
French preparing to act in the Baltic, they should be warned that
Great Britain would certainly intervene.[32] The cabinet ministers
were preoccupied with this affair all through the winter and spring
of 1772-3, until it was finally resolved by a diplomatic confrontation
in which the French appeared to climb down in face of a British
threat of naval mobilization. There is no direct evidence of the in-
teraction of this crisis with colonial concerns—but George III at any
rate was aware then, as he was a year later, of the need to avoid en-
tanglements on both sides of the Atlantic at the same time.[33]

During the same period East India affairs produced a domestic
crisis of the first magnitude and provoked a long, hard parliamentary tussle with the Rockinghamite opposition. During the course of
this business, almost inadvertently, the train leading to an explosion
in America was ignited, not by the colonial secretary but by the
Treasury.[34] After several years of boom conditions, a crisis of confidence hit British commerce in 1772. Badly guided, the East India
Company fell into serious difficulties, with business moribund and
substantial debts owing both to the Treasury and to the Bank of England. North and the Treasury officials seized the opportunity for a
thorough overhaul of the Company's position, culminating in the
passage of the Regulating Act of 1773. At the same time as they
pursued this specifically political object, various ideas were canvassed
for reviving the Company's trade: in particular, attention was
directed to facilitating the disposal for profit of the excessive surpluses of tea which the recession had caused to be left on its hands.
The directors sought customs drawbacks on tea exported. With an
eye on the potentialities of the colonial market, on 7 January 1773
they suggested also the abandonment of the Townshend duty of 3*d*.
per pound on tea. If both these reliefs were granted, they calculated,
perhaps erroneously, that they would be able to undersell the Dutch
tea which everyone knew was smuggled in vast quantities into North
America.

When the government turned from Regulation to the commercial problem, they granted the first of these concessions but not the second. Instead the Company was authorized to dispose of tea in America through its own agencies. As presented to Parliament on 26 April 1773 the scheme made no mention of the Townshend duty, which was left intact. When the opposition moved for its repeal on the ground that the duty, not the price, prevented legitimate sales of tea in America, North jibbed. He pointed out that since a fairly substantial amount of tea, over 600,000 pounds, had been imported into America paying duty over the last two years, the tax did not appear by its nature a barrier to the trade. The drawback would, he thought, cheapen tea sufficiently to cause an increase in demand, and he looked for an additional yield from the American tax. Despite considerable pressure in the Commons he declined to adopt a suggestion that the remaining levy on tea should be collected in British instead of American ports, so that the Treasury would lose nothing while removing a political obstacle to the tea trade.[35] Although North was extremely evasive in debate, he made it sufficiently clear that his concern was to maintain the source of revenue from which Parliament had, during the past two years, authorized payments of salaries to governors and other officials in some of the royal colonies. If the tea tax were abolished, either these arrangements must lapse and the payments be made out of the King's civil list, which was already running steadily into debt; or the payments must be abandoned, to the confusion of the policy of tightening up imperial control; or else Parliament would have to be asked to authorize their continuance out of other revenues collected in America which it had specifically earmarked for defence purposes only. This last course would have brought the controversial topic out into the open again—a result which the ministers clearly seem to have wished to avoid. On the other hand, the loss of a colonial civil list revenue must have appeared peculiarly undesirable at a time when ministers were receiving unpalatable reminders of the obduracy of the provincial legislatures over the question of parliamentary supremacy.[36] The conflict over rights remained in the deadlock reached in 1769, and in 1773 North and his colleagues were no more ready than they had been four years before to make concessions until the colonists had acknowledged the authority of Parliament. Such reasoning led North to dig in his heels over the 3d. tea duty. It remained in force when, on 10 May 1773, the East India Company received statutory authority to market its tea in the colonies through its own agencies.[37]

Sweden, India, and then the long summer vacation thus conspired to delay ministerial and parliamentary consideration of the state of Massachusetts. Not till 1 December did Dartmouth notify Hutchinson that steps were imminent.[38] That day the assembly's and council's addresses for the removal of Hutchinson and his deputy were referred to the Privy Council; but the final hearings were deferred till the end of January and were then coloured by the emotional backwash of the Boston Tea Party.

2. *The Boston Tea Party*

Throughout the summer of 1773 rumours of the East India Company's intention to send tea to America swept through the colonies. Gradually the full details became known. The Company planned to ship 600 chests of tea each to New York and Philadelphia with smaller quantities destined for Boston and Charleston. There it would be sold in wholesale lots by designated consignees at prices as low as two shillings per pound for the cheapest variety of black tea. Even as the details were being published in late September the first signs of opposition appeared. From London a correspondent wrote to his friend in New York that the 'great schemer' Lord North had initiated the East India Company plan 'hoping thereby to outwit us' and thereby establish the Townshend duty as a precedent for further taxation. The reputable Virginia merchant John Norton reported from London that some of the Company's directors themselves suspected they were being made a 'cat's paw' by the ministry to establish the duty. Another gentleman in London wrote that he had warned Company officials to expect their ships and tea to be burnt, for Americans would never allow an act of Parliament to be crammed down their throats. Suggestions such as these stirred up the colonists' deepest suspicions and assured the Company's tea a hostile reception.[39]

Organized opposition appeared first at New York, where the consignee firm of Pigou & Booth reported two major themes emerging in the opponents' camp—that if the tax were submitted to in this instance, others would follow; and that if the East India Company were allowed a monopoly in the tea trade, it would soon control all of America's foreign trade. A series of newspaper articles entitled *Alarm* appeared over the signature HAMPDEN and was joined by a flurry of letters to the editors threatening dire consequences to the consignees if they refused to resign their commissions. Already the opponents had turned to history in adopting the method so successful in blocking the Stamp Act. The consignees at New York managed to hold their enemies at bay throughout most of the autumn, spreading rumours that the tea was duty-free after all, and charging that the opponents were all tea-smugglers who complained only because their illegal trade with Holland was about to be put out of business. On behalf of Pigou & Booth POPLICOLA pointed out that all

American trade would suffer if the East India Company went bankrupt. Another supporter cited the increased revenue that would come from the city's tax on auction sales.[40]

But the campaign against the tea mounted steadily. The harbour pilots were told that whoever among them dared bring the tea ship up harbour would face 'the vengeance of a free people, struggling to preserve their liberties.' In late November a broadside signed THE MOHAWKS warned anyone helping to land and store the tea would receive 'an unwelcome visit, in which they shall be treated as they deserve.' By the end of November the consignees had had enough. They announced to the public and wrote to the Company that they were resigning their commissions. Their letter gave evidence that they considered the opposition to centre on the issue of the duty rather than the threat of monopoly. They urged the directors to work for total repeal of the Townshend Act; then, they estimated, New Yorkers would eagerly buy between 1,500 and 2,000 chests of English tea each year (although not more than twenty-five chests had entered from England in the past five years).[41]

The tea expected at Philadelphia was consigned to several mercantile firms (as was the case in all of the ports). The principal burden fell on the partnership of James & Drinker and Thomas & Isaac Wharton, as the two most prominent firms. Like all consignees, these men had little notice of their selection and no instructions at all in advance of the actual shipments of tea. In mid-October appeared a broadside signed SCAEVOLA (actually the patriot Thomas Mifflin) attacking the tea plan as a means of affirming the Townshend duty and of establishing the East India Company's monopoly over all American trade. SCAEVOLA pointedly reminded the consignees of what had happened to the stamp commissioners in 1765. Unlike their New York counterparts the opponents to the tea shipment at Philadelphia called for a mass meeting to assemble in mid-October. About seven hundred people met at the State House and adopted resolutions condemning the Company's scheme as a plot to enforce the Townshend duty. Those assisting in landing the tea were considered 'enemies to their country', and the consignees were called upon to resign.[42]

Both Philadelphia firms equivocated for several weeks, in the face of local opposition. James & Drinker seemed to take a harder line than did the Whartons, and the patriots exploited the difference to drive a wedge between the two consignees. Meanwhile the public clamour against the expected tea mounted ever higher. Benjamin Rush wrote under the pseudonym HAMDEN [sic] that the chests of tea contained 'a slow poison . . . the seeds of *slavery*'. Another writer pointed out how bad tea was for the system. As November came to an end and the tea was daily expected, the big gun of Philadelphia's patriot camp opened fire. John Dickinson, writing as RUSTICUS, expressed firm opposition to the Company's tea and called upon merchants to deny use of their wharves, longshoremen to refuse unloading the cargo, and shopkeepers to ban the tea from their shops. Let the watchmen making their rounds call out *'past twelve O'Clock, beware of the East India Company'*, suggested RUSTICUS. Meanwhile THE COMMITTEE FOR TARRING AND FEATHERING warned the Delaware River pilots that whoever among them dared to bring the tea-ship in would receive an appropriate award. And the captain himself was asked, 'What think you of a Halter around your neck, then gallons of liquid tar decanted on your pate—with the feathers of a dozen live geese laid over that to enliven your appearance?' By the first of December James & Drinker joined the other consignees in resigning their commissions from the Company.[43]

At neither New York nor Philadelphia had the governor intervened in the dispute concerning the impending arrival of the East India Company's tea. At Boston, however, the situation was quite different. There Governor Thomas Hutchinson had already suffered a decade of abuse from the patriot leaders. His house had been ransacked during the Stamp Act crisis, his assertion of parliamentary supremacy ridiculed, his letters stolen and then published, and finally a petition demanding his removal from office sent to the King. Now British soldiers manned Castle William overlooking the harbour, where warships under Admiral Montagu rode at anchor. What better circumstances for a showdown with his tormentors? Besides, among the consignees of the tea were two of his sons, Thomas and Elisha Hutchinson, as well as the Clarkes, close family friends. The governor himself had applied for a leave of absence; he could hardly wish to depart for England a loser.[44]

For their part the people of Boston were equally determined. Two of the principal firms chosen as consignees were notorious violators of the non-importation agreement of the late 1760s and had continued to import dutied tea after the general boycott broke down in late 1770. It was because of Thomas and Elisha Hutchinson and the Clarkes that Boston had been held up to ridicule. Had the patriots known that Lord North had retained the Townshend duty partly because Boston's importations had encouraged him, they would have been even more angry. But when news of the tea plan reached Boston the Committee of Correspondence there at first seemed preoccupied with its campaign to alert other towns about the issue of the judges' salaries. It also planned to widen its communications to include towns in other colonies as well.[45]

Toward the end of October the campaign against the tea plan

began at Boston, as elsewhere, with a barrage of letters to the several
newspapers complaining about the threat of monopoly as well as the
taxation issue. Noting the approach of Guy Fawkes Day, PRAEDICUS
thought it 'not too late to free ourselves from popes, devils, and
locusts'. Edes and Gill linked the scheme with the ministry's effort to
make the governor and judges independent of the people, while
others worried about the amount of specie that payment for the tea
would drain from the province. The North End caucus voted to oppose the scheme with 'their lives and fortunes'; a moderate merchant
predicted the tea would be destroyed 'by fire and water' unless it
were returned; and other correspondents threatened the Clarkes,
the governor, and 'the two children' with revenge from 'a betrayed
people'.[46]

At the end of October Richard Clarke, one of the consignees,
issued a rebuttal under the signature z. He pointed out the economic advantages of buying tea directly from representatives of the
Company in America and denied that the scheme would drain specie from the province. He rationalized payment of the Townshend
duty by reminding the public how much dutied tea had already entered at Boston, a touch of irony considering his own role in that
trade! Besides, he added, why make a fuss about 'this small branch
of the revenue whilst we silently pass over the articles of sugar, molasses, and wine,' from which large sums have regularly been raised.
Another defender taunted the opposition with the claim that he had
just sold a pound of dutied tea to a well-known local patriot and
promised to note the names of future customers 'in hopes of being
able shortly to furnish you with a pretty handsome list, to be dis-
canted upon the next Town Meeting.' Telling debater's points, but
less likely to win support for the tea plan than to anger Bostonians
sensitive to previous leaks in their boycott.[47]

On 3 November the patriots turned from words to action. Clarke
and the other consignees were summoned to appear at Liberty Tree
to resign their commissions. When they failed to show up some of
the crowd of five hundred stormed the Clarkes' warehouse, where
the consignees managed to barricade themselves on the second floor
to escape injury. A few days later the inhabitants were further
goaded by the publication of a letter from Philadelphia casting
doubt on the Bostonians' ability to resist the tea scheme. If they
failed, 'it will confirm many prejudices against them and injure the
common cause . . .', the Pennsylvanian predicted. A town meeting
on the 5th, moderated by John Hancock, issued its own demand for
the consignees to resign, but again they refused, offering only to
give a fuller response after they received their instructions from the
Company. 'Daringly Affrontive to the town,' was the judgement of an

adjourned session the next day. Now the consignees were in defiance of the town meeting itself.[48]

For the next two weeks Bostonians waited with anxious anticipation for the next development in the drama. Then on 17 November John Hancock's ship *Hayley* entered Boston from London with young Jonathan Clarke, son of the consignee Richard Clarke, on board. Captain James Scott reported that several vessels were on their way with the East India Company's tea. That night, as the Clarkes were celebrating the reunion with their son, a small band of people gathered to show their disrespects. One of the sons fired a pistol at the crowd. Enraged by this unexpected response the mob turned ugly, smashed the windows, and then hurled brickbats and stones through the openings. Despite considerable damage to their furnishings, the Clarkes held fast until finally the tumult subsided, and the mob went home. Convinced that the Clarkes had finally received their long-awaited instructions from the Company, a committee of the town renewed its demand that they resign, but once again the consignees defied the will of the townspeople by refusing.[49]

The consignees petitioned the Governor's Council for protection both of their own persons and of the property they were expecting from the Company. Unlike similar bodies in other colonies the Council of Massachusetts Bay was elected by the lower house, not appointed by the King. Since the governor could take little effective action without the advice and consent of his Council, this condition gave the popular branch an effective check on the executive. Now the Council refused to act on behalf of the consignees. As the editors of the *Boston Gazette* tried to rationalize, the Council owed protection only to those citizens who were 'in the peace of God and the King'. In their opinion the consignees did not qualify, for they were party to an attempt 'to overthrow the Civil Government' by agreeing to sell the Company's tea. Besides, the editors lamely added, the Council had more important duties to attend to than to become involved in the private affairs of every individual. This blatant failure on the part of the Massachusetts Council to extend the protection sought by the consignees would not be ignored by the ministry when it reviewed these events some months later.[50]

Opponents of the tea scheme turned to the network of Committees of Correspondence in their quest for outside help. The Boston committee invited their counterparts from the neighbouring towns of Roxbury, Dorchester, Brookline, and Cambridge to meet together on 22 November at Faneuil Hall. There they agreed to act jointly in preventing the landing and sale of the Company's tea. A subcommittee was established to draft a warning to other towns in the province against 'the evil tendency of the late Ministerial maneuver'. The meeting then adopted a circular letter explaining its case against the tea plan. By refusing to accept dutied tea perhaps the colonists could force the Company to renew its efforts for a repeal of the Townshend duty. Acceptance of this tax was to invite more to follow— revenue 'to support the extravagance and vices of wretches whose vileness ought to banish them from the society of men.' The Boston committee added further arguments of its own in a covering letter.[51]

Early Sunday morning, on 28 November, the bluff-bowed ship *Dartmouth* beat its way into Boston harbour with the first of the East India Company's tea to reach America. Slowly the vessel worked its way up the channel, past Castle William, and came to anchor under the stern of Admiral Montagu's flagship, *Captain,* about 400 yards off the waterfront. That evening two customs officers came aboard. Under various laws and procedures that governed such matters the ship's owner, who was represented in Boston by his son Francis Rotch, was now required to remit all duties owed on his cargo (in this case the Townshend duty on tea) before his vessel could be unloaded or permitted to depart. Failure to pay the duties within twenty days after arrival made the cargo liable for seizure by the custom-house officers. Still another law prohibited any tea, once exported from England, from being returned there.

Opponents of the tea plan found themselves in a difficult position with the actual arrival of the dreaded cargo. To allow the tea to be landed risked the possibility that the duties would be paid and that the tea would somehow be purchased by weak-willed or profit-minded shopkeepers. Permitting it to be stored in the custom-warehouse was likewise a gamble, for who could trust those 'vile wretches', the customs officials, or Governor Hutchinson himself? So far as Bostonians knew, no tea had yet reached the other ports. With the rest of the continent watching them without much confidence, the leaders of Boston knew that their very reputation as patriots was on the line.

The Committee of Correspondence, ignoring the fact it was Sunday, met in emergency session. The group persuaded Rotch not to enter his vessel at the custom house until Tuesday, hoping thereby to ease the way for the *Dartmouth*'s departure. The committee also called for a joint meeting with neighbouring committees, this time in public, in order to generate maximum pressure from popular opinion. Intent on maintaining control of the situation themselves, the selectmen also met on Sunday in expectation that the consignees would have a new proposal for a compromise solution of some sort. But the consignees reported through an intermediary that they would have nothing new to say until the next day. The initiative thereby went to the Committee of Correspondence almost by default.[52]

The gathering of inhabitants on Monday morning, the 29th, was not a legal meeting of the town of Boston. The thousands of people who flocked to Faneuil Hall included inhabitants from neighbouring towns as well as Bostonians not qualified to vote in town affairs. Soon Faneuil Hall was filled to overflowing, and the meeting moved to Old South Church, where over 5,000 people reconvened. They immediately resolved that the tea should be returned to England without payment of the Townshend duty and adjourned until mid-afternoon to give Rotch and the consignees time to respond. When nothing concrete ensued, the meeting voted to post a watch of twenty-five men who would board the *Dartmouth*, now lying at Griffin's Wharf, and see that none of the cargo was surreptitiously unloaded. Meanwhile the Governor's Council also met to consider further the consignees' request for protection. The councillors recommended that the justices of the peace were the proper officers to assure personal protection and that as for the tea the Council could not assume responsibility for its safekeeping. With a pious hope for the preservation of good order the Governor's Council thus washed its hands of the affair. The consignees saw what lay ahead and that night retired to Castle William or into neighbouring country towns for safety. Governor Hutchinson himself spent most of the ensuing days after 29 November at his country seat in Milton, safe from the mobs but also out of touch with day-to-day developments.[53]

'The Body', as the general meeting was called, gathered again at Old South Church the next day. There the people learned that the consignees were willing to permit storage of the tea until they received new instructions from the Company, but the gathering remained sceptical. When the sheriff appeared with a proclamation from the governor ordering the crowd to disperse in the name of His Majesty the King, he was met with a loud hiss. "He, he?" Sam Adams taunted the absent governor. 'Is he—that shadow of a man, scarce able to support his withered carcase or his hoary head? Is he a *representation* of *majesty*?' The crowd ignored the order to disperse, and the sheriff wisely withdrew.[54]

But now contradictory results began to frustrate the Body. While Rotch and the captain of the *Dartmouth* reluctantly agreed to return the tea, the consignees reported from their sanctuary that sending it back was beyond their power. The hours of wrangling began to take their toll of human patience. John Singleton Copley, whose wife was the daughter of the consignee Richard Clarke, attempted to intercede on behalf of his in-laws. The artist denied that the consignees were acting in concert with Governor Hutchinson; he pointed out how they might be ruined if forced to return the tea; but, he suggested, the inhabitants could themselves send it back 'by the political storm, as they termed it', although he was not very specific. Copley managed to cool the resentment of the crowd considerably. 'I think all stands well at present,' he reported to the Clarkes.[55]

Copley also warned the consignees not to discuss the matter of the tea with Governor Hutchinson, even if he should visit the Castle. Obviously in the artist's opinion the principal confrontation at Boston lay between the inhabitants and the governor. Later Hutchinson would claim that he had tried to prevent the *Dartmouth* from entering the harbour in the first place, to facilitate the return of the tea. He charged that the patriots forced the vessel to enter under threat of violence in order to precipitate a crisis. And yet the historical record is clear: on 28 November the *Dartmouth* sailed into the jurisdiction of Boston harbour in the early morning hours under full command of Captain Hall. Once within the harbour the captain was obliged to report his cargo at the custom house without delay, and later that morning the vessel came in past the Castle and anchored off the waterfront. The record shows no evidence that either the Bostonians or the governor tried to prevent the *Dartmouth* from entering the harbour. Nor did either side force Hall to bring his ship in against his will. Interestingly enough, Hutchinson and the consignees did not even try to block the two remaining tea ships from entering when they arrived off the harbour in early December. Copley's subtle warning to the consignees was indeed perceptive. Hutchinson had decided to make the contest his own; the consignees had best keep clear.[56]

The patriots of Boston and vicinity surely recognized the governor as their principal antagonist in the confrontation. Although they had harried the consignees by both word and deed, their choicest rhetoric was reserved for the governor himself. 'Can you deny, Mr. Hutchinson,' asked E. LUDLOW at the end of November, 'that an absolute despotism is establishing itself here. . . . Blood has already besmeared the streets of that metropolis which afforded you the first vital breath. . . . You are again laboring to draw on a repetition of the tragedy,' he charged. 'Ruthless barbarian . . . ! You cry Peace! Peace! But there is no peace, saith my God to a trampler on the rights of his country,' LUDLOW taunted. Rumours that Hutchinson had applied for a leave of absence brought a flurry of jibes. 'By removing yourself, family, and principal accomplices from among us . . .', wrote LUDLOW, 'you might prevent much mischief and obviate numerous evil consequences which your perseverence will render inevitable.' PRAEDICUS reached into his store of classical knowledge to remind the governor that 'I never read of more than one Sylla who was suffered to retire and live in peace, after having injured his country as much as you have done.' Still more directly threatening was the warning from 'A Friend to the Community': 'If you do not very soon take your departure from this abused land, *never to return again,* I will ring you such a peal about Dutch Tea, etc., as will make your ears tingle! [57]

As the showdown at Boston deepened the governor appeared to hold most of the trump cards. The vessel was within the harbour; the law prohibited its departure until the duties were paid; British military and naval forces commanded the channels out to sea; and finally at the end of twenty days—17 December 1773—the customs officials could, with the assistance of the navy if necessary, seize the ship and land the cargo. All the governor needed to do was to wait patiently until the morning of the 17th to gain his sweet revenge over the troublesome likes of Sam Adams and his supporters. Time worked for Hutchinson in another sense as well. The ships carried various goods in addition to the East India Company tea; owners and merchants expecting this cargo wanted the vessels unloaded, not sent back to England. Furthermore, Francis Rotch was eager to get his father's ship cleared of its tea so that he could get a cargo of whale oil on board for the passage to London.[58]

Events seemed to move slowly through early December, but almost every day brought a new development as the tension slowly mounted. On the 2nd the ship *Eleanor* came in with over one hundred chests of tea, and its captain was ordered by the patriots to bring his vessel up alongside Griffin's Wharf, where the *Dartmouth* already lay. Then the brig *Beaver* arrived with small-pox as well as tea and had to lie in quarantine before joining the two other vessels. Still another tea-ship, the brig *William,* came ashore on the backside of Cape Cod, a total loss.

Public opinion grew increasingly bellicose as the days slipped by. A RANGER wrote of how he had marched against the French and Indians 'when they attempted to enslave us, and I am as ready to fight enemies from Britain as Indian from Canada.' He went on to suggest that the Americans should let the enemies land without opposition and then 'we can bush fight them and cut off their officers very easily,' as the French and Indians had done to General Braddock, he unkindly added. A report out of Salem asserted that the people from towns around Boston 'are determined upon hazarding a brush,' if the tea were landed. The editor called upon those wishing to preserve the rights of the country, 'to get suitably prepared.' Bostonians had apparently already done so, for on 1 December the merchant John Andrews had written that 'Twould puzzle any person to purchase a pair of p[isto]ls in town, as they are all bought up with a full determination to repell force with force.' Admiral Montagu reported soon after that the men guarding the tea ships at Griffin's Wharf were armed with muskets and bayonets and paraded 'in military order . . . like centinels in a garrison'. On 8 December Governor Hutchinson asked Montagu to manoeuvre his ships into position to block all channels out to sea. Rumours suggested that Colonel Leslie's troops had charged the cannon at Castle William and were establishing a battery on nearby Governor's Island as well.[59]

On Monday, 13 December, Bostonians learned that the consignees at Philadelphia, like those at New York, had resigned their commissions. The implication was that no attempt to land the tea would be made at either port. No Bostonians could yet know that a tea ship had already arrived at Charleston; thus they had no precedents upon which to base their subsequent actions. So far as Bostonians knew, they stood alone. The letter from Philadelphia minced no words: 'You have failed us [before] in the importation of tea . . . , and we fear you will suffer this to be landed [also].' [60]

As the deadline for seizing the cargo approached, the patriots increased their efforts to get the tea out of the harbour. Rotch was summoned before a joint meeting of the area's Committees of Correspondence on the 13th. The young merchant had agreed at the public meeting of 30 November to send the tea back; now the committee demanded to know whether he intended to keep his promise. Rotch replied that for the *Dartmouth* to leave without a clearance would violate the customs laws and make his vessel liable for seizure. Surely he could not be expected to bear such a loss alone. But when he asked other merchants present to share in the risk by purchasing the ship from him, only young Josiah Quincy, Jr., stepped forward.[61]

Now the only peaceable recourse open to the patriots lay in Rotch's efforts to obtain a legal clearance. Another mass meeting of the Body was therefore called for the 14th at Old South. There both Rotch and Captain Bruce of the *Eleanor* agreed to seek clearances for their vessels from the collector. Escorted by Sam Adams and other patriots, Rotch went to the custom house. That Richard Harrison should be the official in charge in 1773 is one of the ironies of history, for Harrison was the young man who was mobbed in the *Liberty* riot five years before. Harrison now took the request under advisement. When Rotch and his escorts returned the next day, the collector announced that it was 'utterly inconsistent with my duty' to grant a clearance. Perhaps Harrison had made his decision because the tea duty had not been paid; or possibly he realized that the tea could not legally be re-entered in England; or the fact that Rotch had made his request under duress might have influenced the collector. In any event Harrison saw no reason to make an exception to accommodate Sam Adams and his supporters. One more door to a peaceful solution was closed.[62]

Thursday, 16 December 1773. More than 5,000 inhabitants of Boston and the vicinity crowded through the rainy streets toward Old South Church. On the morrow the customs officials could seize and land the tea; then the consignees would undoubtedly pay the duty, and Boston would be disgraced for having failed to block the infamous tea scheme. When the meeting convened, Rotch was once more told to order his ship out of the harbour; again he refused to do so without a proper clearance. Only one recourse seemed open. The Body instructed Rotch to seek from Governor Hutchinson himself a permit to allow the *Dartmouth* safely past Castle William. Rotch agreed to make the seven-mile journey out to Milton; the meeting adjourned until the young merchant could return in mid-afternoon.[63]

We cannot know for certain what was in the governor's mind when Rotch arrived. From his correspondence of the period, however, it is clear that Hutchinson had determined not to give in. 'Surely, my Lord,' he had written Dartmouth two days before, "it is time this anarchy were restrained and corrected by some authority or other.' Hutchinson and Rotch apparently discussed the possibility of authorizing Admiral Montagu to take the vessel under his care, but Rotch realized the consequences of his complicity in such a scheme and decided against it. Hutchinson then explained that while he had always tried to oblige such requests when there was a good reason, 'he could not think it his duty [to do so] in this case and therefore should not.' In what must have been one of the most reluctant journeys in American history Francis Rotch rode back to Boston.[64]

A few candles flickered in the darkness as Rotch returned to Old South Church late in the afternoon. The crowd had grown impatient, and when the young merchant announced that the governor had refused to grant a pass, cries went up around the hall, 'A mob! A mob!' Dr. Young rose to defend Rotch's conduct and assured him that his person and property would not be harmed. Sam Adams then announced in words recalled later by some of those present that 'as for me, I shall go home, set down and make myself as easy as I can, for this meeting can do nothing further to save the country.' As though on a pre-arranged signal a war-whoop came from the gallery, answered by another from the doorway. 'Boston harbor a tea-pot tonight!' 'Hurrah for Griffin's Wharf!' 'The Mohawks are come!' These and other shouts rent the air in a tumult loud enough to arouse John Andrews from his house three blocks away. 'You'd have thought that the inhabitants of the infernal regions had broke loose,' Andrews later recalled, as he approached the meeting-house. Out of the building swept the crowd on their way to Griffin's Wharf, where the three tea-ships lay moored.[65]

As the crowd converged on the wharf small bands of men roughly disguised as Indians broke off and pushed their way on board the vessels. Some of these men were apparently members of various organizations—the North End Caucus, the Long Room Club, the Masons, and Hancock's corps of cadets. A number of them were young, in their twenties, variously employed as common labourers, mariners, or apprentices. Some were mere teenagers. A few, like Thomas Melvill, were men of business; others like James Brewer, were artisans. Mrs. Brewer had helped her husband and friends to blacken their faces with burnt cork that night. Most were men whose names would never be remembered except by their families; others, like William Molineux, Dr. Thomas Young, and Paul Revere, were well-known patriots. About sixty men or more climbed aboard the tea-ships. Some pried off the hatch-covers while others prepared block and tackle. Then they hoisted the chests out of the holds, broke them open with axes, and dumped the contents over the rail and into the dock, nearly dry at low tide. The ebb current carried much of the tea out into the harbour, where men in boats guarded against salvage efforts. On 16 December 1773 within three hours 340 chests of tea, worth about £10,000 were destroyed at Boston.[66]

'This is the most magnificent movement of all,' wrote John Adams in his diary the next day. 'There is a dignity, a sublimity in this last effort of the patriots that I greatly admire. . . . This destruction of the tea 'is so bold, so daring, so firm, intrepid, & inflexible, and it must have so important consequences and so lasting, that I cannot but consider it as an Epocha in history.' His cousin Sam Adams noted in a letter to Arthur Lee, 'you cannot imagine the height of joy that sparkles in the eyes and animates the countenances of all we meet on this occasion. . . .' The authorities seemed almost resigned to the outcome. Admiral Montagu reported that he could have prevented the whole affair 'but must have endangered the lives of many innocent people by firing on the town.' Hutchinson too seemed remarkably detached from the episode in his subsequent reports, writing more as a bystander than as a key figure. But soon Hutchinson learned that of the four governors whose colonies were sent the tea, he alone had taken a firm stand against its return. Willingly or not, Thomas Hutchinson had also been a participant in the Boston Tea Party.[67]

In the first of his historic rides Paul Revere carried the news of the tea party to New York, where it was published and sent on to Philadelphia and points further south. Upon his return Revere brought word of what had happened at Charleston, South Carolina. The tea ship *London* had arrived there in early December 1773 so suddenly that local patriots were totally unprepared. The captain entered his cargo, tea and all, at the custom house, but the next day a mass meeting demanded and received the resignations of the consignees. When the twenty-day period expired and no one had stepped forward to pay the duties, the Charleston customs officials seized the cargo and stored it in their warehouse. Apparently local patriots did not fear that the consignees would try to sell the tea, for there it sat until the outbreak of the Revolution, when according to one account it was sold for the benefit of the war effort. Governor William Bull made no attempt to interfere in the proceedings.[68]

Matters were more complicated at Philadelphia. Inhabitants greeted news of the Boston Tea Party with joyous enthusiasm. Although their consignees had resigned in early December, the tea-ship had not yet arrived and tension steadily grew. The pilots had been warned not to bring the vessel upriver, but moderates had disapproved of that action. Then suddenly on Christmas night the tea-ship *Polly* was reported proceeding upstream without benefit of pilots! On board were 598 chests of East India tea. Patriots tried to stop the vessel at Chester the next day, but it had already passed on its way toward Philadelphia. Later that afternoon Captain Ayres finally brought the *Polly* to anchor off Gloucester Point, several miles below the city but well within the Philadelphia customs district. The patriots invited Ayres ashore to let him sense the temper of the people for himself. A mass meeting of 8,000 inhabitants gathered on the 27th at the State House. There they voted thanks to Boston 'for their resolution in destroying the tea rather than suffering it to be landed.' Captain Ayres had no difficulty in getting the point. After formally asking the consignees to accept his cargo of tea, an invitation hurriedly declined by all concerned, Ayres agreed to depart. On the afternoon of the 28th, less than forty-eight hours after his arrival, Captain Ayres boarded his vessel, weighed anchor, and dropped down the Delaware on his return passage to England. Neither Governor John Penn nor the customs collector made the slightest effort to collect the tax due on his tea (about £900) or to impede his departure.[69]

New York had a far easier time of it that December. A fierce Atlantic storm had driven the tea-ship *Nancy* off its course and inflicted serious damage. Captain Lockyer then put into Antigua for repairs. There he learned of the Boston Tea Party and of the determined opposition awaiting his arrival at New York. One cannot blame him for lingering as long as possible in the Caribbean warmth before making a conscientious effort to deliver his cargo in the spring. When Lockyer finally arrived in mid-April, he wisely anchored below Sandy Hook, outside of the customs district, and came ashore alone. His experience at New York duplicated that of Ayres at Philadelphia. A large crowd showed its determination to block the landing of his cargo; the consignees refused responsibility; and after obtaining provisions for his return passage, Lockyer left the city midst the ringing of bells and cheers of the people. Thus it was that among the four ports to which the Company had dispatched its dutied tea Boston alone had actually destroyed the cargo.[70]

IX

The Coercive Acts

———•—•———

AUTHENTIC REPORTS ABOUT the tea party at Boston reached East
India House about 19 January 1774. In a brief note written that day
to the colonial secretary, George III expressed what was to be the
prevailing belief, that leaders of a faction in Massachusetts had over-
stepped the mark: 'I am much hurt that the instigation of bad men
hath again drawn the people of Boston to take such unjustifiable
steps.' [1] Dartmouth for his part was by then busy amassing information about the boycott of tea which was being reported from points
all along the American Atlantic coast.[2] It was clear that resistance
was widespread. But the events at Boston seemed to deserve particular reprobation, not only because here resistance had expressed itself
in riotous destruction of property, but because it followed in a
sequence of challenges to the imperial constitution: the Boston resolves of November 1772; the dispute with Governor Hutchinson
over parliamentary powers in January 1773; the assembly's petition
of May against civil list salaries for the governor and superior
judges; the publication of Massachusetts officials' correspondence
with Thomas Whately; and finally the legislature's consequent petitions for the dismissal of Governor Hutchinson and Lieutenant Governor Oliver—petitions even then about to be heard before the Privy
Council.[3] Ministers enmeshed in current concepts of the nature of
the Empire and unable to conceive how it could survive if limits were
set to parliamentary supremacy, felt themselves faced by a treasonable conspiracy in Massachusetts. Nor were they alone in this belief ;
a few days later the King wrote to Lord North: 'Indeed all men seem
now to feel that the fatal compliance in 1766 has encouraged the
Americans annually to increase in their pretensions [to] that thorough independency which one state has of another, but which is
quite subversive of the obedience which a colony owes to its mother
country.' [4]

The ministers seem to have had a preliminary cabinet meeting on the American reports on 27 January 1774.[5] Two days later most of them were present at the Privy Council meeting on the Massachusetts' petitions and voted to reject them, applauding the dressing-down given by the solicitor-general to Franklin for his part in the disclosure of the Whately correspondence.[6] The same evening, at a further cabinet meeting, they agreed that the crucial issue must be faced, and 'that effectual steps be taken to secure the dependence of the colonies on the mother country.'[7] The sense of crisis is reflected a day or two later in a letter of General Gage, the commander-in-chief in America then on leave in London: 'People talk more seriously than ever about America: that the crisis is come when the provinces must be either British colonies, or independent and separate states.'[8] No serious disagreement divided the cabinet at this time. If Lords Suffolk, Gower, and Sandwich were the hottest for coercion, nevertheless North and Dartmouth fully accepted the necessity, and Rochford and Lord Chancellor Apsley heartily concurred with the majority view.

Dartmouth, as the responsible departmental minister, now had the task of preparing detailed plans and his under-secretary, John Pownall, was ready with proposals. On 4 February the cabinet provisionally accepted Dartmouth's suggestions, that the seat of government and the custom house should be moved out of Boston, and that the law officers should look into the possibility of mounting prosecutions for treason.[9] Next day the cabinet decided that if the law officers favoured action, an investigating commission should be despatched to Boston with powers to send over suspects for trial in England.[10] It is possible that from this point onwards the ministers were acting over-confidently as a result of misleading information, for General Gage was spreading the view that firm action would bring submission. At an audience on 4 February he told the King that the colonists 'will be lions, whilst we are lambs, but if we take the resolute part they will undoubtedly prove very meek'; and he thought four regiments at Boston would prevent any disturbance.[11]

Gage disastrously misjudged the spirit of Massachusetts. But regardless of Gage's opinions, given their premises the ministers had no alternative. Concession in face of continued colonial pressure seemed no longer possible until it was at least proved that an imperial relationship still existed.[12] Pressed by an American correspondent to repeal the tea duty Dartmouth replied that only a madman would try to do it in present circumstances, though he hoped for eventual repeal.[13] Had the ministers been prepared to give way, their position would have become untenable, not only in relation to the King, but to Parliament and to the main political forces in the country at large. The Boston Tea Party provoked strong condemnation in the London press. Potential parliamentary difficulties were underscored when a former Grenvillite hard-liner, the Earl of Buckinghamshire, moved for the immediate punishment of Massachusetts with a naval blockade and an army of occupation of 10,000 troops. Dartmouth succeeded in persuading Buckinghamshire to withdraw a motion which might have tied the government's hands only by forceful pleas that further reports from America were due.[14]

On 16 February the cabinet, hoping still to mount treason trials, and encouraged by an interim report from the law officers, arranged for sworn evidence to be taken from persons lately arrived from Boston, and it ordered that two guard ships complete with complements of marines be made ready for detachment to the North American squadron.[15] Further steps to this end were projected at a meeting on the 19th, but at this stage the cabinet faced the first set-back in its plans. The law officers expressed doubt whether the port of Boston could be closed by action under the royal prerogative. They reported that captains of ships who produced their clearances were legally entitled to require that a customs officer should attend them at any particular port. Thereupon the cabinet recommended, 'That it be moved for leave to bring in a Bill to take away from the town and district of Boston the privileges of a port, until the East India Company shall have been indemnified.'[16] At the same time ministers approved in principle legislation to alter the constitution of the province of Massachusetts, but left open for the present whether it should be brought forward that session or held over till the next in order to give the General Court an opportunity of making representations.[17]

On 28 February the law officers struck out of the ministers' hands the weapon of treason trials. They reported that on the sworn depositions of evidence taken in the past few days no charge of treason could be sustained. Dartmouth and the cabinet therefore fell back on action in Parliament. Ministers resolved that all the depositions and other papers should be laid before the two Houses and that an address should be moved, giving assurances of support in maintaining the authority of Parliament over the colonies.

On 7 March the ministers laid the American papers before both Houses of Parliament and secured formal addresses of support for the Crown in taking measures to secure the execution of the laws and the dependence of the colonies.[18] On the 14th North moved in the Commons for leave to bring in the Bill closing the port of Boston. The cabinet had further considered this Bill at a meeting on the 10th. The heads of the discussion at this meeting included a 'Bill for making certain offences in Boston triable in Great Britain', and note of a resolution that Gage, after his return to America, should be empowered to take over the governorship of the province if Hutchinson pursued a desire he had aired to come to England.[19] Thus the abortive proposal for judicial enforcement of the Declaratory Act was still under consideration; but by about this time the colonial secretary was veering against it, contemplating the possibility instead of making such cases from Massachusetts triable in Nova Scotia, and 'much taken' with a suggestion made by Buckinghamshire for disabling present offenders by Act of Parliament from holding any office in the province or being members of the assembly.[20]

North's opening speech on the Boston Port Bill on 14 March ranged over both the immediate and the long term preoccupations of the government. He observed that the addresses voted the week before set two objectives: the ending of the present disturbances in America, and the securing 'the just dependence of the Colonies on the mother country.' He outlined at length the difficulties experienced in enforcing the customs laws at Boston, and proposed the closing of the port, in part as a retaliation, in part as a lever for securing restitution for the East India Company. While hinting at further measures to come he made no disclosures about their possible nature but pointed out that the very existence of the Empire in its traditional form now seemed to be at stake: 'At Boston we were considered as two independent states; but we were no longer to dispute between legislation and taxation, we were now to consider only whether or not we have any authority there.' If the agitators could get away with defiance of one parliamentary statute, 'they might set their faces equally against all.'[21]

Opposition to the Port Bill was slight. Many moderates felt that the Bostonians had gone too far and that the destruction of property was inexcusable.[22] Some of them may have hoped that Boston would soon make restitution to the Company and that the Act would therefore be in force only briefly. American merchants based in London were strongly of this opinion and tried to secure a postponement of the operation of the Bill by private treaty with the government. On 18 March a committee secured an interview with North and offered to put up £16,000 to clear the Company's losses if he would give them six months to settle with the town before any measure to close the port became effective. But they admitted that they could not be answerable for Boston quietly receiving consignments of tea in future—the point which was of main concern to the ministers—and on this ground their offer was brushed aside, as was a similar one from the Lord Mayor on behalf of the City of London. Ignorance of the government's further intentions also contributed to the weakness of the opposition. Only the London radical, John Sawbridge, rejected outright Parliament's right to tax the colonies. Even the Chathamite Isaac Barré supported the Bill.[23]

Firm opposition came only from members of the hard core of the Rockingham party. Apart from technical arguments and attempts to score party points, of mere passing interest, these men, even at this stage of the American business, sounded a note of realism fundamental to their whole attitude but unacceptable to the general run of the politicians. On 7 March Burke observed: 'An English government must be administered in the spirit of one, or it will that moment cease to exist. As soon, I say, as the civil government of these colonies shall depend for support on a military power, the former will be at that moment at an end.' On 14 March Lord George Cavendish declared: 'He looked to the mutual interests of the two countries . . . he wished that no idle ideas of superiority might prevail, for that country which is kept by power is in danger of being lost every day.' On the 25th Burke again insisted, that readjustments of imperial relations must be, 'not founded upon your laws and statutes here, but grounded upon the vital principles of English liberty.' [24]

Nevertheless, despite these discordant notes, the opposition knew that it was useless to push matters to a division. On a proposal on 25 March to hear William Bollan, agent for the Massachusetts council, at the bar of the House, before the final passage of the Bill was voted, the minority mustered only forty votes against a ministerial majority of 170.[25] The Bill was sent up to the Lords the same evening and hurried through all its stages there by 30 March. Little opposition was offered. On the 31st it received the royal assent. Boston was to be closed to inward shipping on 1 June and to outward shipping a fortnight later, except for vessels bringing in military supplies and coasters providing supplies and fuel for the inhabitants. Closure would last until such time as compensation was paid to the East India Company and 'reasonable stipulation' given to customs officials who had suffered during the riots.[26] By administrative authority the custom house was moved to Marblehead in the port of Salem. Parliament had thus accepted the first of the coercive acts, despite various criticisms of detail and principle, 'from a general notion that *some act* of power was become necessary.' [27]

On 28 March, almost immediately the Port Bill was out of the Commons, North introduced the Massachusetts Regulating Bill. It is difficult to know just what weight is to be placed on suggestions that during late March Dartmouth and North wanted moderation but were overruled by the rest of the cabinet. Dartmouth's desire for leniency is attested by conversations he held with Shelburne and Grafton, but it is not clear that this meant dissent from either the

Port Bill or the Regulating Bill. There is no evidence in his own correspondence or in that of the King—and had there been any serious disagreement among the ministers this would probably have left its traces in the King's papers.[28] North had sounded the call for restoration of good government on 7 March, and his exposition of the Regulating Bill on 28 March followed logically from the position he had then adopted.

In a close-packed speech North outlined the case and heads of the government's proposals: 'An executive power was wanting' in Massachusetts. 'It was highly necessary to strengthen the magistracy.' The governor was at present powerless and could get no support from the magistrates. The council gave no co-operation. The intention therefore was, 'to take the executive power from the hands of the democratic part of government.' The governor should have full control over civil appointments (many of which were then elective) but should not have power himself to remove the superior judges. Town meetings were to be put under control and restricted to their natural functions of local government. Popular election of juries was to be curbed. Without going into further detail he moved for leave to introduce a Bill.[29] At this stage no mention was made of the mode of choice of the council in Massachusetts, and it seems clear that the ministers were not yet agreed upon any alteration of the existing system of indirect election.[30]

The most marked feature of the ensuing debate was a powerful intervention in support of the government by Lord George Germain. This speech may have been the outcome of a ministerial bargain by which office was to be found for Germain,[31] but there can be no doubt that it reflected Germain's genuine conviction. He ranged widely over various points of detail, calling for an end of the elected council, the replacement of town meetings by closed corporations, the regulation of the jury system, and the strengthening of executive government.[32] North welcomed his proposals with acclaim: 'Every proposition the noble lord has mentioned coincides with my mind; I see the propriety of them and I would wish to adopt them.' Few speakers, so he reported afterwards, appeared against the principle of the Bill, and leave was given to introduce it without a division.[33]

The Easter vacation now imposed a check on parliamentary proceedings, and the government took a step which had been contemplated for several weeks, the temporary replacement of Hutchinson as governor of Massachusetts by General Gage. The scheme had the attractive simplicity of placing in the hands of the civil administrator, who was in what seemed to be the hottest seat in North America, the full resources of the American military command. Difficulties about the use of troops were considered in cabinet on 30 March, when Gage and Amherst both attended and gave it as their opinion, that in the event of bloodshed, no soldier could expect acquittal for murder from a Boston jury. Gage's commissions were prepared at the end of March and issued to him on 7 April.[34] On that day, in response to questions submitted by Gage to Dartmouth, the cabinet, with the law officers and Gage in attendance, confirmed that he could deploy any force needed to suppress riots without the concurrence of the council. At the same time it was recommended that he should be given the power of pardon in capital cases as a protection for soldiers or civilians prosecuted for killing rioters. A commission to this effect was issued two or three days later.[35]

Dartmouth's first formal dispatch to Gage, dated 9 April, ordering him to take up his post, instructed him to remove the seat of government to Salem and take all necessary steps to enforce the Port Act. Furthermore, he was told to investigate the possibility of bringing treason charges in the local courts against the leaders of the tea riots and was furnished for that purpose with copies of the sworn evidence and other documents prepared in February. 'If however', Dartmouth continued, 'the prejudices of the people should appear to you to be such as would in all probability, prevent conviction, however clear and full the evidence might be, in that case it would be better to desist from prosecution, seeing that an ineffectual attempt would only be a triumph to the faction and disgraceful to government.' Finally four named leaders of the popular party were to be vetoed from re-election to the council. Nothing in this dispatch foreshadowed any of the changes to be made by legislation in the constitution of Massachusetts.[36]

With these instructions Gage left Plymouth on 18 April, arriving at Boston on 13 May. With him went three regiments of replacement troops, diverted from their original destinations of Quebec, Halifax, St. Augustine, and New Providence.[37]

The Regulating Bill did not reach the Commons till 15 April. This delay may in part have reflected a reluctance on the part of Dartmouth, and perhaps North, to add the reform of the council to the other provisions already under consideration; but, if so, the weight of the rest of the cabinet was against them, and also the prestige of the chief justice of the King's Bench, Lord Mansfield, to whose expertise appeal had been made.[38]

Alternative drafts, one omitting any alteration of the council, had been prepared. At the King's urging North arranged for the fuller draft to be submitted to Parliament.[39] On introducing the Bill he made special note of the introduction of the proposal to reconstitute the council and also drew attention to his adoption of suggestions from Germain about the method of choosing juries, which should henceforth be in the hands of the appointed sheriffs.[40] The Bill also affirmed the governor's power to appoint and dismiss administrative and judicial officers. Following a suggestion which may have come from ex-Governor Bernard, special town meetings were no longer to be held without the governor's consent,[41] but Germain's proposal for select corporations was not adopted.

There was little debate, and as soon as the Commons had approved the first reading, North introduced a Bill for the impartial administration of justice in Massachusetts. This third measure appears to have arisen directly out of the cabinet discussions of 30 March and 7 April over Gage's use of troops against rioters, though it cannot have been formulated until after the latter date. As North explained, its purport was to ensure that anyone causing death to a rioter by an act of law-enforcement might be removed for trial out of Massachusetts, either to another province or to Great Britain; he would thus run no risk of condemnation by a biased jury. It might be thought that the power of pardon granted to Gage was a sufficient safeguard, and it is possible that the cabinet decided to bring this Bill forward mainly for the moral effect it might have in Massachusetts, not least upon potential rebels. North was reported as saying: 'I would not wish to see the least doubt or imperfection remain in the plan which we have adopted: if there does, the consequence may be that it may produce bloodshed: that the whole plan may be clear and decisive; that every part of it may be properly supported; and I trust that such a measure as this, which we have now taken, will shew to that country that this nation is roused to defend their rights, and protect the security of peace in its colonies.'[42]

The Regulating Bill and the Justice Bill pursued their course through the Commons during the following three weeks. The Rockinghamite opposition was still in some degree of disarray. Rockingham's ally, the Duke of Manchester, though he later changed his mind, felt on 20 April that the Regulating Bill had much to commend it and declared he would rather pass it as it stood, 'than have the people at Boston in such a state of democratic anarchy.'[43] But the debates languished mainly due to the opposition's decision to hold fire until the third reading of the Regulating Bill, which took place on 2 May.[44]

In the meantime opponents of the government gave full backing to an independent member's contribution to a peaceful settlement, Rose Fuller's motion of 19 April for the repeal of the Townshend tax on tea. In this debate, which evoked from Burke one of his greatest oratorical performances, a number of speakers stressed the inadvisability of using Parliament's taxing power save on great occasions. However, they could not persuade government supporters that a retreat over tea would not involve a complete surrender to the colonists' denial of Parliament's right to tax them and perhaps to legislate for them also, and Fuller's motion was defeated by 182 votes to 49.[45]

On 2 May the forces of opposition put out their whole effort against the government's American measures. Dunning denounced their policy as a system of tyranny. Barré declared the question now was, 'whether we will choose to bring over the affections of all our colonies by lenient measures, or to wage war with them', and forecast an early conflict with all the colonies if the Bills went forward. Charles Fox declared the only way the Americans would think they were attached to Britain would be by laying aside the right of taxation. 'If you govern America at all', Burke pointed out, 'it must be by an army.' Savile denounced the violation of chartered rights. But opinion in the House was overwhelmingly against them. Sir William Meredith, finally deserting the Rockinghams on the American issue, declared: 'We must . . . either relinquish at once the right of enacting laws, or take the execution of them out of the hands of those that have denied our authority to make them.' Stanley voiced a common belief, that the colonies must take their law from a metropolitan state: 'Their submission to the laws of some country is necessary, as I cannot conceive the independence of an American colony to exist, whilst the balance of power remains in Europe, supported and protected by armies and navies.' Lord Carmarthen reflected another widely held view, that there was a systematic opposition in America to 'every part of the law of this country.' Attorney General Thurlow reaffirmed the supremacy of Parliament including the taxing power. North posed the question as many in the House then saw it, with the words: 'We are now to establish our authority, or give it up entirely.'[46] In a fairly full House 239 members agreed with him: only 64 voted in opposition. Public feeling in general supported the decision. Burke as early as 6 April had warned his correspondents at New York: 'The popular current both indoors and without, at present sets strongly against America. . . . Such is . . . the temper of Parliament and of the Nation at this moment, which I thought it my duty to lay before you without heightenings or without palliation.' On 20 April the Duke of Manchester pointed out to Rockingham that 'the high spirit of the people of England is certainly at the moment irritated against the outrages of the Bostonians; and the doctrine they now hold of their absolute independency of this kingdom leads many a moderate man to wish Government may succeed to reduce them within the bounds of law and order.'[47] Given this prevailing outlook, it is no wonder that a series of attempts to present colonial views before Parliament by petition were rebuffed.[48] During early May a handful of friends of Rockingham and Chatham continued to oppose both Bills in the House of Lords, but each was passed by overwhelming majorities.

The ministry's American legislation was rounded off with a Quartering Act, which was intended specifically to facilitate the stationing of troops within the town of Boston. In substance this measure was a reaffirmation and strengthening of the Quartering Act of 1765, and the main change it made was an addition to the powers of the governor. The Act of 1765 required any two or more justices of the peace in a district concerned to requisition uninhabited houses, outhouses, barns and other buildings for quarters if other accommodation was insufficient. The new Act of 1774 gave direct power to the governor to make requisitions. In particular, it defined his right to take over private buildings in a locality where he wished to place troops, regardless of the existence of barracks elsewhere—a provision clearly intended to forestall any complaints from Bostonians that Castle William remained empty while soldiers were billeted in the town. It was also more peremptory in its direction that local officials must, on demand from the commander-in-chief in America, find billets for troops in barracks, livery stables, taverns, and victualling houses. It passed in the Commons between 2 and 9 May with apparently little comment—no debates are reported—and completed its stages in the Lords on 26 May.

With the royal assent to the Quartering Act (2 June), the government's measures for restoring imperial authority in Massachusetts were at last complete. The following day Dartmouth signed the first long dispatch sent to Gage since his departure six weeks before. The packet contained the texts of all the three Coercive Acts enacted since Gage sailed, and the covering letter gave elaborate instructions about the selection of the appointed council and the appointment of a lieutenant governor. Dartmouth expressed the prevailing British concern that the very existence of the Empire depended upon Gage's success: [49]

> Whatever violences are committed must be resisted with firmness; the constitutional authority of this kingdom over its colonies must be vindicated and its laws obeyed throughout the whole empire.
>
> It is not only its dignity and reputation, but its power nay its very existence depends upon the present moment; for should those ideas of independence which some dangerous and ill-designing persons here are artfully endeavouring to instil into the minds of the king's American subjects, once take root, that relation between this kingdom and its colonies, which is the bond of peace and power, will soon cease to exist and destruction must follow disunion.

The last four words of this passage deserve attention, because they underline a motive for British action at this time which is commonly overlooked. From the King downwards a majority of the political nation was impelled by fear for national security. America provided Great Britain with the balance of strength which gave her the edge over her formidable French rival. Take that away and, it seemed, the country would no longer have the power to keep itself safe in the jungle of international politics. The defence of provincial liberties by the men of Massachusetts appeared to observers in London to lead straight to that result. As Dartmouth put it a few weeks later in a letter to an American correspondent, Joseph Reed: 'The question then is whether these laws are to be submitted to: if the people of America say no, they say in effect that they will no longer be a part of the British Empire.' Moreover, assuming that the Americans could not alone maintain their independence—an assumption which troubled some American as well as British leaders—a break with Britain would end with American resources absorbed into the hostile Bourbon power-block, to the still greater peril of the parent kingdom. British action, Dartmouth continued, was not provoked merely by abstract argument: 'It is not the mere claim of exemption from the authority of Parliament in a particular case that has brought on the present crisis: it is actual disobedience and open resistance that have compelled coercive measures.' He concluded with hopes that, despite the efforts of 'a few desperate men' to create a more widespread resistance, the 'thinking part' of the people of Massachusetts would shun the 'miseries' which a continuation of the dispute would entail, and would rally to the support of the civil power.[50] The future was soon to show that these hopes were illusory: to the American colonists the Coercive Acts were 'intolerable'.

Legislation concerning Canada placed these Acts in a still more sinister light from the viewpoint of the colonists, and in this regard it was a misfortune for the British ministry that long overdue adjustments in the government of Quebec had not been made at an earlier date.[51] The scheme of government adumbrated for the province in the Proclamation of 1763 had not proved satisfactory, and could not be fully implemented. The Test Acts, as part of English law, barred the Roman Catholic population from public life, and as only a handful of British Protestant settlers drifted into the two chief towns, an electorate on which to base an assembly did not exist. In the absence of any rapid influx of British settlers the governors of the province declined to bring one into being under the terms of the Proclamation. In consequence they were left without adequate revenues. The imposition of English civil law was resented by the Canadian seigneurs, as it seemed to threaten the structure of land law on which their tenure of property was based. Toleration had been conceded to the Roman Catholics in accord with the peace treaty of 1763, but this was soon seen to be an inadequate concession as the population remained almost exclusively of that persuasion. Successive governors found themselves obliged to modify the practice of government, and the provisional unsettled situation of public affairs became prejudicial to the state of the province.

A major enquiry into Canadian conditions was set on foot by the Rockingham ministry in 1766. By 1773 the American department had a vast mass of reports on which to base further action. There is no clear evidence to link the coincidence in time of the ensuing Quebec Bill and the American Coercive Acts, though the assumption is usually made that the crisis at Boston hastened the British government into producing a settlement which they understood would be acceptable to the Canadians and resolve their grievances. In one respect circumstances emphasize the distinction drawn by ministers between the two questions: 'The Ministry seems never to have discussed its Canadian policies in Cabinet at the same time as it considered the problem of the American colonies.' [52] Moreover, Dartmouth's correspondence indicates that all the main outlines of the future measure were in mind well before the Boston Tea Party. On 1 December 1773 Dartmouth reaffirmed to Lieutenant Governor Cramahé his wish that subjects of the Roman Catholic persuasion might 'find within the colony a resource for every thing essential to the free exercise of it.'[53] As soon appeared, this intention included ensuring to the clergy by law the payment of tithes and fees by their congregations. By this date other decisions had also taken shape. The Canadian seigneurs were to be satisfied by the abolition of the jury system in civil cases and the restoration of French and local customary civil law. The assembly promised under the Proclamation of 1763 was to be abandoned. Such a body based on the small Protestant minority would be ludicrous and fiercely resented by the French Canadians, whilst these latter in the main had no interest in representative institutions. Legislative power was therefore to be entrusted to a nominated council representing both groups of the population. An adequate revenue was to be provided.

Finally, it had been decided before December 1773 to annex to the province all the back country north of the Ohio as far west as the Mississippi and around the Great Lakes, and also the Labrador coast with its share of the fisheries. Various considerations gave rise to these territorial changes. They would provide civil government for scattered groups of Frenchspeaking settlers then subject to military control and bring under administration areas which Dartmouth foresaw might become 'the assylum of the lawless and the repair of the most licentious inhabitants of His Majesty's already most extensive colonies in America.' [54] Dartmouth was also concerned about relationships with the Indians from whom came complaints about the depredations of traders based in other colonies. The extension of the boundary to include the Indian reserves north of the Ohio was one way of excluding European settlement there (at least on paper) and of providing means for a better regulation of the Indian trade. The annexation of the Labrador fisheries was intended to revitalize a part of the province's economy, the loss of which had been seriously felt since 1763.

On 2 May the government submitted the Bill drafted along these lines to the House of Lords, partly perhaps anticipating less difficulty there, but no doubt also because the session was well advanced and that House was not clogged with business, whereas the Commons was still busy with the coercive Bills. The Bill was remitted on 17 May to the House of Commons. There acrimonious debates on its various stages continued at intervals till 13 June. During this period the ministers came under heavy fire from the opposition for establishing French despotism and popery and for denying the inhabitants essential freedoms guaranteed by English law, particularly jury trial in civil cases and Habeas Corpus. Some speakers, including Dunning and Burke, charged the government with seeking to use Canada to curb the liberties of the old colonies. However, evidence given before the bar of the House by Sir Guy Carleton, governor of the province, and other witnesses, substantially upheld the ministers' policies. While they stood firm on these main arrangements, various concessions were made. Phrasing was introduced, together with minor boundary adjustments, saving the rights of various older colonies, especially Pennsylvania and New York, in the area north of the Ohio. To implement the principle of political inclusiveness which motivated the Bill, a new form of oath on admission to office in the province was prescribed, which Catholics might swear without violating their religious principles. Other alterations related to the English criminal law, which was kept in force with certain modifications, and to the encouragement of the Protestant church. On 22 June the Bill received the royal assent. One matter—a provincial revenue—now remained outstanding. Rather than propose taxing powers for the unrepresentative council the ministers steered through a separate Quebec Revenue Act. By this piece of parliamentary colonial taxation various preferential import duties were imposed, a licensing duty on places of entertainment was specified, and various former French revenue provisions within the province were confirmed in force for the future. The sums collected were to defray the charges of local civil administration.

Although the Canadian legislation was highly necessary, its coincidence with the Acts directed against Massachusetts added to colonial apprehensions. The New England colonies were virulently anti-Catholic in sentiment and imbued with the belief that popery and despotism went hand in hand. The abrogation of the promise of a representative assembly and the conferment of law-making power on a mandamus council seemed to fall into place alongside the alteration of the Massachusetts council as part of a general intention to reduce the popular or democratic element in provincial government. After all the wrangling about courts of admiralty and judges' commissions, the abrogation of Habeas Corpus and of jury trial in civil suits seemed equally sinister. So too did the westward extension of the bounds of Quebec. The alarmist views expressed in debate by opposition politicians deepened the suspicion with which the Quebec Act was regarded in the American colonies.

X

The Continent Unites

―――•◆•―――

THE BOSTON TEA PARTY had the immediate effect of revitalizing opposition to Great Britain in those parts of Massachusetts where a return to 'business as usual' had followed the end of non-importation three years before. In numerous small towns the action of Boston met with enthusiastic approval and expressions of support. Deeds more than words truly measured sympathy for Boston. A wave of minor 'tea parties' broke out during the first months of 1774. In every case dutied tea was the object of popular disapproval. At Charlestown, Massachusetts, householders were asked to surrender all their tea, and a central committee arranged a public bonfire for its destruction. Lexington and other towns held similar purging ceremonies. Dutied tea had once again become a symbol, as the town of Hull, Massachusetts, made clear by its pledge, if ever the duty were repealed, to 'give preference to England whose true interest we have always considered as our own.' [1]

One of the difficulties, however, was to distinguish dutied 'English' tea from smuggled 'Dutch' varieties, and as the mania against tea spread, bands of patriots destroyed the commodity wherever they found it. The innkeeper Isaac Jones, at Weston, Massachusetts, suffered devastating destruction to his hostelry at the hands of an angry mob of townspeople disguised as Indians, who suspected him of selling dutied tea. Carts were searched, bundles examined, and suspected shopkeepers carefully watched. When a man at Newport, Rhode Island, fell into the water with a small bag of tea in hand, the town laughed. 'Be careful how you travel with this baneful article about you, for salt water seems to attract it. . . .' At the same time the patriots applied more traditional tactics against tea—group pledges not to drink it and newspaper stories concerning various ailments attributed to its consumption.[2]

Boston's resolve against dutied tea received another test in March 1774 when the brig *Fortune* arrived with twenty-eight and one-half chests on board, sent as a private venture by Davison & Newman in London. The brig's owners were as surprised as the patriots to discover the tea on board and immediately agreed to send it back. But they had not reckoned on the obstinacy of Collector Harrison, who rejected their request to allow the vessel speedy departure. Instead he ordered the captain to make an immediate entry at the custom house. This time the patriots did not wait out the full twenty-day period before the duties were payable. The night after the *Fortune* arrived, a band of sixty men, again disguised as Indians, climbed aboard and dumped all the tea into the harbour. The episode reinforces the fact that the patriots' principal quarrel was with the duty, not with a vague fear of monopoly, for this tea came from a private London firm, not from the East India Company. Furthermore, Boston's second tea party shows how incredibly obstinate officials like Harrison could be. After what had happened in December and after noting the prudence exercised at Philadelphia, Harrison might have been somewhat more flexible himself. Nor did Hutchinson make any mention in his report that the owners had requested permission to send the tea back. Finally, by unceremoniously dumping the *Fortune*'s tea into the harbour Bostonians made it clear that they felt no remorse for their December actions.[3]

The anti-tea mania spread rapidly south and west out of New England. The students at Princeton had their own tea party and threw in several effigies of Governor Hutchinson for good measure. And the good ladies of Edenton, North Carolina, became the subjects of a political cartoon when they took the pledge against tea. The patriots of Annapolis, Maryland, protested the arrival of 2,000 lb. of tea on board the brig *Peggy Stewart* by burning vessel and cargo together. One witness to the scene expressed his shock to a friend: 'I think Sir I went to Annapolis yesterday to see my Liberty destroyed. . . .' A Philadelphian probably spoke the mood of more Americans in the wake of the Boston Tea Party when he wrote to an English friend:

> There is not an American from New England to South Carolina who would so far shame his country as to accept this baneful diet at the expense of his liberty. Fleets and armies will never subdue the noble spirit of freedom which fills our breasts. . . . I love Great Britain and rever the King; but it is my duty to hand down Freedom to my posterity, compatible with the rights of Englishmen; therefore no tea duty, nor any unconstitutional tax whatever.

And yet fleets and armies were precisely what Lord North and Parliament had determined upon.[4]

First definite news of the Port Act reached Boston on 10 May

1774. As inhabitants began to recover from their initial shock and ponder their future, they instinctively resorted to the patriots' traditional means of retaliation—economic boycott. This time, however, the New Englanders proposed an immediate and total suspension of trade with both Great Britain and the West Indies. Paul Revere carried the proposals to New York and Philadelphia, for the Bostonians knew that only by joint action could such a boycott have effect. 'At length the perfect crisis of American politics seems arrived,' wrote Dr. Thomas Young to a friend in New York. 'A very few months must decide whether we and our posterity shall be slaves or freemen.' [5]

Elsewhere Americans shared Boston's shock at the imminent closing of the port, and messages of sympathy began pouring into the town. Communities both large and small expressed indignation at the ministry's measure. Farmington, Connecticut, burned a copy of the Port Act and denounced its authors as 'pimps and parasites'. The patriot leaders at New York, Isaac Sears and Alexander McDougall, urged Boston to stand firm. At Philadelphia the patriots planned a general suspension of business on 1 June in sympathy with the closing of Boston port that day. Virginia's House of Burgesses voted that a day of 'Fasting, Humiliation, and Prayer' be observed throughout the colony on the fateful occasion. The moderate George Washington wrote from Williamsburg in early June: 'The cause of Boston, the despotick measures in respect to it I mean, now is and ever will be considered as the cause of America (not that we approve their conduct in destroy[in]g the Tea).' The colonial union that Lord North had struggled so hard to prevent now seemed closer than ever, the result of his own policy of retaliation against Boston.[6]

But as always words proved cheaper than action. Not even the New England ports were unanimous in their willingness to close up in sympathy with Boston. New London, New Haven, and Portsmouth, New Hampshire, were among the hold-outs and enthusiasm elsewhere seemed to waver. At New York the old DeLancey-Livingston feud reappeared. Moderate merchants dominated a new 'committee of fifty-one' and succeeded in blocking any move toward an immediate cessation of trade. Instead the committee proposed that a general congress of delegates from all the colonies convene to decide such an important issue. Both moderates and more radical colonists could support the idea of a congress, the former as a way of postponing and perhaps even preventing non-importation, the latter as an expression of colonial unity.[7]

At Philadelphia a radical group had rallied behind Charles Thomson and Thomas Mifflin to reject the shipment of tea in December 1773 and to endorse Boston's violent solution to its dilemma. Now, however, these leaders needed the support of moderates for the long haul ahead. Instead of endorsing an immediate cessation of trade, as Boston had requested, a public meeting supported the idea of a general congress to petition the King for redress of grievances, with non-importation to depend on the outcome. Thomson apologized to the Bostonians as he reported these proceedings, reminding them that although Philadelphia had also lagged behind during the non-importation movement five years before, 'none were more steady once they were engaged.' Further along the coast the radicals at Annapolis gained approval for an immediate suspension of trade whenever other colonies agreed. At Williamsburg a rump session of the House of Burgesses met at Raleigh tavern after Governor Dunmore dissolved the body in retaliation for its commemoration of 1 June as a fast day. There the legislators called for a colony-wide boycott of East India goods and endorsed the plan for a continental congress.[8]

In Massachusetts Bostonians prepared for life under the Port Act as best they could. General Thomas Gage, Hutchinson's replacement as governor, made a ceremonious entry into the town on 17 May, and two weeks later Hutchinson himself departed for England, never to see his homeland again. On 1 June the Boston custom house moved to Plymouth and the capital of the colony to Salem, as a regiment of troops staked out their tents on Boston Common. Memories of the 1768–70 era under military occupation remained fresh in the minds of many citizens. And still more troops were expected by mid-summer. Meanwhile, Admiral Samuel Graves took over command of the North Atlantic station at Boston. He spared no effort to enforce every jot and tittle of the Port Act. Coastal vessels bringing in food and firewood were forced to unload outside the district and forward their cargoes to Boston overland in wagons that became known as 'Lord North's coasters'. Watercraft within the harbour itself were severely harassed on every pretext.[9]

The Boston Committee of Correspondence attempted to establish a boycott against English goods. It circulated through the colony a 'Solemn League and Covenant' for the signature of those willing to give up the use of British manufactures. But wrangling between the various towns, the refusal of many Bostonians to cancel their fall orders, and distrust of the Committee of Correspondence itself all combined to impede endorsement of the covenant. Not until Governor Thomas Gage made the tactical blunder of denouncing it as a 'traitorous combination' did the movement get off the ground. Thereafter subscription to the Boston covenant and other less stringent versions improved somewhat.[10]

One of the most remarkable results of the Port Act was the response made in other towns and colonies to the plight of Boston. Donations came pouring in from communities near and far—cash from the more prosperous seaports and market towns, wheat and other foodstuffs from agricultural areas, and even livestock directly from farmers themselves. Inhabitants of interior towns who had for decades chafed under the economic heel of Boston now swallowed their previous resentment of the seaport and gave it succour in its hour of need. In Boston a special 'donations' committee was formed, having a considerable overlap of membership with the Committee of Correspondence. It planned for the employment of workmen, distributed incoming contributions to the needy, and most important of all acknowledged virtually all donations with individual responses. And each letter reminded the contributors of Boston's sorrowful plight.[11]

From distant Cape Fear, North Carolina, came a sloopload of provisions in July. And Boston replied: 'The tender sympathy and brotherly kindness expressed in your letter and so fully evidenced by the very liberal donations of our worthy and patriotic brethren of Cape Fear, are truly affecting.' The inhabitants of the little community of Brooklyn in Connecticut sent 125 sheep ('hoping thereby you may be enabled to stand firm, if possible, in the glorious cause. . . .'). And Boston replied: 'The unexampled charity and munificence with which this distressed town hath been treated by their brethren of the continent, must strike Europe with astonishment, as it doth our enemies with dismay. . . .'[12] When the Committee of Correspondence in New Castle, Delaware, wrote to ask whether the beleaguered town preferred money or goods, the Boston Committee tactfully answered that 'Tis a well known saying that "money answers all things"; and yet, so it happens sometimes, that some particular articles cannot be had for money. Either cash, iron, hemp or flax may be sent, as our friends shall find most convenient.'[13]

The opportunity to contribute to the support of Boston during the summer and autumn of 1774 became for thousands of colonists their first personal commitment to the opposition against Great Britain. A farmer who sent his grain or sheep to Boston sent the fruit of his land and of his labour. He could make no more precious gift than that, short of life itself. In the months following the closing of Boston port the resistance movement came to the grass-roots level throughout the colonies. The abstractions that inhabitants of the seaports had talked of in earlier years now took a concrete form recognizable by any citizen—the systematic destruction of a community's livelihood. Perhaps the town of Windham, Connecticut, put the matter most eloquently:

'Tis with pity mixed with indignation that we have beheld the cruel
and unmanly attacks made by the British Parliament on the loyal and
patriotic town of Boston, who seem destined to feel the force of ministerial wrath, the whole weight of parliamentary vengeance levelled
at them in a manner so replete with cruelty and injustice, as must
strike every heart with horror and fill every breast with rage. . . .[14]

Inhabitants of the towns and counties of provincial America had
yet another commitment to make during the summer of 1774—
whether to send delegates to the proposed Continental Congress
and if so, with what instructions. The idea of a congress was not new
in itself—one had met in Albany twenty years before to discuss colonial union, and of course delegates had convened at New York in
1765 to protest the Stamp Act. Even so, there was no established
procedure for the selection of delegates, and as a result the men who
gathered at Philadelphia in September came from a wide variety of
constituencies. In New Jersey, for instance, and a half-dozen other
colonies, the general assembly was not in session, and the governor
refused to convene it. Voters in each county therefore sent representatives to a provincial convention which in turn chose delegates for
the Philadelphia congress. In three other colonies including Massachusetts and Rhode Island the lower branch of the legislature
selected the delegates, while Connecticut left the choice to the Committee of Correspondence. Still other variations appeared in the two
Carolinas.[15]

In most colonies the moderate-to-radical patriots controlled
preparations for the Congress. In some, however, the conservatives
waged fierce battles to govern the choice of delegates and to determine the nature of their instructions. One of the major struggles
took place in New York, where the conservative Committee of Fifty-
one nominated a middle-of-the-road slate. Sears and McDougall
proposed the requirement that the delegates be approved by the
radical Committee of Mechanics but were voted down. They then
called a public meeting to instruct the delegation to favour a strong
non-importation agreement among the colonies represented at the
Congress, but the more conservative forces disavowed the proceedings. Sears, McDougall, and nine other radicals thereupon resigned
from the Committee of Fifty-one. They soon gained revenge when
in late July the public meeting called by the Committee of Fifty-one
to approve its proceedings rejected them instead. After a considerable amount of manoeuvring the moderates' choice for delegates
won approval only after their public commitment to support a non-
importation agreement at the Congress.[16]

An even more significant struggle took place in Pennsylvania. In
early June Governor John Penn rejected a request from moderates

to convene the general assembly. Long weeks of political manoeuvring and debate followed. The cautious proposal of petitioning the King for redress before considering a cessation of trade had strong support in Philadelphia. Conservatives there also insisted that only delegates chosen by the various colonial legislatures should be considered legitimate representatives at the Congress. Radicals and moderates particularly in the interior counties grew increasingly frustrated at the impasse. In mid-July they arranged a convention of delegates from each county to meet at Philadelphia, chose the congressional delegates and adopted instructions. This development promptly goaded Governor Penn into summoning the assembly itself, and its members gathered at Philadelphia while the more radical convention still sat. There ensued a mighty tug-of-war between the two bodies. The convention of men from the various counties was roundly denounced as 'the beginning of republicanism. . . . Nip this pernicious weed in the bud before it has taken too deep root,' A FREEMEN pleaded among members of the legislature. The assembly responded by electing their own more moderate slate of delegates to the Congress and by instructing them to try obtaining a redress of grievances while avoiding 'every thing indecent or disrespectful of the mother country'. As at New York the forces of moderation had won a key victory in Pennsylvania.[17]

Meanwhile, the full details of the so-called 'Coercive Acts' became known throughout the colonies. Although more recently some historians have viewed the Massachusetts Government, the Administration of Justice, and the Quartering Acts as reformative in intent rather than punitive, it was difficult for most contemporaries to see them in that perspective. We know that the British ministry had longed for the chance to alter the Governor's Council from an elective to an appointive body, as in other royal colonies, and the failure of the Council to support Hutchinson at the tea party crisis offered the opportunity. But to prohibit town meetings from gathering except for annual elections went far beyond the scope of a 'reform'. Although far from democratic the town meeting was nevertheless the principal means by which localities in New England governed their affairs, instructed their representatives, and adopted resolutions expressing their opinions on matters effecting their welfare. These latter two functions particularly annoyed the ministry, and the limitation on meetings was apparently designed to muzzle grass-roots opinion. But the towns of Massachusetts Bay ignored the law, merely adjourning their annual elections meetings from day to day through the year. Colonists elsewhere concluded that if Parliament could alter the charter of Massachusetts their own was equally vulnerable. What the Pennsylvanian Edward Shippen wrote about the Port Act he might well have applied to all the Coercive Acts: 'Whoever will scrutinize the late act of Parliament may plainly discover that we are all included . . . the words Rhode Island, Connecticut, New York, etc. . . . are written with lime juice and only want the heat of the fire to make them legible. . . .' [18]

The Coercive Acts produced a major change in the basis of the dispute between the mother country and her American possessions. Until 1774 the quarrel had centred on the question of whether Parliament could impose taxation on the colonies, although as we have seen numerous other issues were also involved. Passage of the Coercive Acts tended to push the matter of taxation aside and focused attention on the basic issue of legislative power within the Empire and its limitations, if any. These questions had been raised in various political pamphlets before, but now they became subjects for discussion by ordinary colonists. In the letters sent from various communities accompanying their donations to Boston are found a number of concerns reaching far beyond the closing of the port itself. Wrentham, Massachusetts, feared for 'the pillars of the Constitution'; Lebanon, Connecticut, thought it 'strange . . . that a K--- possessed of any just and humane sentiments should be so regardless of the merits and rights of h-s American and the interest and welfare of his B-----h su-- j--ts . . .' And the plain folk of Kingston, New Hampshire, believed that unless there were a speedy repeal of the Coercive Acts 'a total disaffection will soon take place, and Britain, instead of being our best friend, will be looked upon as an enemy. . . .' Then, these men of New Hampshire concluded, 'a final separation in all respects will no doubt soon follow, the thoughts of which fill our minds with trouble, anxiety, and concern.' [19]

The Coercive Acts generated an upsurge in the number of political pamphlets published on various aspects of the controversy from a total of eleven in 1773 to forty-eight in the following year. And for the first time a substantial number (at least twelve) defended the colonial policy of the mother country. Several of these essays were written as open letters to the delegates about to convene at Philadelphia. William H. Drayton, a South Carolinian who by his own admission had opposed 'the local popular policy' of his colony, announced his change of heart in *A Letter from a Freeman of South Carolina to the Deputies of North-America.* 'The tragedy of five Acts, composed in the last session of Parliament in my opinion violates all of the rules of the political drama, and incapacitates me from saying one word in favor of Administration.' The same indignation which had led him to oppose the non-importation movement of 1769 as a violation of his freedom now prompted him to oppose the Coercive Acts. 'The question now', Drayton asserted, 'is not whether Great Britain has a right to tax Americans against her consent, but whether she has a constitutional right to exercise Despotism over America.' On the other side of the argument, however, was *A Letter from a Virginian to the Members of the Congress* . . . which attacked the patriots for their demagoguery. The author cautioned the delegates to the Congress not to stir up the people too much lest the storm they raise 'burst upon your own heads.' He urged instead that the Congress devise 'some means of reconciling taxation, the indispensable obligation of every subject, with your ideas of the peculiar and inestimable rights of an Englishman.' [20]

One of the most remarkable essays written during the summer of 1774 was the material prepared by John Dickinson for Pennsylvania's convention of county representatives. The convention separated Dickinson's 'Argument' from his 'Instructions' and printed it as *An Essay On The Constitutional Power of Great-Britain Over The Colonies In America*. Here Dickinson revealed how far his thoughts concerning the limits of parliamentary power had advanced since the writing of his *Letters from a Farmer in Pennsylvania* of six years before. Now he declared that any power of government 'in its nature tending to the misery of the people, or in other words, a power in which the people have no share', was not a legal power. Dickinson conceded to Parliament only the right to regulate colonial trade. Even that power, he argued, derived not from Parliament's claim as supreme legislature over the colonies but from the fact that it was 'the full representative of the parent state and the only judge between her and her children in commercial interests'. Furthermore, this power was itself restricted to those regulations of mutual benefit to both mother country and colonies.[21]

The 'Instructions' drafted by Dickinson underwent considerable alteration by the convention in the process of adoption. In the end the Pennsylvanians authorized their congressional delegation to concur in a cessation of trade with Great Britain if such measures were endorsed by other delegates, although they hoped a respectful petition of redress would be offered first. In the end the Pennsylvania assembly under the domination of the conservative Joseph Galloway ignored the convention's candidates for the Congress and its instructions as well.[22]

Another essay written under similar circumstances to that of Dickinson has become far more famous. Young Thomas Jefferson, chosen as delegate to Virginia's mid-summer convention, had also prepared a statement of his philosophical position which denied the power of Parliament in America and limited that of the King as well. When illness prevented his attendance, he forwarded his document to Williamsburg anyway. There the convention delegates considered it somewhat too extreme for adoption, but several of Jefferson's friends without his knowledge caused it to be printed under the title *A Summary View of the Rights of British America,* and it received wide circulation in both America and Great Britain. Although Jefferson was not the first American to make the major arguments appearing in *A Summary View,* he was still substantially ahead of his time. Nevertheless, the essay remains an important statement of the position that increasing numbers of American patriots would come to take in 1775.[23]

Jefferson based his argument on both natural rights and historical precedent. Comparing the early American settlers to the Saxons who had immigrated to England, Jefferson claimed for the colonists the right to establish their own system of laws as the Saxons had done. They 'thought proper', in Jefferson's words, 'to adopt that system of laws under which they had hitherto lived in the mother country, and to continue their union with her by submitting themselves to the same common sovereign. . . .' The young Virginian went on to claim for the colonies a natural right to free trade throughout the world, a right that was first abridged by Cromwell's Parliament in 1651 and then by subsequent Parliaments after the Restoration. Here is ground that few Americans had yet dared to take, at least in such specific terms, partly perhaps for fear of offending potential allies among the British merchants. In reviewing more recent events in the history of imperial relations, Jefferson saw a 'connected chain of Parliamentary usurpation' linking the various revenue acts of the mid-1760s to the act suspending the New York Assembly and the Coercive Acts themselves. Here, in Jefferson's words was 'a series of oppressions, begun at a distinguished period, and pursued unalterably through every change of ministers, [which] too plainly prove a deliberate systematical plan of reducing us to slavery.'[24]

Yet it was not Parliament alone that bore responsibility for America's distresses. In his *Summary View* Jefferson became the first American directly and publicly to criticize George III. He denied the Crown's claim to ownership of American lands, which belonged instead to that society within which the lands lay. Nor had the King a right to send troops into the American colonies. In short, Jefferson reduced the King to a 'chief magistrate', who possessed power to execute the laws of each state within its own boundaries but who had no authority to exercise the laws of one state [England] within the limits of another [Virginia, say]. Here was heady doctrine indeed, for now the King became a mere arbiter between otherwise separate states, a man whose duty was to hold 'the balance of a great, if a well poised, empire'. Despite a pious suggestion that the Americans were willing 'to sacrifice everything which reason can ask to the restoration of . . . tranquility,' Jefferson in fact offered nothing but defiance. 'The God who gave us life, gave us liberty at the same time,' he concluded. 'The hand of force may destroy, but cannot disjoin them.' [25]

As the delegates from twelve continental colonies began their various journeys toward Philadelphia, they carried with them the prayers of thousands of well-wishers among their constituents. The zealous patriot Samuel Patterson of Delaware supposed that 'never in any part of the world ever appeared so many bright luminaries in all probability,' as would at the Congress. 'They will make all people [in England] surprised and if they won't listen I hope will *Weather burn* them all by the beams of their Rhetorick and Continuance.' The more moderate Joseph Shippen of Philadelphia looked to the Congress as the best means of 'preserving the blessings of liberty and promoting peace and harmony with our mother country.' And New York's conservative Thomas Chandler asked in a pamphlet 'whether full confidence ought not to be reposed in the wisdom, the prudence, and patriotic spirit' of the delegates, who, as men of property, 'have much more to risque than most of their constituents.' [26]

Although men of widely different views might support the idea of a congress, one would hardly expect them to agree on what sort of action that body should take to achieve the 'peace and harmony' sought by most colonists. The range of possibilities might begin at one end with a condemnation of Boston's destruction of the tea and a call for its inhabitants to compensate the East India Company for its losses. The few advocates of such a policy were handicapped by the fact that the Port Act laid down as a condition for its repeal that Boston bring the culprits to justice and guarantee the future good behavior of its inhabitants. Such conditions imposed an almost impossible handicap on conservatives and moderates seeking a solid reconciliation. At the other extreme, the Congress could adopt the position advanced by Thomas Jefferson and separately stated by the Pennsylvania lawyer James Wilson in his pamphlet *Considerations on the Nature and Extent of the Legislative Authority of the British Parliament:* that is, a sweeping denial of parliamentary authority over any American affairs whatsoever including its right to superintend colonial commerce. Such a statement might then be followed by a total cessation of trade with the mother country, as Virginia itself intended to do even without the endorsement of the Congress. [27]

For many of the delegates the trip to Philadelphia marked their first journey from home. Not surprisingly, they did a little sightseeing along the way. Fortunately, the Massachusetts delegation had allowed themselves three weeks to reach their destination, for they were wined and dined at every stopover. It was fortunate too, that an anonymous group of friends had arranged to outfit Sam Adams in a complete new wardrobe more suitable to his high station than the old clothes he usually wore. Silver-buckled shoes, a gold-headed cane, and sleeve-buttons with embossed Liberty-cap devices gave Adams at least the outward appearance of a gentleman. Cousin John kept a careful record of all the men he met *en-route*, and his sketches of his fellow congressmen remain a priceless source of information. 'Phill. Livingston [of New York] is a great, rough, rappid Mortal. There is no holding any conversation with him. He blusters away . . . Seems to dread N. England—the levelling spirit, etc.' Of John Dickinson he noted, 'He is a shadow; tall, but slender as a Reed— pale as ashes.' 'Caesar Rodney [of Delaware] is the oddest looking man in the world . . . his face is not bigger than a large apple. Yet there is a sense and fire, spirit, wit and humour in his countenance.' Since turnabout is fair play, we should note Benjamin Rush's recollection of his first meeting with Adams himself: 'This gentleman's dress and manners were at that time plain, and his conversation cold and reserved.' [28]

George Washington arrived in company with Patrick Henry and Edmund Pendleton on 4 September. In the first ten days thereafter he dined out at nine different places, mostly local homes, along with other delegates. On the evening of 16 September, the gentlemen of Philadelphia played host at a dinner for five hundred guests at the State House. And Silas Deane of Connecticut reported to his wife on the 17th: 'Am engaged to dine out every day this week. . . . You will begin to think we do nothing else, but I assure you it is hard work.' John Adams complained the next day about 'the hurry of business, visits, ceremonies, which we are obliged to go through.' Yet more vital business probably transpired outside of Carpenter's Hall than within.[29]

The men who gathered at Philadelphia, for all their anger or at least frustration over British policy, were nevertheless predominantly men of moderate ideas and temperate personalities. Only a few among them had abandoned hope of reconciliation—Sam Adams almost certainly, and perhaps John Adams, Thomas Mifflin, Richard Henry Lee, Christopher Gadsden, and a few others. But the remaining delegates, some fifty in all, expected to find a means of achieving that peace and harmony which they fervently believed had characterized the Empire prior to the year 1763. It is somewhat surprising, therefore, that in the end they should adopt policies based so closely on the radical positions of Jefferson and Wilson.

A major factor leading the delegates toward such a stand was the set of fiery resolves adopted by the county of Suffolk, Massachusetts, in which Boston lay. Rushed by Paul Revere to Philadelphia, the document arrived while the delegates were still in the first flush of dedication for their work together and while their sympathy for the plight of Boston which had brought them to Philadelphia remained fresh in their minds. The Suffolk Resolves outlined a strong programme of defiance for the inhabitants of that county to pursue, including a posture of civil disobedience in respect to the royal government under General Thomas Gage and a call for weekly military training by the militia of the county. On 18 September, 'taking the foregoing [resolves] into consideration', the Congress unanimously approved 'the wisdom and fortitude with which opposition to these wicked ministerial measures has hitherto been conducted and earnestly recommend to their brethren, a perseverance in the same firm temperate conduct,' as expressed in the Suffolk Resolves. Although the vote committed the Congress to no programme of action, advocates of the more radical point of view had gained the all-important initial momentum at the Congress.[30]

On behalf of the numerous moderates and conservatives Joseph Galloway soon counter-attacked. The influential speaker of the Pennsylvania assembly had already lost two battles—the choice of a meeting place (Carpenter's Hall instead of Galloway's home grounds, the State House) and the selection of a secretary (Galloway's old rival, Charles Thomson). Now Galloway proposed to the Congress a thorough reorganization of the Empire as a means of permanently resolving the crisis between mother country and its American colonies. His 'Plan of Union', as he called it, centred upon a Grand Council, composed of delegates elected every three years by the several colonial assemblies and a president-general appointed by the King. Galloway gave to his Grand Council and president-general joint jurisdiction with the English Parliament over all matters involving the relations between two or more colonies and between the colonies as a whole and the mother country. All legislation thus defined required the approval of both English and American legislatures, so that the Grand Council held in effect a veto power over acts of Parliament pertaining to the American colonies. At the same time, however, Galloway considered the Grand Council 'an inferior and distinct branch of the British legislature'.[31]

Galloway's proposal was one of the few concrete suggestions for the reformation of the Empire to come from either America or England during the crisis preceding independence. Here was a constructive effort to resolve the root cause of the dispute—the distribution of political power within the Empire. One can only speculate how such a proposal from the Continental Congress might have been received in Great Britain. The Earl of Dartmouth opined in

January 1775 that 'the idea of union on some general constitutional plan is certainly very just . . . ,' but Dartmouth's paltry influence within the cabinet had already begun to wane. The question was rendered invalid by the failure of the Congress to adopt the proposal. It had come at a time when many Americans wished to loosen rather than to strengthen the bonds between England and America. As Patrick Henry explained to his fellow delegates, such an American legislature as suggested by Galloway would be exposed to the same corrupt influence which in his view plagued the British Parliament (Henry would feel somewhat the same way toward the Federal Constitution thirteen years later). From London Benjamin Franklin concurred in this criticism of Galloway's plan, despite his long personal and political friendship with its author. 'When I consider the extreme corruption prevalent among all orders of men in this old rotten state, and the glorious public virtue so predominant in our rising country,' he wrote to Galloway in February 1775, 'I cannot but apprehend more mischief than benefit from a closer union.' [32]

After discussion of the plan on 28 September the Congress voted six colonies to five to lay it on the table for consideration at a future date. Historians have disagreed in their interpretation of this action—some believing it suggested tentative approval of the idea, others that it was simply a delaying tactic. In any event when the time came one month later there was sufficient opposition not only to reject the plan but to expunge from the official journal all reference to the proposal itself and to the September discussion as well. With Galloway's plan died the only serious proposal made by the moderates and conservatives for compromise.[33]

Meanwhile, the momentum of the Congress had clearly moved its members toward more radical measures. Indeed, two key decisions bracketed the discussion of Galloway's plan in late September. On 27 September the Congress unanimously resolved to prohibit the importation of all goods sent either directly or indirectly from Great Britain and Ireland. On the 30th the delegates further agreed to prohibit the exportation of all commodities from the continental colonies to Great Britain after 10 September 1775 unless the Americans' grievances were redressed prior to that date. Most of the delegates and their constituents had already determined upon non-importation before the meeting of the Congress (it was after all hardly a new idea in 1774), but non-exportation met strong opposition, especially from the southern colonies whose principal produce depended upon the English market. Postponement of its effective date for a year, along with an exception for rice to Europe, swung sufficient support from the plantation colonies to assure adoption, but probably few delegates actually expected that non-exportation could be permanently avoided.[34]

Earlier economic campaigns against the mother country had begun on the local level and had depended solely upon local sentiment for effectiveness, with somewhat uneven results. Now the Congress took the initiative in proposing a means of enforcement. The Continental Association, as it was called, received the signatures of virtually all the delegates on behalf of their respective colonies. In addition to the provisions concerning importation and exportation of British goods, the Association prohibited the slave trade and the use of imported tea from whatever country. It also proscribed 'every species of extravagance and dissipation, especially horseracing, and all kinds of gaming, cockfighting, exhibitions of shows, plays, and other expensive diversions and entertainment. . . .' In a more positive vein the colonists were to improve the breed of domestic sheep, encourage frugality and industry, and promote agriculture and manufactures, all in an effort to increase American self-sufficiency. Each county or town was to elect a watchdog committee to observe the conduct of local inhabitants and to publish the names of violators in the local newspaper 'to the end that all such foes to the rights of British-America may be publicly known.' Any colony failing to enforce the Association would receive from the others the same ostracism that individual violators might expect from their neighbours. The Congress had in fact authorized the creation of a series of extra-legal quasi-governmental bodies throughout the colonies.[35]

Before adjourning at the end of October, the delegates adopted a series of petitions and addresses stating their grievances in now-familiar language and seeking either redress or support for their cause. In its Declaration and Resolves the Congress listed what it considered natural and constitutional rights of the colonies. Included was the right 'to a free and exclusive power of legislation in their several provincial assemblies subject only to the negative of their sovereign.' But 'from the necessity of the case, and a regard to the mutual interest of both countries', the delegates 'cheerfully' consented to the *bona fide* regulation of colonial commerce by the British Parliament, without, however, conceding that body any right to do so. The restoration of harmony within the Empire depended first of all on the repeal of all previous revenue measures, along with the Coercive Acts and the Quebec Act. Furthermore, the Congress proclaimed that the maintenance of a peacetime standing army without consent of the colony concerned was against the law. 'To these grievous acts and measures Americans cannot submit', the document concluded. The delegates offered nothing in return, unless one considers their refusal to demand repeal of the Navigation Acts a concession.[36]

In its petition to the King for redress of grievances the members of Congress complained of several measures in addition to the revenue laws, Coercive Acts, and standing armies. The great increase in official fees, the broadened powers given customs officers, and the independent salaries granted judges, were all on the list. Furthermore, the congressmen protested that their previous petitions had been put aside and their agents in London ignored. And the petitioners also complained that their commerce 'has been burthened with many useless and oppressive restrictions', although again they stopped short of explicitly denying Parliament the right to regulate imperial trade. As in earlier statements and petitions the members of the Congress suggested that the source of all the mischief came from 'those designing and dangerous men, who daringly [interpose] themselves between your royal person and your faithful subjects. . . .' The moderation of its language testified to the fact that Americans were still loyal to the King even though the extent of their demands indicated their total disenchantment with Parliament.[37]

One of the most interesting documents endorsed by the Congress was the 'Address to the People of Great Britain'. Years before, Benjamin Franklin had complained from London that 'Every man in England seems to consider himself a piece of a sovereign over America; seems to jostle himself into the throne with the king and talks of *our subjects in the colonies.* . . .' Now the delegates to the Congress made clear that they considered themselves as free as 'our fellow-subjects in Britain'. Can there be any reason, they asked, 'why English subjects who live three thousand miles from the royal palace should enjoy less liberty than those who are three hundred miles distant from it?' Having established to their own satisfaction the principle of equality, the Americans then catalogued the various ways in which they had been treated unjustly. 'Permit us to be as free as yourselves, and we shall ever esteem a union with you to be our greatest glory and our greatest happiness. . . . But if you are determined that your ministers shall wantonly sport with the rights of mankind . . . ,' they concluded, 'we must then tell you that we will never submit to be hewers of wood or drawers of water for any ministry or nation in the world.' [38]

In their Address to the People of Great Britain the delegates had especially condemned the Quebec Act for establishing a religion 'fraught with sanguinary and impious tenets'. They played on English anti-catholicism by expressing a fear that the ministry would use the French Catholics of Canada 'to reduce the ancient free Protestant colonies to the same state of slavery with themselves. . . . May not a ministry with the same armies enslave you?' the delegates asked. At the same time, however, the Congress drafted a long appeal to the inhabitants of Quebec that literally dripped with hypocrisy. When after 'a gallant and glorious resistance' the Canadians were incorporated into the body of Englishmen 'we rejoiced in the truly valuable addition . . .', the delegates said. Now they explained that the Quebec Act gave the *habitants* nothing at all; in fact it deprived them of their natural rights. And the Americans piously concluded that 'we are too well acquainted with the liberality of sentiment distinguishing your nation to imagine that difference of religion will prejudice you against a hearty amity with us', and they invited the Canadians to send delegates to the next Congress. Not surprisingly the inhabitants of Quebec failed to accept the invitation. Having indeed determined to meet again in May 1775, unless American grievances were by that time redressed, the first Continental Congress dissolved at the end of October, and the delegates made their weary way home for a winter of hope for the best, and preparation for the worst.[39]

XI

The Point of No Return

1. Whitehall: 'The Dye Is Cast'

IN LONDON there was a prolonged pause in American concerns after
Dartmouth had sent Gage the official texts of the last three Coercive
Acts. Wind, weather, and three thousand miles of rolling water
stood between the government and news of the response to its unyielding policy. The slow trickle of Gage's dispatches kindled moderate optimism and revealed at first no signs of disaster to come. On
19 May he wrote that the Port Act had 'staggered the most presump-
tuous.' On the 30th he reported there was little likelihood of the
other colonies joining in a trade boycott; furthermore, 'the violent
party seems to break and people fall off from them, but no means
are yet adopted to comply with the Act.' He anticipated that the
extra regiments following him across the Atlantic would change the
atmosphere for the better: 'Many are impatient for the arrival of the
troops and I am told that people will then speak and act openly,
which they now dare not do.' On 26 June he stated that some of the
covert support for royal government had now declared itself. Other
letters written up until the arrival of the text of the Regulating Act
continued to report difficulties with patriot activity but no serious
deterioration of the situation.[1]

At the beginning of July, talks with the retired governor of Massachusetts, Thomas Hutchinson, immediately after his arrival in
London, further reassured the ministers. In particular much was
built upon various parting testimonials of support for Hutchinson
from merchants, lawyers, and the episcopal clergy at Boston.[2] After
seeing Hutchinson the King wrote to North on 1 July that he was
'now well convinced they [would] soon submit.'[3] But the ex-governor had no knowledge at first hand of his province's reaction to the
Port Act, and his testimony now, and later, was coloured by an emo-

tional reluctance to believe that American Englishmen would ever go so far as to fire on redcoats. For his part, critical as he was of all the coercive legislation, he gained the impression that submission would win a ready response from the government. King and ministers were anxious, he thought, to relieve Boston from the consequences of the Port Act at the earliest opportunity, as soon as they saw clear evidence of compliance, and would 'forbear from any act for taxation', provided the authority of Parliament was not denied or counteracted.[4]

Private letters of a warning or exhortatory nature, and official dispatches from other centres in the American Empire, presented a similar confusing pattern of information. One or two American correspondents, notably Joseph Reed, warned Dartmouth of the increasing seriousness of the situation, but their known partisanship made their views suspect. Ministers tended to feel that attempts were being made to pressure them into concessions by painting the situation blacker than it really was. Gleams of optimism in official letters were naturally given more weight.[5] Despite the more gloomy newspaper reports, which made the Lord President write from his seat at Trentham of fears for a 'troublesome' session of Parliament, ministers remained set on their course.[6] After a busy month of almost continuous political discussions Hutchinson reported to Gage early in August: 'I hear no other language at court or in the city, among the favourers of the late Acts of Parliament and among those who disapproved of them but this: "We have gone so far that it will never do to go back." '[7]

Behind the government stood the country. A great groundswell of opinion was rising against the apparent tendency of the Americans to seek their independence. Burke told the New York Committee of Correspondence on 2 August that during the spring, 'in general discourses and . . . in publick debates the predominant and declared opinion' had been in favour of the Massachusetts Charter Act.[8] The ministers, had they wished to do so, could only have ignored this feeling at their peril, and it greatly strengthened their hand. Opposition leaders were gravely embarrassed, both by their loss of public support and by their commitment to the principle of parliamentary supremacy. On this situation the evidence provided by Hutchinson is of prime value—and if, in writing to American correspondents, he was tempted into vivid emphasis to make his point, nevertheless his testimony carries weight as much as that contained in such patriot letters as those of Joseph Reed to Dartmouth. On 8 August he pointed out: 'I have not met with one person in the kingdom—and I have seen flaming patriots, as well as fawning courtiers—who thinks the avowed principles, either of the House or Council [of Massachusetts] admissible.' [9] On the 27th he set down a more extensive analysis: [10]

> I am fully persuaded there never has been a time when the nation in general has been so united against the colonies. The opposition is considered not against the Ministry, but the kingdom in general, and even Lord Chatham, Burke, and Barré, who don't vote for Bills which concern the colonies, condemn, notwithstanding, the principles of the people there, and the actions consequent upon them. In travelling about the country, I find all sorts of persons of the same sentiments. This unanimity, I take it, causes the Ministry to be determined not to recede from any measure in which they have engaged, until the end proposed is effected. They could do nothing which would so much tend to destroy their own political existence. They, nevertheless, most heartily wish to see the colonies in peace and quiet, and I easily believe are disposed to indulge them in every point which can consist with their remaining a part of the British dominions.

Early in September Hutchinson visited Norwich, a town where the manufacturers catered for the Baltic markets and had little concern with the American trade. He dined in company with the dissenting minister and a group of aldermen, some friendly and some hostile to North's administration. In his diary he noted, that when conversation turned to the colonies: [11]

> All seemed to suppose that America only wished to be put upon the foot they were upon before the Stamp Act, and that upon such concession they would promise to return to their former state of subjection: but upon hearing that the authority of Parliament in all cases had been denied, they all declared against any repeal, until the right was admitted.

This was a very different viewpoint from that reported to America by Franklin or by the brothers William and Arthur Lee, who seem to have had little contact outside the ranks of the Wilkesite party in the City of London and grossly overestimated the strength and importance of what they had once described as the 'constitutionalist' party.[12] King, ministers, Norwich aldermen, and many others thought alike. To the King any surrender to American views was out of the question. In mid-September he wrote that the policy adopted in the spring must be maintained: [13]

> The dye is now cast, the colonies must either submit or triumph; I do not wish to come to severer measures, but we must not retreat; by coolness and an unremitted pursuit of the measures that have been adopted, I trust they will come to submit; I have no objection afterwards to their seeing that there is no inclination for the present to lay fresh taxes on them, but I am clear there must always be one tax to keep up the right, and as such I approve of the tea duty.

DESTRUCTION OF TEA IN BOSTON HARBOUR, 16 December 1773. *Published by Prentiss Whitney. Engraving, 1773. American Antiquarian Society, Worcester.*

Below: THE ABLE DOCTOR, OR AMERICA SWALLOWING THE BITTER DRAUGHT. America regurgitates into North's face the tea he is pouring down her throat. On the left France and Spain look on with interest. *Engraving, 1774. Department of Prints and Drawings, British Museum, London.*

Above left: A New Method of Macarony Making, as Practised at Boston in North America. The number 45 on the patriot's hat refers to issue No. 45 of John Wilkes's opposition weekly paper the *North Briton*. *Printed for Carington Bowles. Mezzotint, 1774. Department of Prints and Drawings, British Museum, London.*

Above right: Meeting of a Society of Patriotic Ladies at Edenton in North Carolina. *By Philip Dawe. Mezzotint, 1775. Library of Congress, Washington.*

Below: George Washington (1732–1799), accompanied by Patrick Henry and Edmund Pendleton, on his way to the first Continental Congress in 1774. *By H. B. Hall. Engraving. Radio Times Hulton Picture Library, London.*

Above left: Samuel Adams (1722–1803). *By Storm, after J. S. Copley. Engraving. Radio Times Hulton Picture Library, London.*

Above right: John Adams (1735–1826) in later life. *By Stephenson, after J. S. Copley. Engraving. Radio Times Hulton Picture Library, London.*

Below left: John Hancock (1737–1793). *Engraving. Radio Times Hulton Picture Library, London.*

Below right: Thomas Jefferson (1743–1826) in later life. *By Jean-Antoine Houdon. Marble, 1789. Museum of Fine Arts, Boston.*

THE BATTLE OF LEXINGTON. In the centre Major Pitcairn, on horseback, directs the fire of the grenadiers on the retreating figures of the Lexington Provincial Company. In the background to the left of the tree is the meeting-house, and to the right the tavern. *By Amos Doolittle, after Ralph Earl. Coloured engraving, 1775. Lexington Historical Society, Lexington.*

On the next page: 'A Plan of the Town and Harbour of Boston, and the Country Adjacent with the Road from Boston to Concord'. This is the earliest known British map to show the engagement where the attack began' when the militia opened fire on the regulars. The map contains some inaccuracies as Lord Percy relieved Smith at Lexington (not west of it as on the plan) and returned to Charlestown via Men-

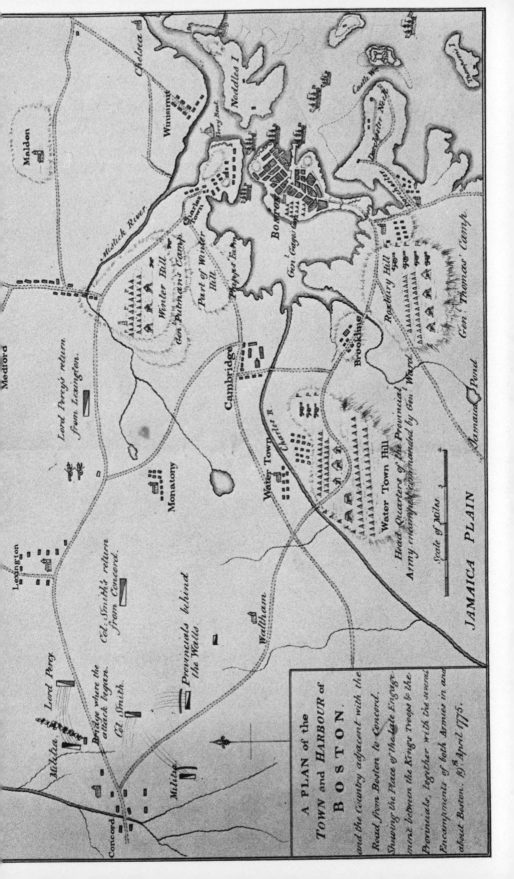

Medford

Chelsea

Maldon

Winisimet

Noddles I

Castle W.

Thompson I.

Mistick River

Charles Town

Winter Hill

Gen. Putnam's Camp

Part of Winter Hill

Pepper's Farm

Dorchester Neck

Boston

Gen. Gage's

Lord Percy's return from Lexington.

Col. Smith's return from Concord.

Cambridge

Brookline

Roxbury Hill

Gen. Thomas' Camp

Lexington

Monatory

Provincials behind the Walls

Water Town

Charles R.

Water Town Hill

Head Quarters of the Provincial
Army encamped & commanded by Gen. Ward.

Jamaica Pond.

Lord Percy

Militia

Bridge where the
attack began.

Col. Smith.

Waltham

Concord

Militia

Scale of Miles

JAMAICA PLAIN

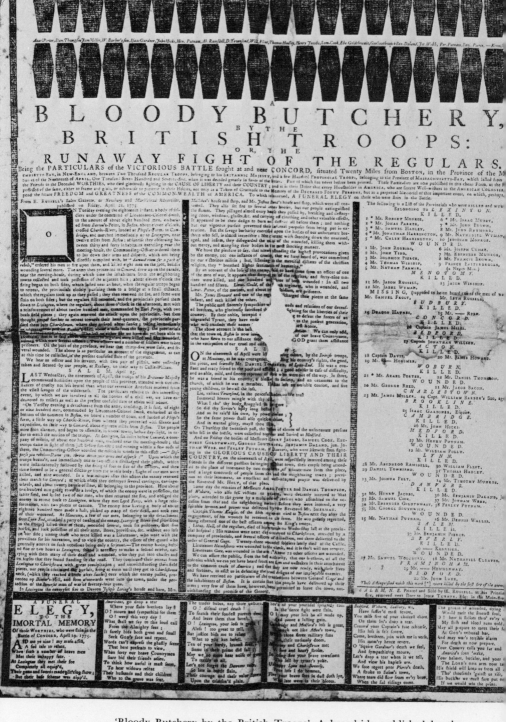

'Bloody Butchery by the British Troops'. A broadside published by the *Salem Gazette* on 21 April 1775 memorializing the men who fell at Lexington and Concord. *Courtesy of the Essex Institute, Salem.*

The State Blacksmiths Forging Fetters for the Americans. A cartoon attacking government measures of 1775 and 1776. *Engraving, 1776. Department of Prints and Drawings, British Museum, London.*

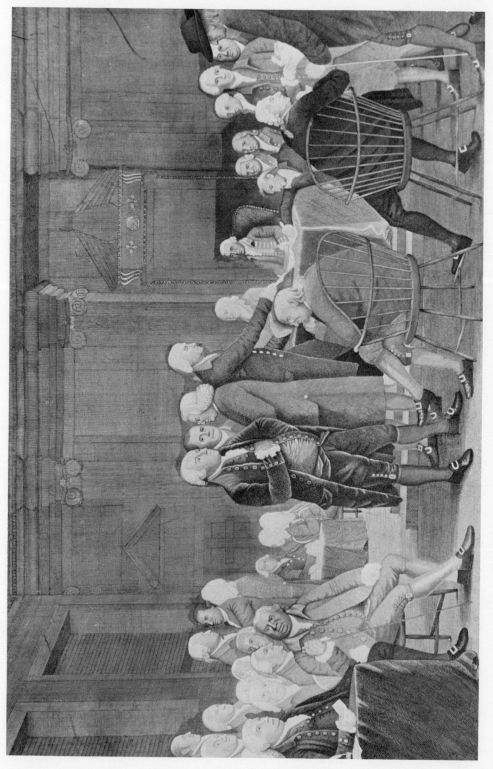

THE CONGRESS VOTING INDEPENDENCE, 2 July 1776. By Edward Savage. Engraving, after

Neither the King nor his ministers had any grasp of the intensity of the colonists' feelings about their constitutional liberties or of their willingness to go all lengths in their defence. Hutchinson's talks with British politicians during the summer gave no indication that they thought armed resistance conceivable, any more than he did himself. The former Rockinghamite, Lord Hardwicke, impelled by his convictions to play a leading part in forwarding the government's American business in the House of Lords, said to Hutchinson repeatedly, 'that he had no apprehensions of rebellion, or forcible opposition to the king's troops.' [14] If the colonists attempted another trade boycott, the ministers were prepared to face it firmly. On 21 September North told Hutchinson that if the colonies refused to trade with Britain, then 'Great Britain would take care they should trade no where else.' [15] But for much of the summer such a development was thought unlikely. Information from the City suggested that, far from joining in any non-importation move, the merchants of New York and Philadelphia were stocking double quantities of goods in order to take over the Boston trade.[16]

But on 1 October 1774 the King and ministers found they were facing the unthinkable. Writing at the end of August, after the arrival of the texts of the remaining Coercive Acts, Gage had to report that 'popular fury was never greater' in Massachusetts 'than at present', and that Connecticut was becoming increasingly involved. A long dispatch of 2 September and a further letter of the 3rd revealed the virtual collapse of royal government and his complete inability to remedy the situation without further large troop reinforcements.[17]

This news could have hardly arrived at a more inopportune moment, for Parliament had just been dissolved and the ministers were engrossed in election business. It seems probable that they had expected no further developments for a month or so; Dartmouth had remarked on 31 August that nothing more could be done until the results of the meeting of the Congress were known.[18] However, further trials clearly lay ahead, and the ministers thought it better to face them with a new Parliament, rather than one bound by law to be dissolved within the next six months. Any policy adopted in the autumn would then be more assured of continued support.[19]

On 3 October, Dartmouth, North, and Lord Chancellor Apsley, the only three cabinet ministers in London, met to discuss the American dispatches. The contents placed them in a quandary. Since home defence and the preservation of order required the retention of the troops left in Britain and none was available from distant garrisons, little reinforcement of Gage was possible. Two regiments might be found from Ireland, but the season precluded their being sent across the Atlantic till the spring. The provision of three more warships and six hundred marines was the best that could be done. This was arranged immediately and the consent of the other ministers obtained by post. But even after this shock ministers' letters revealed an inability to grasp American realities. Rochford declared he still hoped the American business would turn out right as, if he followed Gage correctly, Bostøn was unlikely to get help from other colonies. Dartmouth agreed, and hoped that 'even in the New England government where prejudice and resentment have taken such strong hold', there were 'many friends to the constitution who would stand forth, under the protection of government.' [20]

Hutchinson's talks with junior ministers at this time point to great perplexity in the government ranks. Men conceded that parliamentary taxation was now out of the question, but were at a loss how to give it up without also abandoning parliamentary supremacy. Dartmouth's under secretary, William Knox, even hoped that that illegal body, the Congress, might find some formula that might serve the turn. He believed that the logic of the situation would force the Congress to acknowledge parliamentary control, 'not only for their protection from foreign enemies, but from irreconcilable disputes and quarrels within themselves, as no other umpire can be so fit.' The nightmare of foreign control over British North America played some part in keeping the government on its course. In one letter home Hutchinson wrote: 'I meet with people of no small importance very often, who say they would most willingly break off all connection with you, if they did not suppose you would immediately fall into the clutches of France or Spain.' [21] To have those vast resources bolster the power of the Bourbons was a thing too dire to contemplate.

During the next few weeks things became increasingly clear to the ministers: a breakdown in the Congress was not going to free King, government and Parliament from the hook on which they had impaled themselves; and the local situation in Massachusetts was completely out of Gage's control. Interim reports from a secret source in Philadelphia spelled out the defiant progress of the committees of the Congress, though its decree of a non-importation policy was not finally known till 10 November. Soon afterwards the government learned from both Gage and the American customs board, that the attempt to move the province's capital to Salem was impracticable and that royal officials had taken refuge with the garrison at Boston. Gage even suggested a temporary suspension of the Coercive Acts until such time as a large military force, including German mercenaries, had been gathered to strike with decisive effect. [22] Ministers and officials were thunderstruck but felt that any concession

was inadmissible and would be disastrous.[23] On news of the approval
at Philadelphia of the Suffolk Resolves, Dartmouth told Hutchinson:
'If these resolves of your people are to be depended on, they have
declared war against us: they will not suffer any sort of treaty.' [24]

As the American news brought closer the prospect of an appeal
to force, the Secretary-at-War interjected a discordant opinion. Barrington was an old friend of Gage, had conducted with him
throughout a private as well as public correspondence, and was well-
informed about American conditions. He thought it futile to contemplate military action. On 12 November he wrote to Dartmouth
urging an immediate withdrawal from Boston. So long as the local
magistrates refused to support imperial authority, 'the riotous mobs,
directed by the factious leaders of that country, must govern it; and
they cannot be quelled or even resisted by the army, which must
therefore remain in a disgraceful inaction; enriching with its pay a
delinquent colony, and in continual hazard of insult and bloodshed.'
Gage's seven regiments there could easily be moved to suitable alternative bases. Barrington advised recourse to a naval blockade, which
he believed capable of reducing the colony to submission without
shedding a drop of blood.[25]

No one paid heed to his warnings. The King backed the government in its course. Gage's suggestion for a suspension of the Acts
seemed to him 'absurd'. Any retreat would encourage further
claims: 'We must either master them or totally leave them to themselves and treat them as aliens.' The New England governments, he
declared, were 'in a state of rebellion', and 'blows must decide
whether they are to be subject to this country or independent.' The
following day North talked in the same strain of two regiments
going across from Ireland next spring and other unspecified measures;[26] but for the meantime the sailing season was over and the
government had no more troops to send. He told Josiah Quincy
that if he were to yield on the question of parliamentary supremacy,
'he should expect to have his head brought to the block by the general clamor of the people, and he should deserve it.' [27]

The new Parliament met on 30 November. Although the opposition launched a strong attack on American policy, the debates on the
address showed that the government's position was assured. The following day the full cabinet considered the American situation. Ministers agreed that, if the law officers concurred in the view that the
acts of the people of Massachusetts constituted overt treason, a proclamation should be prepared, requiring all who were guilty to surrender themselves by a given day, on pain otherwise of being treated
as rebels and traitors.[28] At first the law officers saw difficulties, and
at another meeting on 10 December the plan was laid aside. As no

letters had arrived from Gage of later date than mid-September, ministers felt it was useless to contemplate further action.[29]

However, on the 13th the law officers revived the proposal for a proclamation against rebellion. They described various letters and accounts laid before them as 'the history of an open rebellion and war in the province of Massachusetts Bay', and asked for further instructions.[30] By that date Dartmouth was at last in possession of fuller knowledge of developments in the colonies, including the texts of the Congress's Declaration of Rights, its address to the people of Great Britain, and its appeal to the Canadians for support. He also knew of the meeting of the Provincial Congress of Massachusetts and its exchanges with Gage.[31] These proceedings, described by the law officers as 'criminal to a great degree', ensured short shrift for a suggestion that Dartmouth seems to have aired about mid-December, for an appointment of commissioners to treat with delegates appointed by the colonists.[32] The King at once pronounced against any concession: 'This looks so like the Mother Country being more affraid of the continuance of the dispute than the colonies, and I cannot think it likely to make them reasonable; I do not want to drive them to despair but to submission, which nothing but feeling the inconvenience of their situation can bring their pride to submit to.'[33] Three days later further dispatches illustrating Gage's helplessness provoked demands that he be replaced.[34] But as ministers dispersed for the Christmas holiday they still had no clear idea what further measures they should pursue.

At this point Barrington once more intervened in a forlorn attempt to ensure that the army was not set an impossible task. In a long letter of 24 December to Dartmouth, he tried to impress upon him the futility as well as impracticability of a military confrontation. Parliamentary taxation, he believed, was now out of the question: it was not within Britain's power, and the contest was now only on a point of honour. New England alone was probably too strong to be subdued by the forces then in America; but even if overcome it could only be held down by force at ruinous and endless expense. Naval action on the other hand, he optimistically urged, would bring New England to its knees, 'with very little expense and less bloodshed'. So far as other colonies were concerned, a strict enforcement of the Acts of Trade would be sufficient. All regiments should be withdrawn to Canada, Nova Scotia, and East Florida. 'If these ideas are well-founded', he concluded, 'the colonies will in a few months feel their distress; their spirits not animated by any little successes on their part or virtue of persecution on ours, will sink; they will be consequently inclined to treat, probably to submit to a certain degree; and in my humble opinion the whole is then over, for with dignity we may make them concessions.' Barrington ended by pressing for an immediate repeal of the tea duty in respect of the colonies not involved in the association of the Congress. This would 'shew the refractory colonies, that obedience is a sure way to be relieved.' [35]

Barrington's expectations from the use of the navy were certainly unrealistic, and the ministers had no sympathy with his views. North could think only of more troops, and on 31 December Dartmouth was talking of four or five regiments from the West Indies, two from Ireland, and a need to raise still further men.[36] But such a scale of reinforcement hardly corresponded with the unpalatable advice which reached the American secretary from Gage a day or two later. 'If force is to be used at length', Gage wrote, 'it must be a considerable one, and foreign troops must be hired.' The Provincial Congress was rumoured to be embodying 15,000 men. He had but 3,000. 'They confide in their numbers, and a small force rather encourages resistance, than terrifys . . . to begin with an army twenty thousand strong, will in the end save Great Britain both blood and treasure.'[37]

Subsequent events were to indicate that Gage was wildly optimistic in thinking that 20,000 men could subdue America at any time. In early 1775 the government shut its eyes to the implications of his advice. North immediately pointed out only a full war mobilization could provide so great a striking force and that twelve months would be needed to assemble it.[38] It is probable that he shrank from the idea of applying to Parliament for the large sums necessary for such a course of action: indeed, seeing the diplomatic barometer set fair, he was actually budgeting for 4,000 fewer seamen for the navy. Supply on this scale was to be voted in 1776, but it is doubtful how the Commons would have reacted in 1775; no one yet took seriously the American will or capacity to fight.[39]

Accordingly, when the cabinet reassembled after the Christmas recess on 13 January the military measures it approved were the dispatch to Boston as soon as possible of two regiments of infantry and one of light cavalry from Ireland and a further detachment of 600 marines. It decided on the 21st to add a third infantry regiment, and it approved an offer from Brigadier Ruggles to raise a force of irregulars in America. Gage was told that with the 4,000 men that would constitute his reinforced army he was expected to be able to put down the rebellion in Massachusetts. With the blind deliberateness of the somnambulist the cabinet set up the very situation which both Gage and Barrington had warned them would be disastrous. The force at Boston would be large enough to give provocation but not nearly sufficient to 'terrify' or act to any effect. The dispatch in which Dartmouth announced this decision must provide one of the classic examples of a purblind ministry rejecting sound, local expert advice: [40]

> It seems to be your idea that matters are come to such a state that this [the restoration of royal government] is no otherwise attainable than by an absolute conquest of the people of the three governments of Massachusetts Bay, Connecticut, and Rhode Island, and that such conquest cannot be effected with less force than 20,000 men.
>
> I am persuaded, Sir, that you must be aware that such a force cannot be collected without augmenting our army in general to a war establishment; and tho' I do not mention this as an objection, because I think that the preservation to Great Britain of her colonies demands the exertion of every effort this country can make, yet I am unwilling to believe that matters are as yet come to that issue.
>
> I have stated that the violences committed by those who have taken up arms in Massachusetts Bay, have appeared to me as the acts of a rude rabble without plan, without concert, and without conduct, and therefore I think that a smaller force now, if put to the test, would be able to encounter them with greater probability of success than might be expected from a greater army, if the people should be suffered to form themselves upon a more regular plan, to acquire confidence from discipline, and to prepare those resources without which everything must be put to the issue of a single action.

Many other passages in this long dispatch indicated that Gage was now expected to act. The conclusion is unavoidable, that it led to his launching of the fatal Concord expedition two days after its arrival at Boston on 16 April.

Ministers considered two other proposals at the cabinet meeting on 13 January. They agreed in principle that the associated colonies should be debarred from the Newfoundland fisheries and from trading anywhere save with Great Britain, Ireland, and the British West Indies. They also discussed again Dartmouth's proposal for sending commissioners to America to negotiate a settlement. Hoping for reconciliation by some such means, Dartmouth had been maintaining indirect lines of contact with Franklin; but Franklin's information about American attitudes disclosed no willingness to move towards the British position on parliamentary sovereignty.[41] At later cabinet meetings other ministers scouted the suggestion, and before the end of the month it had been abandoned.[42]

North seems to have introduced his own plans for conciliation at a meeting on 17 January.[43] These were hammered into shape in a cabinet minute on the 21st: [44]

> Agreed that an address be proposed to the two Houses of Parliament to declare that if the colonies shall make sufficient and permanent provision for the support of the civil government and adminis-

tration of justice, and for the defence and protection of the said
colonies, and in time of war contribute extraordinary supplies in a
reasonable proportion to what is raised by Great Britain, we will in
that case desist from the exercise of the power of taxation, except for
commercial purposes only, and that whenever a proposition of this
kind shall be made by any of the colonies we will enter into the consideration of proper laws for that purpose, and in the meanwhile to
intreat his Majesty to take the most effectual methods to enforce due
obedience to the laws and authority of the supreme legislature of
Great Britain.

This formula went as far as the ministers felt possible, in yielding the
practical exercise though not the theoretical claim of parliamentary
supremacy. Some of them felt that even this was a concession which
might encourage the colonists to fresh assertions of their more extreme demands.[45]

The government's course was now set, though there were still
wrangles over detail. Hutchinson, anxious to relieve and to
strengthen the personal positions of loyalists, pressed for exemptions from the restrictions of any Restraining Act for those who took
a suitable oath or subscription; but the cabinet discarded the idea as
impracticable.[46] On 17 February the cabinet momentarily conceded
to pressure from Dartmouth, 'that Parliament in some way or other
should signify that if the several assemblies would agree to comply
with such requisitions as shall be judged fit, that then Parliament will
dispense with its right of taxation.'[47] This proposal may have arisen
out of the continued indirect contacts with Franklin and have
broken down on the failure of Franklin to guarantee very substantial
surrenders of points insisted on by the Congress.[48] But as reported it
contained in any case an inherent contradiction—for the judging
that requisitions were 'fit' would presumably entail some overriding
control by Parliament. Nothing more was heard of it.

During these weeks information coming across the Atlantic still
encouraged the ministers in the belief that American resistance
would be strangled by enforcement of a Restraining Act. Two letters
from Gage reported signs of a loyalist reaction in Massachusetts.[49]
Governor Dunmore of Virginia, despite his complete loss of control
over his province, declared that debtor interests were the core of the
rebel movement and foresaw its early collapse under the pressure of
a naval blockade. He thought that the non-importation and non-
exportation agreements would soon reduce Virginia to ruin and
thus to compliance, since the inhabitants could not manage without
the products of the mother country.[50] What neither Dunmore nor
the ministers who read his dispatches realized was the vigour with
which the Virginians would defy law and blockade and trade else-

where—two tobacco ships were at Dunkirk by the beginning of April.[51]

Up to the end of January the ministers conducted holding operations in Parliament. A full dossier of American reports was laid before the Houses on the 19th, though the government felt it necessary to expurgate the more pessimistic passages, especially those in letters from General Gage. The Congress's petition, and petitions seeking conciliation submitted by various British commercial groups were shunted off into committee by decisive majorities. Favourable addresses and petitions removed any impression that the general trend of public opinion was against the ministers, and the government noted that a number of M.P.s formerly associated with opposition were now giving regular support in divisions and contributing to its overwhelming majorities.[52] On 20 January in the Lords the ministers threw out Chatham's proposal for the immediate removal of the army from Boston, a step intended both to avert the danger of a fatal incident and to lay grounds for conciliation. On 1 February they killed at the outset his 'Provisional Act' for settling the troubles in America.[53]

On almost all counts Chatham's conciliation scheme was unacceptable to majority opinion in Great Britain. It met many of the Congress's demands, including the repeal of recent unacceptable legislation and the guarantee of jury trial in the vicinage, but it failed to satisfy crucial American aspirations. While abandoning Parliament's exercise of the taxing power, it attempted to preserve a parliamentary supremacy the colonists had now foresworn. It reserved the Crown's right to keep an army in America, providing only the paper guarantee of intent, that this could never be lawfully used against the liberties of the people. Furthermore, it proposed a formal elevation in constitutional importance of the Congress which debates on Galloway's proposal had shown to be repugnant to many colonists,[54] and it set as one condition that this body should vote a permanent revenue to the Crown.[55]

On 2 and 6 February the ministry carried in the Commons by very large majorities an address upholding its policy of maintaining parliamentary supremacy in America, with special reference to the existence of a state of rebellion in Massachusetts. In the Lords it achieved equally decisive success. On 10 February North introduced in the Commons a Non-Intercourse Bill directed against the New England colonies only—a limitation based on the hope that even at this late stage the other colonies would draw back from supporting Massachusetts in open revolt. In the next few days the Commons approved modest increases to the armed forces—2,000 seamen, and an extra 4,000 troops to enable the force at Boston to be raised even-

tually to about 10,000 men. With steady majorities of over three
to one,[56] on the 20th North next introduced the other main government measure, his conciliatory propositions as defined in the cabinet
minute of 21 January.[57] Some of the objects of this proposal are
clear; others can be inferred. It preserved parliamentary sovereignty. It held out hopes that British taxpayers would still be suc-
coured by their American brethren. Some M.P.s concerned about
these two points even feared, however, that North had conceded too
much.[58] North also hoped this measure would assist the passage of
the Non-Intercourse Bill by reassuring those M.P.s who felt the government ought to make some conciliatory gesture.[59] Possibly it might
drive a wedge between New England and some of the other colonies: its wording carried a clear implication that no deal would be
done with the Congress.[60] Relying on the recent reassuring dispatches,[61] North scouted suggestions that the colonists would spurn
his scheme: 'I have better hopes: there are people, and I hope whole
colonies, that wish for peace.'[62]

Both these Bills passed through their parliamentary stages before
the end of March. They were quickly followed by a further Bill extending the prohibitions of non-intercourse to the other old colonies
except New York, Georgia, and North Carolina, where the government still hoped a loyalist reaction would develop.[63] On 30 March
the cabinet finally approved the form of proclamation against rebellion to be issued by Gage in Massachusetts.[64]

As the legislative machine ground on its inexorable way Burke
on 22 March made one more spirited and forlorn attempt to avert
the coming collision. His conciliatory proposals were a triumph of
creative political imagination. His great speech outlining them was
distinguished for its grasp of the realities of the American situation—the impossibility of indicting a people, the need to govern a
great Empire by consent. Burke advocated wholesale concession to
the demands of the Congress: the abandonment of taxation in practice, the repeal of all acts objected to by the colonists, a return to the
requisition system of the 1750s. He would rely solely on sentiment
and self-interest to keep the colonists in some sort of relationship
with Great Britain. He went further than Chatham in abandoning all
claims to a colonial contribution to revenue as a condition for a settlement. His plea that a veil should be drawn over the question of
parliamentary supremacy went far to meet colonial contentions, for
in the general context of the whole speech it was strongly implied
that supremacy would be buried in oblivion, the British being spared
a formal renunciation of a power which would henceforth only be
evoked with the colonists' consent.

This splendid vision foreshadowing the future British Commonwealth lay far beyond the grasp of most of Burke's contemporaries. In their view even a tacit abandonment of parliamentary supremacy entailed the loss of the Empire and of all the wealth and power derived from it, and probably a French take-over of America would spell the final decline of Great Britain into a minor power. The crushing rejection of Burke's motion by 270 votes to 78 reflected the almost total unacceptability to the political world at Westminster of any radical scheme for restructuring the constitution of the Empire.[65] A week later a like fate met David Hartley's proposals to return to a dependence on requisitions in place of parliamentary taxation and to suspend the Coercive Acts.[66] In the decision to crush rebellion the North ministry was carrying out Parliament's—indeed, the country's—will.[67] To the question, how this was to be done, no one had given adequate consideration.

2. Outbreak of War

As the delegates to the Continental Congress made their various ways toward Philadelphia at the end of August 1774, the situation around Boston was growing increasingly tense. Late in the month General Gage had threatened to break up a town meeting in Salem, called in defiance of the Massachusetts Government Act. But as his troops advanced toward the town house with loaded muskets, the meeting completed its work and adjourned. Meanwhile, militia from neighbouring towns had begun their own march toward Salem but dispersed when the crisis eased. Early on the morning of 1 September Gage dispatched 260 troops from Boston by water to seize a large quantity of provincial gunpowder that was stored in Charlestown. A smaller detachment took two field pieces belonging to the militia of Cambridge. By nightfall militia units had assembled throughout Middlesex county and early the next morning marched toward Cambridge. Rumours spread like wildfire all the next day. Down in Connecticut the old war-horse Israel Putnam was spurred to action by reports that the British fleet had bombarded Boston. Thousands of militiamen from towns all over eastern New England headed for Boston with muskets, pitchforks, clubs or whatever other weapons they could find. As the true story emerged, the men turned back toward their homes.[68]

These developments jarred Gage out of his earlier optimism. In July he had reported to Dartmouth from Salem that 'the terror of mobs is over; the press is becoming free.' By late August (after the Salem confrontation) he wrote to Barrington that if war broke out in New England 'you would be able to overcome them, no doubt, in a year or two.' In the midst of the Charlestown-Cambridge affair of early September, however, he reported that while he intended 'to avoid any bloody crisis as long as possible . . . nothing can be done but by forcible means. Tho' the people are not held in high estimation by the troops,' he continued, 'yet they are numerous, worked up to a fury, and not the Boston rabble but the freeholders and the farmers of the country.' And by the middle of the month Gage had concluded that 'it was absolutely necessary to make an entire conquest of the New England governments, and not less than twenty thousand men could venture to take the field.' Gage strengthened his position by moving back to Boston while calling for reinforcements from England. He proceeded to fortify the narrow neck which carried the only road into the seaport and gradually turned the town into an armed camp. By November over 3,000 British troops were jammed into the confines of Boston proper.[69]

Meanwhile, patriot forces in towns around Boston stepped up their own programme of military preparedness. Marblehead's militia agreed to hold four training sessions per week; a Bostonian reported that the country people were busy making carriages for cannon, 'so that preparations for war are carrying on as if the last reason [resort?] of states was soon to be tried.' From an inhabitant of Norwich, Connecticut, came the suggestion that the colonies raise 'an army of observation' and send it to the 'expected scene of action' where it would be ready for the outbreak of hostilities, which the author expected at any moment. By the end of October correspondents in the Boston newspapers openly discussed such topics as 'the horrors of civil war' ('not comparable to those of slavery'); Americans as soldiers ('the most expert marksmen in the world'); and the suitability of the interior country for defence ('foreign troops would soon desert to settle in America'). When war becomes an acceptable subject for conjecture, it is an indication that a society's constraints against a resort to violence have begun to crumble.[70]

Throughout the long, mild autumn and winter Gage faced mounting difficulties. His efforts as governor to placate the inhabitants not only had little positive effect among the colonists but in fact seriously undermined the morale of his army. Encouraged by inviting handbills, many soldiers deserted. The officers complained that 'Tommy' Gage was too soft on the Americans. Admiral Samuel Graves, in charge of the North American station, quarrelled openly with Gage on matters of policy almost from the time he had arrived in June 1774. But Graves himself was equally ineffective; for neither commander thought he had sufficient forces to take any decisive action against the inhabitants surrounding them.[71]

As the autumn turned into winter the New Englanders did what they could to strengthen their defences against the expected attack.

Farmers returning from Boston's markets smuggled muskets out in their wagons. Under cover of darkness other patriots even succeeded in carrying off several cannon from under the British noses. (In desperation Admiral Graves spiked the guns of the North Battery to prevent their capture.) From the colonists' standpoint most of these weapons were 'fair game' because they belonged to the province, not to the British army, a distinction which neither Gage nor Graves countenanced. After the New Englanders learned in December that George III had ordered a ban on all exports of powder and other munitions from England to the colonies, they stepped up their preparations. The citizens of Newport, Rhode Island, commandeered the cannon installed on Fort Island there and sent them up to Providence. A similar episode occurred at New London, Connecticut. At Newcastle, New Hampshire, a band of inhabitants 'liberated' one hundred barrels of gunpowder, sixteen cannon, and other military supplies from Fort William and Mary, commanding Portsmouth harbour. By the time the marines and warships sent by Graves in response to Governor Wentworth's urgent call for help arrived, the materiel had disappeared into the countryside.[72]

Despite (or perhaps because of) his policy of leniency Gage discovered that the government he nominally headed was crumbling all around him. In opposition to the Massachusetts Government Act and the other 'coercive' measures of the North ministry the inhabitants of the colony adopted a policy of civil disobedience. As the fourth article of the Suffolk Resolves put it, 'no obedience is due from this province to either or any part of the [coercive] acts.' Conventions in other counties throughout the province adopted similar measures. As a result judges who accepted appointment under the new laws were considered 'Under undue influence' and the courts over which they presided were to be ignored. Jurors for the Superior Court of Suffolk County in Boston refused to serve under such judges, while in Newburyport the Inferior Court of common pleas sat 'upon the old constitutional form of government', as though the Massachusetts Government Act did not exist. Bands of patriots demanded the resignation of officials who accepted appointment as 'mandamus' councillors in accordance to the new law, just as they had required Stamp Act distributors and tea consignees to do in earlier crises. Perhaps the most blatant disregard of the governor came in early October, after he had declared that the General Court scheduled to meet at Salem should not convene. The delegates assembled anyway and immediately resolved themselves into a 'provincial congress' to conduct their business. Gage was now isolated in Boston not only militarily but politically as well. By the end of the year he might more accurately have been described as the governor of Boston, for the rest of the colony was controlled by the people's representatives at the local and provincial level, under general guidance from the Provincial Congress.[73]

Three factors combined in Massachusetts to generate the military confrontation that was developing in the autumn of 1774. The severity of the Coercive Acts, the presence of British troops at Boston under the direct command of the governor, and most of all perhaps the long and intense history of struggle within that colony between British and American authorities, now in its twelfth year since passage of the Sugar Act. Although in no other colony had factors quite so divisive come together, yet opposition to British authority took a new turn throughout continental America with gradual adoption of the Continental Association. Here at last was a common mechanism of protest that reached far beyond the non-importation agreements of seaport merchants. The Association called upon inhabitants of all communities, rural as well as maritime, to boycott British goods and to promote frugality, economy, and other measures aimed toward American self-sufficiency. Furthermore, the Continental Association called for the formation of extra-legal committees on the local level (county, city, town) 'to observe the conduct *of all persons* [italics mine] touching this association, and to expose violators of the agreement in the public press.' The opportunity (or the necessity?) of taking a stand against Great Britain was now brought to the grass-roots level.[74]

Within weeks committees of inspection, or observation, or safety, as they were variously called, sprang up in rural communities from Maine to Georgia. In New Hampshire, where Governor John Wentworth had kept a strong hand on the helm of royal government, the Continental Association encouraged the first organized opposition to British authority. The governor reported in December that his province had implicitly accepted the measures recommended by the Congress. In January 1775 an extra-legal convention met in place of the assembly (which Wentworth had refused to convene) and endorsed the Association on behalf of the entire colony. In southern New England the Rhode Island and Connecticut assemblies both approved the proceedings of the Congress and called for appointment of local committees. Only in Connecticut's Fairfield county, hard by the New York border, did serious opposition take shape, partly along the Anglican vs. Congregationalist split that had long polarized the area.[75]

In New York advocates of the Association ran into the determined opposition of conservatives led by the Anglican cleric Samuel Seabury and others. Although the city's Committee of Fifty-one called for cooperation from rural counties, communities in only three of them responded in substantial numbers before the end of 1774. A prolonged effort by patriot forces to gain the Assembly's en-

dorsement of the Association met with continuing failure throughout the winter. In the rural counties of New Jersey, Pennsylvania,
and Delaware proximity to the proceedings of the Congress at Philadelphia prompted swift endorsement of the Association. New Jersey's Assembly approved the programme in late January 1775, as
Pennsylvania's House had already done in December and Delaware's
would do at its first session in March 1775.[76]

In the Chesapeake region counties throughout Maryland and
Virginia promptly established committees to enforce the Association
as soon as the Congress adjourned. The provincial convention meeting at Annapolis approved the proceedings in late November and
reaffirmed its support in mid-December. Sixteen of Virginia's counties had endorsed the Association before the end of 1774. When a
provincial congress met in March 1775 the delegates from all sixty-
two counties gave it unanimous approval. Lack of enthusiasm combined with stiff opposition from the back country delayed endorsement in North Carolina. The special convention that met in the
spring was not altogether representative, and its ratification of the
Association was therefore considerably less effective than actions
taken in other colonies. In Georgia, which had even failed to send
delegates to the Congress, less than half of the counties chose delegates to a provincial convention called for January 1775. The agreement finally adopted by this body included substantial modifications
of the Association drawn up by the Congress, and Georgia remained
seriously divided. South Carolina had its own problems with divisiveness. At the Continental Congress several of the colony's delegates
had demanded and won for their constituents the special right to
continue exportation of rice to Europe as their price for approving
the Association. Now the ill-feeling generated by this demand came
home to roost as a number of South Carolinians proposed that the
colony forego its advantage. The delegates gained support for their
actions by a narrow margin in the Provincial Congress, but the rancour continued for some time.[77]

As in earlier American efforts at commercial warfare against the
mother country, the major battleground was again the seaports. The
degree to which the Association could be enforced there would determine its overall success. The old non-importation movement had
depended upon committees of merchants for enforcement backed
up by the Sons of Liberty and other self-appointed groups. But now
the patriots took steps to broaden the base of support for the Association. Not only were the committees popularly elected, but they were
far larger than their predecessors and included tradesmen and mechanics as well as merchants. Among Boston's Committee of Sixty-
three were men notorious for their radical inclinations: Paul Revere,

John Pulling, John Winthrop, Jr., and many others who had partici-
pated in various activities such as tarring and feathering, Pope's Day
mobs, and the Boston Tea Party itself. New York's Committee of
Fifty-one was already large, but it had been dominated by merchants
no longer acceptable to the Committee of Mechanics. In the shakeup
that followed only the more radical members of the old group
gained election to the new Committee of Sixty. Most of those who
were rejected became loyalists or neutrals in the ensuing years.[78]

The change at Philadelphia has been particularly well docu-
mented, and perhaps its characteristics are representative of other
seaports as well. Philadelphia's earlier committee, chosen in June
1774, numbered forty-three. In November the inhabitants elected a
Committee of Sixty-six to enforce the Association. Less than half of
the June committee members were re-elected, so that two-thirds of
the November group were newcomers to this sort of political force.
The proportion of merchants declined from about 80 percent to just
two-thirds while the share of mechanics correspondingly rose from
10 to 27 percent. And the average wealth of members dropped from
£112 in June to £82 in November. Another change, reflected in the
average ages of the two groups, shows not only a slightly younger
group taking over but that they were significantly younger than the
assemblymen or councillors who sat in the legislature. When one
considers the power that accrued to these local committees enforcing
the Association, the full significance of these changes becomes more
apparent. The forms taken by resistance to the Coercive Acts were
themselves revolutionary. No longer was opposition to British policy
a matter of free and voluntary choice; under the Continental Association resistance became compulsory by decision of the majority.[79]

Adoption of the Association precipitated a polarization of opinion toward the imperial crisis that gained momentum through the
winter. Many Americans of diverse political views had in the wake of
the Coercive Acts supported the idea of a congress. Except in the
minds of a few men at the extreme ends of the political spectrum
(royal officials like Thomas Hutchinson or outspoken radicals like
Sam Adams) 'loyalty' as such was not yet the issue. Not *whether* to
seek reconciliation but rather *how* to achieve it was still the question
as the Congress sat. Until the first Continental Congress men could
discuss this subject in general terms without committing themselves
to a particular scheme. Debates on the local level over ratification of
the Continental Association, on the other hand, compelled many colonists for the first time to take a stand for or against a specific mode
of action. In many regions those in opposition could avoid trouble
only by keeping their beliefs to themselves and by outwardly complying with the various requirements of the Association. Failure to do

so might well lead to exposure, followed by public condemnation as 'an enemy to the country' or worse.

Conservatives and some moderates had been saying all along that the patriot leaders merely offered their own tyranny in place of the British version they complained of so vehemently. Adoption of the Continental Association etched more sharply the lines that differentiated American opinion. In September 1774, customs comptroller Benjamin Hallowell had reported that 'in fact, Sir, those who are not for them [the mob] they say are against them; as I observed to you in a former letter that a neutrality would not be allowed of much longer, the time that I have been expecting is now come.' Boston under Gage became an asylum for men like Hallowell, as did New York city and Philadelphia further south, but thousands of other moderates and conservatives remained to face the resentment of their more radical neighbours. One writer, terming himself A CONVERTED WHIG, bitterly complained that the patriots 'allow not to others who differ from them the same liberty of thinking and acting that they claim themselves, but shamefully abuse them and treat them with spite, malice, and revenge.' [80]

A February 1775 issue of the *Boston Newsletter* listed twenty-five incidents of intimidation and worse that had occurred in the area since July. Aside from the numerous court-closings and house-wreckings there were episodes of personal abuse that bordered on torture. One man was forced to straddle a fence rail on which he was violently bounced up and down. One of the 'mandamus' councillors was confined to a room with a fire, the chimney and windows having been blocked up, until the smoke forced him to sign a resignation. In one of the more bizarre episodes another man was stuffed into the belly of a slaughtered ox while the mob carted him from town to town as he nearly suffocated among the entrails. No wonder that conservatives could view the lofty pronouncements of the patriots with considerable scepticism. [81]

Printers of moderate and conservative views like 'Jemmy' Rivington of the *New York Gazetteer* or Margaret Draper of the *Boston Newsletter* were singled out for particular abuse. The *Gazetteer* enjoyed the largest circulation of any American newspaper and was the only one with a readership in all the colonies. Furthermore, Rivington printed numerous pamphlets and other tracts on behalf of the conservative cause. The printer had *élan;* when abused in the patriot press he replied in kind, labelling the *Boston Gazette* 'Monday's Dung Barge' and the editor of the *Newport Mercury* 'Solomon Saphead'. When patriots in New Jersey hanged him in effigy, he countered by publishing a woodcut of the scene, representing himself in gentleman's attire and terming his opponents as 'snarling curs'. But all of

Rivington's courage and wit could not overcome the boycotts and seizures of his publications, and finally, in late 1775, the destruction of his press.[82]

Adoption of the Continental Association at the local level generated several lively exchanges of opinion in newspapers and political pamphlets during the winter of 1774-5. In New England Daniel Leonard and John Adams matched their considerable grasp of constitutional history as MASSACHUSETTENSIS and NOVANGLUS, respectively. At Philadelphia Joseph Galloway took on John Dickinson and Charles Thomson. In New York Thomas Chandler's *Friendly Address to All Reasonable Americans* provoked responses from two other writers. One of the most widely read series was that between 'the Westchester Farmer', Samuel Seabury, and the young Alexander Hamilton. Seabury initially attacked the Continental Association for the distress it would bring upon innocent inhabitants of England, Ireland, and the West Indies as well as upon Americans. Addressing the farmers of New York, Seabury predicted that their inability to sell their produce under the Association would bring about wide economic distress. Foreshadowing his later fame as an economist, Hamilton attempted to parry Seabury's pessimistic prophecy by analysing the trade patterns of the Empire. He tried to demonstrate that under the Association the Americans could get along well by themselves. He doubted that the colonists would be delivered by the remonstrances and petitions that Seabury and others relied upon. 'The system of slavery, fabricated against America, cannot at this time be considered as the effect of inconsideration and rashness,' he asserted. 'It is the offspring of mature deliberation.'[83]

A few weeks later Seabury widened his attack on the Congress for its failure to make any concession to the British point of view. In closing, Seabury asked his readers whether they were sure that 'while you are supporting the authority of the congress and exalting it over your own legislature, you are not nourishing and bringing into maturity a grand American Republic, which shall, after a while, rise to power and grandeur upon the ruins of our present constitution.' Seabury's thinly veiled accusation that the patriots were striving for independence became a regular theme in his later writings and in those of his fellow conservatives. By concentrating so heavily on this issue they further polarized the political spectrum by separating men into 'loyalists' like themselves or advocates of independence. In succeeding months American conservatives and almost all Englishmen became firmly convinced that colonial opponents of Great Britain sought total independence. Repetition of the charge would in time have the effect of a self-fulfilling prophecy.[84]

Through the first months of 1775 General Gage took advantage of the unseasonably mild weather to maintain careful watch on the activities of the patriots who controlled the countryside around Boston. Spies reported the doings of the Provincial Congress meeting at Concord; others told him where caches of gunpowder and munitions had been concealed. Hearing rumours of several cannon at Salem, Gage dispatched Colonel Alexander Leslie to investigate the reports and to seize whatever military supplies he could find. Upon approaching the town, however, Leslie discovered the drawbridge pulled up and a crowd of stubborn inhabitants who refused to let him cross. Meanwhile, the spreading alarm brought reinforcements from neighbouring communities marching toward Salem. A crisis was averted only by negotiating a compromise; the patriots would lower the bridge if Leslie would agree to march his troops only a token distance beyond. Having fulfilled the letter of his orders (and discovering no munitions), the colonel withdrew just before the militia from Danvers arrived.[85]

How much longer a clash of arms could be postponed under such conditions was problematical. The moderate Bostonian, Thomas Cushing, feared that once the minutemen were mustered by order of the Committee of Safety 'they will suppose it their duty to fight and for fear of being impeached of Cowardice it is more than probable they will commence hostilities. . . . Once they are begun', he concluded perceptively, 'they must be continued.' In mid-February the conservative Peter Oliver predicted that a military engagement would soon break out 'and the sooner it comes the better—the sooner we shall get to be a peaceable People. . . .' A colonel of the militia at Worcester resigned his commission in early March because he could not 'with a good conscience toward God and toward man take up arms and rebel against that prince that we and all our congress own and acknowledge to be our rightful sovereign. . . .' Three weeks later the colonel repudiated his resignation, but the agonizing dilemma that he and thousands of other colonists faced could not be easily be forgotten.[86]

Instead of the thousands of reinforcements that Gage had argued were necessary for offensive action, spring brought him (other than a few marines) only promises of the troops he needed and three generals, Howe, Burgoyne, and Clinton, whom he did not need. Spring also brought Gage something else he did not need— orders from Lord Dartmouth 'to take a more active and determined part', specifically by arresting the principal leaders of the opposition. 'Even though such a proceeding should be, according to your own idea of it, a signal for hostilities,' Dartmouth opined, 'any efforts of the people, unprepared to encounter with a regular force, cannot be very formidable.'[87]

The news that Gage expected reinforcements soon leaked out. Reports of the Restraining Act, which would now exclude New Englanders from the West Indies trade and their traditional fishing grounds, added more fuel to the simmering tempers at the Provincial Congress at Concord. The delegates began to re-examine the loose arrangement of local militia units, the now-famous 'minutemen', and proposed the establishment of a provincial army composed of over 13,000 men on eight-month enlistments. In the meantime, however, the burden of defence fell on the militia forces of each community, raw troops with little combat experience, and reluctant to obey orders despite (or because of?) the fact they elected their own officers. The best efforts of both patriots and profiteers to equip these men fell dismally short. A few soldiers had regulation Brown Bess muskets left over from service in the French and Indian War nearly twenty years before. Others possessed still older weapons from still earlier colonial wars, while most at least had some sort of hunting piece that had dropped a few deer or rabbits in its day. The rifle was as foreign to Yankees as it was to the British soldiers. Few militia had either bayonets or the experience of facing an enemy so equipped. They had something to look forward to.[88]

At the beginning of April Gage had under his command about 4,000 British regulars in eleven different regiments or parts thereof and about 500 marines from Graves's fleet. Morale was not very high, as we have seen, but these men were professionals, well drilled and disciplined, and equipped with Brown Bess muskets fixed with bayonet. This gleaming piece of steel, nearly two feet in length, made a particularly effective weapon in close combat. But the British were accustomed to fighting against troops massed as themselves; they would soon discover that the Americans had developed a somewhat different style of combat.[89]

Faced with Dartmouth's unequivocal expectation that he take some sort of immediate action, Gage decided to go ahead with his intention to raid the town of Concord, where, according to his spies, the patriots had stored a large cache of military supplies. Far from an attempt to capture the patriot leaders at the Provincial Congress (an impossible assignment) Gage's attack was in fact timed to follow close upon the adjournment of the session, while the delegates were *en route* homeward and therefore unable to mobilize resistance. But the patriots had their own spies, the unemployed workers of Boston under the leadership of Paul Revere and Joseph Warren, who had remained behind while the Provincial Congress met. In mid-April they noted that the British were collecting boats and making other preparations for military action. The patriots concluded that Concord was the probable target but could not discover whether Gage meant to send his men over Boston neck ('by land') or across the Charles River ('by sea') to Cambridge. Revere arranged to signal the Charlestown militia from the tower of the North Church to indicate which route the British were taking in case he and his fellow express rider, William Dawes, could not spread the alarm themselves. Despite every effort by Gage to cover the impending attack all of Boston seemed to know of it by nightfall on the 18th. Both Revere and Dawes made their escape by separate routes and aroused the communities along the way toward Lexington. There they were joined by a third rider, Dr. Samuel Prescott, who was the only one to carry the alarm all the way to Concord, as a British patrol intercepted both Dawes and Revere.[90]

Around midnight the British forces crossed the Charles River. Gage had assigned his grenadier and light infantry companies to the expedition, a total of about 700 men under the command of Lieutenant Colonel Francis Smith. Unaware that his mission was no longer secret, Smith took elaborate precautions. The light infantry under the command, oddly enough, of a marine major, John Pitcairn, seized the few passers-by they encountered to prevent disclosure. Meanwhile, on Lexington green Captain John Parker and his 130 minutemen began to assemble in uncertain anticipation of the ominous news Revere had brought. As hour succeeded chilly hour, however, the men grew weary and were allowed to return to nearby homes or the tavern until summoned.

A little before dawn on 19 April 1775, the signal came to the Lexington minutemen that the British had arrived. About seventy militiamen managed to find weapons and fall into two ranks on the green about a hundred yards from the road. Seventy militia were opposing ten times that number of professional soldiers, now coming into sight. Major Pitcairn rode ahead and shouted to the villagers 'Lay down your arms, you damned rebels, and disperse!' Parker apparently ordered his men to comply, and gradually some of them began to move away, but without dropping their weapons. Each commander had ordered his men not to fire, but suddenly a shot rang out, followed by a few more. Then a volley from one of the British platoons ripped into the confused mêlée of Americans. Pitcairn rode among his troops and repeatedly commanded them to cease fire, but before he could regain control, eight Americans were killed, another ten wounded. Old Jonas Parker, a cousin of the militia captain, was bayoneted as he tried to reload his musket; young Jonathan Harrington, mortally wounded, crawled back to the door of his own house facing the green and died, nearly at the feet of his wife and son; Isaac Muzzy fell not far from the line in which he had stood with his father. The war that came to America that day came close to the people.

Although suffering only one minor casualty, the British forces abandoned Pitcairn's original aim of disarming the colonials and instead marched off toward Concord as the sun rose over Lexington green. Meanwhile, patriot riders had fanned out to alert most of the other communities around Boston. Hundreds, then thousands of minutemen grabbed their weapons and headed toward the scene of action. The men of Concord made good use of their advance warning to hide as much as possible of the provincial war materiel in their care.

As the British forces entered the town, the Americans fell back without offering resistance. Reinforced by units arriving from neighbouring towns, they took up defensive positions across the North bridge, which led to the farm where most of the munitions had been stored. Part of the British force remained in the village, wrecking a few cannon, damaging some flour, and throwing gun carriages and other combustibles into several bonfires. Another group took control of the bridge, while a third detachment headed off to destroy the cache of provincial weapons.

When the Americans on the far side of the river saw smoke rising from the village, they concluded that the British were about to burn down the town. They decided, as they said, 'to march into the middle of the town for its defense or die in the attempt.' Under strict orders not to fire unless fired upon, they advanced toward the much smaller British force covering the bridge. Now the redcoats hastily retreated but found themselves jumbled together on the village side of the bridge. As the Americans started across, a few shots came from the British troops, then a volley or two, and the colonial band returned the fire, killing two soldiers and wounding several others—the first British casualties to fall in the first actual battle of the American Revolution.

The Americans did not press their advantage, and Colonel Smith succeeded in reuniting his forces for the march back to Boston. As more minutemen swarmed to the scene, this meant running a seventeen-mile gauntlet along the same country roads he had followed to Concord that morning. At noon they set out, but as they reached the edge of town, the British troops ran into an ambush at the crossing of a small stream. For long stretches the road to Lexington ran between stone walls, from behind which the Americans poured withering volleys into the columns of redcoats. Smith sent out flankers who exacted a toll of colonial militia, but newly arriving minutemen took up positions further along the road. As they approached Lexington the British began to run out of ammunition, and they were dog-tired besides.

Shortly after beginning his march the night before Smith had sent word back for a relief force to cover his return. Now 1,000 soldiers and marines under the command of General Earl Percy met them at Lexington in mid-afternoon. After allowing time for Smith's men to rest, Percy led the way back toward Boston. Along the route were at least 2,000 minutemen, firing away from behind walls, trees, and buildings. Flanker parties smashed their way into numerous homes, mostly to rout out their adversaries, but also to harass the occupants and loot their possessions. The line between soldier and citizen was impossible to draw when one was fighting a citizen-soldiery. Toward nightfall the long weary column of regulars reached the comparative safety of Charlestown and were ferried across to Boston. In twenty hours Smith's men had marched thirty-five miles, the latter half of it under almost continuous fire, while Percy's men had covered more than twenty miles since morning. Altogether the British suffered 273 casualties, including 73 dead, out of a total force of about 1,800. Of the nearly 4,000 colonial militia who fought sometime during the day (not more than half at any one time), 49 were killed and another 46 wounded or missing.

While Colonel Smith and his troops were carrying out Gage's orders, the General himself remained behind. He wrote a routine letter that day to Lord Dartmouth without mentioning Smith's expedition to Concord. Three days later writing to his friend and superior in London, Lord Barrington, Gage opened with the usual acknowledgement of correspondence received. 'I have now nothing to trouble your lordship with,' he then continued, 'but of an affair that happened here on the 19th instant.' There followed a brief factual account of the expedition in which the only mention of British casualties was a postscript reference to 'a return of the killed and wounded' accompanying the letter. Gage was after all not particularly surprised to learn that Smith had met with opposition, and the actual outbreak of hostilities, though costly to his forces, seemed to have relatively little immediate effect on a professional soldier like Gage. Officers engaged in the day's operation, not quite prepared for the tenacity with which the Americans fought, seemed somewhat more surprised. But for them too, the expedition was a part of their professional work. For the 4,000 Americans who bore arms against His Majesty's troops, however, the day had a far different meaning. On 19 April 1775 their resistance became a revolution.[91]

XII

'Tis Time to Part'

———•—•———

1. Lexington Blues

AFTER APRIL 1775 the British ministers were firmly committed to the policy of suppressing rebellion in Massachusetts, if necessary by force. While still hoping for the best, they were prepared to extend action in support of this policy to any other part of the North American continent where this seemed necessary. Moreover, the terms which they believed indispensable for the continuance of the British Empire had been spelled out in North's so-called 'conciliatory' propositions, and they were not prepared to budge from them. Developments at Philadelphia or elsewhere in the rebellious colonies during the remaining fourteen months up to the Declaration of Independence could make no change in the policy and, indeed, their only effect was to reinforce it: the ministers simply reacted to American events in accordance with their previous decisions.

On 15 April, four days before the engagement at Lexington and Concord, Dartmouth sent Gage a long dispatch full of instruction and exhortation. Gage was to seize such strong points as he could and destroy any fortified places he could not hold, collect any guns or arms that might be put to rebel use, and arrest the men whom the law officers had advised might be charged with treason and rebellion. There could be no hesitation in employing troops against open resistance: 'The authority of government must be maintained, let the consequence be what it may.' The ministry assumed that, with the reinforcements about to set out, Gage would have ample forces available to restore legal government in New England. It was suggested that, if possible, he should also establish a substantial corps at New York.[1] Save that Gage now received a copy of the Act restraining the trade of the New England colonies—the conciliatory resolution had already been sent to him [2]—this message marked no new departure since Dartmouth's dispatch of 27 January.[3] It crossed with an urgent plea from Gage to Barrington for the deployment of all forces that could be made available. 'If you yield', Gage wrote, 'I conceive that you have not a spark of authority remaining over this country.' [4]

As in the previous spring the government now faced a period of waiting. Measures were taken: it remained to be seen what the results would be. Parliament's business was nearly finished. In mid-May the Houses received, but declined to consider, the remonstrance from the assembly of New York, on the ground that it challenged parliamentary supremacy. A day or two later the ministers beat off an opposition proposal for the repeal of the Quebec Act. Parliament rose on the 26th. The next day the first news of the clash at Lexington and Concord reached England from rebel sources.

Open warfare had thus begun before the assembly of the forces the ministers thought necessary to deal with the situation; but for the first fortnight they made light of it, dismissing the report of heavy casualties as a rebel exaggeration for propaganda purposes. 10 June brought Gage's confirmation in almost every detail, and the need for a reassessment of the situation became evident. The same ship brought news that New York had declared for the Congress. Under these blows King and ministers stood firm. To Dartmouth George III wrote that day: 'America must be a colony of England or treated as an enemy. Distant possessions standing upon an equality with the superior state is more ruinous than being deprived of such connections.' On 14 and 15 June the cabinet hammered out initial proposals, which were cast into final form on the 21st.[5] Units were to be brought up to strength at augmented establishments, Carleton in Canada was to recruit 2,000 light infantry; six regiments were to be withdrawn from Minorca and Gibraltar to permit an equivalent force to be sent across the Atlantic, and the King was asked to provide Hanoverians in their place. Orders were given for extra frigates and naval transports. 'No situation', the King wrote to Sandwich on 1 July, 'can ever change my fixed resolution, either to bring the colonies to a due obedience to the legislature of the mother country or to cast them off.' [6] For the present the second alternative was thought out of the question.

Between 24 June and 16 July Dartmouth received more reports from Gage dated between 13 May and 12 June, and a further detailed appreciation sent possibly by Howe or Burgoyne.[7] These made it clear that Gage's augmented force was now besieged within Boston with little hope of undertaking any effective operation, and that still larger forces would be required. Gage proposed a three-pronged attack upon New England, with 15,000 men from Boston, another 10,000 from New York, and 7,000 from Canada—32,000 troops in all, including Canadians and Indians in the northern force. He urged the immediate employment of foreign troops, knowing that such forces could not readily be raised in Great Britain.[8]

It was in the light of these reports that on 26 July the cabinet reached a series of short and long term decisions. Further immediate reinforcements were scraped together for Gage. In such a crisis the normal establishment in Ireland must be cut, and five regiments sent across from there. Another 1,000 was added to the proposed Canadian force. Recruiting was to be stepped up with the idea of placing 20,000 regulars in America by the following April.[9] Thus the government accepted that a full-scale war had now broken out in New England, but they proposed to work from Gage's estimate of the previous autumn instead of the more realistic demand he had just formulated. Pessimism about recruitment may have contributed to this decision. Secretary-at-War Barrington was aghast when he learned the April target of regulars for America and expressed strong doubts both to Dartmouth and to George III about the country's capacity to achieve it.[10] The King, however, urged that everything possible must be done: 'as I now look upon ourselves as in an avowed state of war every means must be adopted to quicken that business.'[11] To North he reaffirmed his determination: 'We must persist and not be dismayed by any difficulties that may arise on either side of the Atlantic; I know I am doing my duty and therefore can never wish to retract; the Resolution proposed by the House of Commons is the utmost that can be come into; and if people will have patience this must in the end be obtained.'[12] Since Gage seemed unable to master the situation, he must go.[13] So confidently did ministers believe that their show of force and determination would suffice to lower the pretensions of the Congress, so badly did they underestimate the colonial will to resist, that Dartmouth wrote expectantly on 6 August to one of his under-secretaries: 'If they mean to admit duties for regulation of trade, and will add to that a revenue for the support of civil government, and such military force as they shall themselves desire to have among them, I think we may soon be agreed.'[14]

During the summer the ministers received reports from Gage, Dunmore, and other sources, leaving them in no doubt that, in terms of their conception of the Empire, the colonists were now set upon winning independence.[15] At the same time, reports from the southern colonies caused them once again to underestimate the forces arrayed against them and so confirmed their belief in their policy. Letters from Governor Martin of North Carolina, in refuge on a British warship, told of addresses signed by thousands of loyalists in the Piedmont and held out the promise of a restoration of royal government if he were sent arms and a small force of regulars. Similar news came from Virginia and South Carolina.[16] The belief that all over the south the grip of the Congress was precarious and easily to be broken encouraged the government to ignore the Congress's 'Olive Branch' petition brought to England by Richard Penn in late September. Since it made no concession to the terms on which ministers had been agreed for the best part of a year, there seemed nothing to discuss. Moreover the petition awakened the liveliest distrust, for various intercepted letters had by now convinced the ministers that they were faced with a deep-laid plot hatched in New England to gain independence.[17]

On the basis of this intelligence, plans for military redeployment in the north became entangled with the scheme of a southern expedition. Following the unanimous advice of Gage and his staff the cabinet agreed that Boston should be evacuated and the main base of British operations against New England be set up at New York. There more loyalist support was expected, supplies would be more readily available, and control of the Hudson valley would isolate the New England colonies. Part of the military reinforcement was to be diverted to the south during the winter, on the assumption that small detachments would make possible the re-establishment of royal government there, and that the force would be able to return to New York for a campaign against New England in the early spring. A force to strike at New England from Canada was also projected. Thus, although Gage no longer had the confidence of the ministers and was recalled 'for consultations'—in fact to be superseded at Boston by Sir William Howe—the ministers adopted in modified form his plan for a concentric campaign to isolate and crush New England. During October they also discussed the setting up of a commission to receive submissions, grant pardons, and authorize the re-establishment of legitimate governments in the colonies. The post was offered to, but declined by Lord George Germain, who had emerged as a strong champion of the cause of imperial unity during the previous parliamentary session.

In view of the gathering crisis the ministers felt bound to assemble Parliament earlier than usual. Weeks before it met North began to express fears that the government would come under 'very powerful' attack. The King refused to believe it: 'If the Opposition is powerful next session it will much surprise me for I am fighting the battle of the legislature, therefore have a right to expect an almost unanimous support, if there should arise difficulties they will not dismay me, for I know the uprightness of my intentions.'[18] In the event there were to be a few shifts of political loyalty on either side, but no serious alteration of the overwhelming balance of parliamentary strength in favour of the ministry. Unable to give support to a civil war Grafton declared himself and received his dismission from the Privy Seal, carrying off into opposition General Conway and one or two other personal connections. The Fitzpatrick family, hitherto part of the ministerial Bedford party, withdrew support, provoking a regretful rebuke from the head of the connection, Lord President Gower: 'I think that in the course of the next six months, it must be seen whether this country must abandon its interests in America for ever or whether it is in the power of this country to reclaim it. Drawn on to this situation with the opinion of my friends, and led by my own conscientious duty to my king and country, I feel myself the most unhappy of men to be abandoned by my friends.' [19]

Parliament met on 26 October. The debate on the King's speech and the address bore out George III's confidence in the support of the legislature. The speech stated that 'the rebellious war now levied is become more general, and is manifestly carried on for the purpose of establishing an independent empire.' Opposition was 'violent but not formidable'. In the Commons a vehement debate continued till 4 a.m. the following morning, but the address was carried by a great majority. 'The tone of measures', wrote one M.P., 'seems to be that of exertion but with every inclination to peace'; and North 'spoke to the admiration of all the House and to the approbation of the greatest part of it.' [20] A fortnight later, opposing in the Lords a motion that the 'Olive Branch' petition provided grounds for a conciliation, Dartmouth, on the last day of his service as colonial secretary, defended the government's rejection of it. A petition from the Congress, he averred, could not be recognized, 'without at the same instant relinquishing the sovereignty of the British Parliament.' The issue at stake was no longer taxation but 'the allegiance of the colonies, which administration were desirous of obtaining.' Moreover, 'the petition, in terms, was unexceptionable, but there was every reason to believe that the softness of the language was purposely adopted to conceal the most traitorous designs.' [21]

Grafton's dismissal made necessary a ministerial reshuffle. Dartmouth had no stomach to be a war minister. At the same time North was unwilling to lose his support from the cabinet, and their joint wishes were satisfied by Dartmouth's transfer to the Privy Seal. Rochford was elderly and ill, and his willingness to retire made it possible to offer the seals of the southern department to Lord Weymouth in lieu of his competing claims to the Privy Seal. Dartmouth's vacant office was given to Lord George Germain. The general effect of these arrangements was to strengthen the more unyielding element in the cabinet and to place colonial affairs and the conduct of war in America in the hands of a former professional soldier who was dedicated to the task of preserving British authority in America.[22]

From then on the government was steadily clearing the decks for action. As the dispatch of regular troops to America created a problem of defence and maintenance of order at home, a Bill empowering the King to embody the militia, introduced at the beginning of the session, was rapidly pushed through, receiving the royal assent on 4 December.[23] On the 22nd assent was given to a Bill prohibiting all intercourse with the colonies while they remained in a state of rebellion, making their ships liable to capture and their crews to impressment, and authorizing the Crown to appoint commissioners to receive submissions, grant pardons, and restore normal government and commercial intercourse to communities which returned to their allegiance.[24] An attempt by Burke to present the outlines of his conciliatory proposal in the form of a Bill received short shrift in the Commons on 15 November. In a long and serious debate, lasting till nearly 4 a.m., critics from all sides of the House pointed out that leaving all the Rockingham ministry's legislation intact, as Burke proposed, would in no way satisfy the colonists, and Thomas Pownall observed that the demands of the Congress implied an overhaul of all laws back to the Navigation Act of 1673. Burke's motion was thrown out by 210 votes to 105. An alternative proposal by David Hartley on 7 December attracted only 21 votes.[25] Meanwhile, at the end of November, in response to a petition from the assembly of Nova Scotia, the Commons took preliminary steps to place the fiscal arrangements in that province on the basis recommended by North's conciliatory propositions. It approved a revenue from port duties, to be voted by the local legislature at a flat rate of eight per cent *ad valorem,* and a proposal for a modification of the Navigation Acts to enable wines and fruits to be imported directly into Halifax from their countries of origin in Southern Europe. Once the province's votes of taxation had been approved by the King in council, all duties laid by Act of Parliament would cease to be levied there. Incidental revenues arising from parliamentary regulation of trade were to be credited to the provincial treasury. The Commons ordered a Bill to be brought in, but there the matter lapsed.[26]

The hiring of foreign troops for service in America was under discussion at least from the beginning of October. In mid-November the cabinet pressed on the King the need to obtain regiments from both Hesse-Cassel and Brunswick,[27] and during the winter negotiations were conducted with urgency. Before the start of the next campaigning season the government secured a series of agreements with minor German states providing for a total of over 17,000 men.[28]

Military planning involved from the first some dispersal of

forces, since the government was committed to send five regiments in hopes of aiding loyalist movements in the southern colonies. But furthermore, the initially successful American campaign into Canada forced Germain to allot larger reinforcements for Carleton than originally intended, and to give their dispatch priority over the main body of troops destined to join Sir William Howe for operations in New York. The organization of expeditions, supplies, and naval escorts, all took longer than expected. Consequently the main forces for Carleton did not leave England until the beginning of April and those for Howe three weeks later. Moreover, Howe, having extricated his force from Boston in mid-March, required time to regroup and gather provisions at Halifax. Summer and the announcement of Independence were to come before British forces were ready for major offensive operations in America.

On 3 May the Howe brothers, Admiral Richard Lord Howe and Sir William, respectively commanding the naval and military forces in America, were appointed commissioners to receive submissions in the colonies, and restore normal conditions, in accordance with the terms of the enabling Act passed the previous December. Negotiation was no part of the commissioners' task. In the spring of 1776 the ministers had no thoughts of conciliation along such lines. They demanded surrender and the restoration of 'legitimate' government. The Massachusetts Charter Act was to stand, and they were intent on remodelling the other New England governments more on the 'royal' pattern, at least to the extent of securing imperial control over legislation and the appointment of governors. They insisted upon the fiscal arrangements sketched in North's proposals of February 1775. Ministers believed these terms were necessary to maintain the constitutional unity of the Empire which was essential to its economic well-being and its continued existence as a Great Power, and they were determined to impose them if necessary by force of arms.[29]

Debates and divisions in both Houses during the last eighteen months before the American Declaration of Independence provide ample illustration of the range of British points of view on the American question.

There is little doubt that the ultimate consideration, steeling British politicians against any concessions to demands which they identified with virtual independence of the American colonies, was fear of the collapse of the power system which enabled the British nation to compete on equal if not superior terms in the international jungle, particularly in relation to its long-standing rival, France. The controlled monopolistic imperial commercial system was regarded as an engine for the continuance of economic defensive and offensive

operations in those periods when war itself was suspended. Time
and again during these debates the alarm was sounded, that to concede the demands of the Congress would mean the end of the Navigation Acts and the destruction of the system. In March 1776 the
Earl of Carlisle declared that if control over America were lost,
Great Britain would sink into obscurity and insignificance, falling at
length 'a prey to the first powerful or ambitious state, which may
meditate a conquest of this island.' [30] Abandonment of commercial
control would mean that America's resources would benefit poten-
tially hostile nations and that the pressures of economic warfare
could not be applied [31]—considerations which put out of court the
suggestion of trading a free American commerce in exchange for
taxation.

Although American taxation had become a secondary issue by
1775, it nevertheless remained among the objectives of the government. The majority of the British politicians believed that in equity
as well as in law the colonists owed a contribution to the costs of
defence—landed gentry conscious of the effects of the land-tax were
particularly hot on this point [32]—and they had come to regard permanent civil lists as an indispensable support for executive government in the colonies. Such an arrangement was seen as equivalent to
the King's civil list at home—a permanent financial allocation for
peacetime government, with which the legislature did not attempt to
interfere. Fear of another sort had also become enmeshed in the fiscal argument—fear that if Parliament did not control all defence ap-
propriations within the Empire, a future sovereign, obtaining independent supplies from legislatures in America, might one day
reduce Parliament's own role to a nullity. [33]

Many of these anxieties were summed up in the speech by John
Dyke Acland, the well-briefed mover of the address at the beginning
of the session on 26 October 1775. [34] 'Whatever the original contest
might be', he declared, 'it is now lost in a contest for independence
and empire.' He believed this had long been the object: 'The Congress, in their observations on the conciliatory plan offered by Parliament last year, triumphantly demand, "What right Britain has to
interfere with her government, since she does not interfere with that
of Britain?" Is not this the language of an independent state?' All the
actions and the intercepted American correspondence of the past six
months signified their intention to found an independent extensive
empire. The question facing Parliament was simply whether 'to acquiesce in the independence of America or to enforce their submission.' Acland argued that American independence would mean the
loss of the American trade, a threat to West Indian commerce, and
the establishment of a rival to British enterprise everywhere: 'I must

maintain, that it would have been better for this country that
America had never been known than that a great consolidated
American empire should exist independent of Great Britain.'

During the opening part of this last stage of the crisis—indeed,
perhaps right up to its end—men in governing circles still grossly
underestimated the degree and the extent of the resistance likely to
be offered in America. At first they thought they were dealing only
with a minority in Massachusetts.[35] In November 1774 ministers
believed that the delegates of the Continental Congress 'were far
from expressing the true sense of the respectable part of their constituents.' [36] The following February Hillsborough, not in office but
still supporting the government's line, suggested more cautiously,
that at least a third of the colonists were willing to submit to Parliament.[37] Right up to Lexington and Concord many had the impression that the colonists would give way to an unyielding display of
force, and some thought that they would find themselves so dis-
traught by their own internal quarrels and by foreign pressures if
Britain withdrew her protection, that they would soon sue to be re-
admitted to it.[38] Faith in the existence of large bodies of loyalists
merely waiting for the protection of some royal troops in order to
restore legitimate government in their provinces died hard. In particular, it seems that no one on the government side could grasp the
vulnerability of a small professional army, however efficient, faced
by inexhaustible numbers of determined guerrillas fighting for
hearth and home and a cause in which they believed.

Opposition attacks upon the government's policy made the most
of this last point. In one guise or another it came up in almost every
debate.[39] Nor was it applied only to the war itself. More than one
speaker pointed out that the rapid growth of the colonies put out of
the realm of possibility any long-term British domination. The question was therefore, 'not . . . how we shall be able to realize such a
delusive scheme of dominion, but how we shall make it their interest
to continue faithful allies and warm friends.' [40] Less frequently than
might be expected, M.P.s and peers referred to the dangers of
foreign intervention.[41] Beyond these arguments unanimity broke
down, and the niceties of constitutional theory which had separated
followers of Rockingham and of Chatham ever since 1766 divided
them still. Burke as chief spokesman of the former party continued
to uphold the principle of the Declaratory Act, while seeking to
define and reconcile with it a political understanding that parliamentary supremacy should only be exercised by agreement, and he apparently failed to see the unacceptability to the colonists of the Revenue Act of 1766.[42] The Chathamite wing of the opposition,
especially Camden and Shelburne, its leaders in the Lords when

Chatham was ill, reverted to and broadened their arguments of 1766, declaring that Parliament had no right to tax the colonists, and they were joined in this by the little band of Wilkesite radicals with whom at this time Arthur and William Lee and Stephen Sayre were closely associated.[43] A variant of this argument advanced on at least one occasion ran to the effect that, even if the parliamentary right of taxation had once existed, it had been applied so little in the century before 1746 that in effect it had gone into disuse.[44] Numbers of opposition speakers, and especially the Wilkesites, persisted in emphasizing the dangers of military power to public liberty. Some of them raised the bogey of a secret junto manipulating the ministers and plotting behind the scenes to erect despotism upon the grave of liberty in both America and Great Britain.[45]

From November 1774 till March 1776 the parliamentary opposition conducted an unremitting and well-fought campaign against government policies which they believed would bring on a disastrous civil war within the Empire. The record provides an impressive vindication of the role of Parliament in this period as an instrument of discussion of great political issues. Opportunities for debate were ample, and every argument on both sides was canvassed to the point of exhaustion.[46] But the opposition could make virtually no impression on the independent country gentlemen, most of whom supported the government and who in so doing reflected the attitude of the informed classes in the country at large. On 7 June 1775 the Scottish M.P., George Dempster, wrote to a friend: [47]

> In Scotland, myself and a very few more excepted, the whole body of the gentry and of the independent and enlightened class of people are to a man on the side of administration. . . . There is a principle against America as well as for her, insomuch that it would not be easy for a ministry more favourable to her to bring the bulk of the House over to their opinion.

When the outbreak of hostilities at Lexington and Concord reinforced the impression that the colonists were indeed seeking independence, most of the hitherto critical merchant groups rallied to the ministry.[48] 'The violent measures towards America are fairly adopted and countenanced by a majority of individuals of all ranks, professions, or occupations in this country', Rockingham wrote to Burke on 24 September.[49] This firm balance of opinion against America was faithfully reflected in the parliamentary divisions. In the Lords on major occasions the government majorities were usually in the proportion of five to two, if not more, and the opposition could never raise more than 29 votes, to which the ministry could oppose a phalanx often rising from 80 to 100. In the Commons the government normally had a majority of about three to one, despite the fact that fifty or so placeholders were usually absent on government service of one kind or another. Only on rare occasions could the opposition bring just over one hundred votes into the lobby. In November 1774 the ministry carried the address by 264 votes to 73. At the end of the following January Edward Gibbon noted that the figures were usually about 250 to 80 or 90. In two divisions on the address of 2 February 1775 on the American disturbances, in which the opposition brought up almost every vote, the government carried the day by 304 to 105, and 296 to 106. Burke's conciliatory motion of 22 March 1775 was defeated by 270 to 78. In October 1775 the address was carried by 278 to 108, in November Burke's conciliatory Bill was dismissed by 210 to 105, and in December the government won by 207 to 55 in the crucial vote on its Prohibitory Bill. As North was to claim long afterwards, the American war was truly the war of Parliament and of the British people.[50]

2. Independence—The Last Resort

Shortly after the battle of Lexington and Concord the printers of Massachusetts published accounts of the day's events which highlighted alleged atrocities such as looting and harassment of civilians by the British troops. A broadside published by the *Salem Gazette* featured forty black coffins across the top of its black-bordered front page, each one labelled with the name of an American killed in action. Headlines (a rarity in the eighteenth century) proclaimed 'A BLOODY BUTCHERY BY THE BRITISH TROOPS: OR THE RUNAWAY FIGHT OF THE REGULARS.' The Provincial Congress ordered the general distribution of its official *Narrative of the Excursion and Ravages of the King's Troops.*

After Lexington and Concord the definition of a patriot sharply narrowed, for now one had to defend the use of arms against the King's troops. Loyalists, on the other hand, had to assume the almost impossible burden of siding with the 'aggressors' of 19 April. The middle ground between those who endorsed a resort to arms by the Americans on the one hand or by the British on the other had all but disappeared in the smoke of battle.

From the beginning of the imperial crisis more than a decade earlier, the goal for most colonists who were concerned at all had been to restore the harmony of the years before 1763 by seeking a redress of specific grievances—such as parliamentary taxation, customs abuses, or currency restrictions. Only a few colonists explicitly denied that these were indeed valid grievances, although many Americans of course ignored these issues altogether. What men did disagree about were the means appropriate for gaining redress, the principal alternatives ranging from respectful petitions and peaceful boycotts to intimidation of officials and mob violence. News of the Coercive Acts initiated a gradual change of focus that was greatly accelerated by the clash at Lexington and Concord. Instead of the somewhat passive goal of restoring earlier conditions, Americans increasingly came to express their objective in more aggressive terms— the establishment and defence of American rights. The change was one of emphasis, for the two goals were at first regarded as mutually compatible. But the movement away from the older goal required the consideration of a different set of means. As hope of persuading the British ministry to change its policies waned, so did belief in the relevance of petitions and boycotts. In their place appeared methods viewed as more suitable to the redefined goal—military action, extralegal governing bodies on both the local and continental levels, and a search for outside support.

Prior to the outbreak of hostilities the enemy who threatened American rights seemed to many colonists rather remote and impersonal in the form of the British ministry. Indeed the rights themselves—life, liberty, property—remained abstractions for many Americans. But Gage's march into the countryside transformed the enemy into the dreaded image of the professional soldier, glistening bayonet fixed to the tip of his musket and with orders to trample all opponents under foot. And because they were dramatically threatened, abstract rights also took more concrete forms—the town, the home, the family. To defend such values as these a man had both the right and the duty to bear arms against the foe, many colonists believed, or to adopt whatever other means might be necessary for self-preservation.

The news of Lexington and Concord was carried by express riders from Massachusetts to Virginia within a week's time. In New York the moderate Committee of Sixty took immediate action to stop shipment of provisions to the British army at Boston. A mass meeting on 24 April approved the proposal to organize a militia and take other defensive measures, and to grant the committee broad powers over the city's civil affairs. A battalion of 700 men 'tolerably well equipped considering how recently a military spirit has prevailed amongst us' took effective control of the city. 'I fear that all hope of reconciliation is at an end,' wrote one New Yorker to the merchant Richard Champion. 'Surely this proceeding on the part of General Gage is not the olive branch held up by government,' wrote another correspondent. New York conservatives managed to retain a voice within the committee after it was expanded to 100 members, but they were forced to make major concessions to the advocates of military preparedness.[51]

News of the battle at Lexington and Concord reached Philadelphia within five days and had in the words of Governor John Penn 'so great an effect on the minds of the People . . . as to engage them to enter into a military association. They have already begun to form into companies and are daily acquainting themselves with the military exercise. . . .' Quaker pacificism could not stem the tide toward the preparations for war that swept through the colony. Some patriots seemed to welcome the change. 'The Americans fight for everything that are most dear to them—their lives, liberties, and fortunes,' enthused Edward Shippen from his home in Lancaster, although he hastened to add his hope that not another drop of blood would be spilt. The news had profound political effects as well: 'It's admirable to see the alteration of the Tory class in this place,' the merchant Christopher Marshall confided in his diary. 'Their language is quite softened and many of them have so far renounced their former sentiments as that they have taken up arms.' [52]

Virginians had their own reasons for anger when they learned on 21 April that Governor Dunmore had sent a detachment of marines to seize the provincial powder stored in Williamsburg. The Independent Company of Fredericksburg prepared to march on the capital, as did similar groups from other localities. News of Lexington and Concord simply added momentum to the military preparations which the Virginia convention held in March had already urged be undertaken. (It was there too that the brash Patrick Henry had allegedly uttered his famous 'Give me liberty or give me death' speech.) Another radical Virginian greeted news of the outbreak of hostilities as proof that 'moderation construed into cowardice would induce the British Parliament to try coercive measures and engage all America in a civil war.' To Thomas Jefferson the battle of Lexington and Concord was an 'accident [that] has cut off our last hopes of reconciliation.' In a draft of the same letter Jefferson reported that 10,000 men in arms had begun to march toward Williamsburg in response to the powder episode, the vanguard turning back only after the intercession 'of the principal people'. Another Virginian, one whose life was to be totally changed by what had happened in Massachusetts, also reflected upon the significance of that day. From Philadelphia George Washington wrote to his friend George Fairfax:

Unhappy it is though to reflect that a brother's sword has been sheathed in a brother's breast, and that the once happy and peaceful plains of America are either to be drenched with blood or inhabited by slaves—sad alternative! But can a virtuous man hesitate in his choice? [53]

As Americans responded to the outbreak of hostilities, their delegates gathered at Philadelphia for the second Continental Congress, convening now under circumstances radically different from those of the previous autumn. The Congress itself became what it had not been before—a continental legislature. Thereafter the body sat with only brief recesses for the duration of the war. On 26 May the Congress denounced the ministry's attempts 'to carry into execution by force of arms several unconstitutional and oppressive acts of the British Parliament. . . .' The delegates thereupon resolved 'that for the purpose of securing and defending these colonies . . . , [they] be immediately put into a state of defense.' Armed resistance, then, became continental policy. At the same time, however, the Congress also resolved to petition the King once again for redress of grievances, notwithstanding George III's rejection of its previous entreaty. The resolutions closed with a decision to open negotiations toward accommodation of the disputes with Great Britain.[54]

The will of the Congress was almost immediately tested by two queries from the Provincial Congress of Massachusetts. First, what advice could the Continental Congress give the provincial body 'respecting the taking up and exercising the powers of civil government' in Massachusetts? Second, would the Continental Congress consider taking over the direction of the army now gathering from different colonies in Massachusetts? In its reply on 9 June the Congress resolved that the inhabitants of Massachusetts owed no obedience to the Coercive Acts nor to any governor who endeavored to subvert the colony's charter by enforcing those laws. Therefore 'the governor and lieutenant-governor of that colony are to be considered as absent, and these offices vacant.' The continental delegates recommended that the Provincial Congress authorize the election of a new assembly and council in Massachusetts to 'exercise the powers of government until a governor of his Majesty's appointment will consent to govern the colony according to its charter.' During the week following the Congress answered the second query from Massachusetts by authorizing ten companies of riflemen from Pennsylvania, Maryland, and Virginia to serve in the 'American continental army' before Boston, and by appointing George Washington as commander-in-chief. On the following day other staff officers were commissioned. The colonies now had, at least on paper, a continental army 'for the defense of American liberty and for repelling every hostile invasion thereof.'[55]

From the day of Lexington and Concord itself militiamen had been flocking toward Cambridge, where the American troops outside of Boston had established their headquarters. Old Colonel Israel Putnam learned of the battle while at work on his farm in

Connecticut. Despite the ridicule and abuse he had suffered for his precipitate response to the false alarm of September, Putnam dropped his tools and hastened to Cambridge with whatever men he could arouse en route. Within days, thousands of New England militiamen had taken up positions around Boston, completely sealing off Gage and his army (and officials) from the territory they were supposedly governing. (No wonder Gage's proclamation in mid-June putting all of Massachusetts under martial law produced snickers among the Americans.) But the mass of men who ringed the seaport during those warm spring days could hardly be called an army. Units and individuals departed as they pleased (or as spring farming chores dictated) and others arrived, the total number fluctuating from 15,000 to 20,000. General Artemas Ward of Massachusetts assumed overall command, and militia from the other colonies for the most part tacitly deferred to the 'home team' leader. Problems of supply and logistics were a nightmare. The troops had precious little powder, not enough tents, and virtually no uniforms. Only half a dozen artillery pieces supplemented the small arms that most of the men could furnish for themselves. The kitchen of Harvard College became the centre of attention as commissary officers wrestled with the challenging task of feeding such a horde of men.[56]

Within the city Gage had his own problems. Now Boston was 'blockaded' from the land as it once had been by the sea. Thousands of patriots wanted to leave, while equal numbers of loyalists sought asylum within. For a time refugees were exchanged, Gage taking precautions not to allow evacuees to take their weapons with them. Skirmishes broke out on various harbour islands and nearby peninsulas as the British scoured the area for hay and provisions, but neither side dared to launch an all-out attack upon the other. At the end of May, Generals William Howe, Henry Clinton, and John Burgoyne arrived. Each would have a turn at diminishing his own military reputation in America.[57]

Elsewhere the Americans were taking decisive action of their own. The smoke had barely cleared from the battlefield at Concord when the eyes of New Englanders were drawn toward Fort Ticonderoga on Lake Champlain, the gateway from New York to Canada. Yankees had helped capture the post in the French and Indian War, and they knew that it harboured both cannon and gunpowder. Furthermore, they realized that in friendly hands Ticonderoga and its companion posts could block a British invasion from Canada or serve as jumping-off points for an American 'liberation' of that province. A committee from Connecticut took the initiative in planning the attack, although the idea seems to have come from Benedict Arnold, a successful merchant and militia captain from New Haven, who even then showed signs of the vanity that would in time make him the most hated man in America. The Connecticut group called upon Ethan Allen, who lived in what was to become Vermont, where he headed a band of frontiersmen calling themselves the 'Green Mountain Boys'. Armed with a commission from Massachusetts, Arnold joined the expedition *en route,* but it was Allen's show. On 10 May his men captured the poorly defended fort at Ticonderoga and with it seventy-eight usable cannon, nine tons of bullets, and vast quantities of other material. When the Congress learned of these riches, however, it ordered a careful inventory 'in order that they may be safely returned' upon the restoration of peace.[58]

In early June the Massachusetts Council of War recommended that Bunker Hill on Charlestown neck just north of Boston be fortified, for reasons that have never been adequately explained. Although the position would give its possessors a commanding elevation overlooking Boston and its harbour, the Americans had no artillery large enough to take advantage of the situation. However, the New Englanders began their task on the night of 16 June, having chosen Breed's Hill for the main redoubt while Colonel Putnam established headquarters on Bunker Hill nearby. By morning the work was only partially completed. The British discovered the scheme and opened fire from their warships anchored nearby. Gage and his staff pondered the situation, and, recognizing the vulnerability of the Americans, planned an immediate assault. By noon about 1,500 regulars under General William Howe embarked for the short trip across the mouth of the Charles River to make their landing. But all this gave the Americans enough time to bring up reinforcements and to extend their lines protecting the redoubt on Breed's Hill. Putnam's men worked feverishly to fortify the path of retreat back over the narrow neck to the mainland.[59]

The battle opened in the mid-afternoon heat of an unseasonably warm day. To rout the colonial militia who were threatening the British left flank, Admiral Graves ordered his ships to set fire to the nearly deserted settlement of Charlestown. Soon the entire community was ablaze. On the right, however, Howe's effort to outflank the Americans was halted in a hail of bullets. The British commander then had only a frontal attack to rely upon. Stone walls, rail fences, and ranks of Americans impeded the way, and Howe's first assault was driven back with heavy losses. He regrouped and struck again, one spearhead driving against a rail fence that protected the approach to Breed's Hill, another against the redoubt itself. Again the Americans cut down the British with deadly volleys, and again the hardened veterans fell back.

The Americans had also had about all they could take of such ac-

tion, and their powder supply was dangerously low. Howe's third assault made use of 400 fresh men, but the American reserves for the
most part refused to move up to the comparative safety of Bunker
Hill. The tide of British regulars finally overwhelmed the outer defences on Breed's Hill and broke into the redoubt itself. Without
bayonets the colonials had great difficulty in the hand-to-hand combat that followed, although most of them succeeded in an orderly retreat. But the British fleet covered the narrow isthmus leading back
to the mainland with a heavy fire, and there the Americans suffered
their greatest casualties. Having finally won the battlefield, Howe
made no further pursuit. Of the 2,400 British regulars who fought
that day, over one thousand fell, a quarter of them killed outright.
All twelve of Howe's own staff were hit, Major Pitcairn of Lexington
fame was killed, and Lord Percy reported that his regiment, which
had covered the retreat from Concord in April, was 'almost entirely
cut to pieces: there are but 9 men left in my company, and not above
5 in one of the others.' The Americans lost about 140 killed, including the Boston patriot Joseph Warren, and another 271 wounded,
out of about 1,500 men who actually fought.

Bunker Hill (as the engagement of the 17th has since been
called) changed the nature of the war for many Americans. The
battle of Lexington and Concord saw colonists fighting *to defend* their
own communities from an invading army. The militia who joined in
driving the British back to Boston were mostly men from surrounding towns clearing their territory, as it were, of a threat. And Ticonderoga was captured by a band of men experienced in such adven-
tures and eager for a scrap. But at Bunker Hill hundreds of soldiers
from Connecticut, New Hampshire, and from distant parts of Massachusetts risked their lives to establish and then defend an advance
outpost against British-held Boston. For the first time they engaged
in a pitched battle, and although they lost the field, they gained the
grudging respect of their opponents. In his report to Lord Dartmouth, Gage admitted that 'the rebels are not the despicable rabble
too many have supposed them to be.' He praised their military spirit,
zeal, and enthusiasm. 'The conquest of this country is not easy,' the
general ruefully concluded. And when Washington took command
of the American forces at Cambridge on 2 July, Gage's task would
become still more difficult.[60]

At the end of May the Congress had agreed to seek a reconciliation with the mother country through petition, negotiation, and
discussion of Parliament's 'conciliatory propositions' of 20 February.
As the weeks went by, however, it became increasingly obvious that
the Congress was sharply divided, not only between individual
members but even more significantly, within the minds of many of

the delegates themselves. 'You will see a strange oscillation between love and hatred, between war and peace—preparations for war and negotiations for peace,' wrote John Adams to his friend James Warren in early July. Although genuinely desirous of reconciliation most congressmen believed that an honourable settlement, one in which American rights (as they saw them) were protected, could only be achieved through continued resistance. The colonists were not the first men to seek peace through war, nor would they be the last, but during the course of the summer of 1775 the basic inconsistency of their position became increasingly apparent.[61]

On 6 July the Congress adopted its 'Declaration of the Causes and Necessity for Taking up Arms', drafted by Thomas Jefferson but substantially modified by John Dickinson, who epitomized the dichotomy that raged within the minds of thoughtful Americans. The authors of this Declaration once more reviewed the events of the previous twelve years, from Grenville's taxation policy to Gage's proclamation of martial law. 'Our cause is just. Our union is perfect. Our internal resources are great, and if necessary, foreign assistance is undoubtedly attainable.' But this thinly veiled threat was balanced with a denial of any intent to dissolve the union with Great Britain— 'necessity has not yet driven us to that desperate measure, or induced us to excite any other nation to war against them.' The colonists had taken up arms in defence of their freedom and property, the document declared. 'We shall lay them down when hostilities shall cease on the part of the aggressors, and all danger of their being renewed shall be removed, and not before.' Designed more to inspire American soldiers to war than the British ministry to peace, however, the Declaration contributed nothing to the cause of reconciliation.[62]

But at the same time Dickinson prepared a new address to the King, known as the 'Olive Branch Petition'. As in the appeal to the crown the previous year, this document suggested that the King was being misled by 'those artful and cruel enemies who abuse your royal confidence and authority.' Far from seeking independence, the delegates asserted, they longed for the restoration of that former harmony enjoyed throughout the Empire and looked forward to the establishment of perpetual accord for the benefit of future generations in both countries. Once again the colonists asked the King to interpose his authority on their behalf. On the same day the Congress adopted another 'Address to the Inhabitants of Great Britain'. To offset what it considered misinformation disseminated by America's enemies in the mother country the delegates once more reviewed the developments of recent years and the reasons for their opposition to British colonial policy. The document also sought to

drive a wedge between the ministry and the people with the suggestion, first made in the Address of October 1774, that Britons themselves might also fall victim to the ministerial soldiers who 'have
sheathed their Swords in the Bowels of their American brethren.
. . .' Despite this effort at divisiveness, John Adams dismissed the
Address as a concoction of 'prettynesses, juvenilities, and . . . purili-
ties'. He seemed to consider the document no more than another futile effort at reconciliation.[63]

For the next two weeks the Congress continued its oscillations between moderation and firmness. It set aside consideration of a plan
for colonial union proposed by Benjamin Franklin that would have
given the Congress, at least temporarily, almost all the powers of
sovereign nations. The delegates also refused to move up the date
for commencing its policy of non-exportation. And most significantly,
they tabled a proposal by Richard Henry Lee to declare American
ports open to the ships of all foreign nations in overt violation of the
Navigation Acts. On the other hand, the Congress called upon every
colony that had not already done so to organize its men of military
age into militia companies, to fortify its harbours, and to appoint
committees of safety to superintend matters of defence. Toward the
end of the month the Congress also authorized the emission of continental bills valued at $100,000, to be redeemed by the individual
colonies in proportion to population.[64]

Then on the last day of the month the Congress voted to reject
Parliament's 'conciliatory propositions'. The privilege of granting
one's own money, the delegates now insisted, included the right to
decide 'whether they will make any gift, and for what purposes it
shall be made, and what shall be its amount.' Earlier in the crisis colonists had been willing to contribute a share to imperial defence by
requisitions—the system used during the colonial wars. But that system had not included any of the 'rights' now claimed by the Congress. The Americans' major objection to the conciliatory propositions, however, lay in Parliament's refusal to abandon its claim to the
right of taxation over Americans. Nor did the colonists wish to give
over their money at 'the point of the bayonet'. Two years earlier,
prior to the Boston Tea Party, such a proposal might well have been
acceptable to so many Americans that its opponents would have
been left with little support. But after the onset of hostilities increasing numbers of colonists required far stronger assurances for the security of their property than were offered by Parliament's proposal
of February 1775. That offer became a classic example of 'too little
too late.'[65]

By summer the pendulum had already begun to swing toward
further hostilities and away from reconciliation. The first concrete

signs came in the American policy toward Canada. Long dreaded by
Americans as the source of Indian raids, Catholic heresies, and
French aggression, Canada after 1763 became an enigma for the colonists. It was a part of the King's American dominions, to be sure,
but different in almost every particular from the other continental
colonies. Extension of Quebec's jurisdiction by the Act of 1774 into
areas claimed by Virginia once more aroused American fears. To
some Americans the continuing failure of Canadians to embrace the
colonists' cause seemed proof of their animosity. And yet others
could not accept the implications of their northern neighbours' apparent contentment under current British rule. They persuaded
themselves that an American force would be welcomed as an army
of liberation. At the end of June the Congress had reversed its earlier resolve to abandon Fort Ticonderoga after stripping it of all armament. Instead it authorized General Philip Schuyler, the new
commander of the region, if he 'finds it practicable and that it will
not be disagreeable to the Canadians, [to] immediately take possession of St. John's, Montreal, and any other parts of the country. . . .' [66]

Two of Schuyler's hot-headed subordinates, General Richard
Montgomery and the impetuous Ethan Allen, did not wait for a Canadian invitation. Neither Schuyler nor the Congress seemed to
mind when, after a series of minor reversals, Montgomery succeeded in driving the British General Sir Guy Carleton out of poorly
defended Montreal in mid-November 1775. In fact George Washington had already decided to dispatch Benedict Arnold and 1,100
men up through the Maine woods in what he assumed would be an
easy assault upon Quebec. When Arnold's men emerged from the
wilderness before the city in early November, however, the arduous
journey had cost him nearly half his force and had reduced the rest
to virtual skeletons, 'their visages thin and meager . . . , much re-
sembling the animals that inhabit New Spain called the Ourang-
Outang.' They were in no condition to launch an attack until joined
by Montgomery from Montreal. Their combined forces of about 800
men assaulted the city on New Year's Day, 1776, but they were no
match for Carleton's 1,800 defenders. Montgomery was killed, Arnold wounded, and hundreds of Americans captured before the
meagre remnant withdrew. Arnold doggedly stayed on in Canada,
but small-pox, poor supplies, and the strength of Carleton's forces
took the starch out of the Americans. In June 1776 they began a
long, costly retreat up the St. Lawrence, out of Montreal, and back
to New York. 'Let us quit [Canada],' conceded a chastened Benedict
Arnold, 'and secure our own country before it is too late.' [67]

On other fronts military affairs went far better for the Americans. During the summer and autumn of 1775 Washington tightened his siege lines around Boston, struggled to whip his assorted thousands of untrained and often unwilling men into soldiers, and built up his war supplies. In December he sent his artillery chief, Henry Knox, to fetch the cannon from Fort Ticonderoga. That gargantuan ex-bookseller succeeded in bringing fifty-two artillery pieces by ox-team and sledges over the frozen Berkshire mountains to Cambridge, greatly strengthening Washington's firepower. At the beginning of March 1776 the Americans fortified Dorchester Heights, overlooking Boston from the south. General Howe, who had succeeded Gage as commander of the British forces there, realized the futility of remaining under the guns that would command both town and harbour. Hastily he planned the evacuation, made the more complicated by his moral commitment to take with him over one thousand loyalists who had sought refuge within the seaport. On 17 March 1776 about ten thousand British soldiers climbed aboard their transports and sailed off to Halifax, Nova Scotia. The colony where war had begun eleven months before had seen the last of the enemy.[68]

Meanwhile, General Sir Henry Clinton had left Boston on board the frigate *Mercury* with a small force of light infantry. After pausing at New York, he sailed for the southward. At Cape Fear, North Carolina, Clinton joined up with a major expedition under General Lord Cornwallis. Together they proceeded to Charleston, South Carolina, with intent to take that strategic seaport by amphibious assault. The British had hoped for assistance by an uprising among loyalists in both North and South Carolina, but a decisive patriot victory at Moore's Creek Bridge in January 1776 temporarily discouraged further threats from that segment of the population. Clinton opened his attack on 28 June 1776 with a fierce bombardment of the fort which General Charles Lee had hastily constructed at the harbour entrance. The British fleet had difficulty manoeuvring in the shoal waters, and three warships ran fast aground. The pounding continued until nightfall, but neither the fort's resilient palmetto logs nor the stout Carolinians within gave way. At length the British were driven off, not to return to that region for more than two years.[69]

In Virginia the threat to patriot control came not from an outside force of British regulars but from the royal governor. In April 1775 Lord Dunmore had seized the colony's supply of powder at Williamsburg and had flung a defiant threat to enlist both Indians and slaves to put down the protestors. In those counties where oppressed blacks outnumbered the whites, and Indians begrudged earlier losses such menaces could not be taken lightly. Unlike Gage to the north, however, Dunmore had no army. As the patriots continued to challenge his government, therefore, he retreated on board the British warship, *Fowey*, anchored off the then little-known settlement of Yorktown. Gradually he gathered about him a small force of sailors, marines, loyalists, a few regulars and a number of blacks. In November he declared from his floating headquarters off Norfolk that Virginia was under martial law and offered freedom to all slaves and servants who would rally to the King's standard. At Great Bridge, a few miles south of Norfolk, a detachment of Virginia militiamen dug in and challenged Dunmore to attack. On 8 December 1775 he obliged. In the pitched battle that followed, however, the governor's force was routed, the survivors fleeing to the safety of the British fleet in the harbor. Three weeks later, on New Year's Day, 1776, Lord Dunmore ordered Norfolk to be bombarded and set afire. By the next evening Virginia's principal seaport lay in ashes.[70]

From Falmouth, in Maine (burned by Admiral Graves in October 1775) to Charleston, South Carolina (attacked by Clinton in June 1776) Americans had come to know the fury of war. Thousands more from almost every colony had joined Washington's army before Boston, had taken part in the ill-fated Canada campaign, or had marched against loyalist forces from the back country. By the summer of 1776 war had come to many parts of the thirteen colonies, and there seemed to be no hope for a cessation in the foreseeable future. Indeed, at the end of June General William Howe arrived in New York harbour with the first units of what would become an overwhelming force: 30 warships, 24,000 British regulars, and 8,000 Hessian mercenaries, along with heavy artillery and tons of equipment. By the time they had all reached shore, however, the ground they trod was no longer part of the British Empire; it was, at least in name, the United States of America.[71]

Contrary to the views of some historians the idea of American independence did not spring full-blown from the forehead of Sam Adams. Long before the imperial crisis broke out in the 1760s the expectation that the colonies would some day become independent had been considered in the abstract by numerous writers on both sides of the Atlantic. Men like Benjamin Franklin who noted the rapid expansion of colonial population and wealth concluded that one day the seat of empire would be found in America rather than in England. Perhaps the two countries would separate instead. Such an outcome would result, they thought, from a natural course of events, a process that did not require or even permit the conscious intervention of individuals. There is little evidence to show that colonists considered American independence as ever becoming a political necessity.

But the long quarrel with Great Britain gradually changed all this. By the summer of 1774, as we have seen, most colonists had come to view the Empire and America's place in it almost exclusively in terms of political power. John Dickinson spoke for many fellow colonists that summer when he denied Parliament any legislative power in America save that of superintending imperial commerce. Yet Dickinson also gave voice to the strong sense of loyalty the colonists had to the King. The status of equality with Englishmen under the British Crown seemed just and logical for Americans. As long as they retained allegiance to the King they regarded themselves as loyal members of the Empire. And when they denied that independence was their goal, they were conceding a dependence on the Crown alone. The gradual change toward a complete independence that developed in the two-year period after the Coercive Acts therefore came most commonly in American minds as a rejection of the King.

One of the earliest public expressions of doubt concerning George III appeared in the *Norwich Packet* in September 1774. 'Whether the King has deprived himself of all right of supremacy and is willing to [dis]solve constitutional sovereignty into that of mere power,' asked REFLECTOR rhetorically, 'I leave others to say.' A few weeks later came a blast in the *Pennsylvania Packet* under the heading 'Political Observations'. 'The history of kings is nothing but the history of the folly and depravity of human nature. . . . The American congress derives all its power, wisdom and justice, not from the scrolls of parchment signed by Kings, but from the PEOPLE.' From Virginia A SCOTCHMAN castigated George III's approval of the Quebec Act establishing 'the Popish religion' throughout the English dominion of Canada in violation of his oath to maintain the Protestant faith. 'I will not say that our King hath committed wilful and corrupt perjury . . . , neither do I assert that the People are now absolved of their allegiance, but,' the author concluded, 'we have an old fashioned adage in my country . . . , "that nobody can be hanged for thinking." ' What A SCOTCHMAN said to the King by implication, SCIPIO declared explicitly in late October 1774: 'Instead of being hailed the happy guardian of your people, you are become their tyrant and oppressor! . . . the hated object of millions!' [72]

The relevance of Locke's contract theory to the crisis was not lost on the colonists. 'The instant a king violates his part of the contract,' wrote a New Yorker, 'the engagement of the subject is at end. . . . The legislative power of course naturally returns into the hands of the people, and they are at full liberty to take arms and drive the tyrant from the throne.' For JOHANNES IN EREMO the moment for that event came in the wake of Lexington and Concord:

> King George the third adieu! No more shall we bleed in defense of your person, your breach of covenant, your violation of faith, your turning a deaf ear to our cries for justice, for covenanted protection and salvation from the oppressive, tyrannical, and bloody measures of the British Parliament and [your] putting a sanction upon all their measures to enslave and butcher us, have DISSOLVED OUR ALLEGIANCE to your crown and government! Your sword that ought in justice to protect us, is now drawn with a witness to destroy us. O George see thou to thy own house.

Indeed, some commentators argued that by such behavior the King 'unkings himself . . . , he in a sense deposes himself.' The Americans were not the rebels but rather the British King and magistrates, who by their tyranny have rebelled against the state. 'In case of such a rebellion,' wrote JOHANNES IN EREMO in January 1776, 'the people are bound by the constitution to take up arms in defence of the state against the rebels. . . .' [73]

Long before the publication of Thomas Paine's *Common Sense* in January 1776, therefore, some Americans had already concluded that George III was ultimately responsible for the crisis of Empire. His refusal to hear American petitions, his use of military force against the colonists (particularly the hiring of mercenaries), and finally his accusation of 26 October 1775 that the Americans 'meant only to amuse . . . by the strongest protestations of loyalty to me whilst they were planning for a general revolt', convinced increasing numbers of Americans that further appeal to the throne was futile. Paine's pamphlet not only gave focus to the specific charges against George III, whom he called 'the Royal Brute of Britain', but also broadened the attack on monarchy in general. In so doing he gave positive support to the idea of republicanism that had for the most part remained unexpressed during the quarrel between America and Great Britain. As colonists throughout the continent read *Common Sense* they found, perhaps for the first time, a specific alternative form of government for America—a republic. The particulars of Paine's scheme were impractical, but the idea was not. In urging independence Paine tapped the latent pride of Americans in the greatness of their country. 'Tis time to part. Even the distance at which the Almighty hath placed England and America', he asserted, 'is a strong and natural proof that the authority of the one over the other was never the design of Heaven.' Thomas Paine, resident in America for little more than a year, had somehow found the words that indeed made common sense to thousands of Americans.[74]

As the great debate on independence reached its climax in the first months of 1776, additional arguments gained attention. Months of warfare with no end in sight, months of self-government on both the continental and local levels, months of waiting for some sort of encouraging sign from Great Britain had led many Americans to embrace independence not as an end in itself, but as a last resort. 'After a twelve year's unsuccessful endeavour to remain reconciled to [Great Britain] on principles of right, equity, liberty, and consanguinity we are at last reduced to the necessity of becoming independent and entering into a war with her to preserve our privileges . . . ,' wrote A RELIGIOUS POLITICIAN almost despairingly in February 1776. Even the conservative James Chalmers seems to have reached his limit. Should the ministry have recourse to foreign aid, America might have to follow its example. Then 'if it be essential to our safety to declare an Independence, I would willingly embrace the necessity.' (Chalmers in fact fought as a loyalist.) Others concluded that a reconciliation now with the mother country would simply give her the opportunity to strengthen her American garrisons and adopt new schemes for oppressing the colonists. In the years of quarrelling and months of fighting many Americans had lost faith that the British ministry would honour for long whatever basis for reconciliation the two sides might agree upon. 'Too late, too late, reconciliation is a phantom,' wrote a correspondent to the *Boston Gazette*. 'Why do ye dream of uniting the brave, the gallant colonists to that power which has burnt our towns, desolated our pleasant fields, turned out thousands to beg, put us to millions cost, made every man a soldier, and murdered some of our valiant heroes whose fame shall never die?' [75]

But if some Americans embraced independence in fear of what reconciliation might bring, others tenaciously clung to the hope of reconciliation in dread of independence. Harassed by their neighbours, denied access to printing press and public office in many parts of the continent, the loyalists and other opponents of independence faced insurmountable odds. The widespread popularity of *Common Sense* (it sold 120,000 copies in its first three months) spread arguments against reconciliation along with its doctrine of separation. Like-minded inhabitants contributed their own views in the local press, private conversation, and public discussion. 'Independence a year ago could not have been publickly mentioned with impunity,' wrote a Bostonian to his London correspondent. 'Nothing else is now talked of, and I know not what can be done by Great Britain to prevent it.' [76]

The opponents of independence were overwhelmed by acts as well as by words. New Hampshire, Massachusetts, and several others had in effect already established independent governments, and in mid-May the Congress called upon the rest to follow suit. The number of royal governors with effective power dwindled each month. In early March 1776 the Congress commissioned Silas Deane to seek military aid from the French; a month later he left on the secret mission that would lead two years later, to an American alliance with Britain's arch-enemy. Also in March the Congress responded to Parliament's Prohibitory Act of December by authorizing American privateers to cruise against British vessels on the high seas. In April it threw open the ports of America to foreign trade excluding British possessions.[77]

In one colony after another throughout the spring regular assemblies and special conventions considered how to instruct their congressmen on the matter of independence. The decision was ultimately made at the grass-roots level by the hundreds of delegates who attended these various meetings. As Virginia's convention called upon its congressmen to introduce a resolution favouring separation, John Adams wrote from Philadelphia that 'every post and every day rolls in upon us independence like a torrent.' On 7 June Richard Henry Lee proposed that the Congress declare the colonies free and independent states, open negotiations for foreign alliances, and draw up a plan of confederation. A three-week postponement then allowed delegates to seek guidance from their provincial governments. Meanwhile, a committee including Thomas Jefferson, John Adams, and Benjamin Franklin was appointed to draft a suitable declaration in case the Congress voted in favor of independence.[78]

One by one the reluctant middle colonies either freed their delegates to vote their consciences or instructed them outright to favour independence. Pennsylvania accepted the idea of separation in late June, as did New Jersey, Maryland, and Delaware. Only New York hung back, distracted by the approach of General Howe and the vanguard of his powerful fleet. When debate opened in the Congress on 1 July, John Dickinson stepped forward to voice his opposition. From the Stamp Act resolves of 1765 to the Declaration of the Causes and Necessity for Taking up Arms a decade later, Dickinson had penned a number of remarkable statements on behalf of the American cause. But he was not yet convinced that reconciliation was hopeless. Nor did he trust France to come to America's aid, especially if England were to offer the return of Canada for French neutrality. Dickinson expressed for thousands of fellow countrymen a fear of the future that few of them had dared to reveal: 'When our enemies are pressing us so vigorously, when we are in so wretched a state of preparation, when the sentiments and designs of our expected friends are so unknown to us,' he confessed, 'I am alarmed at this Declaration being so vehemently presented.' [79]

John Adams rose to reply, 'after waiting some time in hopes that someone less obnoxious than myself . . . would move.' The Massachusetts delegate had spoken in favour of independence many times before, 'the pillar of its support on the floor of Congress', Jefferson would later recall, and now he countered Dickinson's arguments with all the logic at his command. When the poll was finally taken, nine delegations favoured independence but Pennsylvania and South Carolina objected, Delaware was divided, and New York was forced to abstain for want of new instructions. On the 2nd, however, Delaware joined in and both Carolina and Pennsylvania switched their votes, the latter through the abstention of two delegates including Dickinson himself. (New York would endorse the proceedings the week following.)

> *Resolved:* That these United Colonies are, and of right ought to be, Free and Independent States; that they are absolved from all allegiance to the British crown, and that all political connexion between them, and the state of Great Britain, is, and ought to be totally dissolved.

Two days later, on 4 July 1776, the Congress adopted Thomas Jefferson's Declaration to proclaim their independence to the world. Now, as General William Howe was landing his troops on Staten Island, they would have to win on the field of battle. [80]

XIII

Conclusion

———•·•———

THE QUARREL which split the British Empire in 1776 was one of infinite complexity. If one ultimate general explanation is to be adduced, it is the inadequacy of human powers of mind and will to grasp the full implications of political situations and discover peaceful evolutionary solutions to the problems which they pose. This incapacity can be observed on both sides of the Atlantic in the period of revolutionary crisis.

It appears that a highly complex array of considerations and circumstances brought British governments over a period of twelve years to the point at which the guns began to fire. On the one hand these included a heritage of ideas about the reasons for the existence of the Empire and about the mode of its organization, a preoccupation with the problem of mobilizing the economic resources of the Empire in a dangerous world of competing nations, a belief that unitary control over the resources of the whole was essential and a conviction that constitutional principles required the location of this control in Parliament. The very struggle for mastery which British governments had directed against France for the past nine years before 1763 seemed to emphasize the necessity for a more highly-keyed and tighter-knit imperial organization to secure and maintain the successes which had been achieved. Hardly any leading politician in Great Britain was prepared to subscribe to the view that the institutional unity focused on Parliament should be abandoned, but they displayed varying degrees of firmness, flexibility or resignation regarding its ultimate preservation. Some like Bedford or Grenville and their friends would stand up for it at any cost; others, like the Rockinghams, were prepared to concede much of the substance to preserve at least some theoretical element of it. On the other hand, in a more immediate context, the British politicians reacted to harsh fiscal pressures generated within Great Britain by a war expenditure of unexampled magnitude; and their attitudes came to be emotionally coloured by a resentment at what appeared to be the much more favourable fiscal position of the colonies. Here, too, considerable divergence of attitudes was displayed, from the relative rigidity of Grenville and his friends, who maintained that the colonies could and should pay the levies laid upon them, to the Rockinghamites and Chathamites, who, looking perhaps to the short-term rather than to the long-term view, thought that efforts to raise revenue weighed light in the balance against the political disruptions of the Empire's economic life to which they appeared to lead.

Leading British politicians—Grenville, Chatham, Rockingham, Burke, for example—all at various times displayed a theoretical awareness, that successful constitutional government could only rest on the consent of the governed. Yet, except perhaps for Burke, and in his case only partially, not one of these four had the political empathy fully to grasp the extent of the emotional affront to the colonists of the new fiscal measures which followed the Peace of Paris. In the years that followed, British leaders consistently underrated the extent of colonial opposition, dismay, resentment, and finally distrust. This was of a piece with their failure to understand that the new economic and fiscal policies of the 1760s were unrealizable owing to the lack of overwhelming power at the centre of the Empire and the infinite opportunity for argument about the suitability of these policies for attaining their ends. Schemes of taxation created new anomalies. It was not easy to refute the colonists' contention that the prosperity of all Britons depended upon the colonists themselves achieving the greatest possible prosperity and enjoying every freedom they thought conducive to that end.

In part British leaders were blinded by the logical compulsions of their situation. The financial burden of the war which had ended in 1763 had been immense and frightening. Some parts of the Empire were certainly not shouldering their share of the consequent burdens, that is, in this context, not the National Debt, but the increased current defence commitments, necessary to hold the position that had been won. After 1763 the international situation remained at least as dangerous, if not more dangerous, than it had been before. It appeared that survival depended upon a systematic redeployment of the actual and potential resources of the Empire, and a continuance of economic pressures upon France which could only be sustained if those resources were directed under the firm control of a single imperial authority. Such a policy involved significant extension of the use of powers hitherto little exercised and little felt in the American colonies.

Misunderstanding and mistrust were multiplied, especially, after 1767, because on both sides of the Atlantic, men opposed to George

III's governments became ensnared by beliefs in the existence of a conspiracy against the constitution and against the civil liberties which it was supposed to safeguard.

It can be argued, that this fear was as much a delusion in America as it was in Great Britain. There was, of course, no logical flaw in John Wilkes's argument, that the invalidation of his final election for Middlesex in 1769 threatened the whole basis of parliamentary representation. The fallacy lay in the assumption that those in power had any intention to proceed to such extremes, and also in the further assumption that there were not ample reserves of political mass available in the country to resist such an attempt if it were ever really launched. Similarly, the colonists saw very clearly the logical threat to the existence of their representative institutions for internal self-government; but they too formed unduly alarmist opinions about ministerial intentions, and they too did not take into account the political mass available to counter such tendencies without flying to extremes of violence. In particular, the colonial preoccupation before 1776 with prevention of the establishment of imperial precedents seems to reveal a curious blindness to the implications of current population trends, which prominent Americans like Franklin could see would enable them, probably within less than two generations, to conduct arguments with Great Britain from a position of material superiority. It also seems as if the colonists, in their preoccupation with absolutes of constitutional right and wrong, did not assess the significance of British responses in the 1760s. Yet in face of colonial protest, three major reversals of British policy took place between 1766 and 1770. In 1766, not only was the Stamp Act repealed, but very considerable changes were made in the tariff provisions of the Plantation Act of 1764. In 1770 North abandoned a large part of the Revenue Act of 1767. These British actions did support British assurances that economic grievances would be given attention and that no oppression of the colonists was intended. Fear and other emotional responses veiled this fact from the eyes of many colonists. This is perhaps the most generalized explanation possible of a colonial over-reaction to the Tea Act of 1773. In turn this provoked an over-reaction by British politicians, who were themselves increasingly oppressed by a fear that the imperial fabric was threatened with destruction by colonial agitators, with all that this implied for the safety and prosperity of the nation.

Suggestions current in the mid-1770s that the British government should simply return to the state of things obtaining in 1763 were less practicable than their makers perhaps realized. From the British point of view, the situation of 1763 was one of deterioration and decay, dominated by centrifugal forces which were apparently hastening the Empire towards disintegration. Fiscal legislation apart,

British measures after that date had been intended to stabilize the Empire and improve the working of the system in the form in which men understood it to have evolved in the previous century. The 'Olive Branch' petition of 1775 was thus unacceptable, since it amounted to a demand that the centrifugal tendencies be allowed to work themselves out to their logical conclusion. Indeed, in the context of pronouncements by such leaders of colonial opinion as James Wilson and Thomas Jefferson, it implied that in some respects the results of this development should be formally recognized.

For by the mid-1770s some colonial leaders were already feeling their way towards the concept of a free association of equal communities bound by voluntary agreement to preserve ties of mutual convenience. British politicians failed to conceive that such a free association might be sufficiently fruitful and solid to preserve national safety and prosperity. But this failure flowed in turn from the constitutional position of George III. No one in London could envisage how a sovereign who though a 'limited' was nevertheless to some extent still an 'efficient' monarch acting through responsible agents, could be placed in a situation where he might be drawn into conflicting policies by different possessions, external limitations on the use of power in one possession being imposed by another. The theoretical solution perceived by such diverse observers as Bernard, Thomas Pownall, and Grenville was the establishment of a united imperial legislature. A similarly intractable problem was to lead the next generation of British statesmen to force through the Act of Union with Ireland. But there was virtually no support for a scheme of this kind embracing the colonies during the 1760s or 1770s. Instead British leaders clung to the new conception of parliamentary supremacy. In their view a state could only be unitary, or else it was no state at all, and their awareness of the constant dangers of international anarchy drove them to maintain the only form of political unity they knew and understood. In another way also the country's circumstances militated against the possibility of their stumbling upon the commonwealth solution to similar problems developed by their successors during the nineteenth century. Early Victorian Britain was the triton among minnows: the nation's industrial progress had given it by then an incomparable superiority in power over any European rival, Germany was not yet unified, and Russia had not yet emerged as a serious competitor. British industrial predominance placed a premium on free-trade policies and made nonsense of the old closed imperial economic system. All this was far removed from the situation facing ministers in the early years of George III's reign.

While in one sense British attitudes were basically unsympathetic towards those of the colonists, they were nevertheless far from monolithic. The chance that brought one man and then another to the place of power in Whitehall played its part in bringing on the imperial civil war. At almost every turn events might have proceeded differently—if George III had not quarrelled with Grenville in the spring of 1765; if Cumberland had not died that autumn; if Grafton and Conway had not been so insistent in early 1766 that Pitt ought to lead the ministry; if Pitt, now Earl of Chatham, had not allowed the reluctant Townshend to be foisted on him by Grafton as his chancellor of the exchequer; if Chatham had kept his health, or if Townshend's had given way twelve months earlier than it did; if the Rockinghams had not, by combining in a trial of strength to bring down Grafton in 1767, forced him into the arms of the Bedford party; if Grafton as head of the Treasury had had the firmness of purpose to insist on his own fiscal policy (with regard to the tea duty) in 1769. Either armed conflict might have come earlier when the colonists' resources were less developed and when they were less prepared, materially and psychologically, than was the case by 1775; or prudence might have prevailed, causing the adjustments within the Empire, which clearly had to take place ultimately, to be pursued with less animosity and without violence. On the British side the characters and fates of individuals, the interplay of British political factions, all fall into their place in the search for explanations of the American Revolution. The events of 1775 and 1776 were not inevitable.

What was it about the particular series of decisions and events during the twelve-year period after the Sugar Act that led ultimately to the Declaration of Independence? Colonial Whigs, like their English counterparts, had grown deeply suspicious of political power in the first half of the eighteenth century. One political faction suspected the motives of others; constituents searched for incorruptible delegates, and then bound them with instructions and insisted on annual elections; even on the local level town meetings sharply reduced the powers of their selectmen and other appointed officials. These misgivings seemed to increase proportionately with the geographical and political distances that separated men from the locus of power. Thus backwoods farmers of Pennsylvania, Virginia, or the Carolinas were generally more suspicious of their colonial governments than their eastern counterparts, who were closer to the source of power. Even outport merchants in New England seemed less confident toward government than were the metropolitan men of trade. 'Country' parties sprang up in opposition to what their members termed 'court' parties.

Under these circumstances then, all the more suspect might be the government at Whitehall, a genuine 'court' party located 3,000 miles away and having no American representation at all. But this distrust remained dormant so long as British rule did not overtly threaten the colonists' perception of their vital interests. We have seen that in fact during the first half of the eighteenth century most Americans viewed their British connection with evident pride. They entered the decade of the 1760s with a large reservoir of good will toward the mother country. For some Americans, however, even the slightest change in government policies or procedures became grounds for suspecting ministerial motives.

Americans protested against Grenville's programme not so much for its immediate costs as for its future implications. Indeed, the ministry itself more than its programme drew the principal fire from the colonists. Their distrust of political power was aroused, and they anxiously searched for Whitehall's motives. By renewing taxation and dispatching troops to Boston, Townshend and Hillsborough seemed to confirm the worst suspicions of the Americans. Thereafter, they saw in virtually every British act clear signs of what they variously described as a 'plot', or 'design', or 'settled plan to enslave' them. Americans did not use the term slavery carelessly. They had ample reason to know its implications far better than did Englishmen—it meant the total and permanent deprivation of one's liberty. Although primarily disturbed by parliamentary taxation, many colonists began to see a myriad of other British acts 'in their true light', as they would have said. The Proclamation of 1763, prohibiting growth west of the Alleghenies, the Currency Act, the Anglican agitation for the establishment of an episcopate, an independent civil list, were all a part of the plan to reduce free-born Americans to a status of slavery. And true to the past history of tyrants, the standing army became a principal instrument by which to achieve this goal. In the absence of any clear explanation from British authorities for their vigorous policies, Americans suspected the worst. Power itself, in their view, had always corrupted otherwise good men.

Not all colonists reached these conclusions at the same pace, of course. The British presence was first and most keenly felt in the seaports. There the Navigation Acts (for almost a century the only parliamentary legislation directly affecting the colonists) were most obvious. There too were located most of the colonial capitals with their governors and other Crown-appointed officials. During wartime British troops and sailors were a not altogether welcome addition to the already rough elements in town. Finally, the presence of newspapers provided a means of exchanging information and opinion (unfortunately much of the news and views of British policy was full of error). When the British ministry introduced what appeared to be basic changes in the pattern of governing America, the inhabitants of the seaports were the first to notice the effects—and consequently the first to protest. They were immediately joined by southern planters dependent upon the British export market, but the great mass of American subsistence farmers did not as yet seem threatened by British policy.

What brought the conflict to the grass-roots level in most colonies was passage of the Coercive Acts. For years radical patriots had predicted that the men who taxed Americans could (and would) also strip the colonists of their livelihood entirely, that men who violated the constitution in the single particular of taxation could (and would) tear up that constitution altogether. The Coercive Acts seemed to prove to those who would look that the radicals' predictions had not in fact been mere rhetoric. But the Acts were significant in other ways. The plight of Boston offered Americans throughout the continent an opportunity to take direct action by giving aid. The appearance of loyalists and others whose refusal to support the Continental Association identified them as 'enemies', provided a local target for resentment and worse. Active opposition to a threat generally tends to make acceptable exaggerated reports of the danger in the absence of a more accurate view, in order to protect against the possibility that one has over-reacted or has responded to a 'false alarm'. Furthermore, after a man changes his attitude or behavior (such as from passive acceptance to active opposition toward Great Britain) his mind will often readjust its image of the past to make it consistent with his new pattern of thought or action. At the same time he frequently becomes even more active than some of the veterans in the group, perhaps in part to compensate for earlier inactivity. The new opposition leaders who emerged in many colonies after the Coercive Acts were for the most part more militant than the men they succeeded.

Those Americans (and there were many of them) who in 1774 still did not view the events of the past decade as 'a settled plan to enslave the colonists' were left in the awkward position of trying to deny the claims of the opposition without having a convincing alternative explanation of ministerial behavior to offer. Still worse, the ministry time and again undermined the position of its loyal American supporters by its essentially negative response to peaceful colonial protests. The failure of the King, for instance, even to receive the petition of the first Continental Congress left American moderates with little ground from which to advocate further petitioning. Before 1774 the loyalists could argue that Great Britain would return to its former benevolent rule as soon as the colonists repudiated the leadership of the radicals. In the face of circumstances that contention was difficult but not impossible. But after 1774 loyalists had the immensely more difficult task of persuading colonists newly committed to the opposition that they too were in error. The ministry offered nothing new to grasp, except for the unconvincing 'conciliatory propositions'. Nor did the ministry offer encouragement to the one concrete plan for reconciliation made by an American—Joseph Galloway's plan of union.

If sending aid to Boston or harassing a neighbouring loyalist intensified a man's commitment to the cause, how much more involved became those who actually fought against the British army. Note the patriots' insistence on labelling Gage's troops the 'ministerial army', in an effort to avoid the implications of bearing arms against the King. Having engaged in war, one finds it hard to turn back until one has gained enough to justify one's resort to violence in the first place. At the same time the enemy becomes a threat to life itself as well as to liberty and property. American self-preservation seemed to require at the very least the maintenance of a military posture in the face of such a threat. Acceptance of Gage's offer of amnesty upon surrender of American arms was unthinkable under the circumstances. Indeed, Gage's offer itself became viewed as an artful device to strip Americans of their last defence against advancing tyranny.

Having lost, after the outbreak of hostilities, what little trust they had toward the ministry, members of the Congress refused to offer any grounds for compromising the dispute. Throughout the rest of the year their distrust widened to include the British people as well. Earlier in the crisis Americans believed that the general British public supported their cause. This misconception was partly due to wishful thinking, partly to a misreading of the Wilkes case, and partly to the inaccurate reports of British opinion that appeared in the colonial press in 1774-6. About eighty percent of items concerning British attitudes suggested wide support for America. This high expectation had a double effect on Americans: not only did it encourage a continuation of opposition to the ministry, but it also deepened the colonists' resentment when they finally realized, after the election of 1774, how badly they had misinterpreted British public opinion. In similar fashion wishful thinking had also blinded Americans to the reality of the King's position. To expect him to favour the colonists in their quarrel with the ministry was a gross misunderstanding of George III's responsibilities as sovereign.

In reaffirming their loyalty to the King the Americans thought they were offering a middle ground between unitary empire on the one hand and total independence on the other. But this made no sense in British terms. George III stood for the general view of his subjects at home when he wrote in November 1774: 'We must either master them, or totally leave them to themselves and treat them as Aliens.' Faced with the alternatives of empire or independence, the Americans reluctantly made their choice.

ABBREVIATIONS USED IN THE NOTES

APC(C)	*Acts of the Privy Council of England: Colonial Series.*
BL	British Library (formerly British Museum Library)
CHS	Connecticut Historical Society
C.J.	*The Journals of the House of Commons*
C.O.	Colonial Office
Documents, ed. Davies	*Documents of the American Revolution, 1770–1783 (Colonial Series)*, ed. K. G. Davies
Fortescue	*The Correspondence of King George III*, ed. Sir John Fortescue
Franklin Papers	*The Papers of Benjamin Franklin*, ed. Leonard W. Labaree and others
H.M.C.	Historical Manuscripts Commission
HSP	Historical Society of Pennsylvania
MHM	*Maryland Historical Magazine*
MHS	Massachusetts Historical Society
NRS	Navy Records Society
P.H.	*The Parliamentary History of England . . . to 1803*, ed. William Cobbett and T. C. Hansard
PMHB	*Pennsylvania Magazine of History and Biography*
P.R.O.	Public Record Office
R.O.	Record Office
s.	series
SCHGM	*South Carolina Historical and Genealogical Magazine*
SP(Dom)	State Papers (Domestic)
WMQ	*William and Mary Quarterly*

NOTES

I. The Empire at the Accession of George III

1. For this revisionist view see Louis M. Cullen, *Anglo-Irish Trade, 1660–1800* (Manchester, 1968), and F. G. James, *Ireland in the Empire, 1688–1770* (Cambridge, Mass., 1973), chapter VIII.
2. Hector St. Jean de Crèvecoeur, *Letters from an American Farmer* (Everyman's Library edn.), (London, n.d.), p. 43.
3. W. T. Baxter, *The House of Hancock: Business in Boston, 1724–75* (Cambridge, Mass., 1945), p. 111.
4. *Franklin Papers*, III, 404.
5. Ibid., IV, 233.
6. Richard Koebner, *Empire* (1961), pp. 90–2.
7. 12 Chas. II, c. 18, 15 Chas. II, c. 7, 25 Chas. II, c. 7, 7, and 8 Wm. III, c. 22.
8. *London Packet*, 4 Jan. 1775, cited in Klaus E. Knorr, *British colonial theories, 1570–1850* (1963), p. 130.
9. See F. J. Hinkhouse, *The preliminaries of the American Revolution as seen in the English press, 1763–1775* (New York, 1926), p. 101.
10. CHS, *Collections*, XVIII, 317–26; Barré's argument is presented at pp. 321–3.
11. See for instance Sir Matthew Decker, *An Essay on the Causes of the Decline of the Foreign Trade* (1744, 2nd edn., 1750). Decker's Dutch background perhaps gave him a wider insight.
12. Knorr, pp. 106–7.
13. Ibid., pp. 95–101.
14. L. H. Gipson, *The Coming of the Revolution, 1763–1775* (1954), p. 24.
15. *A Discourse about Trade* (1690), p. 166, cited Knorr, pp. 80–1.
16. *Discourses on the Publick Revenues . . .* (1698), II, 204, cited Knorr, p. 106.
17. For evidence of the very widespread expression of this view in the 1760s and 1770s, see Hinkhouse, pp. 100, 108. In 1746 an anonymous New Englander had written that if the colonies were lost Britain would lose its independence too (R. W. Van Alstyne, *Genesis of American Nationalism*, 1970, pp. 37–8).
18. See Koebner, *Empire*, pp. 87–9, and on Franklin's views especially, pp. 105–18.

II. George Grenville and the Problems of Empire

1. Henry Fox to Bute, 17 Mar. 1763, Ilchester, *Henry Fox, first Lord Holland* (2 v., 1920), II, 231. Cf. James Oswald to Bute, [13 Apr. 1763], *Memorials of James Oswald of Dunniker* (Edinburgh, 1825), pp. 414–15.
2. *P.H.*, XVII, 1238–40.

3. A. H. Basye, *The Lords Commissioners of Trade and Plantations* (1925), pp. 32–104.

4. Sir Lewis Namier, *Charles Townshend: his character and career* (The Leslie Stephen Lecture, Cambridge, 1959); Sir Lewis Namier and John Brooke, *Charles Townshend* (1964), pp. 37–40, 140–1, 147, 172–9.

5. See for instance, T. C. Barrow, *Trade and Empire. The British Customs Service in Colonial America, 1660–1775* (Cambridge, Mass., 1967), pp. 160–8; John Shy, *Toward Lexington. The Role of the British Army in the coming of the American Revolution* (Princeton, 1965), chapter II, esp. pp. 54, 59–61, 62–5; Jack M. Sosin, *Whitehall and the Wilderness* (Lincoln, Neb., 1961), pp. 28–51, and *Agents and Merchants* (Lincoln, Neb., 1965), pp. 25–8.

6. The case for this view is made in T. C. Barrow, 'The Background to the Grenville Programme, 1757–1763', *WMQ*, 3rd s., 22 (1965), 93–104, esp. 102–4.

7. *P.H.*, XVII, 1240.

8. Barrow, *Trade and Empire*, chapters V and VII, and pp. 169–72.

9. For example, O. M. Dickerson, *The Navigation Acts and the American Revolution* (Philadelphia, 1951), pp. 69–70; L. A. Harper, *The English Navigation Laws* (New York, 1939), p. 268.

10. P.R.O., T.1/434:119. 'Calculation concerning the molasses duty', 1764. This estimate seems not unjustified in the light of the probably incomplete figures for the first years of the Union—1790: 6,418,040 galls., 1791: 6,868,532 galls; see Adam Seybert, *Statistical Annals of the United States of America* (reprint, New York, 1970), pp. 158 seqq.

11. P.D.G. Thomas, ed., 'Parliamentary Diaries of Nathaniel Ryder', Royal Historical Society, *Camden Miscellany XXIII* (1969), pp. 327; 323–5, P.R.O., T. 1/434:120. 'Evidence before the House of Commons concerning the Molasses Duty, 1766.'

12. 'Ryder Diaries', p. 321; *Observations on the trade and revenue of North America* (1763), cited L. H. Gipson, *The Coming of the Revolution, 1763–1775* (1954), p. 63.

13. B. W. Labaree, *The Boston Tea Party* (1964), pp. 9, 7.

14. Thomas Whately, *The Regulations lately made concerning the colonies . . .* (1765), p. 93.

15. Barrow, *Trade and Empire*, p. 149.

16. 'Ryder Diaries', p. 234; Whately, *The Regulations lately made. . . ,* p. 93.

17. Barrow, *Trade and Empire*, pp. 160–2.

18. Ibid., pp. 163–5.

19. Ibid., pp. 165–73.

20. 'Ryder Diaries', p. 234.

21. Barrow, *Trade and Empire*, p. 166; 'Ryder Diaries', pp. 234–5.

22. For evidence that this was under discussion at least as early as the beginning of 1760, well before Pitt left office, see *Archives of Maryland*, XXXI, 527–8.

23. Shy, *Toward Lexington*, pp. 45–6. Shy's subtle and sophisticated discussion of this subject (pp. 45–83) forms the basis of the following summary.

24. Hardwicke to Newcastle, 2 Apr. 1762, B.L. Add. MSS. 32936, fos. 310–12; R. W. Van Alstyne, *Genesis of American Nationalism*, pp. 36–40, 43–5, 47–8.

25. For this paragraph in general see also Sosin, *Whitehall and the Wilderness*, pp. 42–8.

26. *Correspondence of John, 4th Duke of Bedford*, ed. Lord John Russell (3 v., 1842–6), III, 210; Namier and Brooke, *Charles Townshend*, pp. 91–2; *Archives of Maryland*, XXXI, 531.

27. J. A. Ernst, *Money and Politics in America, 1755–1775* (Chapel Hill, N.C., 1973), pp. 34–41.

28. Ibid., pp. 43–83; L. H. Gipson, *The British Empire before the American Revolution* (15 v., New York, 1936–70), X, 158–70.

29. 3 Geo. III, c. 22.

30. Barrow, *Trade and Empire*, pp. 176–80.

31. Charles Jenkinson to commissioners of stamps, 23 Sept. 1763, P.R.O., T.27/28:432. For earlier suggestions about colonial stamp taxes see Gipson, *British Empire*, X, 252–8.

32. Allen S. Johnson, 'The Passage of the Sugar Act', *WMQ*, 3rd s., 16 (1959), 512.

33. For detail see Sosin, *Whitehall and the Wilderness*, pp. 52–65; and for the subordinate role of the Board of Trade, R. A. Humphreys, 'Lord Shelburne and the Proclamation of 1763', *English Historical Review*, 49 (1934), 241–64.

34. The official publication of the Proclamation is in the *London Gazette*, no. 10355, of 8–11 Oct. 1763. See also the *Annual Register* (1763), *Appendix to the Chronicle*, pp. 208–13.

35. Cited in Sosin, *Whitehall and the Wilderness*, p. 31.

36. Egremont to Amherst, 27 Jan. 1763, CHS, *Collections*, XVIII, 224.

37. For an illustration of these considerations see Whately, *The Regulations lately made . . .*, pp. 9–17.

38. *English Historical Review*, 49 (1934), 259. Cf. Whately, *The Regulations lately made . . .*, pp. 19–20.

39. Ibid., pp. 58–9; 'Ryder Diaries', pp. 234–5.

40. Whately, *The Regulations lately made . . .*, pp. 58–9.

41. Ibid., p. 89.

42. Loc. cit.

43. Ibid., pp. 45–56, 78–9, 86–7. See, on hemp and flax, 4 Geo. III, c. 26; on beaver, 4 Geo. III, c. 9; on rice, 4 Geo. III, c. 27; on whale fins, 4 Geo. III, c. 29.

44. Whately, *The Regulations lately made . . .*, pp. 58–9, 68–72.

45. Ibid., p. 92.

46. Ibid., pp. 94–100. On the system of provincial vice-admiralty courts and the establishment of the superior court at Halifax, see Carl Ubbelohde, *The Vice-Admiralty Courts and the American Revolution* (Chapel Hill, N.C., 1960), pp. 3–54. For an instance of the administrative follow-up see Halifax's direction to Governor Sharpe to provide information about illicit trade, 11 Aug. 1764, *Archives of Maryland*, XXXI, 550.

47. Whately, *The Regulations lately made . . .*, p. 54.

48. Ibid., pp. 74–5.

49. Ibid., pp. 78–87. The unreality of North American complaints about the molasses duty is established in Gipson, *The coming of the Revolution*, chapter 5, and Sosin, *Agents and Merchants*, pp. 42–9 and notes.

50. 'Ryder Diaries', pp. 236–8.

51. Cited in E. S. Morgan, *Prologue to Revolution. Sources and Documents on the Stamp Act Crisis, 1764–1766* (Chapel Hill, N.C., 1959), p. 25.

52. For three such instances see ibid., p. 24.

53. *American Historical Review*, 17 (1911–12), 572. Cf. Edmund Burke in the Commons, 19 Apr. 1774, *P.H.*, XVII, 1243.

54. 'Ryder Diaries', p. 235; and see the full account of the debate in P. D. G. Thomas, *British Politics and the Stamp Act Crisis* (Oxford, 1975), pp. 72–5.

55. *English Historical Review*, 54 (1939), 647.

56. Ernst, *Money and Politics in America*, pp. 87–8.

57. Cited in Gipson, *British Empire*, X, 168–9.

58. Charles F. Adams, ed., *The Works of John Adams* (Boston, 1856), X, 247–8.

59. Adams, *Works*, X, 282–4.

60. Bernard Bailyn, ed., *Pamphlets of the American Revolution* (Cambridge, Mass., 1965), I, 411–12; John J. Waters, *The Otis Family* (Chapel Hill, N.C., 1968), pp. 122–4.

61. Edmund S. and Helen M. Morgan, *The Stamp Act Crisis: Prologue to Revolution* (Chapel Hill, N.C., 1953), pp. 21–7.

62. John R. Bartlett, ed., *Records of the Colony of Rhode Island and Providence Plantations* (Providence, 1861), VI, 378–83.
63. *Journal of the Votes and Proceedings of the General Assembly of the Colony of New York* (1766), II, 776–9.
64. Ibid.
65. Ibid.
66. Ibid.; E. B. O'Callaghan, ed., *Documents Relating to the Colonial History of the State of New York* (Albany, 1856), VII, 399–400.
67. John P. Kennedy, ed., *Journals of the House of Burgesses of Virginia, 1761–1765* (Richmond, 1907), pp. 302–4.
68. Ibid.
69. Morgan, *Stamp Act Crisis*, pp. 29–34; Henry D. Biddle, 'Extracts from the Letterbook of Samuel Rhodes', *PMHB*, XIV (1890), 423.
70. James Otis, *The Rights of the British Colonies Asserted and Proved* (Boston, 1764), as printed in Bernard Bailyn, *Pamphlets*, I, 447–8, 454.

III. The First Crisis over Taxation

1. Edmund S. and Helen M. Morgan, *The Stamp Act Crisis. Prologue to Revolution* (new revised edn., New York, 1963), pp. 78–80, 269–77. For an edition of Hutchinson's text with fuller comment, see Morgan, 'Thomas Hutchinson and the Stamp Act', *New England Quarterly*, 21 (1948), 459–92.
2. MHS, *Collections*, 6th s., IX, 44–5, 45–8.
3. Grenville's speech, 6 Feb. 1765, as reported by Nathaniel Ryder, 'Ryder Diaries', pp. 253–6. Cf. CHS, *Collections*, XVIII, pp. 324–5, and *English Historical Review*, 54 (1939), 649–50. All these points had already been analysed for the political audience by Thomas Whately in *The Regulations lately made*, especially pp. 100–14.
4. *Horace Walpole's Memoirs of the reign of King George III*, ed. G. F. R. Barker (4 v., 1894), II, 49, 56; *Archives of Maryland*, XXXI, 558–9.
5. CHS, *Collections*, XVIII, 334.
6. Ibid., 316; 'Ryder Diaries', pp. 256–7. But for a contrary view see Thomas, *British Politics and the Stamp Act Crisis*, p. 93.
7. 'Ryder Diaries', p. 257.
8. Jackson's notes for his speech, *Franklin Papers*, XII, 37–40; CHS, *Collections*, XVIII, 316.
9. 'Ryder Diaries', p. 259.
10. To John Temple, 9 Feb. 1765, cited Morgan, *Stamp Act Crisis*, p. 87. Cf. H.M.C., *Tenth Report*, appendix, pt. 1, *Weston Underwood MSS.*, p. 382, *Franklin Papers*, XII, 69n., and *Annals of Maryland*, XXXI, 560.
11. CHS, *Collections*, XVIII, 332–5; *English Historical Review*, 54 (1939), 650–1.
12. MHS, *Collections*, 6th s., IX, 50.
13. CHS, *Collections*, XVIII, 335.
14. Thomas Whately, *Considerations on the trade and finances of this kingdom . . .* (1766), pp. 44, 71n.
15. For example, Whately (a) in *The Regulations lately made*, p. 102; (b) to John Temple, MHS, *Collections*, 6th s., IX, 51, 59–60; (c) retrospectively, in *Considerations on the trade and finances of this kingdom*, pp. 77–9. On this subject see J. M. Sosin, 'A postscript to the Stamp Act. George Grenville's revenue measures: a drain on colonial specie?', *American Historical Review*, 63 (1957–8), 918–23.
16. 5 Geo. III, c.45.
17. For a critical analysis of this provision see Barrow, *Trade and Empire*, pp. 189–91.

18. CHS, *Collections*, XVIII, 335–6; MHS, *Collections*, 6th s., IX, 56; Ubbelohde, *Vice-Admiralty Courts*, pp. 61–2, 71–3.
19. *The Correspondence of General Thomas Gage*, ed. C. E. Carter (2 v., 1931–3), I, 49.
20. Shy, *Toward Lexington*, pp. 163–81.
21. Ibid., p. 188.
22. 31 Chas. II, c. 1; *Grenville Papers*, ed. W. J. Smith (4 v., 1852–3), III, 11–12.
23. Shy, *Toward Lexington*, p. 187. Shy states (ibid., p. 189) that in the past this burden had been largely born by the Crown. According to C. M. Clode, *The military forces of the crown; their administration and government* (2 v., 1869), I, 235, before 1765 'barracks had been provided by the colonists sufficient for the accommodation of the troops under *ordinary* circumstances.' The point seems to require further investigation.
24. 5 Geo. III, c. 33, ss. 7, 8.
25. CHS, *Collections*, XVIII, 337–40.
26. For Barré's view see the dramatic, oft-quoted account by Jared Ingersoll, ibid., 321–3. For Jackson and Meredith, see p. 47 above.
27. Edmund S. and Helen M. Morgan, *The Stamp Act Crisis: Prologue to Revolution* (Chapel Hill, N.C., 1953), pp. 53–66; Michael G. Kammen, *A Rope of Sand: The Colonial Agents, British Politics, and the American Revolution* (Ithaca, N.Y., 1968), pp. 108–15; Edmund S. Morgan, 'Postponement of the Stamp Act', *WMQ*, III (July 1950), 363–71; John R. Bartlett, ed., *Records of the Colony of Rhode Island and Providence Plantations* (Providence, 1861), VI, 414–16.
28. William Smith jr. to [Robert Monckton], 30 May 1765, in MHS, *Collections*, 4th s., X (1870), 570–2.
29. 'Journal of a French Traveller in the Colonies, 1765, I', *American Historical Review*, XXVI (July 1921), 745.
30. 'Journal', *loc. cit.*, p. 746; the most thorough discussion of the Henry resolutions is in Morgan, *Stamp Act Crisis*, pp. 89–98. See also Edmund S. Morgan, ed., *Prologue to Revolution: Sources and Documents on the Stamp Act Crisis, 1764–1766* (Chapel Hill, N.C., 1959) for convenient reference to the various documents cited in this paragraph.
31. Bartlett, *Records of Rhode Island*, VI, 451–2.
32. These resolutions are most conveniently collected in Morgan, *Prologue to Revolution*, pp. 50–62.
33. Morgan and Morgan, *Stamp Act Crisis*, pp. 105–12.
34. Thomas Pownall, *Administration of the Colonies* (London, 1765), as quoted in Bernard Bailyn, ed., *Pamphlets of the American Revolution* (Cambridge, Mass., 1965), I, 600.
35. Soame Jenyns, *The Objections to the Taxation of our American Colonies by the Legislature of Great Britain, Briefly Consider'd* (London, 1765), p. 1.
36. Thomas Whately, *The Regulations Lately Made Concerning the Colonies and the Taxes Imposed upon Them, Considered* (London, 1765), p. 104.
37. Ibid., p. 109.
38. Daniel Dulany, *Considerations on the Propriety of Imposing Taxes in the British Colonies, for the purpose of Raising a Revenue, by Act of Parliament* (Annapolis, Md., 1765), as reprinted in Bailyn, *Pamphlets*, I, 611.
39. Ibid., p. 612.
40. Ibid., p. 615.
41. Ibid., p. 619.
42. Ibid., pp. 637–8.
43. Ibid., pp. 619–20.
44. Ibid., p. 652.

45. For discussion of American interest in English Whiggism see Bernard Bailyn, *The Ideological Origins of the American Revolution* (Cambridge, Mass., 1967), esp. pp. 1–93; also Pauline Maier, *From Resistance to Revolution: Colonial Radicals and the Development of American Opposition to Great Britain, 1765–1776* (New York, 1972), pp. 27–48.

46. The events related in this and ensuing paragraphs will be found in Morgan and Morgan, *Stamp Act Crisis,* pp. 119–43; Maier, *Resistance to Revolution,* pp. 53–60; and Hiller B. Zobel, *The Boston Massacre* (New York, 1970), pp. 24–47.

47. Thomas Hutchinson to William Jackson, 30 Aug. 1765, quoted in Morgan, *Prologue to Revolution,* pp. 108–9. See also 'Diary of Josiah Quincy, jr.', MHS, *Proceedings,* 1st s., IV (April 1858), 47–51.

48. Arthur M. Schlesinger, *The Colonial Merchants and the American Revolution, 1763–1776* (New York, 1918), pp. 77–80; Morgan, *Stamp Act Crisis,* p. 264; W. T. Baxter, *The House of Hancock: Business in Boston, 1724–1775* (Cambridge, Mass., 1945), pp. 232–4.

49. Maier, *Resistance to Revolution,* p. 106; Benjamin H. Newcomb, 'Effects of the Stamp Act on Colonial Pennsylvania Politics', *WMQ,* XXIII (April 1966), 257–72, concludes that 'a whole series of crises, not merely one Stamp Act, was necessary to produce, and demand, a mature and intensive revolution.'

IV. The Rockingham Ministry and the Colonies, 1765–1766

1. For details of George III's quarrel with Grenville, see John Brooke, *King George III* (1972), pp. 106–22, Stanley Ayling, *George III* (1972), pp. 122–33, and Thomas, *British Politics and the Stamp Act Crisis,* pp. 115–19; and for the formation of the Rockingham ministry, Paul Langford, *The First Rockingham Administration, 1765–1766* (Oxford, 1973), pp. 4–39.

2. For Cumberland's position see Langford, chapter 3.

3. 'Minutes of a meeting of his M's servants at his R.H. the Duke of Cumberland's', 30 Aug. 1765, B.L. Add. MSS 32969, fos. 257–8; Conway to Fauquier (copy), 14 Sept. 1765, ibid., fos. 382–3.

4. Copy, ibid., fos. 380–1.

5. Grenville to Thomas Whately, 4 Aug. 1765, Grenville letter books, v. 2, Stowe collection, Huntington Library, cited Gipson, *British Empire,* X, 371; memorandum by Newcastle for Rockingham, B.L. Add. MSS. 32969, fos. 364–5.

6. Langford, pp. 114–15; Sosin, *Agents and Merchants,* pp. 74–5 and n.

7. Langford, pp. 77–9, 111–15.

8. B.L. Add. MSS. 32973, f. 25.

9. For example, Thomas Whately to John Temple, 11 Oct. 1765, MHS, *Collections,* 6th s., IX, 71–2.

10. To Bernard, to the governors, copies, B.L. Add. MSS. 32971, fos. 93–5, 96–8, the former printed from another copy in *The Barrington-Bernard Correspondence,* ed. E. Channing and A. C. Coolidge (1912), pp. 240–2; to Gage, *Gage Correspondence,* II, 28–9.

11. Langford, pp. 81–3; *American Historical Review,* 17 (1911–12), 583; Northington MSS., cited Langford, p. 127.

12. Thomas, *British Politics and the Stamp Act Crisis,* pp. 144–6; M. G. Kammen, *A Rope of Sand. The Colonial Agents, British Politics, and the American Revolution* (Ithaca, 1968), p. 94; Langford, pp. 109–10; and for a complementary representation of the American economic situation from Rockingham's kinsman, John Wentworth of New Hampshire, see Gipson, *British Empire,* X, 372n.

13. *Franklin Papers*, XII, 362–3.
14. Richard Jackson to Governor Bernard, 8 Nov. 1765, *Speeches of the governors of Massachusetts*, ed. Alden Bradford (Boston, 1818), pp. 69–70.
15. *Franklin Papers*, XII, 364–5.
16. Langford, pp. 119–25; Thomas, *British Politics and the Stamp Act Crisis*, pp. 146–50.
17. Ibid., pp. 160–4; Langford, pp. 128–9.
18. Gipson, *British Empire*, X, 375–6, citing Adolphus's account based on private information and ministerial memoranda; Langford, p. 130; Albemarle, *Memoirs of the Marquis of Rockingham and his Contemporaries* (2 v., 1852), I, 287.
19. B.L. Add. MSS. 32973, f. 12.
20. CHS, *Collections*, XVIII, 383.
21. B.L. Add. MSS. 32972, f. 214; William Strahan to David Hall, 11 Jan. 1766, J. A. Cochrane, *Dr. Johnson's printer. The life of William Strahan* (1964), p. 186; *P.H.*, XVI, 83–90; *Correspondence of William Pitt, Earl of Chatham*, ed. W. S. Taylor and J. H. Pringle (4 v., 1838–40), II, 350–5; G. F. S. Elliot, *The Border Elliots, and the family of Minto* (1897), pp. 396–7.
22. *P.H.*, XVI, 91–3.
23. *A Selection from the Family Papers preserved at Caldwell* (Glasgow, 1854), part II, v. ii, 59; Elliot, *Border Elliots*, pp. 397–8; *SCHGM*, 26 (1925), 71.
24. The conclusion which it is possible to deduce from the unreliable account of this debate in the *Parliamentary History* (XVI, 95–110), that Pitt declared *all* taxation of the colonies unconstitutional, does not stand up to investigation of the many other accounts available. On feeling against Pitt in the House see Elliot, *Border Elliots*, pp. 398–9; H.M.C., *Stopford Sackville MSS.*, I, 105–6; *Caldwell Papers*, II, ii, 64; *SCHGM*, 26 (1925), 71; B.L. Add. MSS. 32973, f. 361.
25. Langford, p. 142.
26. Ibid., pp. 143–7.
27. *Chatham Correspondence*, II, 351; B.L. Add. MSS. 32972, f. 231, 35430, f. 32.
28. Ibid., f. 33; 32973, fos. 235, 244–7, 260. See Lord Hardwicke's note on Yorke's conduct, ibid., 3548, f. 26.
29. To Rockingham, 25 Jan. 1766, copy, B.L. Add. MSS. 32973, f. 275.
30. B.L. Add. MSS. 35430, fos. 37–8. For a more detailed analysis of the wrangle over policy between 19 and 26 Jan., see Thomas, *British Politics and the Stamp Act Crisis*, pp. 180–4.
31. *Benjamin Franklin's letters to the press, 1758–1775*, ed. V. W. Crane (Chapel Hill, N.C., 1950), p. 27, cited J. A. Ernst, *Money and Politics in America*, p. 99.
32. *Franklin Papers*, XIII, 448–9; Sir Lewis Namier and John Brooke, *Charles Townshend* (1964), p. 188; *SCHGM*, 28 (1927), 232.
33. *P.H.*, XVI, 133–6; *MHM*, 6 (1911), 282–7; see also Langford, pp. 153–4.
34. *MHM*, 6 (1911), 290.
35. Ibid., 291–302; *SCHGM*, 26 (1925), 76–85; 'Ryder Diaries', pp. 261–76; *American Historical Review*, XVII (1911–12), 565–74; *Caldwell Papers*, II, ii, 70.
36. Ibid., 68–70; *MHM*, 6 (1911), 302; *The Correspondence of King George III*, ed. Sir John Fortescue (6 v., 1927–8), I, no. 226.
37. The suggestion is made in Morgan, *Stamp Act Crisis*, pp. 349–50.
38. Albemarle, *Rockingham*, I, 271–2; *A narrative of the changes in the ministry, 1765–1767*, ed. Mary Bateson (1898), p. 50.
39. Fortescue, I, nos. 223, 225.
40. Bute MSS., quoted Langford, p. 171.
41. B.L. Add. MSS. 35430, fos. 256–7, 32973, f. 361.
42. *Caldwell Papers*, II, ii, 68–9. For a good account of this debate see *Archives of Maryland*, XIV, 267–72.

43. 'Ryder Diaries', pp. 276–82 (Ryder numbered the resolutions in sequence to the Declaratory Resolution passed on 3 Feb.); B.L. Add. MSS. 32973, fos. 359–60, 361–2, 363–4, 35374, fos. 284–5.

44. *Caldwell Papers*, II, ii, 70–1; cf. H.M.C., *Stopford Sackville MSS.*, I, 106–7.

45. 'Ryder Diaries', pp. 282–91.

46. *The Letters of David Hume*, ed. J. Y. T. Greig (2 v., Oxford, 1932), II, 20.

47. *Horace Walpole's Memoirs of the reign of George III*, éd. Barker, II, 204.

48. The affair is ably discussed in Langford, pp. 163–8.

49. For a more detailed analysis of what follows see ibid., pp. 173–86.

50. *MHM*, 6 (1911), 302; Namier and Brooke, *The History of Parliament. The House of Commons, 1754–1790* (3 v., 1964), III, 558. Surviving accounts of the hearings fully bear out this comment.

51. W. J. Shelton, *English hunger and industrial disorders. A study of social conflict during the first decade of George III's reign* (1973), pp. 24–7.

52. On this point see *Franklin Papers*, XIII, 132, including Franklin's note on questions put by John Huske.

53. Aldworth-Neville Papers, Berks R.O., D/EN 034/23.

54. B.L. Add. MSS. 32973, f. 430.

55. 'Ryder Diaries', pp. 302–10, especially speeches of Conway, Yorke, and Burke; *Archives of Maryland*, XIV, 274.

56. On some of these points see Langford, pp. 185–9, and Ernst, *Money and Politics in America*, pp. 6–15, 65–70.

57. This is especially clear from the abundant evidence available about the careful preparation and the incidence of the 3*d.* duty on molasses; see p. 38 above.

58. Grenville's figures for supplies for the forces and debt interest are derived from 'Parliamentary notes of Nathaniel Ryder', Harrowby MSS., doc. 62. We are grateful to Dr. P. D. G. Thomas for communicating this information. For other aspects of this line of argument, see Thomas Whately, *Considerations on the trade and finances of this kingdom . . .* (1766), especially pp. 44, 73–4, 76–7.

59. Langford, pp. 181–2.

60. 'Ryder Diaries', pp. 272, 288, 312–13, 314, 317; Lords' protests, 11, 17 Mar. 1766, *P.H.*, XVI, 181–93.

61. *Franklin Papers*, XIII, 132, 168–9.

62. 'Ryder Diaries', pp. 310–20; Aldworth-Neville papers, D/EN 034/23; B.L. Add. MSS. 32974, fos. 45–6, 47–8, 49–50.

63. Ibid., fos. 67–8, 107–8.

64. The Lords' proceedings on the Bills began on 6 Mar. and ended on the 17th. *Chatham Correspondence*, II, 403–4; *P.H.*, XVI, 177–93; *Original letters to . . . Henry Flood* (1820), pp. 13–17. *American Historical Review*, XVII (1911–12), 576–86; B.L. Add. MSS. 32974, f. 153; H.M.C., *Stopford Sackville MSS.*, I, 108. W. G. Hamilton to John Calcraft, Saturday [8th], Monday [10th], Wednesday [12th], Thursday [13th Mar.], *Chatham Correspondence*, II, 382–6, all misdated by the editors, include further detail. For a detailed account of these debates see Thomas, *British Politics and the Stamp Act Crisis*, pp. 243–7.

65. Langford, pp. 193–4; *American Historical Review*, XVII (1911–12), 582–3.

66. *The Correspondence of Edmund Burke*, volume I, ed. T. W. Copeland (Cambridge, 1958), pp. 239–40.

67. For a fuller exposition of these points see Langford, pp. 199–203.

68. This appears from the evidence given at the bar of the House of Commons, and from the legislation discussed below.

69. Langford, p. 205.

70. 'Ryder Diaries', pp. 320–9; B.L. Add. MSS. 32974, fos. 348–9, 370–1; *Franklin Papers*, XIII, 237–8; John Huske to Charles Townshend, 9 Apr. 1767, Namier

and Brooke, *Charles Townshend,* p. 187; *WMQ,* 3rd s., 27 (1970), 90–1 and n.; John Yorke to Hardwicke, 19 May 1766, B.L. Add. MSS. 35374, fos. 291–2.

71. B.L. Add. MSS. 32974, fos. 439, 441, 32975, fos. 58–9, 81, 85, 97, 98, 110, 114, 112, 35607, fos. 255–6.

72. B.L. Add. MSS. 32975, f. 147; *SCHGM,* 28 (1927), 230.

73. Ibid., 232, 234–5.

74. 6 Geo. III, c. 52.

75. Whately, *Considerations on the trade and finances of this kingdom,* p. 115. The Chatham administration rectified this error in Dec. 1766 by the statute 7 Geo. III, c. 2.

76. Whately, op. cit., pp. 92–102.

77. 6 Geo. III, c. 51.

78. See p. 80 above. On the initial Bill see *Archives of Maryland,* XIV, 280, and on the amendments, *SCHGM,* 28 (1927), 232.

79. Franklin so represented it, *Franklin Papers,* XIII, 186–7.

80. *P.H.,* XVI, 141, 142, 144, 149, 158–9; *Franklin Papers,* XIII, 135, 137, 139, 143–5, 156; 'Ryder Diaries', pp. 300–2.

81. The rates are conveniently listed in *Sources and Documents illustrating the American Revolution, 1764–1788 . . . ,* ed. S. E. Morison (2nd edn., 1965), pp. 79–80.

82. Langford, p. 207; Dickerson, *The Navigation Acts and the American Revolution,* p. 201.

83. See p. 84 above.

84. See p. 76 above.

85. *Franklin Papers,* XIII, 238–9.

86. Ibid., 240–1.

87. B.L. Add. MSS. 35361, fos. 271–2; Whately, *Considerations on the trade and finances of this kingdom,* p. 102.

88. Langford, pp. 208–10; Conway to Gage, 20 May 1766, *Gage Correspondence,* II, 37.

89. Lyman H. Butterfield, ed., *Diary and Autobiography of John Adams* (Cambridge, Mass., 1961), I, 308–9. Adams remained sceptical *despite* having noted Pitt's speech.

90. As quoted in Edmund S. and Helen M. Morgan, *The Stamp Act Crisis* (Cambridge, Mass., 1953), p. 288.

91. Ibid., pp. 284–8.

92. Richard Bland, *An Enquiry into the Rights of the British Colonies* (Williamsburg, Va., 1766), as reprinted in Jack P. Greene, *Colonies to Nation, 1763–1789* (New York 1967), p. 89.

93. Bland, loc. cit., p. 90.

94. Bland, loc. cit., p. 91.

95. John Shy, *Toward Lexington: The Role of the British Army in the Coming of the American Revolution* (Princeton, N.J., 1965), p. 142.

96. Henry Moore to Secretary Conway, 20 June 1765, in E. B. O'Callaghan, ed., *Documents Relative to the Colonial History of the State of New-York* (Albany, 1856), VII, 831–2; Nicholas Varga, 'The New York Restraining Act: Its Passage and Some Effects, 1766–1768', *New York History,* XXXVII (July 1956), 233–8.

97. Earl of Shelburne to Governor Moore, 9 Aug. 1766, in O'Callaghan, *N.Y. Col. Docs.,* VII, 847–8.

98. Governor Moore to the Earl of Shelburne, 19 Dec. 1766, in O'Callaghan, *N.Y. Col. Docs.,* VII, 823–4.

99. O'Callaghan, *N.Y. Col. Docs.,* VII, 832–4; *Acts and Resolves of . . . Massachusetts Bay* (Boston, 1890), IV, 903–4.

100. Jack P. Greene and Richard M. Jellison, 'The Currency Act of 1764 in Imperial-Colonial Relations, 1764–1776', *WMQ,* XVIII (October 1961), 490–4; see

also, Jack M. Sosin, 'Imperial Regulation of Colonial Paper Money, 1764–1773', *PMHB*, LXXXVIII (April 1964), 174–98; Joseph A. Ernst, 'The Currency Act Repeal Movement: A Study of Imperial Politics and Revolutionary Crisis, 1764–1767', *WMQ*, XXV (April 1968), 177–211.

101. Greene and Jellison, 'The Currency Act', pp. 494–5; Sosin, 'Imperial Regulation', pp. 186–7; Ernst, 'Currency Act', pp. 192–3; O'Callaghan, *N.Y. Col. Docs.*, VII, 820–1; Leonard W. Labaree, *Royal Instructions to British Colonial Governors, 1670–1776* (New York, 1935), I, 228–9.

102. Varga, 'New York Restraining Act', p. 239; Lawrence H. Gipson, *The British Empire Before the American Revolution* (New York, 1965), XI, 54–5.

103. Charles M. Andrews, 'The Boston Merchants and the Non-Importation Movement', *Publications* of the Colonial Society of Massachusetts, XIX (1917), 174–5; O'Callaghan, *N.Y. Col. Docs.*, VII, 920–1.

104. Thomas C. Barrow, *Trade and Empire: The British Customs Service in Colonial America, 1660–1775* (Cambridge, Mass., 1967), p. 191; Neil R. Stout, *The Royal Navy in America: A Study of Enforcement of British Colonial Policy in the Era of the American Revolution* (Annapolis, Md., 1973), pp. 66–8, 72, 119; Herbert A. Johnson and David Syrett, 'Some Nice Sharp Quillets of the Customs Law: The New York Affair, 1763–1767', *WMQ*, XXV, (July 1968), 432–51; Jesse Lemisch, 'Jack Tar in the Streets: Merchant Seamen in the Politics of Revolutionary America', *WMQ*, XXV (July 1968), 381–4; Samuel G. Arnold, *History of the State of Rhode Island and Providence Plantations* (New York, 1860), II, 255–6; *Annual Register* (London, 1765), VII, 19, as quoted in Alfred S. Martin, 'The King's Customs: Philadelphia, 1763–1774', *WMQ*, V (April 1948), 204–5.

105. Barrow, *Trade and Empire*, p. 202.

106. Carl Ubbelohde, *The Vice-Admiralty Courts and the American Revolution* (Chapel Hill, N.C., 1960), pp. 47–54.

107. Ubbelohde, *Vice-Admiralty Courts*, pp. 60–4; David S. Lovejoy, 'Rights Imply Equality: The Case Against Admiralty Jurisdiction in America, 1764–1776', *WMQ*, XVI (October 1959), 462–7; Charles F. Adams, *The Works of John Adams . . .* (Boston, 1851), III, 466–7.

V. Charles Townshend and the Colonies

1. The most detailed recent account of the Chatham ministry's dealings with America is in P. D. G. Thomas, *British Politics and the Stamp Act Crisis*, pp. 283–363.

2. R. J. Chaffin, 'The Townshend Acts of 1767', *WMQ*, 3rd s., 27 (1970), 91–2.

3. John Huske to Townshend, 9 Apr. 1767, Namier and Brooke, *Charles Townshend*, pp. 187–8.

4. *Franklin Papers*, XIII, 446–7.

5. *Burke Correspondence*, volume I, ed. Copeland, p. 280 n. 1; *Grenville Papers*, III, 334–5.

6. Shelburne to Gage, 11 Dec. 1766, *Gage Correspondence*, II, 49–50; to colonial governors, same date, *Documents relating to the colonial history of New York* (15 v., Albany, 1856–87), VII, 880.

7. For an account of this debate see P. D. G. Thomas, 'Charles Townshend and American Taxation in 1767', *English Historical Review*, 83 (1968), 35–8, and references cited, and also explanations by Thomas Townshend, 8 Feb. 1769, and by Grafton, 5 Mar. 1776, *Sir Henry Cavendish's debates . . .* , ed. John Wright (2 v., 1841–3), I, 213–14, and *P.H.*, XVIII, 1227.

8. For the petition see p. 91 above. *C.J.*, XXXI, 158–60; Gipson, *British Empire*, XI, 54–5; *Chatham Correspondence*, III, 186–7.

9. Ibid., 186–7, 188–9, 191; CHS, *Collections*, XIX, 82.
10. *Chatham Correspondence*, III, 206–10.
11. To Chatham, [16 Feb. 1767], Chatham MSS., P.R.O. 30/8/3, omitted from *Chatham Correspondence*, III, 206–11, at p. 210; Barrington to Gage, private, 6 July 1767, Gage MSS.
12. *C.J.*, XXXI, 158–60; *SCHGM*, 29 (1928), 217.
13. 'Ryder Diaries', pp. 330–1; *Caldwell Papers*, II, ii, 106–7; *Chatham Correspondence*, III, 210–11n.
14. Ibid., 215.
15. Ibid., 225; *Horace Walpole's memoirs*, ed. Barker, II, 296; MHS, *Collections*, 5th s., IX, 486–8, 6th s., IX, 79–80; *SCHGM*, 29 (1928), 217–18; H.M.C., *Stopford Sackville MSS.*, I, 120.
16. For the following account of the cabinet meeting of 6 March, see Shelburne to Chatham, 'Sunday', Chatham MSS., P.R.O. 30/8/56, part i, fos. 86–90. The endorsed later attribution, 'April 26th', is certainly incorrect: this letter must have been written *before* Grafton's and Shelburne's descriptions of the *next* cabinet meeting on Thursday, 12 Mar. (*Chatham Correspondence*, III, 231–6), since Shelburne's description refers to its contents. As this letter twice refers to the proceedings as having taken place on the previous Friday, it cannot itself be describing the discussions on the 12th, and in it Shelburne drew Chatham's attention to the fact that the next meeting would be on 'Thursday' (i.e. the 12th). The correct date of the letter is Sunday, 8 Mar. 1767.
17. *Gage Correspondence*, II, 406 (probably received on 17 Feb., cf. ibid., 405).
18. *Chatham Correspondence*, III, 231, 232–3.
19. *Autobiography and political correspondence of Augustus Henry, third Duke of Grafton*, ed. Sir William R. Anson (1898), p. 127. Cf. remarks by Thomas Townshend, 8 Feb. 1769, *Sir Henry Cavendish's debates*, I, 213.
20. *Chatham Correspondence*, III, 232, 233–6.
21. Memorandum by Barrington, [10 May 1766], Fortescue, I, no. 454, misplaced by the editor; Barrington to Gage, private, 12 Sept. 1766, 10 Feb., 13 Mar. 1767, Gage MSS.
22. *Chatham Correspondence*, III, 235.
23. Shelburne to Chatham, 'Thursday Nt.' [19 Mar. 1767], Chatham MSS., P.R.O. 30/8/56, part i, fos. 74–5. For the dating of this letter, by reference to the provision for the King's brothers, see Fortescue, I, nos. 496–7, *Chatham Correspondence*, III, 236, and *C.J.*, XXXI, 236–7.
24. *Horace Walpole's memoirs*, ed. Barker, II, 318–19; B.L. Add. MSS. 32981, fos. 32, 34, 65; *SCHGM*, 29 (1928), 221–2; Townshend to Grafton, n.d. (?—early April 1767?), Grafton MS. 453.
25. *Horace Walpole's memoirs*, ed. Barker, II, 454–5; *Chatham Correspondence*, III, 248–9; B.L. Add. MSS. 35361, fos. 265–6, 32981, fos. 137–8; MHS, *Collections*, 5th s., IX, 224–6, s., IX, 81–3; *Franklin Papers*, XIV, 108–9.
26. B.L. Add. MSS. 32981, fos. 137, 141.
27. *Franklin Papers*, XIV, 125; MHS, *Collections*, 5th s., IX, 227.
28. *Chatham Correspondence*, III, 240–1; Barrington to Gage, private, 10 Apr. 1767, Gage MSS.
29. B.L. Add. MSS. 35608, fos. 14–15.
30. Townshend to Grafton, 23 Apr. 1767, Grafton MS. 452.
31. Fortescue, I, nos. 504–6; B.L. Add. MSS. 32981, f. 313.
32. J. Norris, *Shelburne and Reform* (1963), pp. 47, 49.
33. Namier and Brooke, *Charles Townshend*, pp. 176–8, and on the 'champagne speech', pp. 170–1; P. D. G. Thomas, article cited, pp. 47–8; for the suggestion that the speech was coercive in intention, R. J. Chaffin, article cited, pp. 112–14.

34. MHS, *Collections*, 5th s., IX, 229.
35. B.L. Add. MSS. 32981, fos. 375–6; *Horace Walpole's memoirs*, ed. Barker, III, 24.
36. For this speech see Thomas, article cited, pp. 44–6, and references given there, to which may be added MHS, *Collections*, 5th s., IX, 230–2; *Franklin Papers*, XIV, 180–1; *Pennsylvania Magazine of History and Biography*, 10 (1886), 322–4.
37. Namier and Brooke, *Charles Townshend*, pp. 187–91.
38. B.L. Add. MSS. 32981, fos. 377, 378; *Autobiography of Grafton*, p. 176.
39. Thomas, article cited, p. 46.
40. Ross J. S. Hoffman, *The Marquis. A study of Lord Rockingham, 1730–1782* (New York, 1973), pp. 173–4.
41. 7 Geo. III, c. 59. For New York's compliance with the Act see p. 105 below.
42. On this episode see *Horace Walpole's memoirs*, ed. Barker, III, 34, 35–6; Fortescue, I, pp. 475–84; *Chatham Correspondence*, III, 255–70; *Autobiography of Grafton*, pp. 132–40; B.L. Add. MSS. 32981, fos. 382–3, 32982, fos. 32–3, 62–3, 89, 95–123, 126–7; MHS, *Collections*, 5th s., IX, 236–7.
43. See Grafton's later explanation, *P.H.*, XVIII, 1227.
44. Townshend to Grafton, [25 May 1767], Grafton MS. 445, printed with explanation of the dating, Thomas, *British Politics and the Stamp Act Crisis*, pp. 354–5 and n.
45. The suggestion is made in R. J. Chaffin, article cited, pp. 118–19.
46. *P.H.*, XVIII, 1227.
47. Thomas, article cited, pp. 48–9; *P.H.*, XVIII, 1227. The lost £60,000 must, of course, have been raised from the British public in other ways, under Townshend's arrangements for balancing his budget.
48. Thomas, article cited, p. 50; Shelburne's observations on Grafton's conduct, during a debate of 7 Feb. 1775, *P.H.*, XVIII, 276.
49. 7 Geo. III, cc. 46, 41; *C.J.*, XXXI, 414–15.
50. H.M.C., *Tenth Report*, appendix, pt. I, *Weston-Underwood MSS.*, p. 406.
51. *Chatham Correspondence*, III, 185.
52. Page 96 above.
53. Nicholas Varga, 'The New York Restraining Act: Its Passage and Some Effects, 1766–1768', *New York History*, XXXVII (July 1956), pp. 251–2; E. B. O'Callaghan, ed., *Documents Relative to the Colonial History of the State of New York* (Albany, 1856), VII, 942.
54. O'Callaghan, *N.Y. Col. Docs.*, VII, 945.
55. Jack P. Greene and Richard M. Jellison, 'The Currency Act of 1764 in Imperial-Colonial Relations, 1764–1776', *WMQ*, XVIII (October 1961), 495–517; Joseph A. Ernst, 'The Currency Act Repeal Movement: A Study of Imperial Politics and Revolutionary Crisis, 1764–67', *WMQ*, XXV (April 1968), 193–211.
56. Thomas C. Barrow, *Trade and Empire: The British Customs Service in Colonial America, 1660–1775* (Cambridge, Mass., 1967), pp. 204–6; Neil R. Stout, *The Royal Navy in America, 1760–1775* (Annapolis, Md., 1973), pp. 82–3.
57. Barrow, *Trade and Empire*, pp. 220–66; Dora Mae Clark, 'The American Board of Customs, 1767–1783', *American Historical Review*, XLV (July 1940), 777–85; Margaret M. Spector, *The American Department of the British Government, 1768–1782* (New York, 1940); Carl Ubbelohde, *The Vice-Admiralty Courts and the American Revolution* (Chapel Hill, N.C., 1960), pp. 128–47.
58. Barrow, *Trade and Empire*, pp. 221–2; Clark, 'American Board', pp. 785–6; Pauline Maier, *From Resistance to Revolution: Colonial Radicals and the Development of American Opposition to Britain, 1765–1776* (New York, 1972), pp. 68, 69, 123.
59. Barrow, *Trade and Empire*, pp. 227–8; Clark, 'American Board', pp. 786–7; Stout, *Royal Navy*, p. 116; Charles Paxton to Viscount George Townshend, 24 Feb. 1768, in George G. Wolkins, 'Letters of Charles Paxton, 1768–1769', in MHS, *Proceed-*

ings, LVI (1923), 348; Commissioners of Customs to Commodore Hood, 12 Feb. 1768, in George G. Wolkins, 'The Seizure of John Hancock's Sloop *Liberty*', MHS, *Proceedings*, LV (1922), 278.

60. Commodore Samuel Hood to John Corner, 2 May 1768, in Wolkins, 'Sloop *Liberty*', pp. 271–2; Stout, *Royal Navy*, pp. 116–18; Commissioners of the Customs to Lords of the Treasury, 28 March 1768, in Wolkins, 'Sloop *Liberty*', pp. 269–70; Maier, *Resistance to Revolution*, pp. 123–4.

61. Barrow, *Trade and Empire*, pp. 228–30; Wolkins, 'Sloop *Liberty*', pp. 248–9; Ubbelohde, *Vice-Admiralty Courts*, pp. 120–1; William T. Baxter, *The House of Hancock: Business in Boston, 1724–1775* (Cambridge, Mass., 1945), pp. 160–2.

62. Jesse Lemisch, 'Jack Tar in the Streets: Merchant Seamen in the Politics of Revolutionary America', *WMQ*, XXV (July 1968), 392; Wolkins, 'Sloop *Liberty*', pp. 249–50; Stout, *Royal Navy*, p. 119; Thomas Hutchinson to Richard Jackson, 16 June 1768, in Wolkins, 'Sloop *Liberty*', pp. 281–4.

63. The numerous accounts of the *Liberty* incident vary, so the reader should consult several before forming his own conclusions. No account is particularly favourable to the British officials but cf. Thomas Hutchinson to Richard Jackson, 16 June 1768, in Wolkins, 'Sloop *Liberty*', pp. 281–4, and Hiller B. Zobel, *The Boston Massacre* (New York, 1970), pp. 73–7. At the other end of the spectrum are the versions by Oliver M. Dickerson, 'John Hancock, Notorious Smuggler or Near Victim of British Customs Racketeers?', *Mississippi Valley Historical Review*, XXXII (March 1946), 517–40, and his *Navigation Acts and The American Revolution* (Philadelphia, 1951), 236–46. In between are the accounts of Ubbelohde, *Vice-Admiralty Courts*, pp. 119–27; Barrow, *Trade and Empire*, pp. 230–4; Wolkins, 'Sloop *Liberty*', pp. 239–62.

64. See references under note 63. For Harrison's account of his ordeal, see D. H. Watson, 'Joseph Harrison and the *Liberty* Incident', *WMQ*, XX (October 1963), 585–95.

65. See references under note 63.

66. See references under note 63; for Adams' defence, see David S. Lovejoy, 'Rights Imply Equality: The Case Against Admiralty Jurisdiction in America, 1764–1776', *WMQ*, XVI (October 1959), 479–82.

67. Charles M. Andrews, 'The Boston Merchants and the Non-Importation Movement', *Publications*, Colonial Society of Massachusetts, XIX (1917), 191–3; Arthur M. Schlesinger, *The Colonial Merchants and the American Revolution, 1763–1776* (New York, 1918), pp. 106–13; Otis as quoted in Benjamin W. Labaree, *The Boston Tea Party* (New York, 1964), p. 21.

68. Thomas R. Adams, *American Independence: The Growth of an Idea* (Providence, R.I., 1965), pp. xi–xii, 37–41.

69. John Dickinson, *Letters from a Farmer in Pennsylvania* (Philadelphia, 1768), as printed in Paul L. Ford, ed., *The Writings of John Dickinson* (Philadelphia, 1895), I, 308–12.

70. Dickinson, *Letters from a Farmer*, loc. cit., pp. 317–22.

71. Ibid., pp. 328, 332–3, 355–6, 364, 367.

72. Ibid., pp. 346, 367, 398–9.

73. Ibid., pp. 328, 402.

74. Massachusetts Circular Letter of 11 February 1768, in Harry A. Cushing, ed., *The Writings of Samuel Adams* (New York, 1904), I, 184–8; E. B. O'Callaghan, ed., *Documents Relative to the Colonial History of the State of New York* (Albany, N.Y., 1856), VIII, 58–9.

75. Merrill Jensen, *The Founding of a Nation* (New York, 1968), pp. 250–2, 256.

76. Jensen, *Founding*, p. 257; Richard J. Hooker, 'The American Revolution Seen Through a Wine Glass', *WMQ*, XI (January 1954), 69; 'Rusticus', 'The Cause of

Liberty and Right', in Jack P. Greene, *Colonies to Nation, 1763–1789* (New York, 1967), pp. 148–54.

77. Schlesinger, *Colonial Merchants*, pp. 113–20; Andrews, 'Boston Merchants', pp. 201–4; Thomas Cushing to Dennys De Berdt, 18 April 1768, in MHS, *Collections*, 4th s., IV (Boston, 1858), 350–1; Dickinson, 'An Address', in Ford, *Writings of Dickinson*, I, 411–17.

78. *Boston Gazette*, 15 Aug. 1768; *New York Journal*, 8 Sept. 1768; Schlesinger, *Colonial Merchants*, pp. 120–1, 124–5; Andrews, 'Boston Merchants', pp. 204–8; Labaree, *Boston Tea Party*, p. 23.

79. Schlesinger, *Colonial Merchants*, pp. 125–30; Andrews, 'Boston Merchants', pp. 208–11; Arthur L. Jensen, *The Maritime Commerce of Colonial Philadelphia* (Madison, Wisc., 1963), pp. 174–80; R. L. Brunhouse, 'The Effect of the Townshend Acts in Pennsylvania', *PMHB*, LIV (October 1930), 360–6; and sources cited in Labaree, *Boston Tea Party*, pp. 23–4, n. 20.

80. Labaree, *Boston Tea Party*, pp. 26–32.

81. Ibid., pp. 25–6, 32–4.

82. Ibid., pp. 24–5; Dickerson, *Navigation Acts*, pp. 185, 201.

83. Schlesinger, *Colonial Merchants*, pp. 131–2.

84. General importation statistics from U.S. Bureau of the Census, *Historical Statistics of the United States: Colonial Times to 1957* (Washington, D.C., 1960), pp. 759–60; statistics on duties, Dickerson, *Navigation Acts*, p. 198.

VI. The Grafton Ministry Marks Time

1. Mary Bateson, ed., *A narrative of the changes in the Ministry, 1765–1767* (1898), pp. 141–2; *Correspondence of John, fourth Duke of Bedford,* ed. Lord John Russell (3 v., 1842–6), III, 382–3; B.L. Add. MSS. 32983 f. 392. For a general account of these negotiations see John Brooke, *The Chatham Administration, 1766–1768* (1956), chapters V and VIII.

2. *Horace Walpole's memoirs,* ed. Barker, III, 81, 83–4; B.L. Add. MSS. 32987, fos. 87, 95, 113; *Franklin Papers*, XIV, 331; *SCHGM*, 30 (1929), 178; MHS, *Collections*, 5th s., IX, 247–8.

3. Ibid., 248–9, 265–6; *Franklin Papers*, XIV, 349, XV, 17, 50, 77; B.L. Add. MSS. 32988, f. 49; *Pennsylvania Magazine of History and Biography*, 10 (1886), 330.

4. *Gage Correspondence*, I, 135–7; Gipson, *British Empire*, XI, 130–1.

5. 8,000,000 gallons (see p. 28 above) at 1d. per gallon represented a revenue of over £30,000. In 1767–8 slightly under £12,000 was collected (Dickerson, *The Navigation Acts and the American Revolution*, p. 185, table 9).

6. 8 Geo. III, c. 22; *C.J.*, XXXI, 661.

7. Shelburne to Gage, 14 Nov. 1767, *Gage Correspondence*, II, 53–4.

8. *Franklin Papers*, XV, 74; cabinet minute, 19 Mar. 1768, Granville MSS., P.R.O. 30/29/3/2:103; Fortescue, II, nos. 597, 598; *Gage Correspondence*, II, 61–6, 66, 67; circular letter to governors, 15 Apr. 1768, P.R.O. C.O. 5/241, fos. 14–16.

9. George III to Grafton, 18 Feb. 1768, Grafton MSS.

10. MHS, *Collections*, 5th s., IX, 296; *SCHGM*, 30 (1929), 234.

11. See pp. 113–14 above.

12. Bernard, P.R.O. C.O. 5/757:28–9; Gage, in *Gage Correspondence*, II, 540, acknowledged in Barrington to Gage, 16 Apr. 1768, Gage MSS.

13. *Gage Correspondence*, II, 68–9; Hillsborough to the Admiralty, 7 July 1768, P.R.O. Adm. 1/4128.

14. Bernard to Hillsborough, 11, 14, 16, 17 June 1768, P.R.O. C.O. 5/757:115–17, 118–20, 138–41, 146–7; Fortescue, II, nos. 637–8; Bradshaw to Grafton, 22 July 1768, Grafton MSS.

15. Fortescue, and Grafton MSS., as previous note, and Hillsborough to Gower, 19 July 1768, Granville MSS., P.R.O. 30/29/3/2:104–5; *Grenville Papers*, IV, 320, 321–2; B.L. Add. MSS. 35374, f. 352.
16. *Grenville Papers*, IV, 364; Fitzmaurice, *Life of William, Earl of Shelburne* (2 v., 1912), I, 386; *Horace Walpole's memoirs*, ed. Barker, III, 156; *Gage Correspondence*, II, 72–4; Barrington to Gage, 1–13 Aug. 1768, Gage MSS.
17. As previous note. Barrington described Botetourt as of 'very good understanding, an undaunted spirit, humanity, decision and activity in the highest degree, with a total disregard for every consideration but that of doing right.' To Gage, private, 1 Aug. 1768, Gage MSS.
18. Bernard to Hillsborough, 14 June, 9 July, 6 Aug., and especially 9 Sept. 1768, P.R.O. C.O. 5/757:118–20, 303–6, 368–70, 388–91.
19. *Gage Correspondence*, II, 479–80.
20. To Hillsborough, 26 Sept. 1768, ibid., I, 197.
21. To Barrington, 26 Sept. 1768, ibid., II, 488.
22. To Hillsborough, 31 Oct. 1768 ibid., I, 205.
23. To Barrington, 4 Mar. 1769, ibid., II, 502.
24. Barrington to Gage, 16 Apr. 1768, 20 Sept. 1769, Gage MSS.; Hillsborough to Gage, 4 Aug., 3 Oct. 1770, *Gage Correspondence*, II, 113, 119.
25. Dennys de Berdt to Thomas Cushing, 2 Jan. 1769, referring to a conversation with Hillsborough some time the previous month, 'Letters of Dennys de Berdt', p. 350.
26. *Autobiography of Grafton*, pp. 216–17.
27. Cited, Brooke, *The Chatham Administration*, pp. 372–3.
28. Ibid., pp. 373–4. Cf. Newcastle to Dowdeswell, copy, 17 Sept. 1768, B.L. Add. MSS. 32991, f. 111.
29. Albemarle, *Rockingham*, II, 80.
30. Brooke, *The Chatham Administration*, p. 369; *Grenville Papers*, IV, 510–13n.; B.L. Add. MSS. 32991, fos. 125, 206–7, 220, 224.
31. R. H. Lee, *Life of Arthur Lee* (2 v., Boston, 1829), I, 188.
32. H.M.C., *Various Collections*, VI, *Knox MSS.*, pp. 97–8.
33. Dowdeswell to Rockingham, 14 Aug. 1768, Dowdeswell MSS.
34. George III to Grafton, 27 Oct. 1768, Grafton MSS., referring to Gage's dispatches nos. 15 and 16, of 26 Sept., and a copy enclosed of Bernard to Gage, of 16 Sept. (*Gage Correspondence*, I, 195–8).
35. *Grenville Papers*, IV, 368.
36. MHS, *Collections*, 5th s., IX, 300. Cf. *Grenville Papers*, IV, 364.
37. MHS, *Collections*, 5th s., IX, 300–1; cf. Rockingham to Charles Yorke, 3 Nov. 1768, B.L. Add. MSS. 35430, fos. 128–9.
38. Brooke, *The Chatham Administration*, pp. 375–84; Fortescue, II, nos. 681–6.
39. *P.H.*, XVI, 469.
40. *SCHGM*, 30 (1929), 230; *PMHB*, 10 (1886), 463–4; MHS, *Collections*, 5th s., IX, 302; *Life of Arthur Lee*, I, 202–4.
41. *Gage Correspondence*, II, 509–10; Barrington to Gage, 12 Feb., 21 Mar., 27 June, 17 July 1769, Gage MSS.
42. MHS, *Collections*, 5th s., IX, 306–9, *P.H.*, XVI, 476–80, 507; George III to Grafton, 15 Dec. 1768, Grafton MSS.
43. *Grenville Papers*, IV, 400–1; *SCHGM*, 30 (1929), 234–5; MHS, *Collections*, 5th s., IX, 304–6; *Franklin Papers*, XVI, 11–12.
44. *C.J.*, XXXII, 123–4, 136–7, 151, 185–6, 207; *P.H.*, XVI, 484–511; *Sir Henry Cavendish's debates*, I, 185–225; B.L. Add. MSS. 35375, fos. 3–4, 35608, fos. 326, 336; MHS, *Collections*, 5th s., IX, 312–16, 6th s., IX, 122–5; *Franklin Papers*, XVI, 29–30, 40; *SCHGM*, 31 (1930), 46–9.

45. Fortescue, II, no. 701. Cf. Barrington to Gage, 21 Mar. 1769, enclosure, Gage MSS.; *Gage Correspondence*, I, 202–4.

46. Fortescue, II, no. 701A.

47. Ibid., no. 701. Cf. *Horace Walpole's memoirs*, ed. Barker, III, 223.

48. 9 Geo. III, c. 18; Barrington to Gage, 21 Mar. 1769, Gage MSS.; *C.J.*, XXXII, 317; *P.H.* XVI, 605–7; *Franklin Papers*, XVI, 69–70; *SCHGM*, 31 (1930), 55–7; MHS, *Collections*, 5th s., IX, 326–9.

49. *Franklin Papers*, XVI, 11. Cf. MHS, *Collections*, 5th s., IX, 318.

50. *Franklin Papers*, XVI, 62–3; MHS, *Collections*, 5th s., IX, 325–6; 'Letters of Dennys de Berdt', pp. 364, 366.

51. *P.H.*, XVI, 603–5.

52. Ibid., 610–22.

53. MHS, *Collections*, 5th s., IX, 336–7.

54. Ibid., p. 338.

55. MHS, *Collections*, 5th s., IX, 339–41; *Sir Henry Cavendish's debates*, I, 391–401; *Horace Walpole's memoirs*, ed. Barker, III, 239; *SCHGM*, 31 (1930), 58–9. So deep was the colonial agents' distrust of the government, that they were soon reflecting that the whole debate was a ministerial scheme intended to cause relaxation of the colonial non-importation agreements (MHS, *Collections*, 5th s., IX, 347, 6th s., IX, 149; *Franklin Papers*, XVI, 79).

56. *Autobiography of Grafton*, pp. 229–30.

57. Ibid., pp. 230–5.

58. MHS, *Collections*, 5th s., IX, 358–9. Cf. *Franklin Papers*, XVI, 173, 176, 177.

59. MHS, *Collections*, 5th s., IX, 383–4. Cf. *Franklin Papers*, XVII, 112.

60. *Grenville Papers*, IV, 480.

61. Hillsborough to Gage, 8 June and 30 July 1768, in Clarence E. Carter, ed., *The Correspondence of General Thomas Gage* (New Haven, Conn., 1931–3), II, 68–9 and 72–4; Gage to Hillsborough, 28 June 1768, in Carter, *Gage Correspondence*, I, 182–3.

62. Richard D. Brown, *Revolutionary Politics in Massachusetts: The Boston Committee of Correspondence and the Towns, 1772–1774* (Cambridge, Mass., 1970), pp. 29–30, and his 'The Massachusetts Convention of Towns, 1768', *WMQ*, XXVI (January 1969), 94–104.

63. Hiller B. Zobel, *The Boston Massacre* (New York, 1970), pp. 99–100.

64. Ibid., pp. 100–6; Gage to Hillsborough, 10 and 31 Oct. 1768, in Carter, *Gage Correspondence*, I, 200–1, 202–5.

65. Hillsborough to Gage, 24 March 1768, ibid., II, 84–7; Gage to Hillsborough, 10 June 1768, ibid., I, 228–30; John Shy, *Toward Lexington: The Role of the British Army in the Coming of the American Revolution* (Princeton, N.J., 1965), pp. 306–13; Zobel, *Massacre*, pp. 132–3.

66. Ibid., pp. 132–44. In this and subsequent paragraphs Zobel's authoritative but somewhat conservative interpretation has been tempered by a consideration of other points of view. Most useful in this effort to achieve a balance have been the writings of Pauline Maier, *From Resistance to Revolution: Colonial Radicals and the Development of American Opposition to Britain, 1765–1776* (New York, 1972), pp. 125–6; Shy, *Toward Lexington*, pp. 302–20; 'Revolutionary Violence and the Relevance of History', *Journal of Interdisciplinary History*, II (Summer 1971), 119–35; and Jesse Lemisch, 'Radical Plot in Boston (1770): A Study in the Use of Evidence', *Harvard Law Review*, LXXXIV (1970), 485–504.

67. Zobel, *Boston Massacre*, pp. 145–77.

68. Ibid., pp. 180–205, for this and following paragraph.

69. Ibid., pp. 209–10.

70. Arthur M. Schlesinger, *Prelude to Independence: The Newspaper War on Britain*,

1764–1776 (New York, 1958), pp. 30–1, 43, 109, 117; Thomas B. Adams, *American Independence: The Growth of an Idea* (Providence, R.I., 1965), pp. 57–65; Philip Davidson, *Propaganda and the American Revolution* (Chapel Hill, N.C., 1941), pp. 196–8, 222.

71. Benjamin W. Labaree, *The Boston Tea Party* (New York, 1964), pp. 46–50; Arthur M. Schlesinger, *The Colonial Merchants and the American Revolution 1763–1776* (New York, 1918), pp. 212–36; Charles M. Andrews, 'The Boston Merchants and the Non-Importation Movement', *Publications* of the Colonial Society of Massachusetts, XIX (1918), 241–54; *Pennsylvania Journal,* 12 July 1770.

VII. Aftermath of the Boston Massacre

1. Barrington to Gage, 7 Mar. 1770, Gage MSS.
2. *Sir Henry Cavendish's debates,* I, 483–500; *P.H.,* XVI, 852–74; MHS, *Collections,* 5th s., IX, 421–3; B.L. Add. MSS. 35631, f. 85; *SCHGM,* 31 (1930), 228–33; *Virginia Magazine of History and Biography,* 12 (1904–5), 168–9.
3. 10 Geo. III, c. 17.
4. Cf. *Grenville Papers,* IV, 480.
5. B.L. Add. MSS. 35609 f. 181; *P.H.,* XVI, 979–1001; *Sir Henry Cavendish's debates,* II, 1–12; MHS, *Collections,* 5th s., IX, 435–6, 6th s., IX, 177, 181; Fortescue, II, no. 788, pp. 144–5. In July the law officers gave a legal opinion firmly in support of Gage's position: Barrington to Gage, 31 July 1770, with enclosure, Gage MSS.
6. *Sir Henry Cavendish's debates,* II, 14–36; *P.H.,* XVI, 1001–10 (misdated 8 May), 1010–27; MHS, *Collections,* 5th s., IX, 436–8.
7. On this Act, 10 Geo. III, c. 35, see Gipson, *British Empire,* XI, 260–1, and Ernst, *Money and Politics in America,* pp. 264–81.
8. Gage to Barrington, private, 14 May, 7 Oct., 16 Dec. 1769, *Gage Correspondence,* II, 509–10, 526, 533.
9. Ibid., II, 103; to Hutchinson, draft, P.R.O., C.O. 5/759:156–7, printed *Documents of the American Revolution, 1770–1783,* ed. K. G. Davies, vol. II (Shannon, 1972), pp. 101–2.
10. For this lengthy report, see ibid., 110–28.
11. *APC(C),* V, 246–64; MHS, *Collections,* 5th s., IX, 442–3.
12. *APC(C),* V, 264.
13. *Documents,* ed. Davies, II, 135.
14. Ibid., I, 137.
15. MHS, *Collections,* 5th s., IX, 442–3.
16. Ibid., 6th s., IX, 196–9.
17. Ibid., 203–4.
18. On 19 July 1770 John Yorke wrote to Hardwicke: 'As to America, I do not believe all the long wigs you enumerate, will be able to fall upon any right, and yet popular system, for quieting that country.' B.L. Add. MSS. 35375, f. 64 (misplaced).
19. *Documents,* ed. Davies, II, 156–7; *Gage Correspondence,* II, 112–13.
20. Draft, P.R.O., C.O. 5/759:241–2; abstract, *Documents,* ed. Davies, I, 156.
21. Routine business was being carried on by John Pownall during September, ibid., I, 163–71.
22. Ibid., II, 200.
23. MHS, *Collections,* 5th s., IX, 466; cf. R. H. Lee, *Life of Arthur Lee,* I, 215.
24. MHS, *Collections,* 5th s., IX, 471.
25. Barrington had speculated about the possibility of the trial leading to military and naval operations to subdue Massachusetts; to Gage, private, 2 Sept. 1770, Gage MSS.

26. See J. Goebel, *The struggle for the Falkland Islands. A study in legal and diplomatic history* (New Haven, 1927), pp. 289–355.
27. *Documents*, ed. Davies, I, 172–3.
28. *Gage Correspondence*, II, 556–7.
29. Gage MSS.
30. So Arthur Lee thought, writing to Samuel Adams, 10 June 1771, R. H. Lee, *Life of Arthur Lee*, I, 215. If Franklin's impression is reliable, during the winter Hillsborough's colleagues began to regard him and his American measures as liabilities to be got rid of if the Spanish crisis developed into a war; to Cushing, 7 July 1773, *Writings*, ed. Smyth, VI, 76.
31. *Documents*, ed. Davies, I, 220.
32. Hillsborough to Hutchinson, to the Treasury, 7 Dec. 1770, ibid., 223.
33. Samuel Cooper to Benjamin Franklin, 1 January 1771, King's MSS. 203 (B.L.).
34. General trade statistics from U.S. Bureau of the Census, *Historical Statistics of the United States: Colonial Times to 1957* (Washington, D.C., 1960), pp. 759–60; Samuel Salisbury to Stephen Salisbury, 14 Nov. 1770, Salisbury Papers (American Antiquarian Society); 'An Account of what Tea has been imported into Boston since the year 1768 . . . ,' MS.L (MHS); for overall tea imports, Customs 3/71 through 3/73 (PRO).
35. Customs 3/71 through 3/73 (PRO); Hutchinson to Hillsborough, 26 July 1770, Sparks MS. 10, New England Papers IV, 8 (Houghton Library); Swift to Commissioners of Customs, 31 Jan. 1771, Customs House Papers, XI, (HSP); Bureau of Census, *Historical Statistics*, pp. 759–60, 766.
36. Kenneth Coleman, *The Revolution in Georgia, 1763–1789* (Athens, Ga., 1958), pp. 34–6; Thomas R. Adams, *American Independence* (Providence, R.I., 1965), p. 68.
37. W. Roy Smith, *South Carolina as a Royal Province, 1719–1776* (New York, 1903), pp. 369–86; Pauline Maier, *From Resistance to Revolution: Colonial Radicals and the Development of American Opposition to Britain, 1765–1776* (New York, 1972), pp. 203–4; Jack P. Greene, 'Bridge to Revolution: The Wilkes Fund Controversy in South Carolina, 1769–1775', *Journal of Southern History*, XXIX (February 1963), 19–52; Leonard W. Labaree, ed., *Royal Instructions to British Colonial Governors, 1670–1776* (New York, 1935), I, 208–9.
38. Hugh T. Lefler and William S. Powell, *Colonial North Carolina* (New York, 1973), pp. 256–7.
39. Maier, *From Resistance to Revolution*, pp. 199–206.
40. Carl Bridenbaugh, *Mitre and Sceptre: Transatlantic Faiths, Ideas, Personalities, and Politics, 1689–1775* (New York, 1962), pp. 260–70.
41. Ibid., pp. 314–23.
42. Oliver M. Dickerson, *The Navigation Acts and the American Revolution* (Philadelphia, 1951), p. 201; Thomas C. Barrow, *Trade and Empire: The British Customs Service in Colonial America, 1660–1775* (Cambridge, Mass., 1967), pp. 244–5.
43. Barrow, *Trade and Empire*, pp. 245–6; Alfred S. Martin, 'The King's Customs: Philadelphia, 1763–1774', *WMQ*, V (April 1948), 214–15; Arthur L. Jensen, *The Maritime Commerce of Colonial Philadelphia* (Madison, Wisc., 1963), pp. 150–1.
44. Martin, 'King's Customs', p. 215; Jensen, *Commerce of Philadelphia*, p. 151.
45. John R. Bartlett, ed., *Records of the Colony of Rhode Island* (Providence, R.I., 1862), VII, 58–9; George G. Wolkins, 'The Seizure of John Hancock's Sloop *Liberty*', MHS, *Proceedings*, LV (March 1922), 261; Neil R. Stout, *The Royal Navy in America, 1760–1775* (Annapolis, Md., 1973), p. 140.
46. Bartlett, ed., *Records of Rhode Island*, VII, 61–4; Stout, *Royal Navy*, pp. 141, 156.
47. Bartlett, ed., *Records of Rhode Island*, VII, 68–81; Stout, *Royal Navy*, pp. 142–3.
48. Stout, *Royal Navy*, pp. 156–60; Virginia resolutions as printed in Merrill Jensen, ed., *English Historical Documents*, IX: *American Colonial Documents to 1776*, (New York, 1955), pp. 763–4.

49. Maier, *From Resistance to Revolution*, pp. 192–4, 221; Roger J. Champagne, 'Liberty Boys and Mechanics of New York City, 1764–1774', *Labor History*, VIII (Spring 1967), 123–35.

50. Maier, *From Resistance to Revolution*, pp. 221–2; R. A. Ryerson, 'Political Mobilization and the American Revolution: The Resistance Movement in Philadelphia, 1765 to 1776', *WMQ*, XXXI (October 1974), 568–9; James H. Hutson, 'An Investigation of the Inarticulate: Philadelphia's White Oaks', *WMQ*, XXVIII (January 1971), 22–3; Benjamin H. Newcomb, *Franklin and Galloway: A Political Partnership* (New Haven, Conn., 1972), pp. 217–24; Charles J. Stillé, *The Writings of John Dickinson* (Philadelphia, 1895), II, 451–2.

51. Richard D. Brown, *Revolutionary Politics in Massachusetts: The Boston Committee of Correspondence and the Towns, 1772–1774* (Cambridge, Mass., 1970), pp. 43–8, 54–7; *A Report of the Record Commissioners of the City of Boston* [XVIII]: *Boston Town Records, 1770–1777* (Boston, 1887), pp. 92–3.

52. *Boston Town Records, 1770–1777*, pp. 94–9; Brown, *Revolutionary Politics*, pp. 62–6, 70–4.

53. *Boston Town Records*, pp. 99–106; Brown, *Revolutionary Politics*, pp. 74–8.

54. *Boston Town Records*, pp. 106–8; Brown, *Revolutionary Politics*, 68–9, 79–85, 94–9, 105–6, 122.

55. Brown, *Revolutionary Politics*, pp. 86–91; Bernard Bailyn, *The Ordeal of Thomas Hutchinson*, (Cambridge, Mass., 1974), pp. 206–8; Alden Bradford, ed., *Speeches of the Governors of Massachusetts, 1765–1775* (Boston, 1818), pp. 336–42.

56. Bradford, *Speeches*, pp. 337–42.

57. Ibid., pp. 363–4.

58. Bailyn, *Thomas Hutchinson*, pp. 210–11. and 211*n*.

59. Ibid., pp. 221–8, 235–6, 238–41.

60. Harry A. Cushing, *The Writings of Samuel Adams* (New York, 1907), III, 45–8.

61. Ibid.; Samuel Adams to Arthur Lee, 28 June 1773, in Cushing, op. cit., pp. 48–9.

VIII. Crisis over Tea

1. No cabinet minute or other document pinning down such a decision has been found.

2. *Franklin Papers*, XVIII, 26.

3. MHS, *Collections*, 5th s., IX, 479.

4. *Documents*, ed. Davies, I, 245–452.

5. Barrington to Gage, private, 2 July 1771, Gage MSS. It seems likely that this scheme was hatched as a result of the war scare eighteen months before.

6. Gage to Barrington, 3 Sept. 1771, *Gage Correspondence*, II, 589–90. Gage listed the military dispositions as follows: Canada, four battalions; Nova Scotia, three battalions (with three companies in Newfoundland); E. Florida, two (with a company at Providence); W. Florida, one; Ohio region, one, scattered at various posts including Fort Chartres, Kaskaskia, Fort Pitt; Great Lakes, one; the middle colonies, three.

7. See pp. 33–4 above.

8. For the development of the Vandalia project up to the end of 1771, see Sosin, *Whitehall and the Wilderness*, pp. 181–201.

9. Hutchinson to Hillsborough, 25 Aug., 10 Sept. 1771, *Documents*, ed. Davies, III, 172–3, 180–1, both received on 29 Oct. He noted the greater vigour of the naval patrols. His estimate of the total annual American consumption of tea receives some support from what appears to be the independent figure of six million lb. quoted to the East India Company by the Philadelphia merchant, Gilbert Barkley, in 1773 (cited Labaree, *Boston Tea Party*, p. 74). Nevertheless, such a level of con-

sumption is so far in excess both of what the Treasury estimated and of the average of about two million lb. imported annually in the years after the Union, that the figure must be regarded as far too high.

10. See pp. 155–6 above.
11. *Documents,* ed. Davies, IV, 99, 100, 122, 141, 159; and see pp. 150, 157 above.
12. Letters of Rear Admiral John Montagu and of Hutchinson to Hillsborough, 12 June 1772, *Documents,* ed. Davies, IV, 102, and V, 118–23. Governor Wanton's report reached London the next week, ibid., IV, 109, and V, 125–7. See also cabinet minute, 30 July 1772, Dartmouth MSS., and *Documents,* ed. Davies, IV, 146–7.
13. Ibid., IV, 150.
14. Sosin, *Whitehall and the Wilderness,* pp. 201–5.
15. Barrington to Gage, 2 Sept. 1772, Gage MSS.
16. J. Pownall to Dartmouth, 29 Aug. 1772, Dartmouth MSS.
17. Cabinet minutes, no. 1 and no. 2, 20 Aug. 1772, Dartmouth MSS.; *Documents,* ed. Davies, IV, 158, 165, V, 173–5, 181–2, 186–9, 189–90; Pownall to Dartmouth, 26, 27 Aug., law officers' reports, 28 Aug., and Dartmouth to Wanton, 4 Sept. 1772 (two copies), Dartmouth MSS.; *APC(C),* V, 356–7; and see p. 156 above.
18. Final report of the commissioners of enquiry, 22 June 1773, received in London, 4 Aug. 1773, P.R.O., C.O. 5/1285, fos. 186–95; *Documents,* ed. Davies, IV, 336–7.
19. Ibid., V, 182.
20. Ibid., 238–40.
21. See pp. 157–9 above. The declarations of rights and grievances, and the resolutions passed at Marblehead, Plymouth, and Roxbury, had all reached Dartmouth by 30 Jan. 1773; ibid., IV, 207, 223–4.
22. H.M.C., *14th Report,* appendix, pt. X (*Dartmouth MSS.* II), 135. (The original appears now to be missing.)
23. See pp. 159–61 above; Dartmouth to Hutchinson, no. 6, 3 Feb. 1773, copy, Dartmouth MSS.; *Documents,* ed. Davies, IV, 243; 242, 256–7.
24. To Hutchinson, [no. 8] 10 Apr. 1773, P.R.O., C.O. 5/762, fos. 108–10, and copy, Dartmouth MSS.
25. P. O. Hutchinson, *Dairy and letters of . . . Thomas Hutchinson,* (2 v., 1883–6), I, 181.
26. 6 Jan., 18 Feb. with encl., 20 Mar. 1773, Dartmouth MSS., summarized H.M.C., *14th Report,* appendix pt. X, 129, 138, 143.
27. H.M.C., *Eleventh Report,* appendix pt. V, 335–6.
28. *Documents,* ed. Davies, IV, 321–2; draft, Dartmouth MSS.
29. 19 June 1773, draft, Dartmouth MSS. A similar, formal reply came back to Cushing through Franklin on 7 July, in reply to the petition to the Crown which Cushing had forwarded protesting against the grant of salaries to provincial officers. Copy, H.M.C., *Eleventh Report,* appendix pt. V, 337.
30. *Documents,* ed. Davies, IV, 338, 358.
31. On the Baltic crisis see Michael Roberts, 'Great Britain and the Swedish Revolution of 1772–3', *Historical Journal,* 7 (1964), 1–46.
32. Rochford to Gower, 10 Oct. 1772 and cabinet minute, 7 Oct., Granville MSS., P.R.O. 30/29/1/14:667–70. Dartmouth received a letter of information of 6 Sept. from the northern secretary, Lord Suffolk, and a very full memorandum about the diplomatic situation from Rochford, about 12 Nov. 1772, Dartmouth MSS.
33. Fortescue, III, no. 1436.
34. For detailed narratives of different aspects of this crisis, see Labaree, *Boston Tea Party,* pp. 58–79, and L. S. Sutherland, *The East India Company in eighteenth century politics* (Oxford, 1952), 213–68.
35. Sir Henry Cavendish's unpublished report of the debate of 26 Apr. 1773 is the only one known to provide much detail. B. L. Egerton MS. 246, pp. 1–16.
36. Pp. 164–6 above.

37. 13 Geo. III, c.44.
38. *Documents*, ed. Davies, IV, 414.
39. This section depends throughout on Benjamin W. Labaree, *The Boston Tea Party* (New York, 1964), chapters V–VIII; *Pennsylvania Journal*, 29 Sept. 1773; *New York Journal*, 7 Oct. 1773; *Boston Gazette*, 11 Oct. 1773; John Norton to Peyton Randolph, 6 July 1773, Sparks MS. volume 71, MSS. of Virginia, 11 (Houghton Library).
40. Alarm Nos. 1, 2, 3, in *New York Journal*, 14, 21, 28 Oct. 1773; Pigou & Booth to James & Drinker, 8, 27, 28 Oct. 1773, Drinker Papers, 1739–79 (HSP); Arthur M. Schlesinger, 'The Uprising Against the East India Company,' *Political Science Quarterly*, XXXII (March 1917), 60–79; *To the Agents of their High Mightinesses, the Dutch East India Company at St. Eustatius*, New York, 28 Oct. 1773; POPLICOLA, in *New York Gazetteer*, 18 Nov. 1773; A FARMER, *New York Gazetteer*, 2 Dec. 1773.
41. 'To the Stated Pilots . . . ', signed LEGION, *New York Gazetteer*, 18 Nov. 1773; THE MOHAWKS, *New York Gazetteer*, 2 Dec. 1773; The Memorial of Henry White, et al. . . . , C.O. 5/1105 (PRO); Henry White et al., to Directors of the East India Co., 1 Dec. 1773, C.O. 5/133, fos. 24–5 (PRO).
42. SCAEVOLA, *Pennsylvania Journal*, 13 Oct. 1773; *Inhabitants of Pennsylvania . . .* , Philadelphia, 13 Oct. 1773; *Pennsylvania Journal*, 20 Oct. 1773.
43. James & Drinker to Pigou & Booth, 19 Oct. 1773 and statement of 22 Oct. 1773, Drinker Papers, 1739–79 (HSP); Report of the Committee appointed to Wait on the Tea Commissioners, 17 Oct. 1773, MSS. Relating to Non-Importation Agreements, 1766–75 (American Philosophical Society); James & Drinker to Pigou & Booth, Drinker Foreign Letters, 1772–85 (HSP); AN OLD MECHANIC and HAMDEN, *Pennsylvania Journal*, 20 Oct. 1773; *A Letter from the Country to a Gentleman in Philadelphia*, signed RUSTICUS, 27 Nov. 1773; *To the Delaware Pilots . . .* , Philadelphia, 27 Nov. 1773; Statement of the Philadelphia Consignees to the Committee, 2 Dec. 1773, MS. relating to Non-Importation Agreements, 1766–75 (American Philosophical Society).
44. Hutchinson to Dartmouth, 15 Nov. 1773, Hutchinson Letterbooks, XXCII, 570–1 (Massachusetts Archives).
45. Richard D. Brown, *Revolutionary Politics in Massachusetts: The Boston Committee of Correspondence and the Towns, 1772–1774* (Cambridge, Mass., 1970), pp. 151–5.
46. *Massachusetts Spy*, 14 Oct. 1773; *Boston Evening Post*, 18 Oct. 1773; PRAEDICUS and Edes & Gill, *Boston Gazette*, 18 Oct. 1773; 'Proceedings of the North End Caucus', in Elbridge H. Goss, *The Life of Colonel Paul Revere* (Boston, 1891), II, 641; Henry to Thomas Bromfield, 25 Oct. 1773, Henry Bromfield Letterbook, 1773 (New England Historic and Genealogical Society); *Massachusetts Spy*, 21 Oct. 1773.
47. Z., *Boston Evening Post*, 25 Oct. 1773; *Boston News-letter*, 28 Oct. 1773.
48. Richard Clarke & Sons to Abraham Dupuis, Nov. 1773, in Samuel A. Drake, *Tea Leaves . . .* , (Boston, 1884), pp. 282–6; Hutchinson to Dartmouth, 4 Nov. 1773, Papers Relating to the Boston Tea Party (House of Lords R.O.); Hutchinson to Tryon, 21 Nov. 1773, Hutchinson Letterbooks, XXVII, 572–4 (Massachusetts Archives); *Report of the Record Commissioners of the City of Boston* [XVIII]: *Boston Town Records, 1770–1777* (Boston, 1887), pp. 141–6; *Boston Gazette*, 8 Nov. 1773.
49. Hutchinson to Tryon, 21 Nov. 1773, loc. cit.; *Boston Post-boy*, 22 Nov. 1773; *Boston Town Records*, pp. 147–8; *Boston Gazette*, 22 Nov. 1773.
50. Consignees' petition, Edes Papers (MHS); Drake, *Tea Leaves*, pp. 309–15; Francis G. Walett, 'The Massachusetts Council, 1766–1774: The Transformation of a Conservative Institution', *WMQ*, VI (October 1949), 605–27; *Boston Gazette*, 22 Nov. 1773.
51. Boston Committee of Correspondence Minutes, 16, 22, 23 November 1773 (New York Public Library): Brown, *Revolutionary Politics*, pp. 158–61.

52. Boston Committee of Correspondence Minutes, 28 Nov. 1773 (New York Public Library); *A Report of the Record Commissioners of the City of Boston* [XXXIII]: *Selectmen's Minutes, 1769–1775* (Boston, 1893), p. 203; Brown, *Revolutionary Politics,* p. 161.

53. 'Minutes of the Tea Meetings', MHS, *Proceedings.,* XX (1882–3), 10–11; L. F. S. Upton, 'Proceedings of Ye Body Respecting the Tea', *WMQ,* XXII (April 1965), 289–91; 'Proceedings of the Town of Boston on the 29th and 30th of November', Drake, *Tea Leaves,* pp. 320–1; Minutes of the Governor's Council, 29 Nov. 1773, Drake, *Tea Leaves,* pp. 315–20; Thomas Hutchinson to Elisha Hutchinson, 30 Nov. 1773, Hutchinson Papers, Egerton MSS. 2659, f. 50 (BL).

54. 'Minutes of the Tea Meetings', loc. cit., 11–12; Upton, 'Proceedings', pp. 292–3.

55. 'Minutes of the Tea Meetings', loc. cit., 11–13; Upton, 'Proceedings', pp. 291–6; John Scollay to Arthur Lee, 23 Dec. 1773, MHS, *Collections,* 383–4; John S. Copley to Jonathan and Isaac W. Clarke, [1 Dec. 1773], *Letters and Papers of John Singleton Copley and Henry Pelham, 1739–1776* (Boston, 1914), pp. 211–13.

56. Copley to Clarke, loc. cit.; Peter O. Hutchinson, ed., *Diary and Letters of Thomas Hutchinson* (London, 1883), I, 100–1; 'Extract of the Journal of the ship *Dartmouth,* from London to Boston, 1773', [Benjamin B. Thatcher], *Traits of the Tea Party; Being a Memoir of George R. T. Hewes . . .* (New York, 1835), pp. 259–60.

57. E. LUDLOW, *Massachusetts Spy,* 26 Nov. 1773; PRAEDICUS, *Boston Gazette,* 1 Nov. 1773; 'A Friend to the Community', *Boston Gazette,* 13 Dec. 1773.

58. Protest of Francis Rotch, et al., 10 Dec. 1773, C.O. 5/763 (PRO), Drake, *Tea Leaves,* pp. 353–4.

59. A RANGER, *Boston Evening Post,* 6 Dec. 1773; *Essex Gazette,* 7 Dec. 1773; John Andrews to William Barrell, 1 Dec. 1773, MHS, *Proceedings,* VII (1864–5), 325; Montagu to Phillip Stevens, 8 Dec. 1773, Dartmouth Papers, I, ii, 942 (William Salt Library); Montagu to Customs Commissioners, 16 Dec. 1773, Treasury 1/505 (PRO); HONON-CHROTONTHOLOGOS, *Boston Gazette,* 13 Dec. 1773.

60. Questions proposed by Francis Rotch . . . , 7 Dec. 1773, and Questions proposed by James Bruce . . . , 11 Dec. 1773, Protests of Rotch and Bruce, in Drake, *Tea Leaves,* pp. 344–8, 353–8; 'Extract of a letter from Philadelphia, December 4, 1773', *Boston Gazette,* 13 Dec. 1773.

61. Boston Committee of Correspondence Minutes, 10, 13 Dec. 1773 (New York Public Library); 'Minutes of the Tea meetings', MHS, *Proceedings,* XX (1882–3), 15; Upton, 'Proceedings', loc. cit., pp. 296–7.

62. 'Minutes of the Tea Meetings', loc. cit., pp. 15–16; R. A. Harrison to Customs Commissioners, 16 Dec. 1773, T. 1/505 (PRO).

63. 'Minutes of the Tea Meetings', loc. cit., pp. 15–16; Upton, 'Proceedings', loc. cit., p. 297.

64. Hutchinson to Dartmouth, 14 Dec. 1773, in Bernard Bailyn, *The Ordeal of Thomas Hutchinson* (Cambridge, Mass., 1974), p. 261; Hutchinson to Dartmouth, 15 Dec. 1773, C.O. 5/763 (PRO); Hutchinson to Israel Mauduit, Dec. 1773, in MHS, *Proceedings,* XIII (1873–5), pp. 171–2.

65. Hutchinson to Mauduit, Dec. 1773, loc. cit., pp. 170–1; 'Minutes of the Tea Meetings, 1773', loc. cit., pp. 16–17; Upton, 'Proceedings', loc. cit., p. 299; Hutchinson to Dartmouth, 17 Dec. 1773, Hutchinson Letterbooks, XXVII, 589 (Massachusetts Archives); Henry C. Watson, *The Yankee Tea Party . . .* (Boston, 1851), pp. 18–21; Andrews to Barrell, 18 Dec. 1773, MHS, *Proceedings,* VIII (1864–5), 326.

66. Drake, *Tea Leaves,* pp. xxiii–xxiv, lxvi–lxvii, lxxvii, xcv–clxxii; Henry Bromfield to Flight & Halliday, 17 Dec. 1773, Bromfield Letterbook, 1773 (New England Historic and Genealogical Society); Protests of Alexander Hodgdon, James Bruce,

and Hezekiah Coffin, 17 Dec. 1773, C.O. 5/137 (PRO); Informations of William Rotch, James Hall, Hugh Williamson, and John D. Whitiworth before the Privy Council, 19 Feb. 1774, C.O. 5/763 (PRO); *Boston Gazette,* 20 Dec. 1773.

67. Lyman H. Butterfield, ed., *Diary and Autobiography of John Adams* (Cambridge, Mass., 1961), II, 85–6; Samuel Adams to Arthur Lee, 21 Dec. 1773, Adams Papers (New York Public Library); Montagu to Admiralty, 17 Dec. 1773, Secretary of State for Colonies In-Letters, C.O. 5/247 (PRO); Bailyn, *Hutchinson,* pp. 262–3.

68. *Boston Gazette,* 3 Jan. 1774; *South Carolina Gazette,* 6, 20, 27 Dec. 1773; Leger & Greenwood to East India Co., 4, 18 Dec. 1773, T.1/505 (PRO); John Morris to Corbyn Morris, 22 Dec. 1773, in Drake, *Tea Leaves,* p. 342; John Morris to Lords of the Treasury, 24 Dec. 1773, T.1/505 (PRO); *South Carolina and American General Gazette,* 24 Dec. 1773; Governor Bull to Lord Dartmouth, 24 Dec. 1773, Drake, *Tea Leaves,* pp. 339–41.

69. 'Extract of a letter from Philadelphia, dated 28 December 1773', *Boston Gazette,* 24 Jan. 1774; *Pennsylvania Journal,* 24 Dec. 1774; Joseph Reed to Dartmouth, 27 Dec. 1773, in W. B. Reed, *Life and Correspondence of Joseph Reed* (Philadelphia, 1857), I, 54–6; *Pennsylvania Packet,* 6, 13, 27 Dec. 1773 and 3 Jan. 1774; *Pennsylvania Gazette,* 8, 29 Dec. 1773; *Captain Ayres' Protest,* 27 Dec. 1773, Papers Relating to the Shipment of Tea . . . (HSP); Thomas Wharton to Thomas Walpole, 27 Dec. 1773, Wharton Letterbook, 1773–84 (HSP); George Clymer and Thomas Mifflin to Samuel Adams, 27 Dec. 1773, Samuel Adams Papers (New York Public Library).

70. *New York Gazetteer,* 23 Dec. 1773, 7, 28 April, 12 May 1774; *New York Journal,* 21 April 1774; *New York Gazette,* 25 April 1774; Lockyer and consignees, 20 April 1774, in Drake, *Tea Leaves,* pp. 359–60.

IX. The Coercive Acts

1. Dartmouth MSS.
2. Gipson, *British Empire,* XII, 108.
3. See pp. 157–62 above, and Labaree, *Boston Tea Party,* pp. 177–8.
4. 4 Feb. 1774, Fortescue, III, no. 1379.
5. Bernard Donoughue, *British Politics and the American Revolution. The path to war, 1773–75* (1964), p. 31.
6. Ibid., pp. 32–4.
7. Cabinet minute, 29 Jan. 1774, Dartmouth MSS.
8. To Governor Hutchinson, 2 Feb. 1774, *Diary and Letters of Hutchinson,* I, 100.
9. Cabinet minute, 4 Feb. 1774, Dartmouth MSS.; Fortescue, III, no. 1377 [5 Feb. 1774].
10. Cabinet minute, 5 Feb. 1774, Dartmouth MSS.
11. George III to North, 4 Feb. 1774, Fortescue, III, no. 1379.
12. Donoughue, pp. 48–9.
13. To John Thornton, 12 Feb. 1774, Dartmouth MSS., cited in B. D. Bargar, *Lord Dartmouth and the American Revolution* (Columbia, S.C., 1965), p. 106.
14. Labaree, *Boston Tea Party,* pp. 179–81.
15. Cabinet minute, 16 Feb. 1774, Dartmouth MSS.; Donoughue, pp. 55–8.
16. Donoughue, pp. 63–6; Labaree, *Boston Tea Party,* pp. 175–6; H.M.C., *Lothian MSS.,* p. 290; cabinet minute, 19 Feb. 1774, Dartmouth MSS.
17. Ibid.
18. *P.H.,* XVII, 1159–63.
19. Dartmouth MSS. 853.

20. George III to North, 14 Mar. 1774, Fortescue, III, no. 1416.

21. *P.H.*, XVII, 1163–7; B. L. Egerton MS. 254, fos. 86–111.

22. Cf. Franklin to Thomas Cushing, 22 Mar. 1774, *Writings*, ed. Smyth, VI, 223.

23. Donoughue, pp. 76–83; Labaree, *Boston Tea Party*, pp. 184–93.

24. *P.H.*, XVII, 1161, 1169, 1185.

25. North to George III, [25 Mar. 1774], Fortescue, III, no. 1426.

26. 14 Geo. III, c. 19.

27. *The Correspondence of Edmund Burke*, volume II, *July 1768–June 1774*, ed. Lucy S. Sutherland (Cambridge, 1960), p. 528.

28. *Chatham Correspondence*, IV, 335; Grafton, *Autobiography*, pp. 266–7, H.M.C., *Various Collections*, VI: *Knox MSS.*, pp. 257–8; and see the discussion in Labaree, *Boston Tea Party*, p. 182.

29. *P.H.*, XVII, 1192–3.

30. See p. 189 below.

31. Donoughue, p. 87n.

32. *P.H.*, XVII, 1194–6.

33. Loc. cit.; North to George III, [28 Mar. 1774], Fortescue, III, no. 1429.

34. Cabinet minute, 30 Mar. 1774, Sandwich MSS., cited C. R. Ritcheson, *British Politics and the American Revolution* (Norman, Okla., 1954), p. 161; *Gage Correspondence*, II, 158–9.

35. Cabinet minute, 7 Apr. 1774, Dartmouth MSS.; *Gage Correspondence*, II, 162–3.

36. Ibid., 158–62.

37. Donoughue, pp. 85–6.

38. George III to North, 14 Apr. 1774, Fortescue, III, no. 1440.

39. North to George III, [14 Apr. 1774], ibid., no. 1441.

40. *P.H.*, XVII, 1197.

41. Bargar, *Dartmouth*, p. 111.

42. *P.H.*, XVII, 1200.

43. To Rockingham, 20 Apr. 1774, Rockingham MSS., printed with inaccuracies in Albemarle, *Rockingham*, II, 242–3.

44. North to George III, [25 Apr. 1774], Fortescue, III, no. 1449.

45. *P.H.*, XVII, 1210–73.

46. Ibid., 1300–16.

47. *Burke Correspondence*, II, 528–9; Albemarle, *Rockingham*, II, 242. The fact was also acknowledged in debate by Rose Fuller (*P.H.*, XVII, 1320).

48. For details see Gipson, *British Empire*, XII, 113, 120–3.

49. *Gage Correspondence*, II, 165–6.

50. H.M.C., *Eleventh Report*, appendix, pt. V, p. 355; for dating see Gipson, *British Empire*, XII, 136.

51. For fuller discussion of this subject see Gipson, *British Empire*, XIII, 144–68, and Donoughue, pp. 105–26.

52. Donoughue, p. 108.

53. Gipson, *British Empire*, XIII, 155.

54. Ibid., p. 156n.

X. *The Continent Unites*

1. *Boston Gazette*, 20 Dec. 1773, 3, 17 Jan., 4 April 1774; *Boston Newsletter*, 4 Jan. 1774.

2. *Boston Gazette*, 14 Feb. 1774; *Massachusetts Spy*, 17 March, 7 April 1774; *Boston Evening Post*, 4 April 1774; *Boston Post-boy*, 4 April 1774; *Newport Mercury*, 14 Feb. 1774.

3. *Boston Gazette*, 7, 14 March 1774; Thomas Walley, Peter Boyer, and William Thompson, in *Boston Newsletter*, 10 March 1774; PHILANTHROP, *Massachusetts Spy*, 17 March 1774; Report of the Collector, Benjamin Gorham's protest, and report of tidesmen, 8–10 March 1774, T.1/505 (PRO); Hutchinson to Dartmouth, 9 March 1774, List of Papers relating to Disturbances in Boston (House of Lords R.O.).

4. *Boston Gazette*, 14 Feb. 1774; Hugh T. Lefler and William S. Powell, *Colonial North Carolina: A History* (New York, 1973), p. 259; 'Account of the Destruction of the brig *Peggy Stewart*, at Annapolis, 1774', *PMHB*, XXV (1901), 248–52; 'Letter from Philadelphia, dated 25 December 1773', [London] *Morning Chronicle*, 1 Feb. 1774.

5. *Boston Newsletter*, 12 May 1774; Richard D. Brown, *Revolutionary Politics in Massachusetts: The Boston Committee of Correspondence and the Towns, 1772–1774* (Cambridge, Mass., 1970), pp. 185–8; *Boston Gazette*, 16 May 1774; *A Report of the Record Commissioners of the City of Boston* [XVIII]: *Boston Town Records, 1770–1777* (Boston, 1887), pp. 170–2; Thomas Young to John Lamb, 13 May 1774, John Lamb Papers (New-York Historical Society).

6. 'Letter from Farmington, Conn., dated 23 May 1774', in *Boston Evening Post*, 30 May 1774; Isaac Sears and Alexander McDougall to Samuel Adams, 15 May 1774, Samuel Adams Papers (Bancroft transcripts, New York Public Library); James & Drinker to Pigou & Booth, 31 May 1774, Drinker Letterbook, 1772–84 (HSP); [Purdie's] *Virginia Gazette*, 26 May, 2 June 1774; George Washington to George W. Fairfax, 10 June 1774, in John C. Fitzpatrick, ed., *The Writings of George Washington, 1745–1799* (Washington, D.C., 1931–44), III, 224.

7. *Political Memoranda Relative to the Conduct of the Citizens on the Boston Port Bill . . . ,* McDougall Papers (New-York Historical Society); *New York Gazetteer*, 23 May, 30 June 1774; *New York Gazette*, 23 May 1774; *New York Journal*, 26 May 1774; Bernard Mason, *The Road to Independence: The Revolutionary Movement in New York, 1773–1777* (Lexington, Ky., 1966), pp. 24–31; Benjamin W. Labaree, *The Boston Tea Party* (New York, 1964), pp. 227–9.

8. 'Joseph Reed's Narrative', and Charles Thomson to William H. Drayton, Thomson Papers, *Collections*, New-York Historical Society (1878) 269–77; W. B. Reed, *Life and Correspondence of Joseph Reed* (Philadelphia, 1857), I, 65–7; *Pennsylvania Gazette*, 25 May 1774; *Pennsylvania Packet*, 6 June 1774; Thomas Wharton to Thomas Walpole, 31 May 1774, Wharton Letterbook, 1773–84 (HSP); John F. Roche, *Joseph Reed: A Moderate in the American Revolution* (New York, 1957), pp. 41–2; Thomas Mifflin to Samuel Adams, 26 May 1774, and Charles Thomson to Samuel Adams, 3 June 1774, Samuel Adams Papers (New York Public Library); *Maryland Gazette*, 26 May, 2 June 1774; [Purdie's] *Virginia Gazette*, 26 May, 2 June 1774; [Rind's] *Virginia Gazette*, 26 May 1774.

9. John R. Alden, *General Gage in America . . .* (Baton Rouge, La., 1948), pp. 206–10; *Boston Evening Post*, 23 May 1774; *Boston Gazette*, 23 May, 6 June 1774; 'Extract of a Letter from Boston, dated 2 June 1774', *Pennsylvania Journal*, 15 June 1774; Neil R. Stout, *The Royal Navy in America, 1760–1775 . . .* (Annapolis, Md., 1973), pp. 161–3; Labaree, *Boston Tea Party*, pp. 224, 238.

10. Brown, *Revolutionary Politics*, pp. 191 seq.; Albert Matthews, 'The Solemn League and Covenant, 1774', *Publications*, Colonial Society of Massachusetts, XVIII (December 1915), 107–9; *Boston Gazette*, 13 June 1774; *Boston Post-boy*, 13 June 1774; Peter Force, ed., *American Archives*, 4th s. (Washington, D.C., 1837), I, 491–2.

11. Brown, *Revolutionary Politics*, pp. 220–4; Labaree, *Boston Tea Party*, pp. 237–8.

12. 'Correspondence in 1774 and 1775 Between a Committee of Town of Boston and Contributors of Donations . . . ,' MHS, *Collections*, 4th s., IV (Boston, 1858), 22–6, 50–3.

13. Ibid., pp. 32–5.

14. Ibid., pp. 4–5.

15. Labaree, *Boston Tea Party*, pp. 239–40; Worthington C. Ford, ed., *Journals of the Continental Congress, 1774–1789* (Washington, D.C., 1904), I, 15–24, 30.

16. Force, *American Archives*, 4th s., I, 307–14, 317–20; Isaac Sears and Alexander Mc-Dougall to Samuel Adams, 25 July 1774, Samuel Adams Papers (New York Public Library); *New York Gazetteer*, 14, 21, 28 July, 8 Aug. 1774; *New York Gazette*, 25 July 1774; *New York Journal*, 28 July 1774.

17. *Pennsylvania Packet*, 20, 27 June, 7 July (postscript), 18 July 1774; *Pennsylvania Gazette*, 13, 29 June 1774; Joseph Reed to Dartmouth, 18 July 1774, Dartmouth Papers, I, ii, 998 (William Salt Library); Force, *American Archives*, 4th s., I, 415–16, 601–8n.

18. Jack M. Sosin, 'The Massachusetts Act of 1774: Coercive or Preventive', *Huntington Library Quarterly*, XXVI (1962–3), 235–52; Edward Shippen to Edward Burd, 28 June 1774; Shippen Papers, VII (HSP).

19. 'Correspondence in 1774 and 1775', MHS, *Collections*, 4th s., IV, 10, 42–3, 74–7.

20. [William H. Drayton], *A Letter from Freeman [sic] of South-Carolina, To the Deputies of North-America, Assemblied In The High Court of Congress At Philadelphia* (Charleston, S.C., 1774), pp. 5–7; [Anon.] *A Letter From A Virginian, To The Members of the Congress To Be Held At Philadelphia. On The first of September, 1774.* ([New York], 1774), pp. 27, 45.

21. Force, *American Archives*, 4th s., I, 568–9, 587, 591.

22. Ibid., pp. 563–4; David L. Jacobson, *John Dickinson and the Revolution in Pennsylvania, 1764–1776* (Berkeley, Calif., 1965), pp. 79–80.

23. Dumas Malone, *Jefferson the Virginian* (Boston, 1948), pp. 181–90; Julian Boyd, ed., *The Papers of Thomas Jefferson* (Princeton, N.J., 1950), I, 669–76.

24. Boyd, *Jefferson*, I, pp. 121–2, 123–4, 125–9.

25. Ibid., pp. 132–5.

26. Samuel Patterson to Levi Hollingsworth, 6 July 1774, Levi Hollingsworth Papers (HSP); Joseph Shippen to Edward Shippen, 21 July 1774, Joseph Shippen Papers (Library of Congress): [Thomas Bradbury Chandler], *The American Querist: Or, Some Questions Proposed Relative To The Present Disputes Between Great-Britain And Her American Colonies* ([New York], 1774).

27. [James Wilson], *Considerations on the Nature and Extent of the Legislative Authority of the British Parliament* (Philadelphia, 1774); Force, *American Archives*, 4th s., I, 686–7.

28. William V. Wells, *The Life and Public Services of Samuel Adams . . .* (Boston, 1865), II, 207–8; Lyman H. Butterfield, ed., *The Diary and Autobiography of John Adams* (Cambridge, Mass., 1961), II, 107, 117, 115 (n.5).

29. John C. Fitzpatrick, ed., *The Diaries of George Washington, 1748–1799* (Boston and New York, 1925), II, 162–4, 164 (n.3); Edmund C. Burnett, ed., *Letters of Members of the Continental Congress* (Washington, D.C., 1921), I, 34–5.

30. Worthington C. Ford, ed., *Journals of the Continental Congress, 1774–1789* (Washington, D.C., 1904), I, 31–40.

31. Ford, *Journals*, I, 49–51.

32. Ibid., p. 51 (n.1); Butterfield, *Adams Diary*, II, 143; Albert H. Smyth, *The Writings of Benjamin Franklin . . .* (New York, 1907), VI, 311–12.

33. Ford, *Journals*, I, 51 (n.1), 102 (n.1); Burnett, *Letters*, I, 54–9.

34. Ford, *Journals*, I, 43, 51–3; Burnett, *Letters*, I, 59–60.

35. Ford, *Journals*, I, 75–81.

36. Ibid., pp. 63–73.

37. Ibid., pp. 115–22.

38. Ibid., pp. 81–90.

39. Ibid., pp. 105–13.

XI. The Point of No Return

1. *Gage Correspondence*, I, 355–65.
2. *Hutchinson Diary and Letters*, I, 158–9.
3. Fortescue, III, no. 1486.
4. *Hutchinson Diary and Letters*, I, 179, 181 and n., 191, 227, 233.
5. Bargar, *Dartmouth*, p. 158.
6. Donoughue, pp. 170–5.
7. *Hutchinson Diary and Letters*, I, 204n.
8. *The Correspondence of Edmund Burke*, volume III, ed. G. H. Guttridge (1961), p. 14.
9. *Hutchinson Diary and Letters*, I, 213.
10. Ibid., I, 230.
11. Ibid., 237.
12. *Writings of Benjamin Franklin*, ed. A. H. Smyth (10 v., 1905–7), VI, 238–9, 244–6, 249–51; *Life of Arthur Lee*, I, 211; *Letters of William Lee*, ed. W. C. Ford (3 v., Brooklyn, 1891), I, 85, 110–14 and note.
13. To North, 11 Sept. 1774, Fortescue, III, no. 1508.
14. *Hutchinson Diary and Letters*, I, 181.
15. Ibid., 245.
16. Ibid., 201.
17. *Gage Correspondence*, I, 369–73.
18. *Hutchinson Diary and Letters*, I, 232.
19. Ibid., I, 253–4, 298.
20. Cabinet minute, 3 Oct. 1774, Dartmouth MSS., and also printed, *The Private Papers of John, Earl of Sandwich . . . 1771–1782*, ed. G. R. Barnes and J. H. Owen (NRS, 4 v., 1932–8), I, 55; Rochford to Dartmouth, 5 Oct., Gower to Dartmouth, 6 Oct. 1774, Dartmouth MSS.; *Hutchinson Diary and Letters*, I, 265; Dartmouth to Gage, 17 Oct. 1774, *Gage Correspondence*, II, 173–5. See the fuller survey in Donoughue, pp. 201–7.
21. *Hutchinson Diary and Letters*, I, 260–3, 267–8.
22. Donoughue, pp. 208–10.
23. *Hutchinson Diary and Letters*, I, 272–3, 279, 291, 292–3.
24. Ibid., 284.
25. Shute Barrington, *The Political Life of . . . Viscount Barrington* (1814), pp. 140–2.
26. Fortescue, III, nos. 1557, 1556; *Hutchinson Diary and Letters*, I, 297–8.
27. Ibid., 300.
28. Cabinet minute, 1 Dec. 1774, Dartmouth MSS.
29. Rochford to Sandwich, 10 Dec. 1774, *Sandwich Papers*, I, 55–7.
30. Law officers to Dartmouth, 22 Nov. 1774, P.R.O. C.O. 5/159:3, cited Donoughue, p. 214.
31. *Hutchinson Diary and Letters*, I, 323; *Gage Correspondence*, I, 378–9.
32. Pownall to Dartmouth, 18 Dec. 1774, Dartmouth MSS.; H.M.C., *Various Collections*, VI, *Knox MSS.*, p. 258.
33. Fortescue, III, no. 1563.
34. Pownall to Dartmouth, 18 Dec. 1774, Dartmouth MSS.
35. *Life of Barrington*, pp. 142–8.
36. *Hutchinson Diary and Letters*, I, 336–7.
37. *Gage Correspondence*, I, 380, 382–3, II, 659, received 2 Jan. 1775.
38. North to Dartmouth, 'Bushey Park, Tuesday' [3 Jan. 1775], Dartmouth MSS.
39. Cf. remarks by C. W. Cornwall, 27 Oct. 1775, *P.H.*, XVIII, 775.
40. Cabinet minutes, 13, 21 Jan. 1775, Dartmouth MSS.; Dartmouth to Gage, 27 Jan. 1775, *Gage Correspondence*, II, 181. Cf. Dartmouth's own explanation in March 1776 of his misunderstanding of the situation in 1775, *P.H.*, XVIII, 1254–5.

41. Donoughue, pp. 214–15, 221–2.
42. *Hutchinson Diary and Letters*, I, 363.
43. Fortescue, III, nos. 1575, 1576, 1579.
44. Cabinet minute, 21 Jan. 1775, Dartmouth MSS.
45. *Hutchinson Diary and Letters*, I, 360, 364–5.
46. Ibid., 365, 392–3, 402–3, 407.
47. Ibid., 379.
48. See the discussion in Donoughue, pp. 244–7.
49. *Gage Correspondence*, I, 390, 391.
50. Dunmore to Dartmouth, 24 Dec. 1774, received 10 Feb. 1775, P.R.O. C.O. 5/1373:15–51 (copy), printed, *P.H.*, XVIII, 313–16.
51. Stephen Sayre to Chatham, 4, 6 Apr. 1775, P.R.O 30/8/55 pt. ii, fos. 130, 132. Cf. Sandwich's declaration in debate on 1 Feb. 1775, *P.H.*, XVIII, 205.
52. Gipson, *British Empire*, XII, 288–94; Barrington to Gage, 6 Dec. 1774, 31 Jan. 1775, Gage MSS.
53. For fuller narrative see Donoughue, pp. 231–8.
54. See pp. 209–10 above.
55. *P.H.*, XVIII, 198–203.
56. Dartmouth to Governor Francis Legge, 22 Feb. 1775, Dartmouth MSS. Cf. *Burke Correspondence*, III, 135.
57. See pp. 230–1 above. The cabinet had given final approval on 16 Feb. (Fortescue, III, no. 1599).
58. *P.H.*, XVIII, 330–2.
59. North to George III, 19 Feb. 1775, Fortescue, III, no. 1599.
60. *P.H.*, XVIII, 320; George III to North, 19 Feb. 1775, Fortescue, III, no. 1600.
61. P. 231 above.
62. *P.H.*, XVIII, 322.
63. The proceedings are outlined in Donoughue, pp. 248–55.
64. Cabinet minute, 30 Mar. 1775, Dartmouth MSS.
65. *P.H.*, XVIII, 478–540.
66. Ibid., 552–74; B.L. Add. MSS. 35612, f. 195; Fortescue, III, no. 1624.
67. *Hutchinson Diary and Letters*, I, 410.
68. Peter Force, ed., *American Archives*, 4th s., (Washington, D.C., 1837), I, 762–63; *Boston Gazette*, 12 Sept. 1774; Lawrence H. Gipson, *The Triumphant Empire: Britain Sails into the Storm, 1770–1776* (New York, 1965), pp. 158–9; Christopher Ward, *The War of the Revolution* (New York, 1952), I, 17–19.
69. Clarence E. Carter, ed., *The Correspondence of General Thomas Gage . . .* (New Haven, Conn., 1931), I, 358–60; 369–72; John R. Alden, *General Gage in America* (Baton Rouge, La., 1948), p. 212; John Shy, *Toward Lexington: The Role of the British Army in the Coming of the American Revolution* (Princeton, N.J., 1965), pp. 411–13.
70. *Essex Gazette*, 6 Sept. 1774; Joseph Palmer to R. T. Paine, 15 Sept. 1774, R. T. Paine Papers (MHS); A MILITARY COUNTRYMAN, *Boston Gazette*, 26 Sept., 10 Oct. 1774; *Pennsylvania Journal*, 28 Sept. 1774; 'An American', *Boston Evening Post*, 24 Oct. 1774.
71. Shy, *Toward Lexington*, pp. 413–15; Neil R. Stout, *The Royal Navy in America, 1760–1775: A Study of Enforcement of British Colonial Policy in the Era of the American Revolution* (Annapolis, Md., 1973), pp. 161–2.
72. Ward, *War of the Revolution*, I, 20–1; J. Duane Squires, *Fort William & Mary, From Colonial Times to the Revolutionary War* ([Concord, N.H.], 1972), pp. 7–9.
73. Force, *American Archives*, 4th s., I, 776–9; Resolves of Hampshire County, *Massachusetts Gazette*, 6 Oct. 1774; Resolves of Plymouth County, *Boston Gazette*, 10 Oct. 1774; courts, *Boston Gazette*, 5 Sept., 3 Oct. 1774; resignations, *Massachusetts*

Gazette, 8 Sept. 1774; Provincial Congress, *Boston Gazette,* 26 Sept. 1774; *Journals of Each Provincial Congress of Massachusetts in 1774 and 1775* (Boston, 1838).

74. Worthington C. Ford, ed., *Journals of the Continental Congress, 1774–1789* (Washington, D.C., 1904), I, 77–9.

75. Ibid., pp. 1013, 1202–3, 1258–60; Arthur M. Schlesinger, *The Colonial Merchants and the American Revolution, 1763–1776* (New York, 1918), pp. 442–7.

76. Ibid., pp. 447–55, 458–60; Bernard Mason, *The Road to Independence: The Revolutionary Movement in New York, 1773–1777* (Lexington, Ky., 1966), pp. 85–6.

77. Schlesinger, *Colonial Merchants,* pp. 460–72; Gipson, *Triumphant Empire,* pp. 224–6.

78. Schlesinger, *Colonial Merchants,* pp. 441, 448–50.

79. R. A. Ryerson, 'Political Mobilization and the American Revolution: The Resistance Movement in Philadelphia, 1765 to 1776', *WMQ,* XXXI (October 1974), 571–88.

80. Benjamin Hallowell to Grey Cooper, 5 Sept. 1774, C.O. 5/175 (PRO); A CONVERTED WHIG, *Massachusetts Gazette and Boston Newsletter,* 9 Feb. 1775.

81. Ibid., 23 Feb. 1775.

82. *Massachusetts Gazette and Boston Newsletter,* 16 Feb., 2 March, 1775; *New York Gazetteer,* 9 March 1775; Arthur M. Schlesinger, *Prelude to Independence: The Newspaper War on Britain, 1764–1776* (New York, 1958), pp. 188–9, 225–7, 240.

83. The complete exchange between Seabury and Hamilton includes the titles listed here and in the note following; page numbers where included refer to passages cited: [Samuel Seabury], *Free Thoughts on the Proceedings of Congress* (New York, 1774); [Alexander Hamilton], *A Full Vindication of the Measures of the Congress* (New York, 1774), p. 7.

84. [Samuel Seabury], *The Congress Canvassed* (New York, 1774), p. 24; [Samuel Seabury], *A View of the Controversy* (New York, 1774); [Alexander Hamilton], *The Farmer Refuted* (New York, 1775).

85. Ward, *War of the Revolution,* I, 21; Carter, *Gage Correspondence,* I, 393–4.

86. Thomas Cushing to Joseph Hawley, 27 Feb. 1775, Hawley Papers (New-York Historical Society); Peter Oliver to Elisha Hutchinson, 18 Feb. 1775, Egerton 2659, fos. 137–8 (BL); Thomas Wheeler to Col. William Henshaw, 1 March 1775, Henshaw Papers (American Historical Society).

87. Dartmouth to Gage, 27 Jan. 1775, in Carter, *Gage Correspondence,* II, 179–83.

88. Ward, *War of the Revolution,* I, 30–1.

89. Ibid., pp. 27–9.

90. The account of the Battle of Lexington and Concord in this and following paragraphs relies primarily upon Ward, *War of the Revolution,* I 32–51. Arthur B. Tourtellot, *William Diamond's Drum: The Beginning of the War of the American Revolution* (New York, 1959) has some useful detail and excellent maps. Allen French, *Day of Lexington and Concord* (Boston, Mass., 1925) and Harold Murdock, *The Nineteenth of April, 1775* (Boston, Mass., 1923) are two older but still valuable accounts.

91. Carter, *Gage Correspondence,* I, 395–7, II, 673–4.

XII. 'Tis Time to Part'

1. *Gage Correspondence,* II, 190–6.

2. Ibid., 186.

3. See pp. 229–30 above.

4. *Gage Correspondence,* II, 671.

5. *Hutchinson Diary and Letters,* I, 466–8, 471–2, 475; King's letter and cabinet minutes of 15, 21 June 1775, Dartmouth MSS.

6. *Sandwich Papers,* I, 63.
7. *Gage Correspondence,* I, 397–405; Fortescue, III, nos. 1662, 1663.
8. *Gage Correspondence,* I, 404–5, II, 684, 686.
9. Cabinet minute, 26 July 1775, P.R.O. SP (Dom) Geo. III, 37/11, f. 53; Fortescue, III, nos. 1686, 1687–91.
10. *Life of Barrington,* pp. 148–50.
11. To Barrington, 31 July 1775, Barrington MSS.
12. Fortescue, III, no. 1683.
13. Ibid., no. 1685.
14. H.M.C., *Various Collections,* VI, *Knox MSS.,* p. 121.
15. Gage to Dartmouth, 12, 25 June, 20 Aug. 1775, *Gage Correspondence,* I, 404–5, 408, 412; Dunmore to Dartmouth, 1 May 1775, P.R.O. C.O. 5/1353:141–4.
16. Fortescue, III, no. 1724. Martin to Dartmouth, 16, 23 Mar., 20 Apr., Dunmore to Dartmouth, 1 May, 2 Aug. 1775, P.R.O. C.O. 5/318:81–2, 70–2, 97–101, C.O. 5/1353:137–40, 231–2.
17. H.M.C., *Stopford Sackville MSS.,* II, 6–7, 8–9, 10, and *Fourteenth Report,* appendix pt. X, *Dartmouth MSS.,* II, 315–16, 326, 331, 335–6; P.R.O. C.O. 5/122:151, C.O. 5/92:248.
18. Fortescue, III, nos. 1708, 1709.
19. Gower to Lord Upper Ossory, c. 4 Nov. 1775, Granville MSS., P.R.O. 30/29/3 (this letter now appears to be missing).
20. *P.H.,* XVIII, 695–7, 730–3; William Phillips to Newcastle, [28 Oct. 1775], Newcastle (Clumber) MSS., and cf. his report of the government triumph on 2 Nov., ibid. [2 Nov. 1775]; Isabella to Hugh Elliot, 30 Oct. 1775, Countess of Minto, *A Memoir of Hugh Elliot* (Edinburgh, 1868), pp. 85–6.
21. *P.H.,* XVIII, 919–20.
22. For the details of the cabinet reshuffle see Bargar, *Dartmouth,* pp. 177–81.
23. 16 Geo. III, c. 3.
24. 16 Geo. III, c. 5. For a general account of the passage of this Act see Gipson, *British Empire,* XII, 346–9. As the two Restraining Acts of the previous session, and the Boston Port Act of 1774, were no longer appropriate to the situation, they were repealed by this Act.
25. *P.H.,* XVIII 963–92, 1042–56.
26. Ibid., 1021–7; *C.J.,* XXXV, 467. No further proceedings are indexed in the *Journals,* and no Act was ever passed.
27. Fortescue, III, no. 1760.
28. *P.H.,* XVIII, 1156–67.
29. For an excellent convenient analysis of the Howes' instructions, issued to them on the 6th, see C. R. Ritcheson, *British Politics and the American Revolution* (Norman, Okl., 1954), pp. 205–7.
30. *P.H.,* XVIII, 163, 186, 208, 226, 269, 713, 1200–1. Cf. p. 226 above.
31. See p. 35 above.
32. *P.H.,* XVIII, 939–40, 1072–3, 1245.
33. Ibid., 538–40. Cf. p. 39 above.
34. *P.H.,* XVIII, 731–2.
35. See pp. 149, 166, 183, 186, 192, 226 above.
36. *P.H.,* XVIII, 166–7.
37. Ibid., 213.
38. Ibid., 175, 208, 243, 606.
39. Ibid., 44, 147–60, 215, 441–2, 709, 735, 743–4, 766, 779, 787–9, 910–19, 965–8, 983, 1177–8, 1181–2, 1200.
40. Ibid., 443, 1200.
41. Ibid., 789, 961–2, 965–8.

42. Ibid., 503–4, 972–6.

43. Ibid., 164, 234–5, 341–2, 734, 1029–31, 1084.

44. *P.H.*, XVIII, 647.

45. Ibid., 225, 859–63, 962, 982, 1005–21. For the belief of members of the Rockingham party in such a conspiracy, see Ian R. Christie, *Myth and Reality in late eighteenth-century British Politics* (1970), pp. 27–54.

46. *P.H.*, XVIII, an incomplete record, contains 1,366 columns for this period. Far more than half of this total reports proceedings concerning American affairs.

47. Cited, Namier and Brooke, *The History of Parliament. The House of Commons, 1754–1790*, II, 315.

48. *Burke Correspondence*, III, 190–1.

49. Ibid., 215.

50. On 5 Dec. 1782, 17 Feb. and 7 May 1783, *P.H.*, XXIII, 255, 445, 849.

51. Lexington Alarm Papers (Maryland Historical Society); Bernard Mason, *The Road to Independence: The Revolutionary Movement in New York, 1773–1777* (Lexington, Ky., 1966), pp. 62, 69–75; 'Copy of a Letter from New York to R. Champion', 4 May 1775, Rockingham Papers, R1–1590a (Sheffield Library); *Pennsylvania Journal*, 26 April 1775.

52. Governor Penn to Dartmouth, 1 May 1775, C.O. 5/1300, fos. 411–13 (PRO); Edward Shippen to Joseph Shippen, 13 May 1775, Shippen Papers (American Philosophical Society); W. Duane, ed., *Diary of Christopher Marshall . . . 1774–1781* (Albany, N.Y., 1877), p. 23.

53. Peter Force, ed., *American Archives* (Washington, D.C., 1839), 4th s., II, 387, 391–2, 395–6, 476–8, 526–9; Thomson Mason to John Dickinson, 17 June 1775, Logan Papers (HSP); George F. Willison, *Patrick Henry and His World* (New York, 1969), pp. 264–9. Thomas Jefferson to William Small, 7 May 1775, Julian Boyd, ed., *The Papers of Thomas Jefferson* (Princeton, N.J., 1950), I, 165–6; George Washington to George William Fairfax, 31 May 1775, John C. Fitzpatrick, ed., *The Writings of George Washington* (Washington, D.C., 1931), III, 290–2.

54. Worthington C. Ford, ed., *Journals of the Continental Congress*, (Washington, D.C., 1905), II, 64–6.

55. Elbridge Gerry to Massachusetts delegates, 4 June 1775, Gerry Papers (Library of Congress); Joseph Hawley to Robert T. Paine, 11 June 1775, R. T. Paine MSS. (MHS); Ford, *Journals*, II, 83–4, 89–95.

56. Christopher Ward, *The War of the Revolution* (New York, 1952), I, 53–5; Gage's Proclamation, *New England Chronicle*, 15 June 1775.

57. Ward, 56–61; *New England Chronicle*, 25 May 1775; *Boston Gazette*, 5 June 1775.

58. Ward, *War of the Revolution*, I, 63–72; [Massachusetts] Committee of Safety to Benedict Arnold, 3 May 1775, John Hancock Papers (Library of Congress).

59. The account of the Battle of Bunker Hill in this and succeeding paragraphs is based on Ward, *War of the Revolution*, I, 73–98.

60. Gage to Dartmouth, 25 June 1775, in Force, *American Archives*, 4th s., II, 1097.

61. *Warren-Adams Letters, 1743–1777* (Boston, 1917), I, 73–5.

62. Ford, *Journals*, II, 140–57.

63. Ibid., pp. 158–61; 163–71; *Warren-Adams Letters*, I, 80.

64. Ford, *Journals*, II, 187–90, 195–202, 221–3.

65. Ibid., pp. 224–34.

66. Ibid., pp. 55–6, 109–10; Benedict Arnold to Continental Congress, 15 June 1775, John Hancock Papers (Library of Congress); 'Ethan Allen', Misc. MSS. (American Antiquarian Society).

67. Ward, *War of the Revolution*, I, 149–201, quoted passages, pp. 180, 200–1.

68. Ibid., pp. 123–4, 126–33.

69. Ward, *War of the Revolution*, II, 667–78.

70. Ibid., pp. 845–9.
71. Ibid., pp. 208–10.
72. REFLECTOR, originally printed in the *Norwich Packet*, [?] Sept. 1774, was reprinted in *New York Journal*, 6 Oct. 1775; 'Political Observations' was similarly reprinted from the *Pennsylvania Packet*, [?] Nov. 1774 in the *New York Journal*, 24 Nov. 1774; A SCOTCHMAN, [Purdie and Dixon] *Virginia Gazette*, 13 Oct. 1774; SCIPIO, [Pinkney's] *Virginia Gazette*, 27 Oct. 1774.
73. *New York Journal*, 9 Feb. 1775; JOHANNES IN EREMO, *Essex Gazette*, 25 April 1775; *New York Journal* 19 Oct. 1775; JOHANNES IN EREMO, *New England Chronicle*, 18, 25 Jan. 1775.
74. Thomas Paine, *Common Sense* [Philadelphia, 1776] (Dolphin Edition), pp. 18–27, 31–41.
75. A RELIGIOUS POLITICIAN, *Pennsylvania Journal*, 7 Feb. 1776; RATIONALIS [James Chalmers], *Pennsylvania Gazette*, 28 Feb. 1776; SALUS POPULI, *Pennsylvania Journal*, 24 Jan. 1776; *Boston Gazette*, 15 April 1776.
76. Andrew Eliot to Isaac Smith, 9 April 1776 (MHS).
77. Ford, *Journals*, IV, 230–3, 257–9, 342; Edmund C. Burnett, *The Continental Congress. . . .* (New York, 1941), pp. 142–3.
78. John Adams to James Warren, 20 May 1776, *Warren-Adams Letters*, I, 249; Ford, *Journals*, V, 425, 428–9, 431.
79. J. H. Powell, ed., 'Speech of John Dickinson Opposing the Declaration of Independence, 1 July 1776', *PMHB*, LXV (October 1941), 458–81.
80. L. H. Butterfield, ed., *The Diary and Autobiography of John Adams* (Cambridge, Mass., 1961), III, 396–7; Charles F. Adams, ed., *The Works of John Adams* (Boston, 1851), III, 55–7; Ford, *Journals*, V, 505–7, VI, 1091–3.

A LIST OF MATERIAL AND
WORKS CONSULTED

1. Principal Manuscript Sources

(a) BRITISH REPOSITORIES

Public Record Office

    T. 1 Treasury Board Papers, original correspondence

    T. 27 Treasury Board Papers, general letter books

    C.O. 5 Colonial Papers, America and West Indies

    Chatham MSS.

    Granville MSS.

British Library (formerly *British Museum Library*), *Department of Manuscripts*

    Additional MSS. 32936, 32957, 32966, 32969–91 (Newcastle Papers)

    Additional MSS. 35374–5, 35428–30, 35607–12 (Hardwicke Papers)

Egerton MSS. 2659–75 (Hutchinson Papers)

King's MSS.

House of Lords Record Office

    Papers relating to Disturbances in Boston

    Papers relating to the Boston Tea Party

Berkshire Record Office

    Aldworth-Neville Papers

Central Public Library, Sheffield

    Rockingham Papers

William Salt Library, Stafford

    Dartmouth Papers

Suffolk Record Office

    Grafton Papers

(b) AMERICAN REPOSITORIES

American Antiquarian Society

    Ethan Allen Papers

    Salisbury Papers

American Philosophical Society

    Manuscripts relating to Non-Importation Agreements, 1766–1775

    Shippen Papers

William L. Clements Library

    Gage Papers (The private letters of Viscount Barrington to General Thomas Gage)

Historical Society of Pennsylvania

    Custom House Papers

    Drinker Foreign Letters

    Drinker Papers

    Hollingsworth Papers

    Logan Papers

    Papers relating to the Shipment of Tea

    Wharton Letter Book

Houghton Library

    Sparks MSS.

Library of Congress
  Gerry Papers
  Shippen Papers
Massachusetts Archives
  Hutchinson Letter Books
Massachusetts Historical Society
  Edes Papers
  Manuscripts L. Collection
  R. T. Paine Papers

New England Historic and Genealogical Society
  Henry Bromfield Letter Book, 1773
New-York Historical Society
  John Lamb Papers
  McDougall Papers
New York Public Library
  Boston Committee of Correspondence Papers
  Samuel Adams Papers

2. Printed Sources

(a) NEWSPAPERS AND PERIODICALS

The Annual Register
Boston Evening Post
Boston Gazette
Boston Newsletter
Boston Post-boy
London Gazette
Maryland Gazette
Massachusetts Gazette
Massachusetts Spy
Morning Chronicle (London)
Newport Mercury
New York Gazette

New York Gazetteer
New York Journal
Pennsylvania Journal
Pennsylvania Packet
[Salem] *Essex Gazette*
South Carolina Gazette
South Carolina and American General Gazette
Virginia Gazette [Pinkney's]
Virginia Gazette [Purdie's]
Virginia Gazette [Purdie & Dixon]
Virginia Gazette [Rind's]

(b) PAMPHLETS

[Anon.], *A Letter from a Virginian, to the Members of the Congress to be Held at Philadelphia. On the first of September 1774* ([New York], 1774).

——, *Observations on the Trade and Revenue of North America* (London, 1763).

[Chandler, Thomas B.], *The American Querist: or, Some Questions Proposed Relative to the Disputes Between Great-Britain and Her American Colonies* ([New York], 1774).

Decker, Sir Matthew, *An Essay on the Causes of the Decline of the Foreign Trade* (London, 1744; 2nd edn., 1750).

Dickinson, John, *Letters from a Farmer in Pennsylvania* (Philadelphia, 1768).

[Drayton, William H.], *A Letter from Freeman of South-Carolina, to the Deputies of Congress at Philadelphia* (Charleston, S.C., 1774).

Dulany, Daniel, *Considerations on the Propriety of Imposing Taxes in the British Colonies, for the Purpose of Raising a Revenue, by Act of Parliament* (Annapolis, Md., 1765).

[Hamilton, Alexander], *A Full Vindication of the Measures of the Congress* (New York, 1774).

——, *The Farmer Refuted* (New York, 1775).

Jenyns, Soame, *The Objections to the Taxation of our American Colonies by the Legislature of Great Britain, Briefly Consider'd* (London, 1765).

Otis, James, *The Rights of the British Colonies Asserted and Proved* (Boston, 1764).

Pownall, Thomas, *The Administration of the Colonies* (London, 1765).

[Seabury, Samuel], *A View of the Controversy* (New York, 1774).

——, *Free Thoughts on the Proceedings of Congress* (New York, 1774).

——, *The Congress Canvassed* (New York, 1774).

Whately, Thomas, *Considerations on the Trade and Finances of this Kingdom, and the Measures of Administration with Respect to those great National Objects since the Conclusion of the Peace* (London, 1766).
———, *The Regulations Lately Made Concerning the Colonies and the Taxes Imposed upon Them, Considered* (London, 1765).
[Wilson, James], *Considerations on the Nature and Extent of the Legislative Authority of the British Parliament* (Philadelphia, 1774).

(c) CORRESPONDENCE AND MEMOIRS

The Diary and Autobiography of John Adams, ed. by Lyman H. Butterfield (4 v., Cambridge, Mass., 1961).
The Works of John Adams, ed. by Charles F. Adams (10 v., Boston, 1856).
The Writings of Samuel Adams, ed. by Harry A. Cushing (4 v., New York, 1904).
'John Andrews Correspondence', Massachusetts Historical Society, *Proceedings*, VII (1864–5).
[Anon.]. 'Journal of a French Traveller in the Colonies, 1765', *American Historical Review*, XXVI (1921–2).
Barrington, Shute, *The Political Life of William Wildman Viscount Barrington, compiled from original papers* (London, 1814).
The Barrington-Bernard Correspondence and Illustrative Matter, 1760–1770, ed. by E. Channing and A. C. Coolidge (Cambridge, Mass., 1912).
Correspondence of John, fourth Duke of Bedford, ed. by Lord John Russell (3 v., London, 1842–6).
'Correspondence in 1774 and 1775 Between a Committee of the Town of Boston and Contributors of Donations . . .', Massachusetts Historical Society, *Collections*, 4th series, IV (1858).
'Bowdoin and Temple Papers', Massachusetts Historical Society, *Collections*, 6th series, IX (1897).
The Correspondence of Edmund Burke, ed. by T. W. Copeland and others (9 v., Cambridge, 1958–70).
A Selection from the Family Papers preserved at Caldwell (Glasgow, 1854).
Correspondence of William Pitt, Earl of Chatham, ed. by W. S. Taylor and J. H. Pringle (4 v., London, 1838–40).
Letters of Members of the Continental Congress, ed. by Edmund C. Burnett (8 v., Washington, D.C., 1921–36).
Letters and Papers of John Singleton Copley and Henry Pelham, 1739–1776. Massachusetts Historical Society (Boston, 1914).
Crèvecoeur, Hector St. Jean de, *Letters from an American Farmer* (Everyman's Library edition, London, n.d.).
'Letters of Dennys de Berdt, 1757–70', ed. by A. Matthews, Colonial Society of Massachusetts, *Publications*, XIII (*Transactions*, 1910–1911), pp. 293–461.
The Writings of John Dickinson, ed. by Paul L. Ford (2 v., Philadelphia, 1895).
The Writings of John Dickinson, ed. by Charles J. Stillé (2 v., Philadelphia, 1895).
Elliot, G. F. S., *The Border Elliots and the Family of Minto* (London, 1897).
Minto, Countess of, *A Memoir of Hugh Elliot* (Edinburgh, 1868).
'The Fitch Papers: Correspondence and Documents during Thomas Fitch's Governorship of the Colony of Connecticut, 1754–1766', Connecticut Historical Society, *Collections*, XVIII (1920).
Original Letters to . . . Henry Flood (London, 1820).
The Papers of Benjamin Franklin, ed. by Leonard W. Labaree and others (v.1 +, New Haven and London, 1959 +).
The Writings of Benjamin Franklin, ed. by Albert H. Smyth (10 v., New York and London, 1905–7).

Benjamin Franklin's Letters to the Press, 1758–1775, ed. by V. W. Crane (Chapel Hill, N.C., 1950).

The Correspondence of General Thomas Gage with the Secretaries of State and with the War Office and the Treasury, 1763–1775, ed. by Clarence E. Carter (2 v., New Haven, Conn., 1931–3, repr. 1969).

'Hon. Charles Garth, M.P., the last colonial agent of South Carolina, and some of his work', ed. by J. W. Barnwell, *South Carolina Historical and Genealogical Magazine*, XXVI–XXXIII (1925–32).

[Garth] 'Stamp Act Papers', *Maryland Historical Magazine*, VI (1911), pp. 282–305.

The Correspondence of King George III, ed. by Sir John Fortescue (6 v., London, 1927–8); L. B. Namier, *Additions and Corrections to Sir John Fortescue's Edition of the Correspondence of King George III* (Volume I) (Manchester, 1937).

Autobiography and Political Correspondence of Augustus Henry, third Duke of Grafton, ed. by Sir William R. Anson (London, 1898).

The Grenville Papers: Being the Correspondence of Richard Grenville, Earl Temple, K.G., and the Right Hon. George Grenville, their Friends and Contemporaries, ed. by W. J. Smith (4 v., London, 1852–3).

Traits of the Tea Party: Being a Memoir of George R. T. Hewes . . . , ed. by [Benjamin B. Thatcher] (New York, 1835).

The Letters of David Hume, ed. by J. Y. T. Greig (2 v., Oxford, 1932).

The Diary and Letters of . . . Thomas Hutchinson, ed. by Peter O. Hutchinson (2 v., London, 1883–6).

The Papers of Thomas Jefferson, ed. by Julian Boyd (v.1 +, Princeton, N.J., 1950 +).

Richard H. Lee, *Life of Arthur Lee, LL.D. . . . with his Diplomatic and Literary Correspondence and His Papers . . .* (2 v., Boston, 1829).

Letters of William Lee . . . , ed. by Worthington C. Ford (3 v., Brooklyn, New York, 1891).

Diary of Christopher Marshall . . . 1774–1781, ed. by W. Duane (Albany, N.Y., 1877).

[Newcastle, Duke of]. *A Narrative of the Changes in the Ministry, 1765–1767*, ed. by Mary Bateson (London, 1898).

Memorials of the Publick Life and Character of James Oswald of Dunniker (Edinburgh, 1825).

'Letters of Charles Paxton, 1768–1769', ed. by George G. Wolkins, Massachusetts Historical Society, *Proceedings*, LVI (1923).

'The Pitkin Papers: Correspondence and Documents during William Pitkin's Governorship of the Colony of Connecticut, 1766–1769', Connecticut Historical Society, *Collections*, XIX (1921).

'Diary of Josiah Quincy, Jr.', Massachusetts Historical Society, *Proceedings*, 1st series, IV (1858).

Life and Correspondence of Joseph Reed, ed. by W. B. Reed (2 v., Philadelphia, 1847).

'Extracts from the Letterbook of Samuel Rhodes', ed. by Henry D. Biddle, *Pennsylvania Magazine of History and Biography*, XIV (1890).

Albemarle, *Memoirs of the Marquis of Rockingham and his Contemporaries* (2 v., London, 1852).

The Private Papers of John, Earl of Sandwich . . . 1771–1782, ed. by G. R. Barnes and J. H. Owen (Navy Records Society, 4 v., London, 1932–8).

'Correspondence between William Strahan and David Hall, 1763–1777', *Pennsylvania Magazine of History and Biography*, X (1886).

[Thomson, Charles]. 'Revolutionary [and Miscellaneous] Papers', New-York Historical Society, *Collections*, XI–XIII (3 v., New York, 1879–81).

'Trumbull Papers', volume 1, Massachusetts Historical Society, *Collections*, 5th series, IX (1885).

Horace Walpole's Memoirs of the Reign of King George III, ed. by G. F. R. Barker (4 v., London, 1894).

Warren-Adams Letters, 1743–1777 (Boston, 1917).
The Writings of George Washington, 1745–1799, ed. by John C. Fitzpatrick (39 v., Washington, D.C., 1931–44).

(d) Printed Collections and other Printed Sources

'Account of the Destruction of the brig *Peggy Stewart,* at Annapolis, 1774', *Pennsylvania Magazine of History and Biography,* XXV (1901).
Acts of the Privy Council of England: Colonial Series [1613–1783], ed. by William L. Grant and James Munro (6 v., London, 1908–12).
American Archives, ed. by Peter Force (9 v., Washington, D.C., 1837–53).
Archives of Maryland (70 v. +, Baltimore, Md., 1883–1964 +), volumes XIV, XXXI.
Sir Henry Cavendish's Debates of the House of Commons during the thirteenth Parliament of Great Britain, ed. by John Wright (2 v., London, 1841–3).
Colonies to Nation 1763–1789, ed. by Jack P. Greene (New York, 1967).
'Debates on the Declaratory Act and the Repeal of the Stamp Act, 1766', *American Historical Review,* XVII (1911–12), pp. 563–86.
Documents of the American Revolution, 1770–1783 (Colonial Office Series), ed. by K. G. Davies (v.1 +, Shannon, 1972 +).
Documents Relating to the Colonial History of the State of New York, ed. by E. B. O'Callaghan (15 v., Albany, N.Y., 1853–87).
English Historical Documents, volume IX: *American Colonial Documents to 1776,* ed. by Merrill Jensen (New York and London, 1955, repr. 1969).
Historical Manuscripts Commission: *Tenth Report,* appendix part 1: *Weston Underwood MSS. Eleventh Report,* appendix part 5, *Dartmouth MSS.,* v.1. *Fourteenth Report,* appendix part 10, *Dartmouth MSS.,* v.2. *Lothian MSS. Stopford Sackville MSS. Various Collections,* volume 6: *Knox MSS.*
Journals of the Continental Congress, 1774–1789, ed. by Worthington C. Ford (34 v., Washington, D.C., 1904–37).
Journals of Each Provincial Congress of Massachusetts in 1774 and 1775 (Boston, 1838).
Journals of the House of Burgesses of Virginia, 1761–1765, ed. by John P. Kennedy (13 v., Richmond, Va., 1905–15).
Journals of the House of Commons.
'Minutes of the Tea Meetings', Massachusetts Historical Society, *Proceedings,* XX (1882–3).
Pamphlets of the American Revolution, volume 1, ed. by Bernard Bailyn (Cambridge, Mass., 1965).
'Parliamentary Diaries of Nathaniel Ryder, 1764–7', ed. by P. D. G. Thomas, Royal Historical Society, *Camden Miscellany XXIII* (1969).
The Parliamentary History of England . . . to 1803, ed. by William Cobbett and T. C. Hansard (36 v., London, 1806–20).
'Proceedings of Ye Body Respecting the Tea', ed. by L. F. S. Upton, *William and Mary Quarterly,* XXII (1965).
'Proceedings of the Virginia Committee of Correspondence', *Virginia Magazine of History and Biography,* XII (1904–5).
Prologue to Revolution: Sources and Documents on the Stamp Act Crisis, 1764–1766, ed. by Edmund S. Morgan (Chapel Hill, N.C., 1959).
Records of the Colony of Rhode Island and Providence Plantations, ed. by John R. Bartlett (10 v., Providence, R.I., 1856–65).
Report of the Record Commissioners of the City of Boston [XXXIII]: *[Boston] Selectmen's Minutes, 1769–1775* (Boston, 1893); [XVIII]: *Boston Town Records, 1770–1777* (Boston, 1887).
Royal Instructions to British Colonial Governors, 1670–1776, ed. by Leonard W. Labaree (2 v., New York, 1935).

Sources and Documents illustrating the American Revolution, 1764–1788, ed. by S. E. Morison (2nd edn., London, 1965).

'Speech of John Dickinson Opposing the Declaration of Independence, 1 July 1776', ed. by J. H. Powell, *Pennsylvania Magazine of History and Biography*, LXV (1941).

Speeches of the Governors of Massachusetts, 1765–1775, ed. by Alden Bradford (Boston, 1818).

Seybert, Adam, *Statistical Annals of the United States of America* (repr., New York, 1970).

The Statutes at Large from Magna Charta to . . .1761 (continued to 1806), ed. by Danby Pickering (46 v., Cambridge, 1762–1807).

Tea Leaves . . . , ed. by Samuel A. Drake (Boston, 1884).

3. Secondary Works

Adams, Thomas R., *American Independence: The Growth of an Idea* (Providence, R.I., 1965).

Alden, John R., *General Gage in America* (Baton Rouge, La., 1948).

Ayling, Stanley, *George III* (London, 1972).

Bailyn, Bernard, *The Ideological Origins of the American Revolution* (Cambridge, Mass., 1967).

——, *The Ordeal of Thomas Hutchinson* (Cambridge, Mass., 1974).

Bargar, B. D., *Lord Dartmouth and the American Revolution* (Columbia, S.C., 1965).

Barrow, Thomas C., *Trade and Empire: The British Customs Service in Colonial America, 1660–1775* (Cambridge, Mass., 1967).

——, 'The Background to the Grenville Program, 1757–1763', *William and Mary Quarterly*, 3rd series, XXII (1965), 93–104.

Basye, A. H., *The Lords Commissioners of Trade and Plantations* (London, 1925).

Baxter, W. T., ed., *The House of Hancock: Business in Boston, 1724–1775* (Cambridge, Mass., 1945).

Bridenbaugh, Carl, *Mitre and Sceptre: Transatlantic Faiths, Ideas, Personalities, and Politics, 1689–1775* (New York, 1962).

Brooke, John, *The Chatham Administration, 1766–1768* (London, 1956).

——, *King George III* (London, 1972).

Brown, Richard D., 'The Massachusetts Convention of Towns, 1768', *William and Mary Quarterly*, 3rd series, XXVI (1969).

——, *Revolutionary Politics in Massachusetts: The Boston Committee of Correspondence and the Towns, 1772–1774* (Cambridge, Mass., 1970).

Brunhouse, R. L., 'The Effect of the Townshend Acts in Pennsylvania', *Pennsylvania Magazine of History and Biography*, LIV (1930).

Burnett, Edmund C., *The Continental Congress. . . .* (New York, 1941).

Chaffin, R. J., 'The Townshend Acts of 1767', *William and Mary Quarterly*, 3rd series, XXVII (1970).

Champagne, Roger J., 'Liberty Boys and Mechanics of New York City, 1764–1774', *Labor History*, VIII (1967).

Christie, Ian R., *Myth and Reality in late eighteenth-century British Politics, and other papers* (London, 1970).

Clark, Dora Mae, 'The American Board of Customs, 1767–1783', *American Historical Review*, XLV (1940–1).

Clode, C. M., *The Military Forces of the Crown; their Administration and government* (2 v., London, 1869).

Cochrane, J. A., *Dr. Johnson's Printer. The life of William Strahan* (London, 1964).

Coleman, Kenneth, *The Revolution in Georgia, 1763–1789* (Athens, Ga., 1958).

Cullen, Louis M., *Anglo-Irish Trade, 1660–1800* (Manchester, 1968).

Davidson, Philip, *Propaganda and the American Revolution* (Chapel Hill, N.C., 1941).

Dickerson, Oliver M., 'John Hancock, Notorious Smuggler or Near Victim of British Customs Racketeers?' *Mississippi Valley Historical Review*, XXXII (1946).

——, *The Navigation Acts and the American Revolution* (Philadelphia, 1951).

Donoughue, Bernard, *British Politics and the American Revolution. The Path to War, 1773–1775* (London, 1964).

Ernst, Joseph A., 'The Currency Act Repeal Movement: A Study in Imperial Politics and Revolutionary Crisis, 1764–67', *William and Mary Quarterly*, 3rd series, XXV (1968).

——, *Money and Politics in America, 1755–1775* (Chapel Hill, N.C., 1973).

Fitzmaurice, *Life of William, Earl of Shelburne* (2nd edn., 2 v., London, 1912).

French, Allen, *Day of Lexington and Concord* (Boston, 1925).

Gipson, Lawrence Henry, *The British Empire before the American Revolution* (15 v., New York, 1936–70), v. X: *Thunder Clouds Gather in the West;* v. XI: *The Rumbling of the Coming Storm;* v. XII: *Britain sails into the Storm.*

——, *The Coming of the Revolution, 1763–1775* (London, 1954).

Goebel, J., *The Struggle for the Falkland Islands. A Study in Legal and Diplomatic History* (New Haven, 1927).

Goss, Elbridge H., *The Life of Colonel Paul Revere* (Boston, 1891).

Greene, Jack P., 'Bridge to Revolution: The Wilkes Fund Controversy in South Carolina, 1769–1775', *Journal of Southern History*, XXIX (1963).

——, *The Quest for Power. The Lower Houses of Assembly in the Southern Royal Colonies, 1689–1776* (Chapel Hill, N.C., 1963).

——, and Jellison, Richard M., 'The Currency Act of 1764 in Imperial-Colonial Relations, 1764–1776', *William and Mary Quarterly*, 3rd series, XVIII (1961).

Harper, L. A., *The English Navigation Laws* (New York, 1939).

Hinkhouse, J. J., *The Preliminaries of the American Revolution as seen in the English Press, 1763–1775* (New York, 1926).

Hoffman, Ross J. S., *The Marquis. A Study of Lord Rockingham, 1730–1782* (New York, 1973).

Hooker, Richard J., 'The American Revolution Seen Through a Wine Glass', *William and Mary Quarterly*, 3rd series, XI (1954).

Humphreys, R. A., 'Lord Shelburne and the Proclamation of 1763', *English Historical Review*, XLIX (1934).

Hutson, James H., 'An Investigation of the Inarticulate: Philadelphia's White Oaks', *William and Mary Quarterly*, 3rd series, XXVIII (1971).

Ilchester, *Henry Fox, first Lord Holland* (2 v., London, 1920).

Jacobson, David L., *John Dickinson and the Revolution in Pennsylvania, 1764–1776* (Berkeley, Calif., 1965).

James, F. G., *Ireland in the Empire, 1688–1770* (Cambridge, Mass., 1973).

Jensen, Arthur L., *The Maritime Commerce of Colonial Philadelphia* (Madison, Wisc., 1963).

Jensen, Merrill, *The Founding of a Nation* (New York, 1968).

Johnson, Allen S., 'The Passage of the Sugar Act', *William and Mary Quarterly*, 3rd series, XVI (1959).

Kammen, Michael G., *A Rope of Sand: The Colonial Agents, British Politics, and the American Revolution* (Ithaca, New York, 1968).

Knorr, Klaus E., *British Colonial Theories, 1570–1850* (London, 1963).

Koebner, Richard, *Empire* (London, 1961).

Labaree, Benjamin W., *The Boston Tea Party* (New York, 1964).

Langford, Paul, *The First Rockingham Administration, 1765–1766* (Oxford, 1973).

Lefler, Hugh T., and Powell, William S., *Colonial North Carolina* (New York, 1973).

Lemisch, Jesse, 'Jack Tar in the Streets: Merchant Seamen in the Politics of Revolutionary America', *William and Mary Quarterly*, 3rd series, XXV (1968).

——, 'Radical Plot in Boston (1770): A Study in the Use of Evidence', *Harvard Law Review*, LXXXIV (1970).

Lovejoy, David S., 'Rights Imply Equality: The Case Against Admiralty Jurisdiction in America, 1764–1776', *William and Mary Quarterly*, 3rd series, XVI (1959).

Maier, Pauline, *From Resistance to Revolution: Colonial Radicals and the Development of American Opposition to Great Britain, 1765–1776* (New York, 1972).

——, 'Revolutionary Violence and the Relevance of History', *Journal of Interdisciplinary History*, II (1971).

Malone, Dumas, *Jefferson the Virginian* (Boston, 1948).

Martin, Alfred S., 'The King's Customs: Philadelphia, 1763–1774', *William and Mary Quarterly*, 3rd series, V (1948).

Mason, Bernard, *The Road to Independence: The Revolutionary Movement in New York, 1773–1777* (Lexington, Ky., 1966).

Matthews, Albert, 'The Solemn League and Covenant, 1774', Colonial Society of Massachusetts, *Publications*, XVIII (1915).

Morgan, Edmund S., 'Postponement of the Stamp Act', *William and Mary Quarterly*, 3rd series, III (1950).

——, 'Thomas Hutchinson and the Stamp Act', *New England Quarterly*, XXI (1948).

——, and Morgan, Helen M., *The Stamp Act Crisis: Prologue to Revolution* (Chapel Hill, N.C., 1953, new edn., New York, 1963).

Murdock, Harold, *The Nineteenth of April, 1775* (Boston, 1923).

Namier, L. B., 'Charles Garth and his Connections', *English Historical Review*, LIV (1939).

Namier, Sir Lewis, *Charles Townshend: His Character and Career* (The Leslie Stephen Lecture, Cambridge, 1959).

—— and Brooke, John, *Charles Townshend* (London, 1964).

——, *The History of Parliament. The House of Commons, 1754–1790* (3 v., London, 1964).

Newcomb, Benjamin H., 'Effects of the Stamp Act on Colonial Pennsylvania Politics', *William and Mary Quarterly*, 3rd series, XXIII (1966).

——, *Franklin and Galloway: A Political Partnership* (New Haven, Conn., 1972).

Norris, John, *Shelburne and Reform* (London, 1963).

Pole, J. R., *Political Representation in England and the Origins of the American Republic* (London, 1966).

Ritcheson, C. R., *British Politics and the American Revolution* (Norman, Okla., 1954).

Roberts, Michael, 'Great Britain and the Swedish Revolution of 1772–3', *Historical Journal*, VII (1964).

Roche, John F., *Joseph Reed: A Moderate in the American Revolution* (New York, 1957).

Ryerson, R. A., 'Political Mobilization and the American Revolution: The Resistance Movement in Philadelphia, 1765 to 1776', *William and Mary Quarterly*, 3rd series, XXXI (1974).

Schlesinger, Arthur M., *The Colonial Merchants and the American Revolution, 1763–1776* (New York, 1918).

——, *Prelude to Independence: The Newspaper War on Britain, 1764–1776* (New York, 1958).

——, 'The Uprising Against the East India Company', *Political Science Quarterly*, XXXII (1917).

Shelton, W. J., *English Hunger and Industrial Disorders. A Study of Social Conflict during the first Decade of George III's Reign* (London, 1973).

Shy, John, *Toward Lexington: The Role of the British Army in the Coming of the American Revolution* (Princeton, N.J., 1965).

Smith, W. Roy, *South Carolina as a Royal Province, 1719–1776* (New York, 1903).

Sosin, Jack M., *Agents and Merchants: British Colonial Policy and the Origins of the American Revolution, 1763–1775* (Lincoln, Neb., 1965).

——, 'The Massachusetts Act of 1774: Coercive or Preventive?', *Huntington Library Quarterly*, XXVI (1962–3).

——, 'A postscript to the Stamp Act. George Grenville's Revenue Measures: a Drain on Colonial Specie?', *American Historical Review*, LXIII (1957–8).

——, *Whitehall and the Wilderness: The Middle West in British Colonial Policy, 1760–1775* (Lincoln, Neb., 1961).

Spector, Margaret M., *The American Department of the British Government, 1768–1782* (New York, 1940).

Squires, J. Duane, *Fort William and Mary, from Colonial Times to the Revolutionary War* ([Concord, N.H.], 1972).

Stout, Neil R., *The Royal Navy in America, 1760–1775* (Annapolis, Md., 1973).

Sutherland, Lucy S., *The East India Company in eighteenth-century Politics* (Oxford, 1952).

Thomas, P. D. G., *British Politics and the Stamp Act Crisis* (Oxford, 1975).

——, 'Charles Townshend and American Taxation in 1767', *English Historical Review*, LXXXIII (1968).

Tourtellot, Arthur B., *William Diamond's Drum: The Beginning of the War of the American Revolution* (New York, 1959).

Ubbelohde, Carl, *The Vice-Admiralty Courts and the American Revolution* (Chapel Hill, N.C., 1960).

Van Alstyne, R. W., *Genesis of American Nationalism* (London, 1970).

Varga, Nicholas, 'The New York Restraining Act: Its Passage and some Effects, 1766–1768', *New York History*, XXXVII (1956).

Walett, Francis G., 'The Massachusetts Council, 1766–1774; The Transformation of a Conservative Institution', *William and Mary Quarterly*, 3rd series, VI (1949).

Waters, John J., *The Otis Family* (Chapel Hill, N.C., 1968).

Watson, D. H., 'Joseph Harrison and the Liberty Incident', *William and Mary Quarterly*, 3rd series, XX (1963).

Watson, Henry C., *The Yankee Tea Party. . . .* (Boston, 1851).

Ward, Christopher, *The War of the Revolution* (New York, 1952).

Wells, William V., *The Life and Public Services of Samuel Adams* (Boston, 1865).

Willison, George F., *Patrick Henry and His World* (New York, 1969).

Wolkins, George G., 'The Seizure of John Hancock's Sloop *Liberty*', Massachusetts Historical Society, *Proceedings*, LV (1922).

Zobel, Hiller B., *The Boston Massacre* (New York, 1970).

INDEX

———•———